Facing Ethical Issues

also by the authors
published by Paulist Press

CHARACTER, CHOICES & COMMUNITY

Facing Ethical Issues
Dimensions of Character, Choices & Community

Patrick T. McCormick
and
Russell B. Connors, Jr.

PAULIST PRESS
New York/Mahwah, N.J.

Cover design by Cynthia Dunne/Interior design by Joseph E. Petta

Library of Congress Cataloging-in-Publication Data

McCormick, Patrick T.
    Facing ethical issues : dimensions of character, choices & community / Patrick T. McCormick and Russell B. Connors, Jr.
        p.   cm.
    Includes bibliographical references.
    ISBN 0-8091-4077-2
    1. Christian ethics. 2. Christian ethics—Catholic authors. I. Connors, Russell B., 1948-   II. Title.
BJ1249 .M238 2002
241′.042—dc21

                                                        2002006696

Published by Paulist Press
997 Macarthur Boulevard
Mahwah, New Jersey 07430 USA

www.paulistpress.com

Printed and bound in the
United States of America

Contents

Dedication

Sean O'Riordan, C.Ss.R. (1916–1998)
Timothy E. O'Connell
Richard C. Sparks, C.S.P.

Acknowledgments

Although there is something solitary about writing, no one ever writes anything—certainly not a book—alone. This is obviously the case with this present work, for indeed we did it together. We undertook this project, like our previous book, with the conviction that the two of us could do something together that neither one of us could do singly. And after the back-and-forth brainstorming, devising, outlining, drafting, critiquing, rewriting, editing and writing again that this book entailed, we still believe that two heads can really be better than one. Whatever the faults of the book, it is enriched because of the collaboration that is behind virtually every paragraph.

But we have relied on far more than each other. A glance at the endnotes displays the host of scholars who have been (and remain) our teachers. Their ideas have informed us, their creativity has inspired us and often their convictions have challenged us. We knew from the start that in regard to many of the complex issues we discuss in the text there were quite a number of scholars whose expertise far exceeded our own. Without embarrassment—and with appreciation—we have relied upon that expertise, hoping that we have represented the ideas of our colleagues well.

We want to acknowledge a group of colleagues to whom we are indebted not only academically, but personally. Lisa Cahill, Charles Curran, Richard Gula, Jim Keenan, Tim O'Connell, Tom Shannon, Dick Sparks and Dick McCormick (whose death on February 12, 2000 has left a kind of hole in the fabric of Catholic moral theology) have not only been colleagues and mentors, but friends who have supported and encouraged us along the way. We are very grateful.

Finally, we want to dedicate this book to three people whose work and friendship have been important to us. Sean O'Riordan was the director of my (RC) doctoral work in Rome roughly twenty years ago. He still embodies for me what a first-rate theologian-scholar-teacher "looks like." In some ways Sean taught me how to think, and he helped me believe in my own abilities as a theologian and as a writer. Tim O'Connell has been and remains a theologian/mentor for each of us. We are better because of his ideas, his encouragement and certainly his laughter. And lastly we owe Dick Sparks "big time." Dick labored over a previous draft of this book and made many comments and suggestions that were sometimes candid, often insightful and always important. The faults of this book remain our own, but Dick's contributions have enriched it greatly.

If it is the case that behind every book there is a network of people who have made the author's work possible, that seems doubly the case here. Our thanks to you all.

Pat McCormick and Russ Connors

CHAPTER ONE

A Workbook on Character, Choices & Community

Carol and Marcus Billings, a middle-aged couple with two daughters in college, have just relocated to Dallas, where Carol has been hired as the CEO of a biotech firm and Marcus has taken a management position with Red Cross. While out looking for a new home they found two particularly attractive houses within their new price range, one on a golf course and the other near a lovely park. Both homes, however, are in gated communities, complete with security gates and patrols, and—aside from the cleaning women and lawn workers arriving in vans each morning—there do not seem to be any minorities living in either of the enclosed neighborhoods. Still, Carol soon discovers that many of the bankers and investors she will need to connect with in her new job do live in these communities and that a membership at the golf course could well provide her with important business contacts. Marcus, on the other hand, appreciates that these contacts would be helpful for his fund-raising work as well, but is troubled by the thought of moving into a community that walls out the poor and working class so intentionally.

Character. What sorts of persons would Carol and Marcus need to be to recognize and face the problem in front of them? Can you think of any virtues that would help them to behave well here? What virtues would they need to behave like good Christians?

1

Choices. How should Carol and Marcus go about solving this problem? Are there any steps or resources you would recommend for making this moral choice? What should they do if they want to make a good choice as disciples of Christ?

Community. What kinds of things are going on in our society that might be contributing to the popularity and growth of these gated communities? What do gated communities say about our society or culture, and what might we need to change? How would a community of authentic Christians deal with this question?

Jeff Charles is the principal of St. Catherine's Prep, a small established Catholic girls' academy in Philadelphia. Karen Moore, one of his most popular and respected teachers, is the honors physics professor and has been with St. Catherine's for seventeen years. During this time she has turned down three offers from other private schools that would have paid her significantly more money. Karen is also a lesbian and has been living with her partner, Jennifer, for nine years. This relationship is not a secret. (Karen and Jennifer have been to some faculty social functions and two or three colleagues' weddings over the years.) Still, given the Catholic Church's public stance on homosexuality, Karen has kept a relatively low profile when discussing her home life. This morning, however, things are different. Jennifer, who has MS, recently lost her job and, with it, her health insurance. Karen has come to Jeff requesting that her partner be put on the school's HMO, as are the wives and husbands of so many of her colleagues. Jeff knows that if he asks the diocese or bishop about this the answer will be no. He knows too that if he acts quietly there could be repercussions later for him and the school.

Character. What sorts of duties do Jeff, Karen and Jennifer have to one another, or to other persons or groups in this case? What kinds of persons would Jeff, Karen and Jennifer need to be to recognize and face the moral duties and challenges in front of them? Can you think of any virtues, any habits of the heart or mind that would help them to behave morally here? What virtues, what attitudes, affections and loyalties would they need to behave like good Christians in this setting?

Choices. How should Jeff, Karen and Jennifer go about solving the problems before them? Are there any steps or resources you would recommend for making these moral choices? What should they do and where should they turn for counsel if they want to make these choices as authentic disciples of Christ?

Community. Why do Jennifer and about forty million other Americans currently lack adequate health coverage? What sorts of policies should our nation have about health care? What kinds of rules should we have about marriage in our society? Or about spouses and gay partners getting access to health care insurance and coverage? How would a community of authentic Christians deal with these questions?

Cassie Ruiz is an eighty-three-year-old widow with ALS living in a nursing facility outside of Portland, Oregon. Confined to a wheelchair and increasingly dependent on her not-so-portable oxygen tank, Cassie is slowly but steadily losing muscle control, and will probably die in four to six years. In the meantime she will need to spend down her life savings before qualifying for government assistance, and she can look forward to more and more weakness and dependence. Saddened and depressed at the thought of being a burden on her adult children, particularly her daughter Angelica (a single mom with four children of her own), and at the prospect of growing infirmity, Cassie had begun to wish God would just take her. Four weeks ago her doctor discovered an obstruction in her bowels, and a biopsy has determined that Cassie has cancer, which, if left untreated, will result in death in less than a year. Her physician and children are recommending surgery and/or chemotherapy, and warn that dying from cancer could be more painful than dying from her present illness. But Cassie believes that she would like to choose another option and inquires about the possibility of physician-assisted suicide, currently legal in her state. At least this way, she reasons, she can choose the way she dies, avoiding much of the pain and indignity of cancer or ALS and leaving her children a small inheritance, instead of being such an emotional and financial burden.

Character. What sorts of obligations do Cassie, her children and her doctor have in this case? What kinds of persons would Cassie, her children and doctors need to be to recognize and face the duties and problems in front of them? Can you think of any virtues, any character traits that would help them behave well here? What virtues, what good habits, attitudes, affections and loyalties would they need to behave like good Christians in this setting?

Choices. How should Cassie, her children and physicians go about solving the problems before them? Are there any steps or resources you would recommend for making these moral choices? What should they do and where should they turn for counsel or advice if they want to make these choices as authentic disciples of Christ?

Community. What sorts of beliefs and practices in our society have contributed to this crisis? Are there shared beliefs, social structures or policies that make it more likely Cassie will feel like a burden, be afraid of dying a slow death or be attracted to suicide? What kinds of social structures or beliefs would make it easier for Cassie and her children to face her illness and death with grace and compassion? What kinds of changes in our health-care system would make us resemble a more just or Christian community?

Facing the Issues

Every day millions of us pick up the morning paper, turn on the radio or catch an item on the TV news that leaves us wondering. AIDS activists demand that research protocols be shortened to get drugs to the market faster. Researchers complain that shortcuts will undermine the safety of the drugs being prescribed. Demonstrators picket against the World Trade Organization and World Bank, complaining of injustices against the poor and harms to the planet. Officials of both groups argue that free trade is the only real way to help the poor and improve environmental safeguards. Church and human-rights groups call for the elimination of land mines, and the U.S. government says it needs an exception in Korea to keep the peace there. Are there moral answers to these dilemmas? Are there Christian answers to them? And just how would we find out what they might be?

Meanwhile, in our homes, workplaces and ballot boxes we face a steady stream of moral questions and problems, some small, others fairly large. What sorts of TV shows, movies or video games are appropriate for our children? What kinds of rules should we have about our teens dating, drinking, smoking or going to church with us? When and how much say should they have in these matters? Are we consuming too much stuff, energy or natural resources? Do we need that new SUV, or should we get a compact or hybrid that would save gas and cut down on pollution? How much privacy do we need on the Web, or in our cubicle at work? What should we do if our pension plan is invested in companies using child labor or cutting down rain forests? Should we have a sexual-harassment policy at work that protects gays and lesbians? Should we vote for the new school levy, support a referendum on clean needle exchanges or come out in favor of increased funding for prisons? Can we vote for a candidate who is pro-choice or one in favor of capital punishment? What are the moral answers to these questions? What would the Christian answers be? How can we figure them out?

This is a book about Christian ethics. As the title suggests, it is also a book about "facing the issues" of Christian ethics, about wrestling with the stream of concrete, complex and often confounding moral challenges, questions and dilemmas we come up against in our personal and social lives. In other words, it is a book on what has traditionally been referred to as "special ethics," where we focus on particular issues, on the concrete moral problems encountered daily in areas like medicine, violence, sexuality, economics and the environment. And it is a book on Christian "special ethics," which means that the focus here is on trying to figure out just how disciples of Christ ought to respond to some of the very specific ethical challenges we face in our homes, communities, offices and voting booths. What should the Christian response (or responses) be to questions like assisted suicide, capital punishment, welfare reform, homosexual unions or global warming? And how do we go about discerning just what that response (or responses) ought to be?

There are other important and valuable books on what is known as "basic" or "fundamental" Christian ethics. Timothy O'Connell's *Principles for a Catholic Morality* and Richard Gula's *Reason Informed by Faith* are excellent models of this genre. Our own *Character, Choices & Community: The Three Faces of Christian Ethics* is a recent example. [1] In books like these the authors tend to focus on more fundamental or theoretical questions in Christian ethics. Different chapters explore the nature of human persons, communities and actions, discuss the meaning, history and perspectives of Christian morality and offer insights into the role of conscience, norms, virtues, conversion, sin, Scripture, tradition, experience and reason in Christian morality. These books on "basic" Christian ethics lay the groundwork for the more practical work of making decisions about particular cases and specific questions.

In *Facing Ethical Issues,* then, our goal is to build on the insights of "fundamental" Christian ethics and apply them to the job of making concrete judgments about a number of very specific moral problems and questions. In this book on "special ethics" we hope to move beyond the basic theories of Christian ethics and figure out some Christian answers to the various moral challenges and problems we encounter in medicine, sexuality and economics or when wrestling with issues relating to violence or the environment. And we hope to show just how Christians like ourselves might go about finding these answers.

We should also note, as we did in our first book, that we write this workbook on Christian ethics as Catholic theologians teaching at Catholic universities. Obviously, our work is an expression of who we are and where we are located. At the same time, a glance at our endnotes will indicate that our work is not sectarian in nature. We have drawn fairly heavily from the contributions of Christian theologians and teachings from a number of denominations. Thankfully, that is the way Christian ethics is done these days.

Character, Choices & Community

Still, even though this is a book on "special ethics," it is not just a book about making tough or messy moral decisions. Learning how to make good choices and coming up with the right answer to a moral question or problem are not the only ethical challenges Christians face in medicine, sexuality or economics or when dealing with questions of violence and the environment. As followers of Christ we are certainly called upon to "do the right thing" and to learn how to make good moral decisions. But that is not all. We also are called to become certain kinds of persons and communities. Indeed, we are called to become a communion of saints preparing for the reign of God, disciples who make up the people of God, holy women and men who are the body of Christ.

As disciples of Christ, then, we have a vocation to become the sorts of persons who have "put on Christ," persons who are immersed in and transformed by the mysteries of the Christian faith. We have a calling to become the sorts of persons who approach concrete moral challenges and problems with a specifically Christian set of attitudes, affections and virtues. We are to become Christlike.

And so in this text on "special ethics" we will need to be concerned not just with what we do, but with who we are becoming, with our choices *and* our character. We will need to ask just what habits of the heart and mind, what loyalties, perspectives, affections and skills are required of us if we are to become and behave like authentic disciples of Christ. That means asking what virtues we will need to be the kinds of persons who can discern and face the moral challenges of medicine, economics and sexuality as faithful Christians.

At the same time we are also aware that our choices and character do not exist in a vacuum, but are profoundly influenced by (and influence) the communities we belong to. We know full well that the shared beliefs and structures embedded in our communities can shape how we see and judge specific moral questions and predispose us to certain ways of thinking, feeling and acting. In a racist or sexist society it is harder to recognize the equality of all persons or the malice of discrimination. And it is harder to practice genuine justice.

And, as already noted, we appreciate that our Christian vocation summons us not just to be holy individuals, but a communion of saints, a society of friends held together by God's love and justice. Therefore it should not surprise us that part and parcel of our calling as Christians is to construct the sorts of communities that are shaped by these and other virtues, communities where doing the right thing and becoming good persons will be easier, not more difficult. So in this book on Christian "special ethics" we will attend not only to our choices and character, but also to our communities, asking ourselves just what sorts of shared structures and beliefs will we require to live out our vocation as Christians.

All of this means, then, that "facing the issues" of Christian ethics must involve more than making choices that are identifiably Christian. It should also include developing the sort of moral character and communities that are consistent with our calling as disciples of Christ.

A Workbook

It is also important to note that we are calling this text a "workbook" on Christian ethics, for that is exactly what we mean it to be. When we are interested in learning information about a subject or finding answers to particular questions we often ask an expert, look up a book or article in the library or turn to a Web site. In the jargon of the day we "download" the appropriate information, get the answers to our questions and go away satisfied. And indeed many works in "special ethics" have served as answer books, encyclopedic reference works providing us with the right answers to a host of particular questions. In the past priests learned moral theology from "handbooks" or "manuals" that offered readers the official or accepted positions on a wide range of moral questions. And lay Catholics often turned to their clergy for solutions to difficult moral dilemmas. In a similar fashion contemporary readers can turn to works like the *Catechism of the Catholic Church* or Richard Sparks's fine little book, *Contemporary Christian Morality: Real Questions, Candid Responses,* to find identifiably Catholic or Christian answers to a number of specific moral questions.[2]

But if we are interested in learning a skill or developing a habit, answer books are not quite so useful. Then we often turn to workbooks, where we can practice doing the work of solving problems or mastering skills ourselves. Here we seek to learn by doing, by studying models or examples and applying the insights and directions offered by our teachers to different situations, cases or problems. In this way we don't just learn answers; we learn how to find and critique these answers. For many of us workbooks were a part of how we learned to write, spell, do math or master a second language.

We have called this text a workbook, not because it has cases attached to each chapter, but because we want to acknowledge and highlight the very real ethical "work" that ordinary Catholics and other Christians are called upon to do today. This is a workbook because it is intended to help interested Catholic and Christian adults in their ongoing struggles to learn how to "do" Christian ethics better and better. It is offered with the hopes that interested readers may find in these pages some assistance or guidance in taking up the task of becoming more and more responsible moral agents living out their vocation as Christian disciples.

In the past ordinary Catholics often depended on their clergy and hierarchy to do much if not most of the work of Christian ethics for them. For many Catholics of an earlier generation obedience was the primary Christian virtue, and being moral usually meant following accepted norms and rules. Today, however, most lay Catholics find themselves in a very different place, one where they are increasingly called upon to do more of the actual work of informing their conscience and making moral choices, and one in which their own prudential judgments play a larger role. Much more so than in the past, today's ordinary Catholics are expected to accept fuller responsibility for their moral lives, choices and communities. Without denying the authority or expertise of the church's hierarchy or theologians, contemporary lay Catholics are called to full partnership in the work of Christian ethics. For many this development has been a liberating experience; for almost all it has been a challenging one.

Three things have brought Catholics to this new place as moral agents: education, ecumenism and engagement. First, the days when the cleric was the only person in the parish with a college degree are long gone. Today's Catholic laity are often as equally or better educated than their priests, and many have academic and professional expertise based upon special competencies in medicine, psychology, politics, economics, human sexuality, violence, the environment and even ethics. Thus, they can and should participate fully in the task of making moral judgments about specific questions in these fields. Second, since Vatican II an ecumenical spirit of dialogue with other Christian churches has meant that today's Catholics know more about the moral teachings of these other communities and are more likely to believe that they have something to learn from these voices. This ecumenical dialogue has also made many Catholics both more appreciative and more critical of their own moral tradition. As a result fewer Catholics now believe that their work as moral agents is done once they have heard the church hierarchy's most recent pronouncement on a particular question. And third, the spirit of engagement with the world fostered by Pope John XXIII and Vatican II's call for *aggiornamento* (updating) has meant that the church is deeply concerned with what is going on in the world and with whatever affects our sisters and brothers for good or ill. But it has also meant that usually the people in the front lines of this conversation between the church and the world are the ordinary (or perhaps extraordinary) lay Christians. And these are the people who have to decide just what it means in the concrete to follow Christ in the worlds of medicine, politics, sexuality, economics and the environment.

As a result of these changes the weight of moral responsibility in the church has shifted rather significantly, so that it now sits squarely (but not only) on the shoulders of ordinary Christians. No longer can anyone say they are just following orders. Every adult Christian has real ethical work to do.

Not everyone has been happy with these changes. Some have argued that contemporary Catholics currently pay too little attention to their bishops and the Vatican on moral issues. Others complain about so-called "cafeteria Catholics," who pick and choose what they like (or don't) about the church's moral teachings, or about theologians who are seen as far too ready to dissent from official church positions on sexuality or church discipline. Still, the general trend toward increased moral responsibility for lay Christians is well supported by recent church teachings, particularly by a series of official documents focusing on the role and place of conscience.

In The Church in the Modern World, the bishops of Vatican II stressed the importance, even sanctity, of the consciences of ordinary Christians and underscored their distinctive duties and roles as moral agents, noting that:

> Laymen should also know that it is generally the function of their well-formed Christian conscience to see that the divine law is inscribed in the life of the earthly city. From priests they may look for spiritual light and nourishment. Let the layman not imagine that his pastors are always such experts, that to every problem which arises, however complicated, they can readily give him a concrete solution, or even that such is their mission. Rather, enlightened by Christian wisdom and *giving close attention to the teaching authority of the Church,* (emphasis added) let the layman take on his own distinctive role.[3]

Later in the same document the bishops reversed centuries of Catholic moral thought and suggested that individual Christians should be allowed to follow their own well-formed consciences when deciding about the morality of war or wars.[4] And in the council's Declaration on Religious Freedom, the bishops again underscored the importance of the consciences of individual Christians. Instead of calling for simple obedience to church teachings, the document stated that "in the formation of their consciences, the Christian faithful ought *carefully to attend* (emphasis added) to the sacred and certain doctrine of the church."[5]

In his 1971 apostolic letter "A Call To Action," Pope Paul VI also highlighted the increased moral responsibilities of lay Catholics when he argued that often enough Christians on the scene were better equipped than Rome to make concrete moral judgments about political and economic options or policies.

> In the face of such widely varying situations it is difficult for us [the Vatican] to utter a unified message and to put forward a solution which has universal validity. Such is not our ambition, nor is it our mission. It is up to the Christian communities to analyze with objectivity the situation which is proper to their own country, to shed on it the light of the Gospel's unalterable words and to draw principles of reflection, norms of judgment and directives of action from the social teachings of the Church.[6]

And in their pastoral letters "The Challenge of Peace: God's Promise and Our Response" and "Economic Justice for All," the U.S. Catholic bishops further acknowledged the moral responsibilities and consciences of ordinary Christians in a particularly striking manner. They did this by consulting broadly with folks in parishes and dioceses around the nation and by incorporating the input and contributions of these groups into subsequent revisions of the documents. By seeking the insights, counsel and expertise of Christians whose education, experiences and competencies allowed them to make critical contributions to the process of moral discernment, the bishops paid tribute to the distinctive moral role and agency of the laity. They also recognized the community of baptized Christians as genuine partners in the work of Christian ethics. And, not too surprisingly, they also wrote a better and more informed letter than they would have done alone.

In order to help ordinary Christians exercise their full responsibility as moral agents and go about the work of forming and informing their consciences, a number of contemporary Christian ethicists have written a host of "how-to" books. Some of these works outline the skills or steps needed to make good moral decisions. Others describe the virtues essential to the formation of a Christian conscience or character. And still others lay out what is needed to build truly Christian communities.

Daniel Maguire's now classic essay, "Ethics: How to Do It," as well as Kenneth Overberg's *Conscience in Conflict: How to Make Moral Choices* and Richard Gula's *Moral Discernment* offer their audiences clear and helpful insights into the processes of making sound moral judgments as Christians. And in their previously mentioned pastoral letters on peace and economic justice the U.S. bishops hold up a particularly clear model of moral decision making, one that pays close attention to the voices of experience, Scripture, church teachings and moral reason. Meanwhile, other recent works, like Anne Patrick's *Liberating Conscience* and William Spohn's *Go and Do Likewise,* not only address the challenges of discerning the right moral choice, but also point out the practices and habits of the heart and mind (i.e., virtues) we will need if we are to fashion well-formed Christian consciences and become authentic disciples of Christ. And in Timothy O'Connell's *Making Disciples: A Handbook of Christian Moral Formation* the author describes the sorts of shared stories, beliefs and practices, indeed the kinds of communities that will empower us to act like and become moral Christians.[7]

It is in line with books like these and out of a growing recognition of the ethical work that ordinary Christians are currently expected to do that we have set out to write this workbook. We are hoping to offer a workbook in Christian ethics for adult believers in the messy middle of things, a book that attempts to take seriously their new location and responsibilities and that seeks to offer them some useful tools. We write this workbook for lay Christians just as earlier authors wrote the manuals of moral theology for clergy—to help prepare them for the work they have to do.

Thus, this workbook in "special ethics" is not a catechism, and its primary goal is not to offer the right or official answer to a slew of moral questions. We are not suggesting that such works are not useful or that they do not represent an important, even critical, resource for Christians seeking to inform their consciences or make tough moral decisions. We think they are quite important, and we ourselves use them regularly. We are only saying that this is not such a text. Rather, it is a workbook in Christian "special ethics," a somewhat messier text in which adult readers are actively encouraged to struggle with the tasks of recognizing, facing and resolving complex moral issues. And it is a book in which they are encouraged to do this by employing a method which recognizes that we are called to become good persons, make the right choices and build just communities, and which attends to the rich range of voices shaping an authentic Christian morality.

And so we are calling this text a workbook because it is our intent in these pages to offer just such a method for approaching the various moral challenges confronting us in the areas of medicine, sexuality, violence, economics and the environment. In the chapters that follow we hope to model a moral method that attends to both the importance of character, choice and community, and the contributions of the four voices of experience, Scripture, tradition and reason. In this way we hope to offer a thoughtful and responsible way to discern our shared moral duties as Catholic Christians. We are trying to teach, then, not so much the specific answers to particular questions, but a path for arriving at them.

Approach of the Text

Our approach in this text is relatively simple. In each of the following five chapters we will ask just how our Christian vocation should shape our character, choices and communities in a particular field of ethics. What sorts of persons will we need to become, what virtues will we require to respond as Christians to the moral challenges and demands we face in medicine, sexuality and economics, or when dealing with issues of violence and the environment? What sorts of choices would authentic Christians make about controversial questions in these differing areas and how would they arrive at these decisions? What types of shared myths and social practices, what kinds of community structures make it more difficult to live out our Christian vocation in these areas? And what sorts of reforms would bring us closer to living out our calling to be a communion of saints, the body of Christ?

Thus, each chapter will focus on one area of "special ethics" and be divided into an introduction, three major sections and a set of cases. After a brief introductory sketch of the history of Christian medical, sexual or economic ethics the first major section of each chapter will explore the issue of character. There we will try to identify some of the moral virtues needed to live out our call to Christian discipleship within the context of the various roles and relationships in which we find ourselves cast when dealing with questions of economics, medicine, sexuality, violence and the environment. In the second section (on choice) we will address three concrete (and often controversial) moral decisions by attending to the four fonts of wisdom—experience, Scripture, tradition and reason. Our goal here is to offer both a Christian response to the particular issue and (more importantly) a method of arriving at such a choice. And in the third section (on community) we will look into the ways our differing communities influence our perception of and response to the issues we face in these diverse areas. We will also offer some suggestions about Christian beliefs and practices that might lead to reform. Finally, each chapter will close with a set of cases offering readers an opportunity to apply some of the insights of the chapter to differing situations.

Character. In the first major section of each chapter we will be looking at our character and our virtues. And we will be asking just what sorts of persons we need to be in order to face the various moral challenges we encounter in the fields of medicine, economics and sexuality, or when dealing with questions of violence and the environment.

As Christians we have a calling, a vocation. And, as we have already noted, this vocation is not just to follow a certain set of rules or even to "do the right thing." It is a calling to become a certain kind of person, a disciple of Christ, a saint. We are not simply to observe the commandments or follow the rules of Christian ethics. Rather, we are to be converted, to "put on Christ," and to do this we will need to address much more than our external behavior or individual choices. We will need to pay attention to our character, to look deep into our hearts and embrace those attitudes, loyalties and affections that we have come to identify with Christ, or the disciple of Christ. The question for us, then, is not so much "What would Christ do?" but "Who is Christ calling us to be?" And this means that we need to discover and embrace those virtues that are characteristic of a disciple of Christ.

In general we suggest that virtues are those good moral habits, attitudes, loyalties and affections that lead to genuine human fulfillment, even perfection, on both personal and social levels. For Christians virtues are those habits that help us to be more Christlike. By contrast, vices are poor moral habits, affections, attitudes and beliefs that hinder human fulfillment or perfection, both personally and socially, and that draw us away from Christ.

Virtues, then, are not simply good ways of acting. They also include those attitudes, affections and beliefs from which actions flow and which are themselves deepened through consistent effort and choice. Indeed, virtues entail not just repeated acts, but a sustained and deepening commitment to be a certain kind of person. This is true whether we are talking about the classical Western virtues of justice, prudence, temperance and fortitude, the three theological virtues of faith, hope and charity, or other important virtues such as openness, hospitality, compassion and generosity. Justice, for example, is not simply a matter of acting justly. It includes all those attitudes, affections and beliefs that help sustain a person's or a community's commitment to *be* just. Understood in this way, virtues are not garments to be worn, but the stuff of one's soul.[8] In Aristotle's words, "virtue is that which makes the one who has it good, and the work that he or she does good."[9]

And just which virtues or dispositions do Christians need to face the moral challenges and demands we encounter in the fields of medicine, sexuality, economics, ecology and when deciding about issues of violence? In this book we respond to that question in two steps. First, we identify what seem to us to be some underlying virtues or convictions that ought to shape any Christian's approach to these areas of our lives. Thus, we would argue that any Christian dealing with economics ought to affirm the central importance and dignity of persons. Likewise, any Christian contemplating medical questions would need to be committed to the sanctity of human life and that the practice of justice and compassion would be essential to both of these settings. Second, we argue that the specific virtues required of us in different settings are usually those we need to be faithful to the duties and obligations generated by our various roles and relationships. For in the ordinary course of our lives we confront medical, economic, sexual and environmental questions or issues of violence within our various roles as parents, spouses, citizens, consumers, educators, workers or employers. And in these roles we have a number of duties to other folks—to our patients, spouses, workers, children, customers, neighbors, and all the other stakeholders (known and unknown) affected by our lives and choices. Thus, as disciples of Christ we can discern the specific virtues demanded of us in these various areas by asking what practices and habits will enable us to be faithful to those with whom we are "covenanted" in differing relationships.

What is critical here is that the virtues we identify as essential to living out our vocation as Christians in these various settings are grounded in the roles and relationships in which we find ourselves, and thus have a deeply "relational" character. That is, these are the virtues required if we are to live out our covenantal obligations to those we are tied to in our various roles.

As Christians we believe that virtues are not simply those habits we practice or acquire for self-improvement or perfection. Rather, we hold that in our baptism we have been called into covenants with God and our neighbors, and indeed with all of creation. And to be authentic disciples of Christ we need to embrace and practice the virtues that will enable us to be faithful to these moral bonds. As the Christian ethicist Paul Ramsey once wrote, "We are born within covenants of life with life. By nature, choice, or need we live with our fellowmen in roles or relations. Therefore, we must ask, What is the meaning of the *faithfulness* of one human being to another in every one of these relations? This is the ethical question."[10] And so, in the first section of each chapter we will try to name the general and specific virtues required of us as we seek to be authentic Christians within these differing arenas.

None of this is to suggest that the virtues we discuss are unique to Christians or that only Christians have a duty to practice virtuous medicine, sexuality or economics. All human persons and communities are called to be good and to practice virtue, and in fact it can often happen that other believers and nonbelievers exceed Christians in the practice of virtue. Still, this is a book on Christian ethics. And our point is to highlight the fact that as disciples of Christ, Christians have a calling to practice virtue and to bring that practice to the moral challenges and dilemmas they face in medicine, sexuality, economics, ecology and with regard to the use of violence.

Choices. In the second major section of each chapter we will look at some of the moral choices we are called upon to make in the various fields of "special ethics." To do this we will identify three current controversies in each of these fields, offer a method for approaching the decision-making process and make some recommendations.

The central method of this second section on choices will be to approach the process of moral decision making by attending to and integrating the different voices of four fonts of Christian morality: experience, Scripture, tradition and reason. For if we are to know how to respond to concrete moral challenges as Christians, we must certainly listen carefully to what the Bible and church teachings have to say to us. At the same time we must also take a long, hard look at the lessons of experience, and bring to bear all the resources of human wisdom. And so in each of the three controversial choices confronted in the second section of every chapter we will attempt to discern the appropriate choice or course of action by first listening long and hard to the moral wisdom, perspectives and insights embedded in these four fonts.

This is not a new or unique approach to Christian ethics. Many Christian ethicists rely on some version of this method in making moral choices, though Catholic authors have sometimes combined experience and reason in the notion of natural moral law, thus reducing the fonts of Christian morality to three. Still, our own use of this method may be slightly different from some others in that we do not see reason as a separate voice to be listened to alongside that of experience, Scripture and tradition. Instead, we understand reason as the way we interpret and integrate the insights and perspectives of the other three voices, the way we pull together the wisdom of experience, Scripture and tradition to fashion a genuinely Christian response to the question at hand.

At the same time, we also want to note that for us reason is not merely a matter of dry logic or sterile calculation. Rather, the reason we are speaking of is both fully human and fully Christian, fashioned of our heads, hearts and consciences, and it encompasses all our ways of knowing. It is a reason, as Richard Gula notes, "informed by faith," and by love and justice. It is also a reason informed by our noblest affections, sympathies and loyalties, as well as our most creative imaginations. And, to bring things full circle, it is a reason fed and watered by experience, Scripture and tradition.

Therefore, we will approach each of the controversial topics in the section on choices by listening to four voices: experience, Scripture, tradition and reason.

1. Voices of Experience. We begin our analysis of each controversial moral issue by first listening to the voice, or rather the voices of experience. Here the challenge before us is to be comprehensive in our listening, to attend to as many of the differing voices of experience as possible and to listen wisely. We need to be careful not to be unduly influenced by a single event or perspective or to let the voices of the powerless be drowned out by those with great wealth or authority.

So we will pay particular attention to three voices: (1) the voice of *history,* so we might understand how the present crisis came about and learn from the wisdom of the past; (2) the competing voices of the *contemporary* debate, so as to grasp the differing sides of the current controversy and acknowledge the complexity of the question at hand; and (3) the voices of those in the *margins,* so we might never forget or overlook those with the least protection or power and thus those most likely to be harmed by our choices.

Christians have a special reason for keeping an ear out for this third voice. The Hebrew prophets were constantly reminding their audiences to remember the *anawim* (Hebrew for "God's little ones"), those widows, orphans, aliens and other poor people who had no protector but God. And today we Christians are constantly being reminded of our own call to make a "preferential option for the poor," to stand with and come to the aid of those who are always falling through the cracks of modern society. We can hardly make such an option for today's *anawim* if we cannot even hear their voices, or the voices of those who cry out on their behalf. Often in these sections the voices we hear will not just be the poor, but also those experts and activists who stand with and advocate for those in the margins.

2. Scripture. Next we seek to attend to the voice (or voices) of Scripture, asking ourselves what relevant moral wisdom or insights are revealed to us in the Bible. What, in effect, does Scripture have to say on this topic or in this general area that will help us to discern a moral course of action? The wisdom or guidance we seek may come in the form of particular citations or specific teachings about the morality or immorality of a certain way of acting. We may even find a rule or saying of Jesus that provides concrete directions on how we are to act in a specific setting. It is often more likely, however, that we will find moral guidance from the shape or direction of a parable or story, from some theme or lesson deeply embedded in the larger fabric of Scripture's narrative or from the experience of being immersed in the parable of Jesus' life, death and resurrection. Often enough the moral wisdom we seek will come not in concrete pieces of advice, but in the distinctive perspectives, loyalties and affections that one "learns" from becoming a conscientious and attentive listener to God's word.

Here, too, the challenge is to listen wisely. For we are to attend to the voice (or voices) of Scripture with ears that have been schooled in faith by a Christian community entrusted with and shaped by this divine revelation. And we are to listen for Scripture's revealed wisdom with ears educated by the insights of contemporary biblical scholarship. In other words, we are to hear and interpret the voice of Scripture as educated believers. And we need to acknowledge that while there can be no genuinely Christian ethics that is not grounded in Scripture, it is often very hard work indeed to discern and apply the moral wisdom of Scripture to contemporary questions, particularly while also seeking to listen to the voices of tradition, experience and reason.

3. Tradition. The third voice we will attend to is that of tradition, or church teachings. Here we will listen to the voices of the *magisterium* (the teaching office of the church), attending carefully and diligently to official documents from the popes and bishops on the various moral issues at hand. At the same time we will also give an ear to the reflections and writings of moral theologians and Christian ethicists who have wrestled with these and related questions down through the ages. And we will pay serious attention to the lives and examples of those saints whose words or deeds offered a particularly striking witness to the Gospel and whose lives promise to teach us something very important about how to be moral in this or that part of our lives.

For Catholic Christians this third voice has a particularly important weight and needs to be attended to respectfully, for we believe that the Holy Spirit inspires and guides the *magisterium* in a special manner. At the same time, this does not mean that the *magisterium* replaces our conscience or that reading church documents is a substitute for doing the hard work of moral reasoning. Rather, church teachings are designed to guide and serve us in the work of moral decision making, and we are to approach such teachings with humility and openness.

With this voice too, then, we must be wise listeners, recognizing the context of particular documents, and the purposes and audiences for which they were written. While attending diligently to official church statements on various questions, we must also have an ear to their historical settings, their conversational partners, their underlying philosophical and scientific assumptions and their place in the ongoing development of church teaching.

Finally, although we give priority in this section to distinctively Catholic voices, we also believe that listening to the voice of tradition in a book on Christian ethics must necessarily mean including a number of other Christian voices as well. And so we will attend occasionally to the contributions of other Christian churches, teachers and theologians, allowing these voices to enrich our understanding of both tradition and Christian ethics.

4. *Formulating a Christian Response.* The task in this final part of the section on moral choices is to use our reason to formulate some sort of specifically Christian moral response to the question or issue at hand. Obviously, given what has gone before, this response needs to be shaped by the insights gained from the conversation among the three voices of experience, Scripture and tradition.

In general, our approach in this part has been twofold. We have sought first to identify a series of general convictions that we believe would need to inform any authentically Christian choice regarding the issue in question and that seem consistent with what we have learned from experience, Scripture and tradition. Then we seek to identify what we believe are some of the really hard questions that must be addressed to resolve the issue at hand. Some of these questions are questions of fact and could be resolved with more research and concrete information. Others are questions of value or judgment, and can only be decided, not necessarily answered. At any rate, we tend to shy away from offering concrete answers to the choices in this section, primarily because it is our goal here to model a method of making choices and not to come up with specific solutions.

Community. Finally, in the third major section of each chapter we will look at two moral issues or problems we face *as* communities, and suggest ways in which these issues challenge us to reform the communities to which we belong. Our method here will be in three parts. First, we will identify what seem to us to be two examples of social sins. Then we will highlight the shared beliefs (or ideologies) and embedded practices that make up these social sins. Finally, we will offer some Christian beliefs and structural reforms that might help to address and correct the problem.

As we noted above, the communities we belong to influence (for good or ill) our moral character and choices. For these communities consist not only of people, but also of the established patterns of believing and behaving that the members of these groups have embraced, and pass on to their children. (Catholics believe in the sacraments and celebrate the Eucharist on Sundays. Citizens of democracies believe in civil liberties and elect their leaders. Pacifists believe in love and practice nonviolence.) And as members of these communities we often internalize the ways of thinking and acting modeled by our communities, accepting them as "the way things are" or "the way things ought to be."

But not all of our community beliefs or practices are good. Not all of them help us to be moral or just persons, treat others fairly or to do the right thing. And not all of them help us to become or act like authentic disciples of Christ. Some beliefs and practices—like racism and apartheid, consumerism and environmental abuse or militarism and arms races—make it more difficult to practice virtue or make the right moral choice. Some encourage us to take care of ourselves and ignore the unjust sufferings of others, to go along with immoral policies or to scapegoat the innocent and weak in society.

In a very real sense these shared beliefs and practices, these social structures, are the ways in which we act *as* communities. They are our communal deeds. And at the same time it could also be said that these patterns of thinking and acting reflect our communal character. They are, in a sense, who we are *as* communities. And when these patterns of believing and behaving harm others unjustly and make it more difficult for us to become and act like authentic Christians, we may speak of them as "social sins." For these sinful social structures embody and magnify our personal sins, embedding them in our communal character and passing them on as an inheritance to our children and grandchildren. Included in these social sins are: "(1) structures that oppress human beings, violate human dignity, stifle freedom, or impose gross inequality; (2) situations that promote and facilitate individual acts of selfishness; and (3) the complicity or silent acquiescence of persons who do not take responsibility for the evil being done."[11]

Addressing or overcoming these social sins means we need to recognize, challenge and replace both the ideologies and practices that underlie and embody them. And to do this we need to identify a counterbalancing set of beliefs and practices. Indeed, we have to reform our community's present ways of thinking and acting, replacing them with alternatives that are informed by an authentically Christian vision and oriented to a just treatment of all persons and communities.

In each of the following chapters, then, we will identify two social sins relevant to the practice of medicine, sexuality or economics, etc. The sins in question might include an "ism" like individualism or consumerism or a more specific problem like domestic violence or our nation's prison-industrial complex. In either case, we will first lay out those shared beliefs or ideologies and embedded practices that constitute this social sin. Then we will recommend a corrective set of Christian beliefs and structural reforms that may help us to repent communally of the social sin in question and move toward a more just and Christian community.

Cases. As we have noted throughout this chapter, our primary goal in this workbook on Christian ethics is to offer a *method* for facing a wide range of specific moral issues and challenges. This method attends to the three dimensions of our character, choices and communities and listens to the voices of experience, Scripture, tradition and reason. We seek to model this method in the following chapters on economics, violence, sexuality, the environment, and medicine, and we encourage our readers to apply it in the cases attached to each chapter.

In each of the next five chapters, then, readers will find five cases, one at the beginning and four at the close of the chapter. These cases are offered to provide readers with an opportunity to apply the method of this workbook to a number of concrete moral issues and challenges.

Readers may work through these cases alone or as part of a group discernment process. We recommend, however, that they attempt to do at least a couple cases in concert with others. This will allow readers to become more aware of their own decision-making priorities and processes while learning something from the strategies and steps of their colleagues. At the same time it could also help to broaden their perspective and teach them something about the challenges and advantages of group decision-making. Because so many of our moral decisions need to be made in collaboration with others and because we can learn so much from others in a good group discernment process, we believe this is an important learning tool.

Following the cases, readers will find a brief list of resources at the end of each chapter. We hope these may prove useful in working through the cases or in learning more about any of a number of ethical issues in economics, sexuality, medicine or regarding violence and the environment. A number of these resources are educational and advocacy organizations providing helpful information and specific programs targeted at a variety of contemporary moral problems and social injustices relating to the differing spheres of our lives. And some of these resources are useful journals or magazines.

In any case, readers should feel free to seek as much outside information, expertise and advice as possible when working through the various cases. For while we tried to put enough information in the cases and chapter to guide our audience through the decision-making process, our judgment can always be enriched by seeking out more input from experience, Scripture, tradition and reason. And it never hurts to seek the good judgment and counsel of wise people with extensive experience.

Finally, as an aid to working through the cases, we conclude this introductory chapter with a worksheet that includes a set of questions on the three dimensions of our character, choices and communities. These questions, offered as one possible way of analyzing the cases, are based on the approach we have used in writing the individual chapters. We begin by asking readers to identify the roles, relationships and duties of the various persons in these cases and to think about the sorts of character or virtues these persons would need in order to behave as authentic Christians. Then, in the questions on moral choices readers are asked to identify the basic moral issue(s) or choice(s) confronting the agents in this case and to attend to the voices of experience, Scripture, tradition and reason as a guide in making their decisions. They are also invited to identify some basic Christian convictions that should inform their decision-making process, as well as any hard questions that need to be addressed. And in the questions on community we ask about the sorts of sinful social structures that have contributed to the problem at hand, and about the kinds of structural reforms that would help us become the types of communities we are called to be as disciples of Christ. We hope this worksheet is useful.

Worksheet

Character

1. *Roles, Relations & Duties.* What are the various roles and relationships in which the central characters in this case find themselves? How do these roles and relationships connect or tie these persons to other persons or groups of persons? As a result of all these differing roles and relationships, what are some of the various moral duties the people in this case have to one another and other persons and/or groups? Are some of these duties more important than others? Which are the most important?

2. *Virtues.* What kinds of persons would the people in this case need to be in order to recognize and fulfill the various moral duties and challenges facing them here? What are some virtues, attitudes, affections and loyalties they would need to behave as authentic Christians?

Choices

1. *Identifying the Choice.* What is the basic or central choice confronting the people in this case? What are some of the conflicting values or goods that the people in this case will need to make choices about? Are there competing duties that the people in this case have to each other or other persons or groups?

2. *Seek Counsel.* What moral wisdom or insight can we gain about the choice(s) to be made from the voices of experience, Scripture and tradition? What persons or resources would be most useful in discovering what these various fonts of wisdom have to tell us about the issues or choices in this case?

3. *Formulating a Christian Response.* What might be some basic convictions that the Christian perspective brings to the central choice or issue in this case? What are some hard questions that need to be answered regarding this choice?

Community

1. *Social Sins.* Are there some social sins embedded in this case? Are there any social ills or injustices, any shared ways of thinking or acting that are contributing to the problems in this case or making it harder for the people here to make good choices or behave well?

2. *Christian Reforms.* What sorts of social practices or beliefs might need to be changed to make the structures and institutions discussed in this case more just, more Christian? What kinds of reforms are needed on the institutional or societal level? Why?

CHAPTER TWO:
Economic Justice

Case #1: What Do We Owe?

Looking for a less hectic lifestyle, Blythe and Tyrone Calder are a professional couple in their early fifties who have recently relocated from San Francisco to Spokane, Washington, a place where they are no longer burdened by the need to make long commutes or pay city and state income taxes. Aside from these advantages, a number of other things drew the Calders to make this move. First, both of them were able to find well-paying jobs. Blythe works as a computer analyst for a moderately large computer corporation, making $66,000 a year, while Tyrone earns $61,000 as an associate dean at a private university. Second, the couple (who had recently become empty-nesters when their two daughters graduated from excellent schools in the California state university system) were able to use the profit from the sale of their relatively modest California home to purchase a spacious luxury condominium located along the Spokane river within easy walking distance of the downtown district. Third, while offering fewer of the amenities of urban life than they might have found in San Francisco, Spokane's location provides them with easy access to dozens of uncrowded recreational areas where they could enjoy canoeing, biking, skiing, golf and hiking in a variety of lakeside and mountain settings. Indeed, after a year in Spokane, the Calders are contemplating purchasing a small summer place near one of the lakes in nearby northern Idaho.

One of the nicer surprises of this move, however, has been the discovery of a vibrant and welcoming faith community at a nearby downtown parish. Having been alerted to St. Vincent's by one of his colleagues at work, Tyrone and Blythe have been attending this small Catholic parish for nearly a year and are grateful to belong to such a hospitable and active church: a place where the laity are deeply involved, where there are several outreach programs connecting parishioners to neighborhood shelters and drop-in centers, where the preaching is often excellent and where working class, homeless and professional people celebrate Sunday liturgy side by side.

As part of the Lenten adult ed program this year the parish's Social Justice Committee brought in Sister Jane Thompson—a social activist who teaches political science at the local Catholic university—to address a proposal supporting a progressive income tax for the state and to explore the moral obligations of Christians to tithe a significant percentage of their income for the poor. Sister Jane offered a threefold argument in support of the tax measure. First, a state income tax is necessary to adequately provide for the state's burgeoning transportation, education and welfare budgets. Second, such a progressive tax would be much more suitable than the present reliance on an 8.3 percent sales tax, an approach that unduly burdens the poor, and would provide for a better distribution of educational resources than real estate taxes do. And third, Christians have a moral duty to provide for both the common good and the protection of our weakest members, a duty not sufficiently met by the relatively small amounts Americans give to charities. Taxes, Sister Jane argued, are the way most of us "tithe" and give alms for the poor, and we should do that in a truly just fashion, even if it hurts.

Walking back to their condominium from church, Tyrone and Blythe spoke about the talk, agreeing that such a tax would make a sizeable cut in their combined income. What, they wondered, did they owe to the common good, or to the poor? Were they, as many Americans believe, entitled to pay low taxes and keep as much of their wealth as possible? What did they intend to do with their money now that the girls were raised and school paid for? Could they excuse themselves from supporting this legislation because they had both worked hard to build up their savings and incomes? Could they argue that having paid high taxes in California all those years entitled them to let others carry the burden? Even if the measure didn't pass, Blythe wondered, just how much of their income ought they to be tithing or sharing with those in need? Now that they were DINKS (double income, no kids), did they have an increased obligation to share with the less fortunate? The following Sunday Father Ignazio asked Blythe if she would be willing to serve on a parish committee working for tax reform and exploring the notion of tithing. What should she do?

Introduction. Indeed, what are any of us, as Christians, to do about money? What are we to think about property, possessions and accumulated goods? Or about poverty, consumption and sharing with others? Are ownership and wealth gracious blessings from God, rewards for our hard work and clever planning? Or are they "the root of all evil," distracting and addictive temptations that lead us farther and farther away from God and harden our hearts to our suffering neighbors? Or, yet again, might they be helpful resources in our struggle to create more humane communities, useful goods in our campaign to meet the needs of the whole human community? At times Jesus seems to suggest that we should give up all our possessions and embrace poverty, and yet it seems clear that for the millions of people in our country (and the hundreds of millions around the planet) who find themselves trapped in poverty this is a cruel, frightening and dehumanizing condition that keeps them from growth or happiness. And yet we also know that wealth, all too often fails to provide any real meaning or dignity to those who spend their lives amassing more and more of it.

And what about the things we do to make money, or indeed the things we do with our wealth once we have received or made it? What is the meaning of our work? How are we to invest or share our resources? What do we owe to the common good, to the poor, to the victims of injustice, to the generations yet unborn? What sorts of rights and duties do we have as laborers, employers, owners? And what kinds of rights or duties do those who cannot work have, or those who do the work of taking care of our children and elders without the benefits of a paycheck?

This chapter, which is about economic justice, tries to address some of these questions from a Christian perspective. We attempt in these pages to think about the ways in which our Christian faith calls us to live and act in a world where wealth and property are both a blessing and a distraction, and where the justice and compassion we are called to show our neighbors is often worked out in our economic behavior and relations. And so we will explore here some of the ways in which Scripture, tradition, reason and experience direct us as Christians to shape our character, choices and communities when dealing with economic questions.

We begin this chapter, then, with the briefest sketch of the roots and history of Catholic social teachings, paying particular attention to what this growing body of work says about our duties in the area of economics. Next we turn to the question of character, exploring some of our various economic roles and relationships and suggesting a number of virtues critical to living out our vocation as Christian disciples in these different settings. Then we examine three controversial choices regarding economic justice—welfare reform, affirmative action and the international debt—and ask about possible Christian responses to these issues. Following that, we explore some of the larger social beliefs and structures shaping our national community's practice of economic justice and suggest how our Christian faith might offer critiques and alternatives. Finally, at the close of the chapter readers will find four more brief cases, offering further opportunities to explore Christian thought on economic justice and apply it to particular situations. As in other chapters these cases will be followed by a list of organizational resources that might prove helpful in getting to know more about the questions addressed in the case and throughout the chapter.

The Roots of Christian Teaching about Economic Justice

The authors of the Hebrew Scriptures believed that Yahweh's covenant with Israel demanded, among other things, economic justice for the poor. In both Deuteronomy (chs. 12–26) and the writings of classical prophets like Isaiah, Jeremiah and Amos, being faithful to Yahweh meant practicing *sedaqah* (covenantal justice), which obliged the Hebrews to show special concern for the needs of widows, orphans, aliens and other poor who constituted the *anawim,* or "God's little ones." Jesus, who began his public ministry by announcing that the Spirit of the Lord had anointed him to "bring good news to the poor," affirmed this tradition by teaching his disciples that whatever they did for the hungry, sick and homeless they were doing for God. As a result, the followers of Christ saw an intimate connection between their faith in Jesus and their obligations to the poor, and down through the centuries Christian communities founded countless institutions offering aid to impoverished persons at home and abroad.[1]

Still, much of what we think of as Christian social thought on economics began in response to the turmoil of the industrial revolution. In the second half of the nineteenth century industrialization and urbanization were transforming life in Europe and the United States, creating both an unprecedented explosion of wealth and a vast chasm separating armies of impoverished factory workers and small clusters of wealthy owners. In Manchester and throughout England Christian Socialists like the Anglican theologian Frederick Maurice attacked the injustices of laissez-faire capitalism and spoke out in defense of workers.[2] On the continent Social Catholics like Archbishop Ketteler of Mainz and the members of the Fribourg Union "condemned the ruthless competition and harsh individualism that typified early capitalism," and called for a just wage and safe working conditions for workers.[3] And in the United States the social gospel movement, which grew out of the experience of Protestant pastors ministering to the working class and urban poor, argued that compassion and cooperation, not competition, should be the rule governing human relations. The Baptist theologian Walter Rauschenbusch, perhaps the social gospel's most ardent (and radical) spokesperson, called for a Christian social order that would transform not just the hearts and minds of men and women, but the very economic life of the community.[4]

At the end of the century Pope Leo XIII joined this growing chorus of Christian voices calling for economic justice for industrial workers and began a tradition of Catholic social teachings that w seek to address the concerns of the world's *anawim* by "reading the signs of the times" in the light of the Gospel's call to discipleship. Speaking as pastors deeply concerned with the ways differing economic, political and social structures were affecting the lives and dignity of all their sisters and brothers, Catholic popes and bishops sought to raise a prophetic voice reminding Christians and all persons of good will of our duty to work for a world in which the poor and marginalized are empowered to develop and participate as fully human persons.

Over the past century Catholic social teaching on economic justice has developed in response to a wide variety of concerns, but has been shaped most significantly by its attention to three central issues: (1) the impact of the industrial (and then postindustrial) revolution; (2) the shift from European colonialism to a neocolonialism managed increasingly by multinational corporations; and (3) the East-West bloc competition of the Cold War. At the same time this growing body of church teachings has also been characterized by a steady commitment to three central values: (1) the dignity of human persons, (2) the common good and (3) a preferential option for the poor.

The Story of Catholic Social Teachings in Three Phases[5]

Phase One (1891–1960): Justice for the Workers. Much of the early writing in Catholic social thought was in response to the terrible condition of industrial workers resulting from the excesses of laissez-faire capitalism. In the first social encyclical, "On the Condition of Labor" (1891), Pope Leo XIII cried out against the workers' desperate poverty, miserable wages, long hours, unbearably poor and unsafe working conditions and utter powerlessness at the hands of a small number of inordinately wealthy employers. Writing two generations later, Pope Pius XI admitted in "The Reconstruction of the Social Order" (1931) that workers had made some real progress, but warned of an increasing concentration of wealth and power in capitalist societies.

Still, Catholic social teaching was also critical of socialist solutions to the workers' problems. Leo XIII rejected the elimination of private property, seeing this as an even greater threat to the long-term security and rights of workers. Meanwhile, both he and Pius XI were deeply concerned about the tendency in socialist societies to reduce persons to mere cogs in the machine of the state.

In general, Catholic social teachings sought to protect industrial labor from the excesses of both laissez-faire capitalism and socialism by doing three things: (1) defending the rights of workers, (2) focusing on the true dignity of human work and (3) reminding the state of its duty to protect the weak. Leo XIII defended workers' rights to a living wage, private property, safe working conditions, sufficient rest and unions; Pius XI and John XXIII addressed the rights to employment and fuller participation in the running of companies, as well as the right to emigrate to find new work and the right to sufficient education. Rejecting the notion that human labor was simply a commodity for exchange or exploitation, Catholic social teachings stressed that the value of human work flowed from the dignity of the men and women who labored, that these workers were more important than mere profits (people, not money, were the bottom line) and that workers and owners needed to cooperate with each other to serve the common good. Finally, church documents argued that the state had a responsibility to address the growing gap between the rich and poor by acting on behalf of the most powerless in society.

Phase Two (1961–91): Justice for the Nations. Although still deeply concerned about justice for workers, in the 1960s Catholic social teaching broadened its focus and began to address more global questions of economic justice. Beginning with Pope John XXIII's "Christianity and Social Progress" and "Peace on Earth" (1963), and later in Vatican II's "Pastoral Constitution on the Church in the Modern World" (1965) and Pope Paul VI's "The Development of Peoples" (1967), church documents took up questions of international trade, the economic development of poor nations and the impact of the arms race on the world's poor.

The central issue addressed by Catholic social teachings in this new era was the growing gap between the North and South. For in spite of the end of European colonialism in the two decades after World War II, many developing nations in Asia, Latin America and Africa were left behind by the postwar boom going on in industrial countries, trapped in a cycle of poverty, dependence and debt. In part this growing gap was the heritage of European colonialism (in which the church itself played a part). In part it resulted from internal problems in less developed countries: government corruption, poor management of resources and the presence of small aristocracies controlling vast amounts of the national wealth and land. But church documents pointed out that other causes were also at work. In many poor countries huge multinational corporations (MNCs) based in North America, Europe and Japan dominated the national economy in a new form of colonialism. Without the restraint of unions or government regulations to hold them in check, these corporations were often allowed to exploit local workers with pitifully low wages and unsafe working conditions while paying little or no attention to the disastrous environmental effects of their operations. At the same time international trade and banking arrangements were structured to protect the advantages of the industrial and postindustrial countries of the North.

Throughout the Cold War, however, Catholic social teachings also addressed the dangers and harms of both the arms race and the increasing competition between the East and West. Repeatedly Popes John XXIII, Paul VI and John Paul II pointed out that the huge global investments in armaments robbed poor nations of the resources needed to meet the basic needs of their peoples and forced these countries to postpone or cancel plans for economic development. Even worse, the competition between the blocs often resulted in regional arms races and conflicts in some of the world's poorest nations, causing intolerable suffering to the poor there.

Overall, Catholic social teachings responded to the gap between the North and South and the competition between the East and West by calling for development, disarmament and solidarity. Particularly in Paul VI's "The Development of Peoples" the church argued that real development meant not merely economic growth, but the full participation of all persons and nations in the various political, economic and social structures of the day.[6] It also involved protecting a full spectrum of personal and national rights and the liberation from every unjust and oppressive structure. Church teaching further affirmed that the nations of the world, particularly the nuclear powers, must take immediate and concrete steps at mutual disarmament, shifting global resources from weapons to development. And finally, Catholic social teachings continued to stress the need to recognize the interdependence of all earth's peoples by working for solidarity between the world's rich and poor.

The Present Situation (1991–Today). Since the end of the Cold War, Catholic social teachings have focused on the challenges facing people around the world as a result of the globalization of the market, the growing power of MNCs and the birth of information capitalism. Church documents address the exploitation of workers and natural resources in less developed nations, the permanent loss of employment for a whole class of people in both the North and South and the growing ecological impact of development around the world. And there is concern about the erosion of social welfare programs in the North and the spiraling international debt of many nations in the South.

CHARACTER:
Bringing Discipleship to the Marketplace

The bishops of Vatican II point out in The Church in the Modern World that we are called to be disciples of Christ not just at church or in our homes, but at work and in the marketplace as well.[7] And in their 1999 social statement on economic life, the Evangelical Lutheran Church of America notes that we live out our calling from God in a wide variety of settings, including the economy. For "through (our) human decisions and actions, God is at work in economic life."[8] Indeed, for most of us our vocation as followers of Christ is largely worked out in the various professional and social settings of our lives, and so the ways in which we behave as economic agents—as workers, employers, shareholders, citizens and/or consumers—comprise an essential part of our identity as disciples. For it is in these various roles that we find ourselves in relationships with all sorts of neighbors (persons and/or groups), relationships generating a wide array of moral obligations and calling Christians to behave with faithful and compassionate justice. It is also in these roles that we need to make important and often difficult moral judgments between competing values and goods, judgments that reveal the shape of our Christian character.

To a large degree our behavior and choices in these various roles and our response to these differing relationships are shaped by our underlying perspectives, dispositions and passions. In other words, *how* we act as workers, employers, shareholders, citizens, and/or consumers is affected by the moral virtues and vices making up our character. The question we need to address here is just which perspectives, dispositions, passions and intentions Christian disciples should bring to these roles and relationships. What virtues should shape and inform our behavior as economic agents in the world?

Before examining the virtues required for the specific roles we take up as economic agents, it is possible to suggest four general convictions that ought to characterize the approach of all disciples to questions in the marketplace. First, the Christian tradition and Catholic social teaching stress the absolute centrality and inviolable dignity of human beings, noting that all persons are made in the image and likeness of God, and reminding us that economies are made for humans and not the other way around. Second, biblical teaching and Christian thought make it clear that we are to see the gifts of creation (and our talent to shape these gifts) not primarily as private property to be owned and disposed of as we choose, but as a sacred trust from God intended for the good of the whole planet, to be cared for with diligence and shared fairly with our neighbors and descendants. Third, Christians are to see all persons and communities as fellow children of the same God, rejecting any stratified divisions of race, gender, faith, occupation or national origin and behaving toward neighbor and stranger alike with both covenantal justice *(sedaqah)* and solidarity. Finally, in the eyes of the disciple the *anawim,* consisting of the world's poor, oppressed and marginalized, have a special status and make a particular claim on our attention. Exercising a preferential option for the poor, we are to be their advocates and allies.

Specific Roles

Workers. There are a lot of things we don't like about work. We often complain that it is frustrating, difficult and tedious, that too many people sacrifice health and family in an obsession with work, or that millions of others are exploited and discarded by their employers. Still, although personal and social sin have in some ways damaged our experience of it, work is basically good for us. Indeed, it is a fundamental good for human persons and communities, and it is in our role as workers that we make what is probably the most important contribution to economic justice. Why is work a fundamental good for us? As the U.S. Catholic bishops point out in "Economic Justice for All," in work we earn our daily bread, share in God's ongoing creation of ourselves and our world and cooperate with our sisters and brothers in contributing to the larger common good.[9] In other words, our work allows us to provide for ourselves and our families, but even more it gives us a way (maybe *the* way) to be creative, to make a mark and a difference in the world around us, and to join with others in building a better and more human community.[10]

Our role as workers places us in various relationships and generates a number of corresponding duties. We work to provide for our families, and have an obligation to make certain they are well taken care of. We work with and alongside other laborers and should do what we can to assure that they are treated fairly by ourselves and our employers. Indeed, this duty to our coworkers also includes those working in other places, as well as those who cannot find sufficient work because of personal disabilities or economic injustices. We work for private and public employers and owe them a fair day's work for a fair day's wage. In our work we also provide products and services for customers who are entitled to goods that are safe and well made and work that meets professional standards. Finally, we work within local, national and global communities, which provide the resources and conditions for our labor, and we have a duty not to exploit the human or natural resources of these communities or to make products that make the world less safe or peaceful.[11]

In our role as workers we are called to practice two types of justice. Commutative justice, which calls for the fair exchange of goods and services between individuals, demands that we meet all our contractual obligations and provide employers and customers with a good product and/or service in return for their monies. We are to give an honest day's work for a fair day's wage. Social justice, on the other hand, concerns our duty to contribute to the common good and obliges workers and unions to make certain that we do our fair share in building up the wealth of the society and providing for the poor. Often the best way to assure that we are practicing both of these types of justice is to be industrious and creative as workers, making certain we are contributing our fair share to the common good. At the same time it is also important for us to be cooperative, both with other workers and with anyone interested in improving the overall conditions of our work and the community. Integrity or honesty is also a critical virtue for workers, for much of our labor depends on being able to trust and work with others. Finally, we require a certain amount of prudence in balancing the demands of work with our duties to family and community, as well as our needs for rest, leisure and prayer.

Employer/Manager. Christians who own or manage businesses also have a critical role in working for economic justice and a particular vocation to contribute to the common good. Indeed, as John Paul II has noted, "...the degree of well-being which society today enjoys would be unthinkable without the dynamic figure of the business person, whose function consists of organizing human labor and the means of production so as to give rise to the goods and services necessary for the prosperity and progress of the community."[12]

Like workers, employers and managers also find themselves in a network of relationships and have obligations not simply to the company's shareholders, but also to its various "stakeholders," including employees, customers and the various communities in which it operates. Indeed, in an age when the power of corporations is often disproportionately greater than that of workers, consumers, or even local communities or governments, employers and managers have a particular responsibility to assure that all parties are treated justly. Along with exercising a prudent stewardship of their stockholders' investments and assuring just wages and safe working conditions for their employees, owners and managers also have a duty to deliver safe, useful and quality products and services to customers and to refrain from harming or endangering the larger community. And, of course, they have an obligation to compete fairly.

Along with commutative justice in their relations with employees and customers, entrepreneurs and employers must also practice social justice in their dealings with larger communities. This is particularly true of huge MNCs operating in places with insufficient protection for human rights, fair business practices or environmental safety.[13] Furthermore, as John Paul II notes in a 1991 encyclical celebrating a century of Catholic social teachings, owners and managers also need such virtues as "diligence, industriousness, prudence in undertaking reasonable risks, reliability and fidelity in interpersonal relationships, as well as courage in carrying out decisions which are difficult and painful but necessary."[14]

Stockholder. Although many working- and middle-class people may not often think of themselves as corporate shareholders, an increasingly large number of us own stock indirectly by way of pension plans, retirement accounts or mutual funds, and the ranks of those purchasing shares directly through brokers, bankers or even off the Internet grow daily. While Catholic social teaching defends the right to the private ownership of productive property, it also teaches that such owners have larger social obligations than simply increasing their profits. In "The Reconstruction of the Social Order," Pius XI reminds us that investors provide an important service in creating opportunities for work and economic development, but they also have duties to make certain that the wealth they hold privately serves the larger common good for which God intended it.[15]

In our increasingly global market middle-class shareholders in Pittsburgh or San Diego often find themselves owning stock in MNCs based in Korea, Germany or the United States and operating plants in Nicaragua, Thailand or Nigeria. While these relationships can seem inordinately complex and remote, they are quite real and generate moral obligations. For shareholders have a duty not just to provide for their own families, but also to treat their companies' stakeholders fairly. At the very least this means not exploiting human and natural resources to pad our retirement accounts or dumping dangerous weapons or chemicals on the market to pay for our children's education.[16]

Practicing social justice in our role as shareholders means being good stewards with our investments. This first requires prudence, as we investigate the companies or funds under consideration for purchase. It also demands compassion, as we seek to understand and care about the workers, customers and communities who will be affected by our companies.

Citizen. Another less immediate but critically important way in which we influence economic justice is through our role as citizens. Catholic social teaching notes that as members of both individual states and the larger human family we are obliged to contribute to the national and global common good. At the same time church documents like Leo XIII's "On the Condition of Labor" and John XXIII's "Peace on Earth" argue that the state plays a key role in assuring economic justice. It does this by establishing a legal framework for the marketplace, protecting the rights of all its citizens—especially the poor, and providing those important services and goods not supplied by the private sector.[17] And it is in our role as citizens that we decide which legislation and what taxes are needed for the state to achieve these necessary goals.

As voters and taxpayers we are obliged to work through our national government to set reasonable boundaries on the scope and authority of the marketplace. We must assure the protection of a full range of human rights for all our fellow citizens—including both civil and political liberties like freedom of speech, religion and assembly and economic rights to basic goods like employment, education and health care. We must do our best to generate full employment and ensure fair labor and trading practices. We also have a duty to provide for the long-term stability and development of our society, making prudent investments in the infrastructures of public health, transportation, education and welfare and assuring that there is an adequate "safety net" for all our citizens, so no one is without access to the basic necessities of life. And while each nation has a particular obligation to care for its own members, the church teaches that we are not just citizens of one country, but of the whole world, and that our civic duties do not stop at the border. Indeed, given the size of our national economy, the grave needs of many poor nations and the absence of a sufficiently powerful international authority, the U.S. bishops argue in "Economic Justice for All" that citizens of this country have a unique responsibility to work for global economic justice.[18] At the very least this would mean providing real support for the UN and other international aid organizations working for fair trade, labor and banking practices around the planet and offering special assistance to developing nations.

In The Church in the Modern World the bishops of Vatican II note that "citizens should develop a generous and loyal devotion to their country, but without any narrowing of mind. In other words, they must always look simultaneously to the welfare of the whole human family, which is tied together by the manifold bonds linking races, peoples, and nations."[19] Thus, authentic patriotism calls us as American citizens to practice social justice by contributing a fair share of effort and capital to *both* the national and global common goods. We are also obliged to practice distributive justice, which mandates that each person or group receives a fair share of the common wealth. This means that we must direct our government to provide adequately for the welfare of all its members while also attending to the needs of the poor everywhere.

Consumer. One final way in which we affect economic justice is through our role as consumers. Choices we make about spending affect the quality of our lives and the lives of our neighbors and descendants. Probably the most important single spending decision we make is done as citizens, when we determine how much of our personal wealth and income will be spent in the public sector, building and maintaining our public infrastructures and providing a safety net for all our citizens. Still, choices we make as individual consumers—what percentage we set aside for savings, charity or the arts, how much we spend on essentials or luxury items, how often we need the newest or latest item or what level of debt we live with—all these can impact our families and our world. So too, our choices about spending money on pornography, violent entertainment, illegal drugs or all sorts of weapons can have real effects, as can our decision to buy another car instead of a bus pass or to save a few bucks by purchasing clothes made in a sweat shop or foods grown with harmful chemicals.

As individual consumers we have an obligation to use our money reasonably, purchasing the goods and services we and our families need to survive and develop as whole persons. We also have a duty to pay a fair price for things, so those who produce and deliver our staples or luxury items, as well as those providing important or even recreational services may be able to take care of their own families. And we should make certain our purchases do not encourage the exploitation of natural resources or introduce harmful waste products into our environment.

As responsible consumers we are called to practice commutative justice and prudence, paying a fair price for goods and services and making informed choices about the safety and usefulness of the products we buy. But even more urgently, we need to embrace a certain simplicity of life. For in a nation and world of sharp economic contrasts, where millions of poor scrounge for scraps from the tables of the rich, and on a planet where overconsumption threatens to rob all our grandchildren of their inheritance, it is essential that we hear the challenge of Catholic social teaching to "live more simply so that others may simply live." Simplicity is required of us as a sign of our solidarity with the world's suffering poor, as a step in our recovery from the increasingly unsatisfying addiction of overconsumption, and as a means of reducing the threat of environmental catastrophe.[29]

CHOICES:
Three Issues of Economic Justice

Welfare reform, affirmative action and the international debt are three contemporary controversial issues involving questions of economic justice. Just what are our obligations to people in need of government assistance, to those belonging to groups harmed by discriminatory practices in our society or to the citizens of nations overwhelmed by debt? As Christians, what are we called to do for and with such persons? What would be just and effective solutions to these problems?

Welfare Reform

The Voices of Experience. As we will do throughout this book, we begin our examination of welfare reform by attending to experience, which involves listening to the voices of history, the contemporary conversation and those in the margins.

The Voice of History.[21] Traditionally, American social policy regarding welfare was influenced by a ruggedly individualistic Puritan ethos, which saw prosperity as God's blessing for hard work.[22] While many Americans felt compassion and solidarity toward their impoverished neighbors, they also believed in a gospel of self-help and were reluctant to offer aid that might encourage sloth or dependency. As a result, government assistance was generally very modest and offered in ways that stigmatized the poor and deterred them from seeking further help.

The widespread poverty and unemployment of the Great Depression, however, caused many Americans to question the link between hard work and prosperity and to see their impoverished neighbors as victims of larger social ills. This change of attitude led to President Franklin Delano Roosevelt's New Deal legislation, offering the first comprehensive federal entitlement programs for the poor (programs recognizing that all persons have a right to certain basic economic goods), and to the Social Security Act of 1935, a bill providing income for the unemployed and elderly poor and initiating the Aid to Dependent Children (later renamed the Aid to Families with Dependent Children) program.

Contemporary Voices. By the 1990s, however, AFDC and other entitlement programs for the poor were under assault from critics on both the Left and Right. Conservatives argued that federal welfare cost too much, contributed to the breakdown of families, undermined the value of work and trapped the poor in a cycle of dependence. Liberals, on the other hand, tended to complain that AFDC was inadequate to the problems of hard-core poverty, overly bureaucratic in its management and humiliating for its recipients.

The result of this dissatisfaction was that in 1996 President Clinton signed the Republican-sponsored Personal Responsibility Act, putting an end to six decades of a federally guaranteed entitlement program for poor families and significantly cutting food stamps, federal assistance to immigrants and supplemental Social Security for disabled children. Under the new legislation AFDC was replaced by block grants (known as TANF: temporary assistance for needy families) that allowed individual states to determine how to spend the money, as long as recipients are off welfare and into work within very short order.

Voices from the Margins. While agreeing that anyone who can work ought to, that many welfare recipients are trapped in a cycle of dependence and poverty and that there was much that was evil and humiliating about AFDC, the poor and their advocates have generally argued that the 1996 legislation signed by Clinton was a step in the wrong direction.

First, they note the modesty of U.S. spending on programs for the poor, particularly when compared with the comprehensive social programs offered in most Western European nations. Total spending on AFDC averaged $25 billion a year, representing about 1 percent of the federal budget. When food stamps, housing subsidies and Supplemental Security Income for elderly poor and disabled are added, federal aid to the poor climbs to $53.4 billion, or about 4 percent of the budget. Second, advocates of the poor argue that while this modest level of support was—unfortunately—never intended to eliminate poverty, most major antipoverty programs have successfully fed, clothed, sheltered and treated millions of people with no place else to turn. Eliminating these safety nets will move 2.6 million more Americans into poverty. Third, there seems to be no solid evidence that many people are trapped in poverty or encouraged to have children out of wedlock as a result of overly generous federal aid. Instead, it is suggested, such problems probably result from a shortage of good jobs, training or child care. Fourth, while demanding that all adult recipients find work within two years, the 1996 welfare reform ignores the fact that a significant percentage of full-time workers are not making enough to pull themselves and their families out of poverty and includes no new funds for job training or child care. Nor does it acknowledge the shrinking number of jobs available to the unskilled workers making up the vast majority of adults on welfare. Fifth, even if charitable giving in America doubled, private organizations could not make up for cuts to the poor in the present legislation. And finally, most of the thirty million poor in America are women and children, and two-thirds of AFDC recipients were children.[23]

Scripture. The Bible offers two insights relevant to our reflections on welfare reform. First, all people have a need, right and duty to work, though our work may take different forms and our inability to work does not rob us of our dignity as persons. Second, while wealth may be seen as God's blessing on the righteous, *sedaqah* (covenantal justice) demands that those with wealth attend to the needs of those overwhelmed by want.

The first chapter of Genesis (1:26–28) reports that humans, made in the image and likeness of their Creator, have been entrusted with the ongoing *work* of creation (1:26–28). Our ancestors were placed "in the Garden of Eden to till it and keep it" (2:15). We are, it seems, made for work, and our labor is not simply a punishment for sin, but an essential part of our vocation as humans. We need and have a duty to work. Indeed, passages in Proverbs (24:30–34) and 1 Thessalonians (4:11–12) underscore the importance and value of work by warning of the evils of idleness.[24]

Still, not all our work takes place in the fields, or in the factory or office. In a hymn to the ideal wife and mother, Proverbs (31:10–31) offers a tribute to the rich tapestry of labors done by those who care for households and raise families, while Sirach (3:1–16) reminds us of the importance of caring for our parents in their old age. The work we do teaching and caring for our children or tending to our elders is also critical to our vocation as humans. This is real work.

And yet, as important as work is, we do not lose our worth as persons when we cannot work. Rather, Scripture teaches that those of us who can work and have more than we need should help those who cannot adequately provide for themselves. As we noted at the start of this chapter, *sedaqah* (God's covenantal justice) demanded that the Hebrews show special concern for the *anawim,* those widows, orphans, aliens and poor overwhelmed by want. So, while righteous persons might be blessed by prosperity for their labors, this wealth generates specific duties to God's "little ones." As the Psalmist (82:3–4) notes, we are to "give *justice* to the weak and the orphan; maintain the right of the lowly and the destitute. Rescue the weak and the needy" (italics added).

Within Scripture we find a number of specific practices designed to implement the demands of *sedaqah* and provide aid for the poor. Leviticus (19:9–10) mandated that landowners and their workers were not to go through their crops a second time, but to leave the gleanings (leftovers) of the harvest for the poor. This would prevent the *anawim* from going hungry. In chapter 25 of the same book we are introduced to the practice of the Jubilee Year. Every fifty years Hebrews were obliged to release any poor neighbor sold into indentured servitude, cancel the debts of all fellow Israelites and return the family lands of Jews who had fallen into poverty. In this way the *anawim* were protected from being permanently imprisoned in their poverty. In Sirach (4:1–6) and Tobit (12:9) readers were encouraged to give alms to the poor, while in the Acts of the Apostles we read that the early Christian community in Jerusalem had its members share their goods with one another (2:44–47) and developed a specific ministry to serve the needs of the poor (6:1–6).

Indeed, the duty to come to the aid of the poor is abundantly clear in the New Testament. As we noted above, Jesus begins his public life with the announcement that the Spirit of the Lord "has anointed me to bring good news to the poor" (Luke 4:18), and in Matthew 25:31–46 Jesus tells his disciples that anyone who fails to take care of their poor, naked, homeless, sick or imprisoned neighbors will be condemned, for "just as you did not do it to one the least of these, you did not do it to me." This point is driven home dramatically in the parable of the rich man and the beggar Lazarus (Luke 16:19–31), when the wealthy man is eternally condemned for failing to hear the cries of his poor neighbor. And in 1 John 3:17 the New Testament author asks, "How does God's love abide in anyone who has the world's goods and sees a brother or sister in need and yet refuses to help?"

Tradition. Early saints like Ambrose (339–97) and Basil the Great (329–79) argued that Christians were not being generous when they shared their goods with the poor, but merely returning a fair share of God's bounty to those in need. Anything else would be theft. And Martin Luther (1483–1546) wrote that Christians who failed to feed the hungry were breaking the fifth commandment and guilty of killing their neighbor.[25] During the middle ages St. Thomas Aquinas (1225–74) agreed that the duty to give alms to the poor was universal and grounded in both justice and charity, and subsequent church teaching has held that after meeting the basic needs of our family we should share some of our abundance with the poor. For, as Paul VI argues in "The Development of Peoples," God has given the bounty of creation for the good of all persons, and both the state and those who hold wealth privately should make certain that this "universal purpose of created things" is not frustrated by a few owning too much while too many go without.[26] Furthermore, as John XXIII makes clear in "Peace on Earth" every person has the right to food, clothing, shelter, medical care and necessary social services, "and the right to security in case of sickness, inability to work, widowhood, old age, or in any other case in which one is deprived of the means of subsistence through no fault of their own."[27] Thus, the consistent teaching of the church clearly supports some form of humane government assistance to those in need, and sees this aid as a duty of those who have enough and a right of those who don't.

In 1995 the U.S. Catholic bishops made their contribution to the debate on welfare reform in a document called "Moral Principles and Policy Priorities on Welfare Reform."[28] Here they offered six moral criteria to be used in evaluating any proposed program, arguing that they could support welfare reform which: (1) protects human life and human dignity, (2) strengthens family life, (3) encourages and rewards work, (4) preserves a safety net for the vulnerable, that is, "for those who cannot work or whose 'work' is raising our youngest children," (5) builds public/private partnerships to overcome poverty and (6) invests in human dignity.

Thus, the bishops affirmed the need for reforms that strengthen families and encourage work, and agreed that Washington should cooperate with state and local governments, as well as charitable organizations, in better organizing the delivery of assistance to those in need. What the bishops were clearly not willing to support, however, was what they saw as: (1) the federal government abandoning its moral obligations to the poor by handing the job over to states or charities clearly incapable of dealing with the task, (2) trimming the federal budget by taking a disproportionate chunk out of spending on the neediest of our citizens, (3) failing to provide training, opportunities or child care to those who desperately want to work, (4) demanding that those who cannot work be pushed off the welfare rolls or (5) removing or reducing significant strands of an already overburdened safety net. As the bishops argue, "...the target of reform ought to be poverty, not poor families."

Similarly, recent statements by the Presbyterian, Episcopal and Methodist churches affirm that our society has an obligation to provide adequate assistance to those in need, that the government has the primary role in providing this assistance and that welfare reform must mean more than requiring recipients to find jobs. It must also include a commitment to provide "individuals with the tools to take responsibility for their own lives, such as jobs, education, training, low cost housing, and language skill."[29]

Formulating a Christian Response. How, then, should Christians respond to the issue of welfare reform? As we will do with the other controversial choices in this book, we attempt to answer this question by naming some basic convictions, convictions that should inform any authentically Christian solution to this problem. And then we identify some of the particularly difficult questions that must be addressed in formulating a response to this issue.

Some Basic Convictions. First, every human person is sacred, and the dignity of all persons must be protected. Fashioned in the image and likeness of God and redeemed by the love of Christ, no person may be considered a possible castaway in our society. Second, our dignity as persons is "realized in community," meaning that each of us is entitled to the liberties, goods and services we need to flourish as human beings and members of our society. Normally we have a duty to provide many of these goods and services for ourselves and families, but in times of real dependence or need our community has an obligation to assist us. Third, the state has a critical role in protecting human dignity and the common good, and a specific obligation to defend the interests of the weakest in society. As citizens we have a duty to insure that a fair share of the common wealth is distributed to those in need. Fourth, work is a right and a duty of all able adults, the primary way in which persons participate in an economy, realize their potential and provide for their families. Thus, able adults have a duty to work, and societies have an obligation to provide work for all those who can and offer assistance to those who cannot. Fifth, the work of those who raise our children and care for our elderly or sick is critically important, and society has an obligation to recognize, provide for and support that work to the same degree that we value the labor of those who work in offices, factories and farms. Sixth, we are called to overcome the growing gap between rich and poor by living in solidarity with those in need and by making a preferential option for the poor. At the very least this means that the poor ought not to bear the brunt of cuts in federal spending simply because they lack the clout to defend themselves.

Some Difficult Questions. First, what specific policies best enable the federal and local governments to work together efficiently and justly in addressing the problems of the poor? Block grants may give local governments more freedom in responding to the specific needs of their citizens. Still, the federal government has a real role to play in exercising responsible oversight, so as to prevent uneven and unfair treatment of the poor in various regions. Second, what sorts of measures will be genuinely helpful in breaking the cycle of poverty and dependence in which millions of Americans find themselves? After decades of attempts at welfare reform it is easy to understand the attractiveness of rigid time limits, but if such time limits are not accompanied by funding programs that make employment viable, or are rigidly enforced on people who cannot find work, will that solve anything? Third, what sorts of measures can help strengthen families and discourage illegitimacy without encouraging abortions or punishing children for the sins of their parents? Indeed, what do we really know about the causes of welfare dependency and illegitimacy? Fourth, just what are our obligations to those resident aliens who find themselves in need? Will we be able to stem the tide of immigration by withholding entitlement to basic services, and if so, do we have a right to treat anybody this way?

Affirmative Action

The Voices of Experience

The Voice of History. In 1562, after attempts to press Native American peoples into forced labor had failed, European colonists decided to "recruit" African workers for their plantations or haciendas, bringing hundreds of thousands of men, women and children to the New World in chains.[30] This "peculiar institution" of slavery lasted three hundred years in America, and was followed by a century of "Jim Crow" laws sanctioning racial discrimination and segregation. In the 1960s federal civil rights legislation sought to overcome four hundred years of brutal injustice and help African Americans secure their full political and economic rights as citizens. The Civil Rights Act of 1964 barred discrimination in the workplace, and a year later President Johnson's Executive Order 11246 empowered the Labor Department to take "affirmative action" in securing jobs for blacks and other minorities. This authority was later expanded to address gender discrimination as well.

In general, affirmative action programs have done more than just outlaw discrimination or compensate its individual victims. Working for what President Johnson called "equality as a fact and as a result," such programs call for employers and educators to take specific steps countering the underrepresentation of women, blacks and other minorities in the workplace and on campus. Weak affirmative action programs involve "outreach" attempts to recruit members of disadvantaged groups, while stronger and more controversial programs call for some preference to be given to such persons, or establish numerical quotas.

Contemporary Voices. Although most Americans oppose discrimination and support equal opportunity for all persons, a growing number of voices have criticized affirmative action and called for either the end or radical curtailment of such programs. The most common complaint is that affirmative action, particularly when it involves preferential treatment or quotas, is simply reverse discrimination, making it unjust. Instead of helping us move toward a just or "color blind" society, affirmative action programs repeat the sins of the past and deepen tensions between blacks and whites. The second most popular criticism is that affirmative action ends up harming innocent third parties (usually white males) who have not discriminated against anyone, while offering aid to many middle- or upper-class blacks who have suffered few or no effects of discrimination. Still other critics suggest that affirmative action programs have harmed minorities and women by undermining their self-confidence, leading preferred candidates and their colleagues to believe they lack the talent to compete on a level playing field. Finally, a small number of persons suggest that the goals of the Civil Rights movement have been met and that there is no longer a need for affirmative action programs.[31]

Voices from the Margins. While victims of discrimination and their advocates admit that there have been excesses and mistakes in specific programs, they continue to maintain that affirmative action has been both useful and necessary. Over the past three decades, they argue, the greatest gains by minorities and women have been made in those companies and sectors of the economy subject to affirmative action programs. As Stephen Steinberg notes, "One thing is clear: without government, both as employer and as enforcer of affirmative action mandates, we would not today be celebrating the achievements of the black middle class."[32] Further, in spite of such progress, discrimination has not been eliminated in our society, and there continues to be a real need for affirmative action programs. Twenty years ago black families made $605 for every $1,000 received by white households. Today that ratio is $577 per $1,000.[33]

Scripture. One of the scandals of the Christian story has been the way in which some believers and ministers of the Gospel have used certain biblical passages to support the practices of slavery and racial discrimination. Those seeking to defend slavery have often pointed to Noah's curse on Canaan, rendering him and his tribe slaves to the descendants of Shem and Japheth (Gen 9:20–27), or to Paul's letter to Philemon, in which the apostle urges his fellow Christian to forgive (but not necessarily free) the runaway slave Onesimus. Later, these same passages were used to justify continuing discrimination and prejudice against blacks and other minorities, as were certain passages in the Hebrew Scriptures stigmatizing other tribes and peoples as enemies of Israel.

In spite of these aberrations, however, the church has consistently taught that the larger biblical evidence supports neither slavery nor discrimination, but instead reminds us of the common humanity and equal dignity of all persons as children of God, of the universal love of Christ and of our duty as Christians to work for the full integration and reconciliation of every person and group into the larger human community.[34]

In the creation accounts of the first two chapters of Genesis we learn two important points; that all humans have been made in the image and likeness of God (1:26–27), and that we are all members of the same family (3:20). Being fashioned in God's likeness means that all humans, regardless of race, creed or gender, possess a transcendent and inviolable dignity, a sacred quality entitling them to basic rights and obliging us to conduct ourselves with respect, reverence and a fundamental equality. Belonging to a common family implies further that, in spite of any superficial differences, we are all sisters and brothers to one another, called to show that love and care owed to members of our own household.

Nor does God's choice of Israel contradict this call to universal love. For the Bible makes it clear that God also has a covenant with the whole human race (Gen 9:11), that hospitality to strangers is a fundamental virtue (Gen 18), and that Israel has been chosen to bring the Lord's grace and blessings to all humanity. As Yahweh tells Abraham, "...in you all the families of the earth shall be blessed" (Gen 12:3).

Christ is the fulfillment of that universal covenant, for through his death and resurrection the divisions of sin have been overcome. The wounds inflicted on the human race at the Tower of Babel (Gen 11:1–9) have been healed by the gift of the Spirit at Pentecost (Acts 2:1–13). "There is no longer Jew or Greek, there is no longer slave or free, there is no longer male and female; for all of you are one in Christ" (Gal 3:28). And as disciples of Christ we are to embody this universal love by living in solidarity with all, imitating the example of the one who associated with Gentiles and Samaritans and brought healing to Romans and Syro-Phoenicians.

Furthermore, Scripture teaches that we not only have an obligation to show compassion for those *anawim* who have been oppressed and marginalized in society, but also to stand with them in the struggle for justice. Quoting from Isaiah, Jesus announces his own vocation to "proclaim release to the captives, [and]…to let the oppressed go free" (Luke 4:18). It is not enough simply to share our food with the poor; we must address the underlying causes of injustice.

Tradition. From the beginnings of the European colonization of the New World popes such as Paul III (1537), Urban XIII (1639), Benedict XIV (1741) and Leo XIII (1888) condemned the practice of slavery and attacked racial theories justifying the poor treatment of native peoples. To their voices was added a chorus of pastors and theologians, including the outspoken Dominican bishop and former slave holder Bartolome de las Casas, as well as the Spanish ethicists Francisco de Vitoria and Francisco Suarez. Unfortunately, these statements were often ignored by members of the clergy and laity, and the actual witness of the church in this area was not always exemplary.

In this century several church documents have described racism as a sin and condemned every sort of discrimination based on race, creed, gender or national origin. In 1937 Pius XI attacked the racist theories and practices of Nazi Germany in the encyclical *Mit Brennender Sorge,* and in 1963 John XXIII's "Peace on Earth" noted that "racial discrimination can in no way be justified."[35] Still, perhaps the clearest Catholic denunciation comes in The Church in the Modern World when the bishops of Vatican II argue that "every type of discrimination, whether social or cultural, whether based on sex, race, color, social condition, language, or religion, is to be overcome and eradicated as contrary to God's intent."[36]

In 1958 the U.S. Catholic bishops issued a document condemning discriminatory laws and enforced segregation of the races, and in 1979 recommended that affirmative action plans be adopted in dioceses across the nation and published a pastoral letter on racism entitled "Brothers and Sisters to Us." While noting that much progress had been made in the years since the Civil Rights movement, the bishops complained in this later document that the enduring presence of racism and discrimination in our society could be seen in the differing experience of blacks and whites in employment, education and housing.

In their 1983 pastoral "Economic Justice for All," the U.S. Catholic bishops again noted the continuing harms of discrimination against minorities and women and argued that, "where the effects of past discrimination persist, society has the obligation to take positive steps to overcome the legacy of injustice. Judiciously administered affirmative action programs...can be important expressions of...true justice."[37] As a result they called upon the country to "renew its efforts to develop affirmative action policies that assist those who have been excluded by racial or sexual discrimination in the past." Nine years later Cardinal Roger Mahoney, speaking against a California proposition calling for the dismantling of state affirmative action programs, reiterated the bishops' position, arguing that such programs continue to address an important need in a society where minorities and women do not compete on a level playing field.[38]

Other Christian voices have also been raised in support of affirmative action. Christian ethicist Franklin Gamwell has argued that affirmative action is just because "discrimination against women and minorities, especially African-Americans, has resulted in acute inequality in the common conditions of human flourishing, [and] we require policies that correct those consequences."[39] So too, the 1995 General Assembly of the Presbyterian Church (U.S.A.) reaffirmed "its commitment to affirmative action as a means of achieving equal employment opportunity and undoing historical and institutional effects of discrimination...(and) urges federal, state, and local legislators to support affirmative action policies in the public and private sector."[40]

Formulating a Christian Response

Some Basic Convictions. It seems evident that discrimination against persons because of their race, creed, gender or nationality is unjust. Such discrimination not only harms the persons denied equal access to employment, education and housing, but also punishes their children by robbing them of the advantages their parents might have provided for them, and harms the common good by depriving us of the gifts and talents of these persons and by increasing the hostility between groups. It seems equally clear that, in spite of the progress resulting from the dismantling of segregation and discriminatory laws in this country, prejudice and discrimination remain embedded in our society and are at least a partial cause of the higher rates of poverty and unemployment among minorities and women. This situation, which cries out for a remedy, generates two sets of obligations. Given the fact that the state has the duty to protect human rights and secure basic justice for all its members, and indeed has a special duty to protect the weakest in society, the government must have some role in addressing the question of discrimination in the workplace. At the same time, as Christians we have an obligation to work for the integration and reconciliation of all groups in the larger society, for real justice cannot occur when some are marginalized and prevented from fully participating in building up the common good. Indeed, the church itself has a special obligation to be just in this area, and in particular needs to address in a convincing manner concerns about discrimination against women. For if Catholic Christians are to offer a persuasive witness to the call to justice we must create institutional practices and structures that help to reverse the lingering effects of sexism in our own community and create real opportunities for the victims of this injustice. Finally, whatever policy is selected, it must not make things worse than they are at present, but must effectively improve the common good without creating new and worse injustices. This does not mean that there could not be some cost to such a program or that it could not have some regrettable side-effects—only that, like any reasonable and just law, it must work effectively for the common good.

Some Difficult Questions. The toughest question about affirmative action is whether policies involving preference and quotas represent an inherent and unacceptable injustice or can be justified as part of a short-term strategy providing the only possible means to address a grave injustice. Although constricting the scope of affirmative action programs, recent supreme court decisions (*Adarand v. Pena:* 1995) continue to recognize the government's right to take such action if it has compelling reasons, as the U.S. Catholic bishops believe it does. Still, other voices warn that these policies violate justice and the constitution's guarantee of equal protection. Another important question is whether affirmative action programs actually help those disadvantaged by discrimination. There is a great deal of evidence suggesting that women and minorities have made significant progress under such policies, but there are also those concerned about the harms done to the confidence of affirmative action candidates. Furthermore, there is the question as to whether affirmative action programs help to build bridges between whites and minorities by bringing more people of color into our schools and workplaces or contribute to growing racial and ethnic tensions. Again, the evidence seems to indicate a significant growth in integration under affirmative action programs and suggests that without such programs the gap between whites and blacks would be worse. Still, some complain that such programs have contributed to a political climate in which racial identity is becoming more, not less, important. Finally, our last question involves just which of the three approaches to affirmative action (outreach, preferences or quotas) might be called for, either as a general rule or in a particular setting. It seems clear that outreach programs generate the least controversy, but they also offer the weakest remedy, and so we are challenged to exercise prudent judgment in determining just how strong a medicine is needed to address the malaise of discrimination.

International Debt

The Voices of Experience

The Voice of History. In 1973, responding in part to U.S. policies devaluing the dollar, OPEC (the Organization of Petroleum Exporting Countries) increased the cost of oil four-fold and invested the huge profits in First-World banks.[41] These banks then made massive loans at low but adjustable rates to developing nations in the Third World, which needed capital to fund their industrialization and pay for the soaring cost of oil. Unfortunately, many of these loans were poorly monitored, and instead of being spent on capital investments improving these nations' economic infrastructure, monies often went to huge, ill-advised projects, military spending or corrupt officials. In the late 1970s OPEC once again doubled the price of oil, U.S. monetary policy helped generate spiraling interest rates and a worldwide economic recession led to plummeting prices for the very goods (i.e., food crops and raw materials) that many Third-World nations had been encouraged to invest in. As a result, these countries now found themselves unable to buy the oil needed to fuel their fledgling industries or to make interest payments. Most sought to "borrow" their way out of the problem.

In 1982 Mexico, the second-largest debtor nation in the world, became the first developing country to inform its creditors that it could not make its debt payments, effectively threatening to declare bankruptcy. Fearing a collapse of the international banking system and perhaps the global economy, the world's major creditors (commercial banks and First-World governments) stepped in and had the World Bank and International Monetary Fund (IMF) negotiate restructured loans to Mexico and (later) other deeply indebted nations. Unfortunately, while this process succeeded in rescuing Western commercial banks, it has offered little respite to debtor nations, whose debts continue to spiral upward. Nor have these countries received much assistance from other international efforts at debt reduction, such as the 1989 Brady Plan or the World Bank's recent Highly Indebted Poor Country (HIPC) initiative.

Contemporary Voices. One way to understand the present shape of the International Debt crisis is to look at some of the numbers. In 1995 developing nations had an external debt of $2 trillion, a figure that had grown fourfold since 1979. This is in spite of the fact that both the principal and a good deal of interest on most of the original loans have been repaid. From 1982 to 1990 developing nations paid about $420 billion to Western banks, and still every year Third-World countries hand over to the West three times more in debt repayment than they receive in aid. And just how much money does this represent for these nations? Latin America's external debt is equivalent to 36 percent of its gross national product, while Africa's debt is equal to 83 percent of its GNP. Indeed, the cumulative debt of sub-Saharan Africa (not counting South Africa and Namibia) is about 120 percent of the total income of that region. Currently, each person in the Third World owes about $420 (significantly more than a year's wage for many) to the West.[42]

And the crippling effects of this debt are not felt only by the poor. Environmental damage often results when developing nations are forced to meet their debt payments by increasing cash-crop exports. Soil is degraded through overuse or saturation with chemical fertilizers. Forests are destroyed by logging or "slash and burn" ranching and farming. Fish stocks are decimated by overfishing of rivers, lakes and oceans. It is the world's largest debtors who can least afford to protect or steward their natural resources. At the same time, when nations are devoting 30 to 80 percent of their GNP to debt, they can ill afford to pay high wages to their citizens or purchase products imported from the West. As a result, the debt crisis contributes to the migration of jobs to the South and robs the First World of potential customers for its products. Furthermore, highly indebted countries often enough turn to illegal drugs as a cash crop. In Bolivia, where half the income from legal exports must go to paying its debt, 40 percent of its workforce is supported directly or indirectly by the drug trade. Finally, when commercial banks in the West claim huge tax deductions for losses resulting from unpaid debt, it is First-World taxpayers who end up paying for these write-offs.

Voices from the Margins. Two things are evident about international debt. First, the original loans did little or nothing for the poor in developing countries, but were largely siphoned off in projects that were either questionable or of primary benefit to a rich elite. Second, the weight of the present debt, as well as the "structural adjustment programs" (SAPs), which the World Bank and IMF impose on debtor nations, works its greatest burden on the poor.

In order for highly indebted nations to make their regular debt payments and/or comply with imposed SAPs, they must cut spending in health, education and welfare. Not surprisingly, then, African nations spend four times as much on debt repayment as they do on health care, and most highly indebted poor countries have significantly higher rates of infant mortality, illiteracy, malnutrition and disease than other developing nations. Furthermore, SAPs require that debtor nations increase their profits from exports, usually encouraging a shift to cash crops and agribusiness. This often results in the loss of small farms, increased unemployment, dropping wages and a growing dependence on imported staples to feed the population. Indeed, for about one billion people on this planet debt has meant the reversal of promised economic development and a steady slow slide back into desperate poverty. And while the World Bank and IMF's SAPs may enable poor countries to make debt payments, many see them as constituting an unjust and intolerable burden on the weakest in society.

Scripture. From the Hebrew Scriptures we learn a number of things about debts and loans: (1) that we are morally obliged to pay back what we owe; (2) that we ought to be generous in offering loans to neighbors who are poor; (3) that we ought not to profit from their desperate need; and (4) that we are to cancel debts to these poor neighbors in the Jubilee Year. Standing behind each of the last three points seems to be a commitment to keep poor neighbors from being irretrievably crushed by the weight of their debts.

On the question of paying our debts, Sirach (29:2–4) offers this advice to his readers. "Repay your neighbor when a loan falls due. Keep your promise and be honest with him, and on every occasion you will find what you need." He goes on to note that borrowers who fail to repay their debts cheat lenders of their wealth and in this way may even discourage loans to other people.

Nonetheless, Sirach argues that we ought to be generous with the poor, lending to our neighbors in their time of need, for "the merciful lend to their neighbors; by holding out a helping hand they keep the commandments" (29:1). Indeed, not only do we have a duty to lend aid to impoverished neighbors, but several passages in the Hebrew Scriptures (Lev 25:36–38; Ezek 18:7–8; Deut 23:20; 24:10–13) remind us that we are not to profit from their need. Exodus (22:24–26) instructs the Hebrews, "If you lend money to my people, to the poor among you, you shall not deal with them as a creditor; you shall not exact interest from them. If you take your neighbor's cloak in pawn, you shall restore it before the sun goes down, for it may be your neighbor's only clothing to use as a cover." There is, then, to be no interest charged on a loan to the poor.

Furthermore, the author of Leviticus (25:8–55) reports on the ancient practice of the fiftieth or Jubilee Year, a time when those Hebrews who had accumulated great wealth and property were commanded to cancel all debts owed by their fellow Israelites, to set free any Hebrew who had been sold into indentured servitude and to return all Jewish properties to their original owner. The idea here seems to be that a periodic canceling of all debts was necessary for two reasons. First, this practice made certain that impoverished Israelites were not permanently trapped in servitude (25:35) nor completely alienated from their tribal lands (25:39). Thus it offered a safety net for "God's little ones," the *anawim.* At the same time the cancellation of all debts in the Jubilee Year offered a periodic readjustment of the growing gap between the rich and poor in Israel, keeping this chasm from growing too large.

Although the New Testament does not contain such explicit proscriptions against lending with interest, it does extend our moral obligations to those in debt in two significant ways. First, by revealing in the parable of the Good Samaritan (Luke 11:29–37) that the biblical command to love our neighbor (Lev 19:18) extends to every human being on the face of the earth, Jesus makes it clear that we are not to profit unjustly from the debts of the poor anywhere. Indeed, when we read in Matthew 5:42 that we are to "give to everyone who begs from you, and do not refuse anyone who wants to borrow from you," we now understand this as a call to come to the aid of all poor people. Second, in Luke 6:34–35 Jesus seems to set a new standard for loans to the poor, telling his disciples that "if you lend to those from whom you hope to receive, what credit is that to you? Even sinners lend to sinners, to receive as much again. But—lend, expecting nothing in return. Your reward will be great, and you will be children of the Most High.…" So too in the parable of the unforgiving servant (Matt 18: 21–35) Jesus presents God as a king who forgives tremendous debts and calls us to show similar mercy to our debtors, which seems to be one of the central lessons of the Lord's Prayer (Matt 6:12) where we ask God to "forgive us our debts, as we also have forgiven our debtors."

Tradition. Until well into the Middle Ages Christian teaching repeated biblical proscriptions against taking interest on loans to the poor, condemning the greed of such lenders and warning about exploitation of the poor.[43] In the thirteenth century Aquinas and other scholastic theologians argued that while generally one ought not to charge interest on a loan of money (which was seen as an unproductive good), lenders might have some external claim to profit from risking their monies in a loan or to compensate them for the loss of some other opportunity to profit from their wealth. These exceptions created a space for loans at modest interest, which were justified in the modern era based on a new understanding of money as a productive good. As many have pointed out, Christian churches currently exercise responsible stewardship of their own funds by placing them in institutions paying interest on investments.

At the same time Christian ethicists have consistently argued that persons incurring debts in fair and open contracts have a strict moral obligation to pay back their creditors in full and on time. Failure to do this was seen as a violation of commutative justice and, if it involved a significant amount of money (i.e., a person's daily wage), represented a grave sin. Nonetheless, the church has also recognized that paying back debts was sometimes a physical or moral impossibility, and argued that persons were to be excused temporarily or even permanently from this obligation if they found themselves in bankruptcy, or if the repayment of the loan would reduce them to starvation or some other desperate situation.[44]

Contemporary Catholic social teaching offers three central insights on the mounting crisis of international debt. First, in many developing nations the present level of debt represents an intolerable and unpayable burden, resting mainly on the backs of the poor. In "At the Service of the Human Community: An Ethical Approach to the International Debt Question," the Vatican argued that "debt servicing cannot be met at the price of asphyxiation of a country's economy, and no government can morally demand of its people privations incompatible with human dignity."[45] As a result, John Paul II's 1994 apostolic letter "As the Third Millennium Draws Near," calls for a substantial reduction, if not outright cancellation of the international debt crushing so many of the Third World's poor.[46] Second, the great indebtedness of many developing nations is both a symptom and result of larger structural injustices in global financial systems. In Paul VI's "The Development of Peoples" and the U.S. bishops' "Economic Justice for All" Catholic social teaching argues that the present international financial structures unfairly benefit First-World nations that set them up and must be restructured if there is to be any equitable solution to Third-World debt.[47] Third, both First-World creditors and Third-World borrowers share responsibility for this debt, and both they and the poor of these countries should be involved in formulating fair solutions to this crisis. Indeed, five of the six guiding principles offered in "An Ethical Approach to the International Debt Question" underscore the need for increased dialogue, parity and participation among all the parties faced with the present crisis, while calling for special attention to be paid to the needs of the poor.

At the same time, a number of other Christian churches have voiced their support for debt reduction, or even cancellation. The 1998 General Assembly of the Presbyterian Church (U.S.A.) issued a resolution calling for the "definite cancellation of international debt in situations where countries with high levels of human need and environmental distress are unable to meet the needs of their people."[48] And the Evangelical Lutheran Church in America's statement on a "Sufficient, Sustainable Livelihood for All," called for "reduction of overwhelming international debt burdens in ways that do not impose further deprivations on the poor, and cancellation of some or all debt where severe indebtedness immobilizes a country's economy."[49]

Formulating a Christian Response

Some Basic Convictions. Although commutative justice normally demands that fairly contracted debts be repaid in full and on time, those debtors who are incapable of making repayment or who would be grievously harmed by attempting to do so are to be temporarily or permanently excused. Given the crushing reality of so much unpayable Third-World debt, it seems mandatory that some substantial reduction or cancellation take place. According to both Scripture and Christian tradition there is a particular obligation to lend money to the poor, and to do so in ways that do not take advantage of their need or permanently entrap them in debt. In "The Development of Peoples" Paul VI recommends the development of a "world fund" for this purpose.[50] In order to offer this aid First-World countries and creditors need to make significant contributions to development funds in organizations like the World Bank, the UN and the IMF. Unfortunately such assistance has been dropping steadily even as Third-World debt has been skyrocketing. Finally, given the ways in which both creditors and debtor nations helped to create the present crisis, it seems patently unjust to suggest that solutions should only meet the needs of the former or be paid for by the poor. Present international financial, trade and development structures, including institutions like the World Bank and the IMF., need to be restructured in ways that allow developing nations full and fair participation.

Some Difficult Questions. The most difficult questions regarding international debt involve the issue of debt reduction or cancellation. If such relief is to be offered, who is to make these decisions, how are candidates to be selected and what sorts of safeguards are to be put in place to prevent the international financial system from being undermined or poor nations from slipping back into debt? Some have recommended the development of a neutral international agency to arbitrate the restructuring of loans or debt relief, an organization in which both debtors and creditors would have equal say. Others have suggested that debt relief be secured by greatly expanding the World Bank's HIPC, funded in part by increased commitments from First-World nations and institutions. A second set of questions involves the use of SAPs to help debtor nations improve their balance of payments. Given the uniqueness of each indebted country, many have wondered if uniformly and rigidly applied SAPs always fit the concrete situation, while others question their effects on the poor and the environment. The problem here is to develop SAPs that encourage human development and protect natural resources while still helping to reduce debt, not an easy task by any stretch of the imagination.

COMMUNITY:
An Examination of Two Social Sins

As we noted in the first chapter, our moral character and choices are deeply influenced by the larger social structures embedded in our communities. For these structures, which include both shared myths and institutionalized practices, help constitute us as a people and create a context in which individual persons find it easier or harder to be virtuous or make the right choice. While the American economy has been shaped by a number of differing structures, we will focus here on two sinful social structures—individualism and consumerism—

examining their effects on economic justice and suggesting some possible Christian responses.

Individualism. In his 1845 classic *Democracy in America*, Alexis de Tocqueville coined the word "individualism," using it to describe what he saw as the most self-reliant and antistatist people on the face of the earth. According to de Tocqueville, "Individualism is a calm and considered feeling which disposes each citizen to isolate himself from the mass of his fellows and withdraw into the circle of family and friends;...[leaving] the greater society to look after itself."[51] Indeed, de Tocqueville adds, this attitude of radical self-reliance leads many citizens of the young republic to think of themselves as having few duties or ties to others and of being complete masters of their own destiny. Though often held in check by other, more communitarian structures, more than a century and a half after *Democracy in America* there can be little doubt that the individualism its French author discerned in our national psyche has in fact endured, profoundly shaping the American experience and exerting a tremendous influence on our economy.

The Myth. For many it would be hard to imagine a more American archetype than that of the rugged individual: Hawkeye, the solitary frontiersman of James Fenimore Cooper's *The Last of the Mohicans,* the rugged, independent hero of Owen Wister's *The Virginian,* the Lone Ranger, and a long list of hard-boiled private eyes waiting in their dusty offices like knight errants eager for a chance to battle the forces of evil and corruption. These are the stuff, as Sam Spade once said, our dreams are made of. And yet, perhaps even more than all these cowboys and detectives, the prototypical American myth, the real American dream if you will, is captured in *The Autobiography of Benjamin Franklin,* or in his *Poor Richard's Almanack.* It is the tale of a scrappy, self-reliant, and successful character who goes out into the world and manages to make a fortune out of nothing more than a lot of sweat, self-discipline, smarts and a pinch of good luck. This, the Horatio Alger story, the fable of the hometown girl or boy who *made* good, is the myth so many of us seem to want to believe in, and the one Hollywood exports to audiences around the world.

The roots of this American myth of the rugged individual in the marketplace can be found in our Puritan ancestors, the writings of Enlightenment philosophers and Adam Smith's early defense of capitalism in *The Wealth of Nations*. Seventeenth-century Puritan settlers landing in Massachusetts brought with them a fierce work ethic forged in a religious ethos that saw self-discipline, sacrifice and hard labor as part of one's personal vocation, and interpreted the economic self-sufficiency or wealth earned through the dint of great effort as a sign of God's blessing. A century and a half later architects of the new republic embraced the Enlightenment's defense of individual political and civil rights and argued that the future success of our nation would depend on the brilliance, initiative and creativity of individual entrepreneurs. It is hardly surprising, then, that Americans should find Adam Smith's notion of "the invisible hand" so attractive, for it allows us to argue that the greatest good for the community is achieved when we all work as hard as we can for our own personal profit. In this schema individualism becomes a sort of heroic patriotism and America becomes that place where personal freedom finds its fullest expression.[52]

Some Practices. In "Economic Justice for All" the U.S. Catholic bishops acknowledge that the American emphasis on individual liberty and private initiative has "encouraged citizens to undertake bold ventures...[and helped] the U.S. economy to provide an unprecedented standard of living for most of its people."[53] Still, this stress on individualism has not been without its problems. For while Americans are generally quite eager to protect the civil and political rights of private citizens—liberties like freedom of speech, religion and assembly—our society has been significantly more reticent to recognize the right to economic and social goods like food, clothing, shelter, health or employment, goods that make it possible to live and participate in modern society. American citizens and corporations pay the lowest taxes of any industrial nation, contributing a smaller proportion of their private wealth to pay for public goods like health, education and welfare than the people of any other modern nation. As a result, the social safety net America provides for its neediest citizens is inadequate, our welfare system fails to address the deeper issues of poverty in America and we remain the only First-World nation without a comprehensive national health-care program. Furthermore, Americans have proven similarly reluctant to contribute aid to poor nations around the world or to support international aid and development agencies. In both of these areas the United States, with the largest national economy in the world, continues to donate a lesser percentage of its GNP (gross national product) than several nations with much smaller economies. Indeed, of late the United States has even fallen behind several other nations in the amount of money donated to international aid.[54]

Still, the most troubling effect of America's stress on economic freedom and individual liberty may be that the most powerful economy in the world also has the greatest economic inequality of any developed nation, allowing nearly forty million of its citizens to live in poverty. America currently has the greatest income gap of any industrial or postindustrial nation, and this gap has been increasing for more than two decades. American CEOs currently make approximately 190 times the salary of factory workers, and the richest fifth of our population makes thirteen times as much as the poorest fifth, taking home 48.7 percent of the nation's income. Today, in an economy where household income reaches nearly $5 trillion, one-fifth of our children live in poverty and millions of full-time workers cannot pull themselves above the poverty line. In the nation that produces more self-made millionaires and wage earners making $100,000 than any other country we also have more citizens in jail or living on the streets than any comparable modern state.[55]

Christian Beliefs. Our religious tradition certainly values individual persons, defends their rights and holds them accountable for their actions. Still, as we have seen elsewhere, the biblical stress on *sedaqah* (covenantal justice) argues that we are social beings who have real duties to our neighbors and, indeed, special obligations to the *anawim,* or poor. So, too, Catholic social teaching calls us to practice solidarity with and a preferential option for the poor, and argues that human dignity is not achieved in isolation, but "realized in community." In the Hebrew Scriptures certain structures were put in place to set limits on the gaps between the rich and poor. Farmers were to allow the poor to pick the gleanings from their crops, and old debts were to be canceled, lands returned and slaves freed in the Jubilee Year. Likewise, the New Testament records practices of early Christian communities sharing their goods with one another and giving alms to the poor.

Structural Reforms. Still, addressing the excesses of American individualism calls for more than personal conversion and corrective myths. It requires structural reforms as well. We need to change some of our shared practices. These could include some or all of the following. To begin with, we need to radically improve the social safety net provided for our neediest citizens, which means (at the very least) welfare reform that addresses the long-term and underlying causes of poverty in our society and the development of an adequate and comprehensive national health-care system. We also need to make a national commitment to provide full employment for all persons who can work, and to provide adequate support for those caring for children and/or elders. Naturally, these commitments will require increased spending in the public sector (even if offset by massive cuts in military spending), which means increased taxation. Such taxes need to be shouldered in a more equitable fashion than at present. Corporations and wealthy individuals should honor the social contract that ties them to the rest of society by paying for their fair share of the common good. Finally, we need to make a renewed commitment to address poverty around the world by increasing our contribution to nonmilitary foreign aid and our financial support of those international organizations that work for peace and development in the Third World.

Consumerism. According to one popular bumper sticker, "The one who dies with the most toys wins." Maybe that's why 70 percent of Americans visit the mall each week, more than go to church or synagogue. Or why we spend six hours a week shopping and only about forty minutes playing with our children. Perhaps this explains why we have more malls (about forty thousand) than high schools in the United States, or why, in spite of the fact that our houses are twice as large as they were in the 1950s, we currently need twenty-five times as many commercial self-storage units to put our stuff in as we had in 1970. Indeed, this may even explain why more than a quarter of the households making more than $100,000 a year claim they can't afford everything they "need."[56]

Once again it is de Tocqueville who gives us an early insight into our American appetite for consumption, noting in us what he considered "an inordinate love of material gratification." Nor was he alone in this opinion. Alexander Hamilton commented on the tendency his fellow citizens had for "multiplying their acquisitions and enjoyments," a penchant that has not disappeared. Since the 1950s Americans have used more resources than everyone who ever lived before them. With less than 5 percent of the world's population, we consume about 60 percent of the world's natural gas, 40 percent of its coal, and 30 percent of its petroleum. Indeed, one estimate indicates that if every other nation copied our patterns of consumption it would take the resources of four earths to keep up.[57]

Two Myths. The twin engines of American consumerism are to be found in the underlying myths of advertising and credit cards, for by means of these two instruments Americans are constantly persuaded of their need to buy more and more, and promised that payment of the full cost of this consumption may be deferred to some far-off date in the (never-to-arrive) future.

The average American sees a million commercials before registering to vote, and another million before collecting Social Security. At present Madison Avenue spends a bit more than $500 a year on every man, woman and child in this country, and we spend about a year of our life watching commercials. Marketers are particularly interested in preaching the gospel of consumption to our youngsters, and have increased spending on children's advertising by tenfold in the last fifteen years, hoping to "brand" them early and produce loyal, lifelong customers. The underlying message of this media barrage is simple—happiness may be achieved through ownership and/or consumption of the latest product. Indeed, such ownership or consumption is necessary to achieve or maintain the grace, beauty, power, popularity and/or status we all supposedly seek.[58]

Fortunately, or not, our unlimited appetite for consumption may be satisfied by charging our purchases. In 1997 Americans received three billion offers for credit cards, about eleven for each person in the country. We also got millions and millions of blank checks from our credit card companies, inviting us to consolidate or take on new debt. The unfortunate message of this "easy payment plan" is that Americans may consume as much as they like, deferring full payment to some future date yet unnamed. Indeed, not only do our credit card bills not hold us accountable for the personal effects of bingeing, but they also tend to hide the fact that there are other, larger social costs for our patterns of consumption. Our monthly charges do not include the social or ecological costs rung up by our patterns of conspicuous consumption. There are no charges for disappearing rain forests, depleted natural resources, polluted rivers, endangered species or decaying infrastructures.

Some Practices. There are a number of practices resulting from consumerism that ought to be of concern to us. First, this conspicuous consumption is going on side by side with desperate poverty at home and abroad. While the United States consumes a quarter of the world's energy and millions of Americans spend disposable income on Lexuses, Rolexes and sports utility vehicles costing up to $40,000, at least 20 percent of the planet is hungry or chronically malnourished. Our overconsumption of resources and our preference for private consumer goods over public spending on basic needs are injustices against the poor. Second, our present patterns of consumption pose severe ecological threats. For, along with consuming a quarter of the planet's energy, the United States accounts for 25 percent of global carbon dioxide emissions and overall pollution, and leads the world in per capita production of garbage. Each of us generates about thirteen hundred pounds of trash and uses up to twenty tons of raw materials a year, recycling only the tiniest fraction of these resources. Third, our present spending patterns are cutting into our savings and running up astronomical bills. In spite of the fact that Americans earn twice what our parents made in the 1950s, we save only half as much, our personal savings rate having plummeted to a paltry 4 percent. These reduced savings are matched by increased debts, with American households currently carrying $1.2 trillion in consumer debt, an increase of 58 percent in the last five years. One result of all this crushing debt has been that in 1997 there were a record breaking 1.3 million personal bankruptcies in this country.[59]

Christian Beliefs. As we have already seen, the church abhors the involuntary and desperate poverty of the world's *anawim* and defends the right of all people to a fair share of the earth's material goods. Still, in "On Social Concern" John Paul II argues that "the mere accumulation of goods and services…is not enough for the realization of human happiness," and there is a real danger that, once having met our basic needs, our ongoing or increasing attachment to material possessions may entrap us in an addiction blinding us to our duties to others and keeping us from fully developing as persons.[60] This argument is offered in the Evangelical Lutheran Church's statement on economic life, which notes that "when consuming to meet basic needs turns into consumerism as an end in itself, we face a serious crisis of faith.…[For the] endless accumulation of possessions and pursuit of wealth can become our god."[61] Jesus warns of this attachment when in Mark 10:21 he challenges the rich young man to "go, sell what you own, and give the money to the poor," and again in Mark 10:25, when he tells his disciples that "it is easier for a camel to go through the eye of a needle than for someone who is rich to enter the kingdom of God." Contemporary Catholic social teaching calls for a practice of simplicity and evangelical poverty and reminds us that our "possession" of the world's goods is a sacred trust from the Creator and that we are to use everything in service of the whole human race.

Structural Reforms. In order to address a few of the more serious effects of consumerism we might consider some of the following proposals. To begin with, as the U.S. Catholic bishops argue, "…meeting fundamental human needs must come before the fulfillment of desires for luxury consumer goods.…This priority presents a strong moral challenge to policies that put large amounts of talent and capital into the production of luxury consumer goods while failing to invest in education, health, [and] the basic infrastructure of our society."[62] In other words, we need to greatly increase our investment in the public sector, particularly in programs addressing basic needs and repairing critical infrastructures. One possible way to do this would be by increasing taxes. At the same time, we also need to find some way to curb consumer debt and encourage an increase in the personal savings rate. This might be achieved by introducing a progressive consumption tax. Such a tax could shift monies to the public sector, encourage savings and set some limits on the growing gap between rich and poor. Also, a progressive consumption tax, like an oil-depletion allowance, could help to defray the greater social and ecological costs of consumption, providing public funds for the clean-up of toxic dumps and investment in critical research regarding alternative energy sources.[63] Furthermore, we need to figure out some way to oversee and regulate advertisements targeted at children, making certain that some protection is afforded to these vulnerable persons. As Americans we are extremely reluctant to support any form of censorship, but we must be equally committed to preserving the very limited freedom of minors. In addition, we must devise some ways to encourage both producers and consumers to create and select reusable, recyclable products that involve a minimal use of resources and production of waste. Finally, our church needs to offer a public witness to the dangers of consumerism. Our religious leaders and institutions need to embrace a simplicity of life, to celebrate and encourage better stewardship of the earth's resources and to model ways of living that do not rely on consumption or ownership for happiness.

Cases and Resources

Along with the introductory case involving Blythe and Tyrone's choices about tithing and taxes, the following four cases offer the opportunity to explore and reflect upon moral choices about a number of other issues relating to economic justice. The resources that follow should be useful in resolving the cases or learning more about economic justice.

Case #2: Whom to Hire?

Brother Alex Thornton, the chair of the theology department at St. Andrew's, a medium-sized Catholic university in Philadelphia, has a problem. Founded in 1867 by the religious community to which Alex belongs, St. Andrew's was originally set up as a men's college designed to serve the mostly German, Italian and Irish Catholic immigrants filling the pews of Philadelphia's parish churches and looking for a way for their children to escape the confines of their ethnic ghettos and move into the American mainstream. For nearly a century St. Andrew's helped waves of first- and second-generation immigrants become engineers, teachers, pharmacists, doctors, attorneys and members of the clergy, over time adding a growing number of Greek, Puerto Rican, Vietnamese and African American students to its roster and opening its doors to women students and faculty in the fall of 1961.

For most of the first century of St. Andrew's existence the university's administration and faculty consisted largely of priests and brothers from Alex's community, with a smattering of lay professors committed to the school's mission of providing an education to the diocese's immigrant and blue-collar constituencies. And, like the population they originally sought to serve, most of these men were of German, Italian and Irish descent. In the two generations after World War II St. Andrew's grew in leaps and bounds, its enrollment climbing from 480 undergraduates in 1946 to nearly seven thousand by 1980, with its faculty increasing from forty-seven to just short of four hundred in the same time. One result of these changes was that the priests and brothers of Alex's order became a shrinking minority among faculty, continuing to direct and influence the school they had founded through the services of campus ministry and a number of key administrative positions. Indeed, it was only in the theology and philosophy departments that the community continued to dominate, holding on to more than half the faculty positions in each department well into the late 1980s.

While many alumni and members of the board of trustees pointed with pride to the strong religious presence in these two departments, and more than a few Catholic parents expressed satisfaction that their children were being educated by the priests and brothers who had taught generations of St. Andrew's students, there was a down side to this strong community presence. For in a school with a great deal of ethnic, racial and gender diversity among its students, teachers and administrators, the faculties of the theology and philosophy departments at St. Andrew's (the two largest departments in the school of arts and sciences) consisted overwhelmingly of white males, mostly middle-aged or older, and largely members of the clergy. Indeed, among the theology department's sixteen full-time faculty there were no people of color and only one woman who was not a religious. The philosophy department as well had only one laywoman (a very junior colleague who complained regularly about the absence of any real consciousness of women's issues among the male members of the department) and no members of any racial minority.

A twenty-five-year veteran of the university, Alex took over as chair of the theology department two years ago, and in that time has overseen the retirement of four of his colleagues, three of them members of his own community. Still, because of budget restrictions, he has only been authorized to fill one tenure-track position at this time, an assistant professor of biblical studies. Supportive of the university's mission statement, which describes St. Andrew's as an institution committed to diversity, Alex wants very much to hire more women and people of color in the department and is hoping that this will be an opportunity to do so. Unfortunately, his own community is also forwarding the application of one of its junior members for this spot, a brother who has recently completed doctoral studies in Scripture in Rome and who has been teaching for the past two years in a Catholic college in Scranton.

After the screening process has winnowed the applicants down to the top three, Alex is faced with a choice among the following candidates: Jeff Stone, the member of his community; Gregory Hahneman, a gifted white male teacher with five years of experience and a small but impressive list of publications; and Louise Carstairs, an African American woman with a brand new degree from Catholic University. The problem for Alex is that while all three candidates prove to be excellent instructors, Louise has less experience than either of the men and fewer publications than Gregory.

Still, he believes that there are good reasons for hiring Louise. First, Alex knows that it is significantly more difficult for laywomen to get advanced degrees in theology at Catholic institutions. They simply do not have access to the sorts of financial supports available to clergy and members of religious communities. Second, he believes that she would bring a unique perspective and contribution to the department and that having a black woman as a teacher in the classroom would make a significant statement about the department's real commitment to diversity. Third, he is deeply concerned about the enduring effects of sexism and patriarchy in the church and supports the U.S. bishops' recent call to work harder for the advancement of women in leadership positions. At the same time he is concerned about being fair to Gregory and about providing for the continued presence of his community at the school he loves so well. What should he do?

Case #3: Take the Promotion?

Qiu Lilin, a thirty-seven-year-old chemist and marketing representative for Carruthers Pharmaceuticals (a multinational drug company based in the United States), needs to make an important decision. This morning she was summoned into her boss's sprawling corner office on the thirty-sixth floor of the company's Dallas headquarters and offered a major promotion. Carruthers is moving into China, Lilin was informed, and the company is looking for someone special to set up marketing operations in Beijing and then to oversee marketing and sales divisions in Shanghai and Guangzhou. The initial work would be quite demanding, her boss warned, calling for between a year and sixteen months of eighty- and ninety-hour weeks, but the rewards, both for her and the company, could be tremendous.

For with a potential market of 1.2 billion customers, the opening of China to Western pharmaceutical companies like Carruthers represents a major financial opportunity. This is true for a couple of reasons, the most important being that country's ongoing shift toward a market economy has meant significant cutbacks in the government's health-care policies. As a result, cash-strapped Chinese hospitals have been given permission to sell prescription medicines at a profit, and the income generated by the sales of expensive (and extremely popular) name-brand Western drugs is substantially greater than those made from Chinese brands. For while there are tight price controls for Chinese-made drugs, hospitals are allowed to sell Western pharmaceuticals at whatever price they choose. Furthermore, Western brand-name drugs are highly touted by Chinese physicians and by a eager public enamored of all things Western and new.

What disturbs Qiu Lilin, however, as she sits in traffic on the commute home that evening, is that these drugs are often unaffordable to the average Chinese person. Indeed, while the profits from these pharmaceutical sales may presently be underwriting the survival of Chinese hospitals, they are also contributing to a whopping 35 percent annual increase in medical costs. And, in a country where government health plans currently pay for fewer and fewer pharmaceuticals, isn't it rather exploitive, she wonders, to be marketing inordinately expensive medications, particularly when they are sometimes not noticeably better than the cheaper Chinese brands available at a tenth of the cost? On top of that, Lilin has heard reports that marketing reps for multinational drug companies are actively courting Chinese doctors (who tend to earn less than $200 a month), enticing them not just with free samples, tote bags and junkets to Hong Kong, but also with "commissions" or kickbacks, a practice forbidden by U.S. laws. How ethical is that?

Still, this would be an extraordinary opportunity for Lilin, whose parents came from China in the late fifties, and who grew up speaking fluent English and Mandarin. To live and work in Beijing, to expose her two daughters to the culture, language and people of their homeland, and—perhaps—even to do some good in the process, bringing the mixed blessings of Western pharmaceuticals and hi-tech medicine to the country of her parents' birth. Of course, there would be personal costs to this move as well. Tim, her husband, had only recently received tenure as an English professor at nearby Southern Methodist University. It would be hard for him to walk away from such a position, even if he could get a leave of absence for a year or two. And they had recently gotten her daughter Grace admitted to a special school for artistically gifted children. What would they do about that? Then, of course, there was always her father, living alone in the family house in Brooklyn. Only a couple of months ago she had asked him again about coming to live with her and Tim and the girls in their home in the Dallas suburbs. Would he even consider going with them to China? And if he did, could she get good medical care for him there? What should she do?

Case #4: Work or Welfare?

At 1:00 A.M. on Tuesday Sheila Rankin is once again at her kitchen table sorting through the stack of monthly bills and trying to figure out which ones she can afford to make payments on. Down the corridor she can hear the sound of her two sons Mike (fifteen) and Charlie (nine) sleeping in their bedroom, and the muffled snores of Debra (six) curled up in her own bed across the hall. Tired from a full day at work, from two and a half hours of commuting on city buses and three hours in the emergency room at Providence hospital waiting for Debra to be seen and treated for an asthma attack, she is also trying to make some other, even tougher, choices.

Two and a half years ago Sheila had been a soccer mom, living with a husband and three children in a modest but comfortable three-bedroom ranch in a suburban development outside of Houston. An active member of her parish, she had taught the third grade Sunday school class on the weekends, been the den mother of her son Charlie's Cub Scout pack and held a part-time minimum wage job working in the cafeteria of the local grade school. This schedule allowed her to supplement her husband's income as an electrician while still getting home in time to meet the returning school buses at 2:30 and 3:45.

But two and a half years ago Sheila the soccer mom had also been the victim of long-term domestic violence and, returning one evening from a Cub Scout meeting with Charlie, she was greeted at the door by a drunken husband brandishing a hot frying pan and demanding to know just where his dinner was. The next seven months were a blur: a flurry of apologies and promises that always ended in more threats and violence. Relocating with the children to an apartment twenty miles away, changing schools, filing for a separation, trying to find work, sitting up nights with frightened, angry, lonely children, wondering if the next phone call or knock on the door would be an harassment or threat from their father, or perhaps one of the many bill collectors who were beginning to make their way into her life.

In the end she had decided for safety's sake to move to another state, even though this took her away from all the family and support systems available in Houston. She also decided to get a divorce, though this left her with an additional $3,600 in debts and didn't result in a steady income of child-support payments from her increasingly out-of-control ex-husband. And she had *decided to go on welfare, just to tide her over until she could find work and get back on her feet.*

Unfortunately, this wasn't nearly as easy as she had thought. For, in spite of her best efforts to pull herself up and out of her present crisis, Sheila soon discovered that a decade and a half as a stay-at-home mom with a year of community college and very limited work experience in minimum-wage jobs had left her incapable of adequately providing for herself and her three children. Even if she were able to find and hold a full-time job at the $6.00-an-hour salary available to folks with her skills and background, she soon learned that such jobs did not pull her up to or over the poverty line, did not solve her child-care or health-care problem, did not give her sufficient flexibility to take care of medical emergencies and often called for ten to fifteen hours a week commuting on city buses. On top of that, the staggered schedules at the three schools Mike, Charlie and Debra attended meant that the younger children would need to spend half an hour to an hour unattended at the beginning and close of every day, and her own work and commuting schedule usually had her out of the house from 6:30 A.M. to 6:30 P.M.

In the last year Sheila had gotten and had to give up three of these jobs— once because of lay-offs, and twice because medical emergencies with Debra had made it impossible for Sheila to make the hour-long commute to work. In that time she had also had the power turned off on her twice, had paid only $176 of her legal bills, had accumulated $7,200 in new medical bills and had been mugged once coming home from work.

So, sitting there looking at her stack of bills, Sheila was thinking about going back on welfare. If she could go on public assistance for two years and get grants and loans to attend the local community college, she could possibly get training as a legal secretary and find a $10-an-hour job that would allow her to work her way out of poverty. She might also be able to find a work study position at the college that would allow her to meet her "Work First" obligations and could, perhaps, set up a schedule that would give her the flexibility to deal with her children's school schedules and any medical emergencies.

But she would also have to deal with the constant harassment, embarrassment and humiliation that came with being on public assistance, with the disappointment and disapproval from her own family members, and with all the hundreds of little shames that came with using food stamps at the grocery store or paying for everything with money orders or hearing other people talk about "those folks" on welfare. And even with welfare and all the paperwork and wait-ing in lines that it would require, Sheila understood that the next two years would be extremely treacherous. Anything from a change in the federal rules to the bad mood of a social worker could see her payments reduced or terminated. Of course, she could provide a little buffer for herself and the children by doing some unreported work for cash, cleaning houses for other people or doing some extra child care on weekends. That would be illegal and, Sheila believes, morally wrong, but it might also mean the difference between paying the light bill one month or spending ten days in the dark. God, she wonders, what should she do?

Case #5: Where to Invest?

Malcolm and Chloe Washburn are trying to make some choices about investments. A thirty-six-year-old history teacher at the local community col-lege, Malcolm has long been convinced that he and Chloe would not be able to depend on Social Security and Medicare alone to provide for their basic retire-ment needs, and would certainly need to put aside significant savings for the education of their two daughters, Sarah (ten) and Holly (six). Furthermore, Chloe is her widowed mother's only child, and over the past several years it has become increasingly clear to the couple that Mrs. Clairborne is going to need financial help from them in the years to come.

And so the couple has decided to plan aggressively for their future, and for the last several years have set aside 10 to 12 percent of their income in savings, a figure well above twice the national average. At the same time they have tried to be conscious of their duties to the larger community and to those in need, designating an additional 5 percent for charitable giving. These choices have occasionally meant making sacrifices and paying pretty close attention to their budget. But they have also provided Malcolm and Chloe with an increased peace of mind, knowing that they will be able to meet their obliga-tions without becoming a burden to their two girls at some later point.

Malcolm has a pension plan at the college to which he contributes 10 percent of his salary, matched by an additional 5 percent from the school. These monies go into a tax-deferred annuity, where they are invested in a mixture of growth (more aggressive) and equity (more stable) mutual funds, which then make *investments in a broad range of national and multinational corporations around the planet. Chloe, who works as a real estate agent at the local branch of a national chain, has no such plan, and so has put $2,500 a year into an IRA account, where her money is likewise invested in a number of mutual funds. To balance out their heavy reliance on the stock market, they have placed the rest of their annual savings in money market accounts at their credit union.*

Recently, however, the couple has become concerned about some of their investments. Two weeks ago Chloe saw a story on Sixty Minutes *about some Catholic nuns whose communities had bought shares in a number of multinational corporations and who were now attending stockholder meetings and raising some very uncomfortable questions about a number of corporate practices they considered immoral or unjust. There were questions about exploiting foreign workers in sweat shops, about profits being made from the production and sales of weapons, about carelessly polluting and despoiling the environment in developing nations and about offering bribes and kickbacks to corrupt officials. What was particularly disturbing to Chloe about this story, however, was that she recognized three of the companies in question. They were corporations in which her and Malcolm's mutual funds were deeply invested. Some of the monies that would pay for their retirement, for her mother's eldercare and for the education of her children at a good Catholic school were being made by youngsters working in sweat shops in Southeast Asia and Central America.*

The following Sunday Malcolm cornered Sister Angela after mass and asked her about the story. She informed him that the members of her own religious community had become increasingly concerned about "socially responsible investing" and were trying to make sure their monies weren't invested in companies engaged in unsavory practices. One way to address the issue, Angela suggested, was to consider investing in a "Social Choice" or "Social Awareness" mutual fund account. Such accounts avoided investing in companies that exploited workers or the environment, that were involved with the sale of tobacco, weapons or alcohol or that supported the nuclear or gambling industries. Sister Angela also suggested that Malcolm and Chloe might consider turning to groups like the Interfaith Center on Corporate Responsibility to get information about socially responsible corporations.

Coming home in the car from church, Chloe and Malcolm expressed concern about what they had learned. Just how responsible were they for things done by

*a company that the mutual fund they had invested in owned shares in? Could
they really be blamed for child labor in Pakistan just because they had invested
their monies in a profitable mutual fund? And how were they to weigh their
duties to their children and Chloe's mom against their obligations to some
unidentified workers in a sweat shop on the other side of the planet? Weren't
they doing enough by saving prudently for the future? What more could be asked
of them? Should they look into this "Social Choice" account? And what if the
returns are less than those of the growth accounts that have been doing so well for
them? Will their changing mutual funds help anyone? What should they do?*

Resources

Bread for the World (http://www.bread.org), 1100 Wayne Ave., Suite
1000, Silver Spring, MD 20910; (301) 608-2400. Information
and advocacy on hunger and poverty issues from a Christian
perspective.

The Catholic Worker (http://www.catholicworker.org), 36 East First
St., New York, NY 10003; (212) 777-9617. A lay Catholic
organization committed to nonviolence and justice for the
poor.

Habitat for Humanity (http://www.habitat), 121 Habitat St., Ameri-
cus GA 31709; (912) 924-6935. Information, advocacy and an
opportunity to work with those in need of adequate housing.

Interfaith Center on Corporate Responsibility (ICCR), 475 Riverside
Drive, Room 566, New York, NY 10115; (212) 870-2295. Information and resources regarding morally responsible investing.

National Conference of Catholic Bishops/United States Catholic
Conference's Office of Social Development and World Peace
(http://www.nccbuscc.org/sdwp), 3211 Fourth St. NE, Washington, DC 20017-1194; (202) 541-3180. Information and resources
on Catholic positions and initiatives on economic justice.

NETWORK (http://www.networklobby.org), 801 Pennsylvania
Ave. SE, Suite 460, Washington, DC 20003-2167; (202) 547-

5556. Education and advocacy on a wide range of social issues from a Catholic perspective.

Sojourners magazine (http://www.sojourners.com), 2401 15th St. NW, Washington, DC 20009; (800) 714-7474. Information and advocacy on a wide range of social justice issues from a Christian perspective.

Christians and Violence

Case #1: Censoring Cyberspace?

At the breakfast table one Saturday morning David Martinez puts down the newspaper and turns to his wife Jackie.

"Honey, according to this piece kids in this country see about 100,000 violent acts on TV by the end of eighth grade, and about 40,000 murders by the time they graduate from high school. And what's worse, most of this hitting, kicking, shooting and killing is portrayed as a perfectly natural way of solving problems. Hardly anybody ever gets badly hurt, hospitalized or arrested. On top of that, lots of studies show that all sorts of kids are affected by this video violence. This reporter said that boys and girls who watch a lot of TV develop what they call a "mean world syndrome," which means they believe the world is a nasty, dangerous place, and so they feel entitled to be aggressive and violent.

"It's kind of staggering," he adds, "thinking about our kids exposed to that much violence. It's like there's some sort of a toxic leak in our living room slowly poisoning our children."

"Oh, I don't know Dave," Jackie responds. "It's not like we didn't watch violent stuff when you and I were kids. Remember Road Runner cartoons on Saturday mornings? Or the Three Stooges and all their slapping and banging? And then there were all those monster flicks in the '50s. And Psycho and Wait Until Dark were certainly major screamers in their day. But you *and I turned out all right. We're not aggressive or paranoid. We don't hit each other or the kids, and we aren't building bombs in the basement. We just like to watch an occasional Hitchcock on cable."*

"Sure, but don't the movies and videos seem more violent to you today? You could show most of Hitchcock's old classics on the Family Channel, but the thrillers they're showing down at the multiplex these days nearly always seem to be about psychopathic serial killers with weird sexual fetishes. Heck, even the comic books seem darker and more violent than the stuff we had. And then there are all those slasher films and the whole video-game thing. Every time some lonely kid shoots up a school it seems like he's spent hundreds of hours playing violent video games or visiting hate sites on the Web. You're not telling me you're not just a little concerned?"

"Sure, I'm concerned. But you and I can monitor what our kids watch. And we can always watch shows with them and talk about what we see. And we can hug them and teach them about working through problems without using violence. And, if all of that's not enough, we could join some parents' advocacy group and petition the networks to put less violent programming on TV.

"But what I don't want to do is get behind the town hall meeting Suzie Bangston and George Harris are organizing for next Wednesday. Those two want to introduce censorship at our library. George wants to adjust the library's computer terminals to restrict access to violent materials on the Internet. OK, I'm sympathetic with their concerns, but I don't know that I want someone else telling me what I can or can't read or look at in the public library. Remember when your brother Carlos wasn't allowed to check out Catcher in the Rye *because the librarian thought it was too dirty? Do we want to go back to that?"*

"No, of course not. But how do you feel about the boys going down to the library and searching the Web for hate-group sites, or violent porn? At least at home we can monitor that sort of activity. Shouldn't we have some safeguards to protect our kids from this sort of garbage? We were pretty happy when the government stepped in and got rid of cigarette advertising targeting minors. We didn't care if Joe Camel's free speech was being violated. Is this really so different? I mean, if we wouldn't let these sites into our home, why should we give them access to our kids at the local library?"

"All right, but if we agree to censorship here, what are you going to say if Suzie and George don't want our kids reading about serial killers like Frankenstein, Macbeth or even King Herod? How are we going to choose which violent entertainment is taboo and which is useful? And who is going to make those choices?"

"Fair enough. I don't know how we'll decide. And I don't know how I'll vote on Suzie and George's proposal. But I've got to hope there's a way for us to protect our kids without becoming some kind of loony Puritans. I guess we'll see."

Introduction. We live in a world and society haunted by violence. On the evening news we hear reports of ethnic cleansing, bombing campaigns and school shootings, and our various forms of entertainment tend to saturate us with images of mayhem and murder. Nations spend huge sums on weapons and armies, while hundreds of millions go without food, shelter or health care. Closer to home, twin plagues of homicide and domestic violence threaten the lives of millions of our neighbors, and our government's "wars" on crime and drugs have led to the most massive incarceration of citizens in human history.

How are we as Christians to respond to this violence? What are we to do in the face of unjust aggression, escalating arms races, widespread domestic violence, international terrorism, ethnic cleansing and astronomical homicide rates? Clearly we must address the underlying tensions and injustices generating this violence, seeking justice and reconciliation whenever possible. But may we ever use force to respond to these evils, or would that violate the gospel commands to forgive our transgressors and love our enemies? In a sinful and fallen world could violence itself ever be the loving thing to do, the only possible path to justice or even a modest sort of peace? Or does it always lead us deeper and deeper into a spiral of retaliation and vengeance?

What is the meaning of those "hard sayings" of Jesus regarding forgiveness, nonresistance and enemy-love? Do they describe impossible ideals, require only that we don't despise our enemies, or just apply to our personal behavior and not our conduct as nations? Are loving Christians allowed to use or threaten force in defense of themselves or others?

And if force could on occasion be (regretfully) justified, what attitudes or rules should Christians adopt regarding its use? What sorts of violence could or couldn't we resort to? What reasons would or wouldn't justify employing or threatening force? Even more than this, however, if we are called to be peacemakers, just what attitudes and practices are we to embrace to prevent or reduce some of the violence in our world? What changes, sacrifices and risks should we make on behalf of peace?

In this chapter, then, we try to think about some of these questions, asking how Christians are to respond to violence and whether and how force itself might ever be part of that response. How, as a people called to be peacemakers, are we to live in a world scarred by sin and violence? What should the Christian position be on war, capital punishment, gun control, abortion, nuclear deterrence, military interventions, arms races or euthanasia? How should we respond to the widespread problem of domestic violence, the pervasive presence of media mayhem, intolerable homicide rates or the massive incarceration of our citizens? And how should we go about shaping our attitudes, behaviors and structures so they're consistent with the Gospel's call to forgiveness and compassion, even for our enemies?

As elsewhere, we begin this chapter with a brief historical sketch, examining the story of Christians and violence in three phases. Next we look at character, suggesting some "peaceable virtues" we might bring to our roles as spouses, parents, teachers, consumers and citizens. Then we examine three fairly controversial choices regarding the use of force—capital punishment, nuclear deterrence and humanitarian military interventions—and ask about possible Christian responses to these issues. Following that, we look at two forms of violence embedded in our communities—domestic abuse and a growing need to punish—and suggest some possible Christian responses to these social sins. Finally, we close the chapter with four more cases and a brief list of organizational resources for those interested in learning more about and addressing some of the issues raised here.

The Story of Christians and Violence

Phase One: The Pacifism of the Early Church.[1] One of the most startling characteristics of the early church is its pacifism. For the first century and a half after Jesus' death there is no evidence of a Christian serving in the military, and until the time of Constantine no major Christian author approved of Christians participating in war. This pacifism was striking for three reasons. Judaism had accepted and occasionally blessed wars like the conquest of Canaan and the Maccabean rebellion. The New Testament offered no clear moral argument condemning war or military service. And early Christians seem to have been the first people in history willing to die rather than serve in the military.[2]

There may have been several causes for this early pacifist stance. Initially, members of the church expected the sudden return of Jesus and the end of the world, and so were less interested in participating in political and social structures. At the same time much of the early growth in the church took place among marginal groups unlikely to join the military or serve in the government. Furthermore, soldiers in the Roman Empire were required to offer idolatrous worship to the emperor, and, of course, this same army had on numerous occasions been instrumental in the persecution of Christians.

Still, a central reason for reticence regarding military service must certainly have been the belief that killing was forbidden for Christians. For though the New Testament does not offer a specific argument condemning war and military service, early (and many later) Christians saw such activities as incompatible with a gospel ethic that called disciples not merely to forgive and love their enemies, but to refrain even from resisting injustice. In the "hard sayings" of Matthew 5:21–48 Jesus instructs his disciples not to hate their enemies. Rather, they are to love, forgive and pray for their persecutors. They are to turn the other cheek when slapped and to go the extra mile when pressed unjustly into service. These lessons of compassion and nonviolence are reinforced by Jesus' own behavior when he prevents Peter from using a sword in his defense (Matt 26:52) and pleads for God's forgiveness for his own executioners (Luke 23:34).

Nonetheless, throughout the third century there is evidence of a growing number of Christians serving in the military. Some were certainly soldiers converted to Christianity, while others were disciples who had joined the army. And though the church disapproved of this practice, such Christian soldiers were not excommunicated, perhaps in part because during this time the army served mainly as a police force keeping the peace, and perhaps because a growing number of Christians were concerned about the threat of barbarian invaders.

Phase Two: The Long Reign of the Just War. The conversion of Constantine and his establishment of Christianity as the religion of the Roman Empire led to a reversal of the church's position on war. Faced with an empire transformed overnight from persecutor to protector, this no-longer marginal sect had to reconcile the gospel mandate to love one's enemies with the need to defend Christian civilization against invasion. The result was a two-tiered ethic in which most Christians were allowed to fight in just wars, while pacifism was demanded only of monks and other religious.

St. Ambrose (339–97), the bishop of Milan and a former governor of northern Italy, was the first Christian to justify participation in war. For though he taught that Christians were not allowed to hate their enemies or kill an attacker in self-defense, Ambrose argued that believers might well use force in coming to the aid of innocent third parties or in defending the peace. Hence, if the cause were just, he believed Christians could participate in a limited war declared by a competent authority.[3] St. Augustine (354–430), the bishop of Hippo, also believed that ordinary Christians might still be loving if they fought for a just cause and sought to restore the peace, but that the clergy were held to a higher standard. For him, going to war could only be justified by the need to respond to the injustice of the enemy. Sin had made war, but it had also made war necessary.

In the thirteenth century St. Thomas Aquinas (1225–74) listed three conditions necessary to justify entering into war. The war must be:

(1) declared by a competent authority, (2) waged in response to an injustice by the enemy (just cause) and (3) fought with the right intent (i.e., seeking peace, not vengeance). Medieval theology later added three other criteria, noting that war must be the last resort, and entered into with both a reasonable hope of victory and an expectation that the good achieved would outweigh the harms involved. Francisco de Vitoria (1486–1546) added to this list by noting two conditions for the just fighting of a war once it had begun. The first was the principle of discrimination (also known as noncombatant immunity), requiring that innocent civilians not be made the direct targets of war. The second principle, proportionality, meant that armies were not to inflict more damage or harm than needed to achieve their peacemaking goal.

The just war tradition was not, however, the only Christian response to war in this period. During the Crusades and the wars of religion that occurred during and after the Reformation many of the restraints of the just war tradition were abandoned, and opponents were treated as demons—entitled to neither justice nor charity. In these so-called holy wars the gospel mandate to love and forgive one's enemies was forgotten, and killing was not just tolerated as a necessary evil but blessed as a holy and Christlike practice. At the same time, the tradition of Christian pacifism has never been completely extinguished. Down through the centuries there has been a steady stream of individual Christian pacifists like Francis of Assisi, as well as a small number of "peace churches" like the Quakers, Amish and Mennonites.

Still, in the main Christian teaching since Constantine has been shaped by just-war theorists. Indeed, "the most prevalent attitude in the West, in the Roman Catholic, Orthodox, and Protestant churches alike, has been approval of combatant service by laymen in wars regarded as just."[4] And recent statements by the U.S. Catholic bishops, the Evangelical Lutheran Church in America, and the United Methodist Church continue to affirm the just war tradition, noting that nations sometimes have no other choice but to turn to force in defense of the innocent.[5]

Phase Three: A Modern Reevaluation. Although continuing to maintain the right of nations to legitimate self-defense, Catholic and

Christian thought on war began to shift in the early 1960s. Pope John XXIII wrote in "Peace on Earth" that "in an age such as ours…it is contrary to reason to hold that war is now a suitable way to restore rights which have been violated."[6] Two years later the bishops of Vatican II noted in The Church in the Modern World that a variety of "considerations compel us to undertake an evaluation of war with an entirely new attitude."[7] In the same document the bishops praised those Christian pacifists who "renounce the use of violence in the vindication of their rights," and offered the Catholic Church's first public defense of conscientious objectors. So too, recent statements by the Presbyterian Church (U.S.A.) and the Evangelical Lutheran Church in America have affirmed the right to conscientious objection and raised questions about modern warfare.[8]

In general this shifting stance toward war, which has shown up in a number of mainstream Christian churches, has been in response to the increasing savagery of modern—particularly nuclear—warfare and weapons. Over the last four decades a growing chorus of Catholic and Protestant leaders has argued that contemporary weapons of mass destruction make a mockery of the principles of discrimination and proportionality and introduce an age of total warfare involving unparalleled butchery and threatening the very survival of human civilization. Moreover, they have been profoundly critical of an arms race that has robbed the poor of their rightful inheritance, threatened the world with nuclear holocaust and endangered the environment. As a result, numerous statements from the Catholic and other Christian churches have condemned any act of total war, repeatedly called for mutual disarmament, accepted nuclear deterrence (if at all) only as a short-term strategy and expressed profound skepticism about the possibility of a discriminate, proportionate or winnable nuclear war.[9]

Still, these reflections on war and deterrence are not the only developments in contemporary Christian thought on violence. Within Christian churches there has been a growing sensitivity to the ways differing forms of violence threaten the lives and well being of persons and communities, as well as a deepening commitment to restrict and resist violence whenever possible. Liberation and feminist theologians have criticized unjust economic, political and social structures as embodying a kind of "institutionalized violence" against the poor and pointed out numerous forms of violence being directed at women and children. Meanwhile, a growing number of Christian churches have recently issued official statements calling for the elimination of the death penalty. More and more, it seems, Christian thought is making a preferential option for peace.

CHARACTER:
Blessed Are the Peacemakers

All people have a duty to work for peace, and as disciples of Jesus we Christians are powerfully reminded of our vocation to be peacemakers. For in his life, death and resurrection Christ proclaimed and initiated God's reign, offering us the first fruits of a reconciling peace that tears down the walls of division, oppression and hostility and calling us to hope and prepare for the fullness of this peace in an age to come. In "The Challenge of Peace" the U.S. Catholic bishops note that "because we have been gifted with God's peace in the risen Christ, we are called to our own peace and to the making of peace in the world. As disciples and as children of God, it is our task to seek for ways to make the forgiveness, justice and mercy and love of God visible in a world where violence and enmity are too often the norm."[10]

In the concrete, we are to live out this vocation within the various roles and relationships that make up the fabric of our daily lives and generate a network of obligations to neighbors both near and far. That is, we are called as spouses, parents, teachers, consumers and citizens to be peacemakers, and the ways we live out our vocation in these relationships will shape and express our character as disciples of Christ and make the world we live in more or less peaceful.

Before suggesting the specific "peaceable virtues" required of Christian spouses, parents, teachers, consumers or citizens, we need to identify some basic convictions or commitments that ought to shape the hearts and minds of every Christian peacemaker.[11] First, Christians need to have a strong preference for peace and a presumption against the use or threat of force. This means being willing to make sacrifices and take risks for peace, and seeing violence as a regrettable last resort. Second, every Christian needs to have a profound respect and reverence for the dignity and sanctity of human life and the human person, and a deep distaste for all that threatens or undermines any of our neighbors anywhere. Thus, there can never be any treatment of any person or group as "less than human." All discrimination, oppression, marginalization, scapegoating or demonizing of others is completely inconsistent with Christianity. Third, all Christians must be committed to working for a peace that is built on love, truth, freedom and justice for all, especially the voiceless and marginalized. Often such a commitment will require both personal conversion and social transformation. Finally, any authentic Christian response to violence must somehow embrace the Gospel challenge to repent of our own sinfulness and heed the radical call to love and forgive our enemies and pray for our persecutors.

Specific Roles

Spouses. Peace, like charity, begins at home, and so our roles as spouses seem like an excellent place to begin the discussion of our call to be peacemakers.

In The Church in the Modern World the bishops of Vatican II described the intimate partnership of marriage as a vocation and a sacrament in which spouses "render mutual help and service to each other through an intimate union of their persons and actions."[12] They also noted that, "as a mutual gift of two persons, this intimate union," grounded in the "equal personal dignity of wife and husband," contributes to the personal and spiritual development and dignity of both spouses, the health of their families and the well-being of the whole community.

Thus, in our roles as spouses we are bound in intimate relationships with our partners and called to foster both their and our own good through a communion nurtured by mutual and generous love and modeled on Christ's own love for humanity. At the same time, this married love is to be a sign of grace and peace for our children and families, and so our role as spouses obliges us to love in a way that reaches beyond our partners. We are to be models of compassion, generosity, forgiveness and respect, and our love is to spill over the walls of our home, showering grace and hospitality on our children, neighbors and local and global communities.

Unfortunately, many spouses do not experience mutual love or peace, but find themselves in relationships profoundly distorted by a partner's sinful desire to dominate. Often fueled by patriarchal and sexist myths, this domination is expressed in a wide variety of abusive and violent practices. Partners (most often women) are threatened, ridiculed, harassed, beaten and terrorized in an attempt to gain and maintain control. In the United States a woman is beaten every eighteen seconds, physical abuse occurs in 28 percent of households and women are in more danger of being assaulted, raped or killed by their current or former male partners than by any other person.[13]

What virtues, then, do we need to be peacemakers within the intimate partnership of marriage? First, we need to be committed to mutual love, a love grounded "in the equal personal dignity" of both spouses and incompatible with any sexist or patriarchal beliefs in the right of one partner to dominate or control another. A genuinely peaceful and loving relationship is only possible when power, responsibility and respect are shared equally between such intimate friends. We do not transcend ourselves and grow into more loving persons by dominating or being dominated, but by facing our mutual frailty and gracefulness in intimate, face-to-face relations of loving trust. We become whole by learning to dance with partners who are friends, not servants. Second, peaceful relations require compassion and empathy, an ability to understand and care about the joys and sufferings of another, a willingness to listen to and learn from another's experience and perspective, and a readiness to negotiate, compromise, repent and forgive. Being peaceful people means we have learned to walk around inside the shoes and skins and joys and sufferings of our spouses. Third, spousal relationships invite us to practice both hospitality and generosity as we seek to enter into an intimate and vibrant communion with another frail but graceful human being. In the generous and mutual sacrifices we make as spouses we seek to forge a community that is greater than our single parts, a community that will be a blessing to us and a light to others. Here, of all places, building peace means being willing to go the extra mile.

Parents / Teachers. We are also called to be peacemakers as parents and educators, whether we practice these roles at home, in the classroom or anywhere else in the lives of our children. In "The Challenge of Peace" the U.S. Catholic bishops described the contribution of parents to the work of peacemaking as "unsurpassed." They also noted that "parents who consciously discuss issues of justice in the home and who strive to help children solve conflicts through nonviolent methods enable their children to grow up as peacemakers."[14] In a similar fashion, all of us who mentor and educate the young are called to teach them the ways of peace and to make the world in which they live a more peaceful place. And indeed our roles as parents and educators tie us not only to our own biological daughters and sons, but to all the children of our community, country, and planet.

As parents and educators we "teach peace" in a variety of ways, in the things that we tell our young people, the stories and entertainment we offer them, and in the rules and norms we direct them to follow. Still, our most powerful tool as educators remains the example we offer. How we behave in front of and toward our children, what sort of regard, affection, respect, tolerance, compassion and forgiveness we show to them and others will offer the most persuasive and lasting testimony regarding peace.[15] If we treat our children with compassion and respect, create a safe, loving environment where they can grow and develop without fear, then they will be more likely to become peaceful, loving persons, capable of forming stable, affectionate attachments to others and of negotiating conflicts without resorting to violence. Indeed, study after study confirms that violence is a learned behavior and that "family influence is the single most likely determinant of an individual's level of violence."[16]

Likewise, as the parents and teachers of our children, there are a variety of things we need to do to make the world in which they live and grow up safer and more peaceful. Every day in America fourteen of our children are killed by guns, 8,470 are reported abused or neglected, and 14.5 million are trapped in poverty. We must address the plagues of gun violence, poverty and abuse that threaten our children, reduce the intolerably high rates of infant mortality haunting many parts of our country and halt the crisis of homelessness and despair threatening too many of our young. And we need to do the same for all the children of our planet.

To be parents and educators who are peacemakers, then, we need to practice nonviolence and compassion in our homes and classrooms, to model tolerance, mercy, forgiveness and honesty in our interactions with others. In these ways we will "teach our children well" to become peacemakers. At the same time we need to commit ourselves to justice and solidarity on behalf of all the children in our society and world who are threatened by every form of violence. And we need to love our children, to be present to them in real, consistent and nurturing ways, to treat them with respect and reverence and to create a safe environment for them.

Consumers. We can also make the world more violent or peaceful by our choices as consumers. As we noted in our discussion of economic justice, our purchasing decisions and patterns can impact the quality of life of workers and communities at home and abroad. And our preference for a cheaper product or service might well result in the exploitation of children in Pakistan or the destruction of a rain forest in the Philippines. Thoughtless, unregulated consumption poses real threats to the safety of our environment and can impede the struggle for peaceful development in many nations around the world. We need to think about where our dollars go and make choices as consumers that will do less and less harm to peoples and environments everywhere.

At the same time, more and more Americans are raising questions about our consumption of violent forms of entertainment, suggesting that this contributes to an escalating cycle of violence in our society. Studies indicate that American children see about 40,000 murders and 200,000 acts of violence on television before they graduate from high school. Three-quarters of this violence goes unpunished (indeed, when "good guys" commit violent acts on television they are only punished 15 percent of the time). Not surprisingly, then, people who watch a lot of television tend to see the world as a more dangerous place than it really is and are more likely to buy guns and support violent responses to crime. Indeed, children who watch a good deal of television violence tend to be less sensitive and more aggressive as youngsters and are more likely to grow into adults who are arrested for criminal activities.[17]

Likewise, a growing chorus of voices in our society cries out for some moderation in our patterns of gun purchasing and ownership. At present there are about 192 million privately owned firearms in this country, and though many purchase these weapons to feel safer, guns kept in the home are forty-three times more likely to be used to commit homicide, suicide or for an accidental killing rather than in self-defense. In 1996 handguns took the lives of 15 people in Japan, 30 in Great Britain, 213 in Germany, and 9,390 in the United States. In this country gunshot wounds are the second leading cause of death for people aged ten to thirty-four, and the rate of gun death among children under fifteen is nearly twelve times higher than in the other twenty-five industrialized nations combined.[18]

As consumers, then, we are challenged to be responsible in our choices. We need first to practice both social justice and a certain simplicity of life, making sure that our patterns of consumption don't violate our duties of stewardship to the planet or justice to our neighbors. We need also to embrace a genuine prudence in making choices about the sorts of entertainment we purchase or choose for our children and ourselves. Not all the violence we encounter in the media is gratuitous or exploitative, but much is, and a significant amount of care must be exercised in choosing what and how much is appropriate for our young. At the same time we need to develop a deep passion for the victims of gun violence in our society, committing ourselves to work on their behalf for a community where our purchase and use of such weapons is much more responsible.

Citizens. Another way in which we are called to be peacemakers is in our role as citizens, both of our own country and of the world. As neighbors, voters and taxpayers we need to confront the various expressions of violence in our society and world. We have a duty to address unconscionably high homicide, infant mortality and abortion rates, to make all our schools, homes and streets safe and to come to the aid of victims of every sort of violence and abuse. And we have an obligation to respond to the underlying causes of so much of the violence in our society—to root out poverty, racism, homelessness and despair. As Pope John XXIII argued in "Peace on Earth," real peace is achieved when all persons in a society enjoy a full range of economic, political, cultural and religious rights, when none are left behind, brutalized or victimized.[19] And in a modern democracy these obligations fall squarely on its citizens.

Likewise, we have a duty as citizens to address our own government's use of force, only critiquing defense budgets, nuclear policies, arms sales, military interventions and our prosecution of the wars on drugs and crime. More than a decade after the Cold War the United States spends just over $280 billion a year on military defense, slightly more than the next nine countries combined.[20] At the same time, the United States has bypassed Russia as the world's premier arms dealer, in part by selling billions of dollars' worth of weapons to developing nations. And at home our state and federal governments have been fighting drugs and crime by building the largest prison system in the world, incarcerating over two million Americans at a cost of more than $40 billion a year.

As citizens called to be peacemakers, then, we need to practice a social justice that will address the underlying causes of violence in our society and world. We also need to develop a profound sense of compassion for and solidarity with all the victims of personal and institutional violence in our communities and around the globe. Furthermore, we must be prudent in our decisions about spending, giving priority to the needs of the poor and marginalized and committing ourselves to building up the common good of our nation and all other nations. And finally, we need to practice a prayerful restraint and forbearance when confronting injustice and conflicts, seeking out first every possible non-violent response, and turning to the use of force not out of any insecure need to prove ourselves "tough," but with the deepest regret.

CHOICES: Three Issues of Violence

There are a number of controversial issues we might examine in this section on choices about violence. How are we to deal with killings in our schools or mayhem in our media? What sorts of gun control legislation ought we to have? What ought to be our position on a ban on land mines? Certainly three that continue to demand our attention are capital punishment, nuclear deterrence and humanitarian military interventions. Just what are we as Christians to think and do about our government's use of force in these three areas?

Capital Punishment

The Voices of Experience[21]

The Voice of History. Widely practiced in the ancient civilizations of Greece, Rome, and the Middle East and throughout Europe in the Middle Ages, the death penalty was prescribed for a large number of crimes and carried out in a variety of ways both brutal and public. In the "spectacle of the scaffold" criminals were hanged, drawn and quartered, beheaded, broken on the wheel, stretched on the rack or burned at the stake, and at the close of the eighteenth century English law still had over two hundred crimes that were punishable by death. In the following century, however, the growth of prisons and the work of Enlightenment thinkers like Cesare Beccaria led to significant reforms in this practice. Public executions all but disappeared, and the number of capital offenses and executions decreased radically. By the middle of the twentieth century capital punishment had been all but eliminated in Western Europe.[22]

American reliance on capital punishment declined radically in the first three-quarters of the twentieth century. During the 1930s 150 to 200 persons were executed annually nationwide, a number that dropped to about 50 by the late 1950s and 15 in 1964. In 1967 concerns about the constitutionality (i.e., due process and equal protection) of the death penalty led to a ten-year moratorium, ending when the Supreme Court affirmed the state's right to execute in *Gregg v. Georgia* (1976). Since then more than 500 people have been executed in the United States, and 3,500 prisoners currently sit on death rows in the nation that has become the world's leading practitioner of capital punishment.

Contemporary Voices. Generally, modern proponents of the death penalty see it as a necessary and effective deterrent to violent crime and argue that in executing certain dangerous criminals the state exercises a just retribution and protects the public from further harm by these persons. Some also suggest that capital punishment is less expensive than life without parole.

Those opposing the death penalty note that in spite of extensive research there has never been any solid empirical evidence that capital punishment deters violent crime, and report that death penalty cases and appeals often cost the state about the same as a life sentence. Not surprisingly, then, they contend that relying on long-term or lifetime prison terms can protect the public just as effectively and economically. Furthermore, many suggest that the state's use of the death penalty is erratic and therefore unfair, and that employing such deadly force against disarmed citizens not only fails to deter criminal activity but actually contributes to a cycle of violence in our judicial system and society. Finally, a number are concerned about the fact that executions leave little opportunity for criminals to reform and none for society to correct mistaken convictions. Between 1976 and 1999 nearly eighty Americans were released from death row after having their convictions overturned.

Voices from the Margins. One of the most common criticisms of the death penalty is that it unfairly targets the poor and minorities. As a former warden of San Quentin once noted, "Capital punishment is a privilege of the poor." Studies repeatedly show that good legal representation is the most important factor in avoiding a death sentence. They also indicate, however, that the vast majority of those sitting on death row could not afford such representation because they were indigent at the time of their arrest. As a result, court-appointed attorneys who were both inexperienced and underpaid generally defended them.

Racial bias shapes the practice of the death penalty in two ways, regarding the race of both the defendant and the victim. In the United States minorities have always been overrepresented among death-row inmates. While they make up about 12 percent of the general population, African Americans constitute a whopping 35 percent of those sentenced to execution, and one recent study indicated that the chances of receiving a death sentence were 3.9 times greater if the defendant was African American. Still, the most significant "race factor" in a death penalty case is the race of the victim. Those who kill a white person are more likely to be executed than those who kill a black person. Indeed, in Florida, Illinois, Oklahoma, North Carolina and Mississippi those who kill whites are four to five times more likely to receive the death penalty.[23]

Scripture. Christian supporters of the death penalty have regularly turned to passages in Scripture, usually in the Hebrew Scriptures, to show that capital punishment is a practice ordained by God. For within the Mosaic Law thirteen different crimes or sins (including adultery, incest, blasphemy, idolatry and contempt of one's parents) were listed as capital offenses.[24]

Generally, two Hebrew Scripture passages have been used to defend capital punishment. In Genesis 9:6 we read that "whoever sheds the blood of a human, by a human shall that person's blood be shed," and in Exodus 21:23–25 we are instructed that when we harm another we are "to give life for life, eye for eye, [and] tooth for tooth." In addition, many proponents cite Romans 13:1–4 from the New Testament.

There Paul instructs Christians that if they do good they have no reason to fear the government, "but if you do what is wrong, you should be afraid, for the authority does not bear the sword in vain. It is the servant of God to execute wrath on the wrongdoer."

There are, however, problems with using these passages to support the death penalty. To begin with, Genesis 9:6 is more of a proverb describing what happens to killers than a command from God. And, indeed, when Cain commits the Bible's first murder, God does not have him executed, but puts a mark of protection on him, "so that no one who came upon him would kill him" (Gen 4:15). Furthermore, Bible scholars agree the law of retaliation in Exodus 21:23–25 was meant to set a limit on tribal vengeance, commanding that the Hebrews not take *more* than a life for a life, or an eye for an eye. And finally, the passage from Romans merely recognizes the state's right to police and punish its citizens, not to execute them.

Three other points should be noted about the death penalty in the Hebrew Scriptures. First, ancient Hebrew legal codes called for the execution not just of murderers but also of adulterers, blasphemers, homosexuals and children who struck their parents. It's hard to believe that any of us would want a modern government to apply such commands literally. Second, it is not at all clear that biblical laws on the death penalty reflected the actual practice of the Israelites or that ancient readers understood these directives as requiring capital punishment in all these cases. Rather, it seems likely that differing mitigating procedures (i.e., requiring two eyewitnesses and excluding any circumstantial evidence) greatly limited the use of this punishment and that over time executions became even more infrequent.[25] Third, the Hebrew Scriptures also stress God's merciful forgiveness for sinners of all stripes and warn against taking vengeance. In Ezekiel 33:11 God tells the prophet that "I have no pleasure in the death of the wicked, but that the wicked should turn from their ways and live."

In the end, however, any Christian reflection on capital punishment must come to grips with the New Testament's central themes of mercy, reconciliation and forgiveness. As already noted, in the

Sermon on the Mount (Matt 5:21–48) Jesus directs his disciples to forgive those who have wronged them and to love and pray for their enemies. And regarding the law of retaliation he notes, "You have heard that it was said, 'An eye for an eye and a tooth for a tooth.' But I say to you, Do not resist the evildoer." Throughout his life Jesus preached and practiced a mercy embracing and reconciling all kinds of sinners, while challenging his disciples to refrain from self-righteous judgments or vengeance. And in the moment of his own death he pleaded for the forgiveness of the very persons responsible for his execution (Luke 23:34). It seems hard to reconcile such a witness with a practice like capital punishment.

Tradition. Some early Christian writers like Tertullian and Lactantius criticized the death penalty as incompatible with Christianity. Still, the *Catechism of the Catholic Church* notes that "the traditional teaching of the Church has acknowledged as well-founded the right and duty of legitimate public authority to punish malefactors by means of penalties commensurate with the crime, not excluding, in cases of extreme gravity, the death penalty."[26]

Traditionally, Christian thinkers justified capital punishment on two grounds: retribution and deterrence. (Clearly, the reform of sinners, normally a third reason for punishment, could not apply here, since the executed prisoner is unable to repent.) The argument from retribution was that executing violent criminals redressed the wrongs they committed and restored a just order to society, while deterrence assumed that the death penalty protected the public by incapacitating criminals and discouraging imitators. So Thomas Aquinas argued that criminals who are dangerous to the community may be executed, and that this example will act as a brake on future crimes. For "the punishment terrifies more than the sin attracts."[27]

Still, other, more troubling reasons have also been offered. Both Aquinas and Pope Pius XII held that those guilty of capital crimes had lost their dignity as persons and thus their right to life. In a passage bound to strike our modern sensibilities as decidedly un-Christian, Aquinas wrote that "it may be justifiable to kill a sinner just as it is to kill a beast, for as Aristotle points out, an evil man is worse than a beast, and more harmful."[28] That is very different from Pope John Paul II's position in his encyclical "The Gospel of Life," where he argues that "not even a murderer loses his personal dignity."[29] At the same time, the *Catechism of the Council of Trent* taught that executing criminals preserved the common good by repressing outrage and violence, suggesting that public executions served not only as a warning to future criminals, but also as a satisfaction of the crowd's passion for vengeance.[30] Fortunately, one no longer finds such arguments in church documents.

Recently, however, there has been a significant reversal of Christianity's traditional support of the death penalty as more and more church leaders and statements call for abandoning this form of punishment. In the 1960s and 1970s the Presbyterian Church (1965), the National Council of the Churches of Christ in the U.S. (1968), the American Friends Service Committee (1972), the American Baptist Churches (1977) and the Episcopal Church (1979) all issued statements calling for abolition of the death penalty. In 1980 these voices were joined by statements from the United Methodist Church and the U.S. Catholic bishops, who noted "that in the conditions of contemporary American society, the legitimate purposes of punishment do not justify the imposition of the death penalty."[31] More recently other Christian communities, including the Evangelical Lutheran Church in America (1991), have also issued statements calling for an end to capital punishment.[32] And in 1995 Pope John Paul II argued that the death penalty ought not to be used except in cases of extreme necessity and that "today...such cases are rare if not practically nonexistent."[33]

In general these statements note that capital punishment has never been shown to deter violent crime and offers no real protection for individuals or communities. Moreover, the authors of these documents express profound concern about the ways in which the practice of capital punishment discriminates against the poor and minorities. Still, for many contemporary church leaders the central argument against the death penalty is that such a brutal penalty is profoundly un-Christian and only adds to our society's deepening cycle of violence. As the U.S. Catholic bishops noted, "...such a punishment might satisfy certain vindictive desires that we or a victim might feel, but the satisfaction of such desires is not and cannot be an objective of a humane and Christian approach to punishment."[34] Similarly, as we read in the United Methodist Church's document, Christians "cannot accept retribution or social vengeance as a reason for taking human life. It violates our deepest belief in God as the creator and redeemer of human life...[and] in the long run, the use of the death penalty by the state will increase the acceptance of revenge in our society and will give official sanction to a climate of violence."[35] In the end, then, there seems to be an evolving consensus among Christian churches that we "should not kill people to show that killing people is wrong.... [and that] in a society already saturated with and sick from violence, capital punishment is a tragically mistaken sentence."[36]

Formulating a Christian Response. What, then, are we to make of capital punishment? After all, it is a practice explicitly sanctioned in numerous biblical passages and officially accepted by the church for centuries. But it is also a practice that contemporary church teaching increasingly sees as inconsistent with a Christian respect for the dignity and sanctity of every human life and the Gospel's mandate to love and forgive our enemies.

Some Basic Convictions. The state has the right and the duty to redress injustices and the disorder created by them, to protect the public by deterring crime and incapacitating criminals, and to provide for the reform and rehabilitation of those who have committed crimes. To preserve the common good, then, the government may justly punish those who do harm. However, the state also has an obligation—perhaps a greater one—to address the underlying causes of violence and crime in society, to combat poverty, discrimination and social injustice. Relying excessively on punishment to address society's ills is itself a sort of institutional violence, particularly when penalties are severe and disproportionately meted out to the poor and disenfranchised. Also, punishment must be proportionate. It must be commensurate with the crime committed without imitating the brutality of the criminal or deepening the cycle of violence. It must involve no more violence than is absolutely required to restore justice and protect the common good. And it should be consistent with contemporary sensibilities about what constitutes humane punishment. Moreover, punishment must be carried out with a right intent. As penalties grow more severe it must be asked whether their increased violence expresses a commitment to deterrence, retribution or vengeance. And any punishment, but especially those that are more drastic, must be administered fairly, free of discrimination against the poor or minorities. Otherwise, these penalties will simply contribute to the violence and injustice in the society. Finally, the ways in which we punish must be consistent with basic Christian beliefs about the sanctity and dignity of all human life and must make some room for the call to repentance, forgiveness and reconciliation. Punishments that ignore or forget the humanity of the criminal are unacceptable.

Some Difficult Questions. What are we, as American Christians, to make of our nation's status as the world's leading practitioner of capital punishment? What lessons are there for us in Europe's nearly complete abandonment of this practice and in the growing rejection of the death penalty by so many church leaders? And just what are our obligations to those on death row, to their victims and to the families of both? What sorts of punishments offer the best hope of restoring justice and preventing further violence? Also, how are we to evaluate the inherent risks of mistaken convictions and executions, especially when so many death-row inmates have received inadequate representation? How strong is our obligation to ensure that innocent persons are not executed? Given our history and all the evidence, is it realistic to expect that the death penalty could ever be applied in ways that do not discriminate against those who are poor or black? And even if we could improve the deterrent value of capital punishment by shortening the appeals process, what would we be sacrificing in terms of due process or human lives?

Nuclear Deterrence

The Voices of Experience

The Voice of History.[37] The nuclear age began on August 6 and 9, 1945, when the United States dropped atomic bombs on Hiroshima and Nagasaki, killing 210,000 people. For the next forty-five years America and the Soviet Union engaged in an unprecedented arms race, based on the premise that only a credible nuclear deterrent could protect the delicate peace of the Cold War. Amassing a combined nuclear arsenal of more than 55,000 warheads, each of the two superpowers possessed the capacity to destroy the other (and their allies) several times over and to precipitate a "nuclear winter" that would effectively end human civilization. In his 1981 farewell address President Jimmy Carter noted that "in an all-out nuclear war, more destructive power than in all of World War II would be unleashed *every second* during the long afternoon it would take for all the missiles and bombs to fall."[38]

Since the end of the Cold War significant progress has been made in arms control and disarmament, with START (Strategic Arms Reduction Talks) I and II calling for American and Russian arsenals to be cut back to ten thousand warheads apiece by 2003. Unfortunately, the Russian Parliament has been unwilling so far to approve or fund these cuts, and there have been recent moves in the U.S. Congress to revive President Reagan's "Star Wars" missile defense initiative. Meanwhile, the world's "nuclear club" has now officially grown to include India and Pakistan.

Contemporary Voices. Two key arguments have been offered in support of nuclear deterrence. Given the regrettable but irreversible introduction of these weapons into the arsenals of (a growing number) of nations, we now (and for the foreseeable future) find ourselves in a world where we require a credible means of deterring their use against us, or other innocent nations. In such a world unilateral nuclear disarmament seems dangerous and irresponsible, while mutual disarmament by all parties seems—at least so far—unlikely. Furthermore, the possession and supposed willingness by our government to use these weapons, or at least to credibly threaten to use them—is believed by many to have been critical to containing Soviet aggression and preventing a nuclear war for half a century. In the same light it is seen as essential to responding to the ongoing danger of nuclear or other similar threats in a post–Cold War world.[39]

Critics, however, like General Lee Butler, the former commander of America's Strategic Air Command, argue that, "nuclear weapons are inherently dangerous, hugely expensive, militarily inefficient and morally indefensible." Indeed, Butler goes on to note that "nuclear war is a raging insatiable beast whose instincts and appetites we pretend to understand but cannot possibly control." Others note that nuclear powers like the United States are obliged by the Non-Proliferation Treaty to take real steps toward total nuclear disarmament.[40]

Voices from the Margins. Since 1945 the United States has spent over $5 trillion on its nuclear arsenal and even after the end of the Cold War our government continues to spend more than $22 billion a year to prepare for a nuclear war. Meanwhile, for nearly five decades universities and research centers across the nation committed a huge percentage of America's intellectual resources to military and defense purposes. Many would argue that this massive diversion of funds and brainpower robbed the poor and undermined development at home and abroad. Monies and minds that should have been directed to correcting social ills, providing food, education, health care and welfare for the poor and assisting in the real economic and political development of impoverished nations were instead spent on building bigger, better and more lethal bombs.

At the same time, the presence of these arsenals threatens the peoples of developing nations in two other ways. First, without being able to participate in any of the decisions involving these weapons, their fates have been held hostage by a small cluster of government officials in a handful of nations often indifferent or even hostile to their plight. Second, the spreading proliferation of these weapons and technology threatens to divert their own national funds into the development of nuclear arsenals and/or to embroil them in regional nuclear arms races.

Finally, our nuclear arsenals pose a significant environmental threat. Even without the danger of fallout from a nuclear war, the manufacture, testing, deployment and disposal of nuclear weapons pose numerous ecological hazards to us and our descendants.

Scripture. As the U.S. Catholic bishops note in "The Challenge of Peace," it is clear that the Scriptures do not provide contemporary Christians with specific answers to the question of nuclear deterrence, a problem "beyond the imagination of the communities in which the scriptures were formed."[41] Still, it is possible to discern within the heart of the Bible some fundamental directions that could aid us in facing this matter.

The Hebrew Scriptures often portray God as a warrior leading the Hebrews to military victory over their opponents (Deut 1:30; Josh 2:224; Judg 3:28), while biblical accounts of the conquest of Canaan and the Maccabean revolt describe these campaigns as holy wars mandated by God. Still, it is also true that the biblical prophets were often suspicious of reliance on military might as a means of securing peace and were likewise critical of any so-called peace built on injustices committed against the poor (Ezek 13:6; Jer 6:14).

In an essay on the New Testament and nuclear arms, Scripture scholar Sandra Schneiders makes a number of important points.[42] First, she argues that at several places in the New Testament the disciples of Jesus are summoned to be peacemakers (Matt 5:9), to preach "the good news of peace" (Acts 10:36) and to hand on the gift of Jesus' peace, a peace that the world cannot give (John 14:27). According to Schneiders, however, the peace Christians are summoned to work for and practice cannot be achieved by preparing for war or threatening others with destruction, but must instead be sought by imitating the compassion of Jesus.

Second, Schneiders notes that the command to love our neighbors, which is at the very heart of the New Testament's call to discipleship, has been radicalized by Jesus in two ways. Christians are to love *all* persons, even our enemies (Matt 5:44), and to offer compassion even to those who attack and persecute us (Matt 5:38–42). Called into friendship with Jesus, Christians are to love as they have been loved by God, even to the point of being willing to lay down their lives for one another. As Schneiders understands this command, Christians are at the very least obliged to make real sacrifices on behalf of those we call our enemies, for we are called to love them as friends.

Third, Schneiders points to our Christian calling to be reconcilers, active agents of peace facing the violence of our world with the compassion and forgiveness offered to us by Jesus. As Paul notes, God has "reconciled us to himself through Christ and has given us the ministry of reconciliation" (2 Cor 5:18). In his life and death Jesus confronted and struggled against all sorts of injustice and violence, but again and again rejected retaliation or the threat of retaliation as a means of responding to these evils. Instead, he sought to break the cycle of violence and vengeance with a compassion and forgiveness that neither fought nor fled.

A similar point is also made by the biblical scholars Marcus Borg and Walter Wink, both of whom argue that Jesus' preaching and practice offered his disciples a third way of responding to injustice, one that was neither timidly passive nor violently reactive. According to these authors Christians are called to confront unjust social structures and break the cycle of violence with a "politics of compassion" and a "creative resistance" that stands in solidarity with the oppressed without demonizing the oppressors. It is hard to see how the threat of nuclear deterrence is consistent with such a call.[43]

Finally, Schneiders refers to Jesus' consistent identification with the poor and marginalized of the world. At the beginning of his Galilean ministry Jesus announces that the Spirit of the Lord "has anointed me to bring good news to the poor" (Luke 4:18). And in the parable of the last judgment (Matt 25:31–46) he identifies himself with all those who are hungry, naked, sick and imprisoned, telling those who had cared for these unfortunates that, "just as you did it to one of the least of these who are members of my family, you did it to me." This "preferential option for the poor," one of the most striking characteristics of Jesus' life, raises serious questions about a policy of nuclear deterrence that has cost so many of the world's poor their daily bread.

Tradition.[44] The Catholic Church's first major attempt to wrestle with the uniquely modern problem of nuclear deterrence came in Pope John XXIII's 1963 encyclical "Peace on Earth."[45] There the pope rejected the notion that real peace could be achieved by a balance of terror and warned of the dangers and harms of a spiraling nuclear arms race that robbed the poor and brought the world ever closer to the brink of disaster.

Since Pope John's critique several points have become staples of Catholic teachings on nuclear deterrence. First, genuine peace depends upon an international order shaped by justice and mutual trust and is undermined by the hostility and suspicion of a nuclear arms race. For though the paradoxical logic of nuclear deterrence may temporarily prevent an enemy's attack, it also tends to provoke an escalating and widening arms race, resulting in increased instability and danger. In The Church in the Modern World the bishops of Vatican II argued that "the arms race is an utterly treacherous trap for humanity....it is much to be feared that if this race persists, it will eventually spawn all the lethal ruin whose path it is now making ready."[46] Second, massive expenditures on nuclear arms rob the world's poor and future generations of basic necessities and inhibit the sort of real development that might lead to peace. As Pope Paul VI argued in a 1978 message to the UN, "the scandal [of the arms race] is due to the crying disproportion between the resources of money and mind that are put at the service of the dead and those that are devoted to the service of life." Third, a credible nuclear deterrent seems to depend on a willingness to use weapons of mass destruction in ways that would almost certainly violate the moral principles of discrimination and proportionality. And finally, nuclear deterrence puts the very survival of humanity at risk. In "The Challenge of Peace" the U.S. Catholic bishops noted that "we are the first generation since Genesis with the power to threaten the created order."[47]

Other Christian churches have raised similar concerns about the morality of nuclear deterrence. The United Methodist Council of Bishops' 1986 pastoral letter "In Defense of Creation," spoke about "the idolatry of deterrence" and warned that, far from building a lasting peace, "nuclear deterrence has become a dogmatic license for perpetual hostility."[48] The Methodist bishops also went on to describe the ways in which the costs of this deterrence policy "are born most directly by those who are most defenseless: the poor, the elderly, and the very young." Not too surprisingly, then, they, along with many other Christian churches, have called for the progressive and ultimate nuclear disarmament of all nations.[49]

In "The Challenge of Peace" the U.S. Catholic bishops offered three specific judgments regarding nuclear warfare and deterrence. To begin with, they noted that "under no circumstances may nuclear weapons or other instruments of mass slaughter be used for the purpose of destroying population centers or other predominantly civilian targets." Even as part of a defensive response such bombings would be indiscriminate and disproportionate acts of total war. Next, they argued that they could not envision "any situation in which the deliberate initiation of nuclear warfare, on however restricted a scale, [could] be morally justified," and so called upon NATO to adopt a "no first use" policy in its defense of Europe. And finally, they expressed deep skepticism about the real possibility of a limited, proportionate or winnable nuclear war and warned that once initiated a nuclear exchange was very likely to grow out of control almost immediately.[50]

Moreover, in their discussion of nuclear deterrence the Catholic bishops argued that "no use of nuclear weapons which would violate the principles of discrimination or proportionality may be intended in a strategy of deterrence," and that "deterrence is not an adequate strategy as a long-term basis for peace." At the same time, they recognized the dangers of unilateral disarmament and offered a "strictly conditional moral acceptance of deterrence." This acceptance was possible, however, only as long as: (1) nuclear deterrence exists only to prevent the use of nuclear weapons by others and includes no plans for "prevailing" in a nuclear war; (2) such policies seek only "sufficiency" to deter, and not superiority over others; and (3) nuclear deterrence is used as a step toward progressive disarmament.

Formulating a Christian Response. What, then, are we to make of our government's continued use of nuclear deterrence, even after the close of the Cold War? What are our obligations as Christian peace-makers regarding the use of this threat as part of our foreign policy?

Some Basic Convictions. Even though we live in a sinful world where nations must sometimes resort to force or the threat of force in the defense of their citizens, the genuine peace given and promised by Christ the Reconciler cannot be achieved by the threat of mutual destruction or a balance of arms. Instead, real and lasting peace is an ongoing work of truth, love, freedom and justice and requires a com-mitment to the sanctity of the human person and the common good of the global community. As the U.S. bishops noted in their 1993 fol-low up to "The Challenge of Peace," building true peace demands that we: (1) strengthen those international institutions and structures con-tributing to cooperation and mutual trust among nations; (2) promote and defend a full range of human rights for all persons everywhere; (3) support the authentic, equitable and sustainable development of all peoples around the planet; (4) commit ourselves to restraining con-flicts flowing from national, ethnic, racial and religious differences; and (5) work to improve the collective security of all nations through diplomacy, demilitarization and disarmament.[51]

Furthermore, nuclear arms present a unique and devastating threat to the human community, and anyone possessing such weapons must be resolutely opposed to any intent to use them except as a deterrent and deeply committed to a process of progressive disarmament. Plans to target civilian population centers, gain superiority over one's opponents, respond to non-nuclear threats with nuclear weapons or "win" a nuclear war are not part of a morally acceptable policy of nuclear deterrence.

Also, the disproportionate allocation of economic and intellectual resources to nuclear weapons and the arms race represents a kind of theft committed against the poor people and nations of the planet. It also undermines authentic development and exacerbates the underlying tensions and problems contributing to war and other forms of violence.

Some Difficult Questions. In an essay on Catholic moral thought and nuclear deterrence Richard A. McCormick, S.J., raises some important questions.[52] First, given a broad based consensus that any real nuclear exchange would soon escalate out of control and lead to completely unacceptable acts of violence, shouldn't we forbid the actual use of these weapons under any conditions? And second, if we are only allowed to possess but never use these weapons, what sort of a credible deterrent is that likely to provide? In order to prevent our enemies launching a nuclear assault, wouldn't we have to make plans and preparations to deploy these weapons ourselves? Wouldn't we need to intend to commit acts that we have already judged to be immoral?

At the same time we also need to ask about the usefulness of nuclear deterrence in a post–Cold War world. How effective are such weapons against non-nuclear powers or rogue states? How does our continued possession of these weapons affect their proliferation among other nations seeking the same dubious security or status they provide for us? What risks does this possession pose in terms of nuclear accidents or environmental harms from testing, storage or disposal? And finally, just which steps will be most effective in progressively reducing and (hopefully) ultimately eliminating the dangers posed by the possession of tens of thousands of these weapons? In other words, how can we get out of this nuclear paradox?

Humanitarian Interventions

The Voices of Experience

The Voice of History. Once a rare phenomenon, humanitarian interventions have become more common since the close of the Cold War. In 1991 the UN supported U.S., British and French troops going into Iraq to protect the Kurdish people from slaughter by their own government. During the years that followed UN or multinational forces have gone into Somalia, Liberia, Rwanda, Bosnia and Kosovo to ensure the safety of populations threatened by genocide, civil war or massive human rights violations, and the United States has sent troops into Haiti to restore a democratically elected government. Furthermore, while not all these incursions have been successful or well received, more and more critics argue that the international community should be prepared to intervene militarily on behalf of peoples threatened by major humanitarian crises that their own government has either caused or cannot control.

There seem to be three reasons for the increased use of humanitarian military interventions. With the close of the Cold War the UN is more able to act militarily without exacerbating East-West tensions (though Kosovo would be an example of how tender this issue can still be). In an increasingly global community national sovereignty and borders are somewhat less sacrosanct. Modern states must cooperate with one another and with all sorts of multinational organizations in dealing with economic, political, environmental and military issues. And nowhere is this new internationalism or cosmopolitan vision more evident than in the matter of human rights. The basic civil, political and economic rights of persons are no longer seen as a matter of internal or domestic policy that a nation may or may not grant at its whim. Instead, human-rights violations are understood as a crime against humanity and a cry for international assistance.

Contemporary Voices.[53] Supporters of humanitarian interventions admit that national sovereignty is an important principle, but contend that it may be overridden when there is no other way to prevent or end major humanitarian crises. Indeed, a number argue that the international community and neighboring states have a duty to intervene when the crisis is serious enough and the use of military force offers a significant benefit without disproportionate harm. In response to concerns that these interventions do not serve national or international interests, supporters suggest that swift and forceful responses to such crises will deter their spread and protect peace in the region. Interestingly enough, humanitarian interventions have found an increasingly receptive audience among a number of pacifists who see these rescue and peacekeeping operations as more akin to police activity than war making.

Critics of humanitarian interventions warn about the dangers of discarding the principle of national sovereignty. Likewise, they worry that ill-defined peacekeeping operations (like Somalia) can all too easily escalate into protracted and costly conflicts with no resolution in sight. Or they argue that neither the UN nor the United States has the right, responsibility or resources to take on the role of global cop. Finally, they are skeptical about the possibility of developing a consistent and coherent set of criteria for such interventions and argue that foreign policy should not be driven by emotional responses to video images of human-rights abuse halfway across the planet.

Voices from the Margins. Often enough the initial call for humanitarian intervention comes from those who have heard the cries and whispers of the victims of genocide, civil war and widespread human-rights violations. Satellite images from refugee camps and war zones, reports from humanitarian agencies and workers attempting to deal with overwhelming losses of life, interviews with victims and survivors—all of these stir the hearts and minds of citizens and policy makers in other lands and generate pressure for action. Without a government that can or will protect them from the crisis at hand, these modern day *anawim* have no one else to turn to, and must count on strangers to rescue them from conditions that "shock the conscience of humanity."

At the same time, a number of smaller, poorer nations have expressed their own fears about a right to humanitarian interventions. After a long history of dealing with colonial and neocolonial powers that defended their empire-building interventions as benign and civilizing, it is easy to see why many people in developing countries might be worried about their larger neighbors exercising undue influence and interference in the name of humanitarian assistance.

Scripture. Even though Genesis 14:13–17 recounts the tale of Abraham's armed rescue of Lot and all his kinfolk, it would be a mistake to argue that Scripture offers a simple approval of humanitarian military interventions. After all, given everything that the New Testament has to say about enemy-love and forgiveness, it should be obvious that the use of violence must always be a troubling matter for Christians. Still, the biblical witness does offer some starting points for our reflections.

To begin with, in the Hebrew Scriptures God is often portrayed as a mighty liberator who rescues the Israelites from their oppressors and enemies. Nowhere is this more evident than in the Exodus narrative, a story of God's powerful deliverance of the Hebrews from their Egyptian captors. In Exodus 3:7–10 Moses encounters God for the first time and is told, "I have observed the misery of my people who are in Egypt; I have heard their cry on account of their taskmasters. Indeed, I know their sufferings, and I have come down to deliver them from the Egyptians....Come, I will send you to Pharaoh to bring my people, the Israelites, out of Egypt."

The God revealed in this story of liberation has heard and been moved by the cries and sufferings of the Hebrews. This is a God with a deep compassion for the oppressed and marginalized, and a profound and active passion for justice. This is a redemptive and liberating God who rescues those in harm's way, a God who sends Moses to confront Pharaoh and forces the Egyptians to set the Hebrews free.

We find this divine compassion for the powerless, this preferential option for the victims of oppression and injustice, throughout both the Hebrew Scriptures and the New Testament. Again and again the prophets portray God as one who hears the cries of widows, orphans and aliens and comes to their aid. As Psalm 103:6 notes, "...the Lord works vindication and justice for all who are oppressed." So too, in the New Testament (Luke 4:18) Jesus proclaims that the Spirit of the Lord has sent him "to bring good news to the poor,...to proclaim release to the captives...[and] to let the oppressed go free."

We also find in Scripture a consistent call to imitate God's compassionate and redemptive justice; a demand that we treat the *anawim* as God has treated us. As the author of Psalm 82:3–4 directs, we are to "give justice to the weak and the orphan; maintain the right of the lowly and the destitute. Rescue the weak and the needy." And in

New Testament passages like the parable of the Good Samaritan (Luke 10:29–37) Jesus extends this obligation to include all strangers and foreigners. So although the biblical authors don't speak about human rights, Scripture repeatedly testifies that we have a duty to help all those in need and to liberate them from every form of danger and harm. Indeed, as the last-judgment parable in Matthew 25:31–46 makes clear, the ultimate measure of our righteousness will be whether we recognize God in the least of our brothers and sisters, and come to their aid.

Finally, it is evident in the New Testament that for Jesus there is no political, economic or religious structure more important than the human person. Neither the state nor the Sabbath takes priority over the suffering neighbor, suggesting that a principle like national sovereignty would not be a sufficient reason to refrain from coming to the rescue of those threatened by a humanitarian crisis.

All of this is to say that the biblical witness consistently testifies to the centrality of the human person, to the absolute importance of the command to love one's neighbor and the duty to make a preferential option on behalf of all those who are the victims of injustice. At the same time, of course, the "hard sayings" of Jesus regarding forgiveness and enemy-love raise serious problems about the use of violence to protect others. These reflections do not resolve the question of humanitarian intervention, but they do help us sketch out some parameters for the conversation.

Tradition.[54] It must first be acknowledged that while the majority of Christian churches continue to accept the morality of some wars, and thus of certain humanitarian military interventions, the Christian tradition also includes—and recognizes as authentically Christian—the voices of individual pacifists and "peace churches." These Christian pacifists would, in general, be opposed to military interventions of any sort and would be unlikely to support the humanitarian interventions being discussed here. Still, among Catholics and Christians who accept the just-war tradition, there may be a case to be made for humanitarian interventions.

Catholic social teaching has three reasons for arguing that a state's right to sovereignty is not absolute, but could be overridden to prevent or stop grave human-rights violations. First, in Catholic thought it is the human person and not the state that is sacred. Fashioned in the image and likeness of God, the person "stands above all things" and is both the basic building block of society and the reason states exist. Indeed, the very purpose of the state is to protect and preserve the common good of all persons, which it does primarily by defending and promoting a broad spectrum of human rights. Second, as Pope John XXIII notes in "Peace on Earth," every moral society is grounded on the premise that the human person is endowed with certain rights and that these rights "are universal and inviolable, so they cannot in any way be surrendered."[55] And third, while recognizing the legitimacy of national citizenship, Catholic teaching affirms that all persons are members of the global human community and that our duties to our neighbors do not stop at the border.

And so, in spite of a deepening discomfort with the horrors and dangers of modern warfare, a number of recent statements from Catholic and other Christian leaders have offered a limited but consistent support for certain types of humanitarian interventions. In a letter on military intervention in the Balkans the presiding bishop of the Evangelical Lutheran Church in America argued that "while we support the use of nonviolent measures, there may be no other way to offer protection in some circumstances than by restraining forcibly those harming the innocent." Furthermore, he noted, Christians are called upon "to make opposition to genocide and other grievous violations of human rights."[56]

Pope John Paul II made a similar point in an earlier address to the diplomatic corps. There he argued that "once the possibilities afforded by diplomatic negotiations and the procedures provided for by international agreements and organizations have been put into effect, and, nevertheless, populations are succumbing to the attacks of an unjust aggressor, states no longer have a 'right to indifference.' It seems clear that their duty is to disarm this aggressor if all other means have proven ineffective. The principles of the sovereignty of states and of noninterference in their internal affairs—which retain all their value—cannot constitute a screen behind which torture and murder may be carried out."[57]

What is striking in particular about the pope's statement is that he goes beyond affirming a right to humanitarian interventions and argues that the international community and neighboring states have a duty to intervene in certain settings. "Humanitarian intervention [is] obligatory where the survival of populations and entire ethnic groups is seriously compromised. This is a duty for nations and the international community."[58] As the Pope sees it, the refusal to act in the face of such crimes as ethnic cleansing or to respond to grave humanitarian crises constitutes a "culpable omission" on the part of those who stand idly by and watch.

In attempting to discern just when, where, and what sort of humanitarian interventions might be justified, various Christian authors have suggested relying on the just-war criteria.[59] First, there would need to be a *just cause* for intervening, which might include genocide, ethnic cleansing, massive losses of life, or human-rights violations that one author described as "egregious, unconscionable and so pervasive as to affect thousands of individuals." Second, parties could only intervene as a *last resort,* after all diplomatic and less violent measures had been exhausted. Third, the intervention would have to be carried out with a *right intent.* The goal must be to protect the rights of the endangered population, not to seek any political or military advantage for the intervening countries. Fourth, prudence would demand that there be a reasonable *prospect of success,* that the humanitarian and peacekeeping goals of the intervention be achievable and that the military force used be capable of achieving them. Fifth, the intervention must be characterized by a certain *proportionality.* The harms inflicted ought not to outweigh the good done by intervening. This is often a particularly tricky bit of calculus to work out, but it is critical in evaluating whether the intervention should be undertaken, for it makes no sense to take an action that will clearly make things worse. Finally, interventions should be made by parties with *legitimate authority* to act. In the vast majority of cases this would mean that incursions should be supported and carried out by groups of nations, preferably sponsored by the UN or some regional international organization. Still, there seems to be some willingness to accept unilateral interventions in extreme cases.

Formulating a Christian Response. How, then, are we to respond to the question of humanitarian interventions? Are they a moral and effective way of dealing with the threat of genocide, ethnic cleansing and other humanitarian crises? Or do they represent a dangerous violation of the international order and invite all kinds of mischief?

Some Basic Convictions. In "The Harvest of Justice Is Sown in Peace," the U.S. Catholic bishops offer five points in their reflection on humanitarian interventions.[60] "First, human life, human rights and the welfare of the human community are at the center of Catholic moral reflection on the social and political order." Our duty to help those facing humanitarian crises crosses all borders, and indifference to the sufferings of others is simply not an option. Second, national sovereignty continues to be an important but limited principle that "may be overridden in exceptional circumstances, notably in the cases of genocide or when whole populations are threatened by aggression or anarchy." As John Paul II has noted, at "the very heart of international life is not so much states as man." Third, intervening parties should seek to use as much diplomacy and as little force as possible, relying first on a mixture of humanitarian aid programs, political and economic sanctions, and various diplomatic initiatives and embargoes before turning to full-scale military interventions. This reticence to use force should reflect a Christian's fundamental presumption against the use of violence and preference for the peaceful settlement of disputes. Fourth, regretfully, "military intervention may sometimes be justified to ensure that starving children may be fed, or that whole populations will not be slaughtered." (Of course, a long line of Christian pacifists would disagree with this conviction, arguing that love of neighbor—even the unjust neighbor—forbids the use of such force or violence.) Still, such interventions should be exceptional and "conform strictly to just war norms and norms of international policing." Particular attention needs to be paid to making certain that interventions are limited, proportionate and have a reasonable probability of success. Fifth, all humanitarian interventions must be evaluated in light of their effect on international peace, and the international community needs to develop clear principles and procedures regarding this practice.

Some Difficult Questions. Christians embracing a pacifist stance are unlikely to acknowledge the morality of any military interventions. But even those Christians who argue that humanitarian interventions are sometimes necessary and moral must still address several hard questions, a number of which the Catholic ethicist Kenneth Himes identified in a recent essay on the topic.[61] To begin with, who exactly may intervene? Clearly, everyone's preference is that all interventions have broad based international support, preferably from the UN, but at least from a multinational coalition of neighboring states. Still, does that mean that the United States ought not to have gone into Haiti if it hadn't had UN support? And does the United States, as the world's sole remaining military superpower, have a particular obligation to support or lead such interventions? Or should it, for the very same reasons, only operate under the umbrella of the UN, NATO or other multinational groups?

Next, what ought to count as sufficient grounds for an intervention? Genocide and ethnic cleansing seem clear, but what about other losses of life and human-rights violations? How serious does the hemorrhaging of human life have to be to risk this procedure? And when are such interventions feasible? Under what conditions is it reasonable to expect that a military incursion will save the lives of thousands or tens of thousands without aggravating the present crisis? It is important to recognize that any military intervention involves the loss of life, and that intervening nations have some genuine obligation to accept proportionate risks and casualties. Still, it is also critical to be prudent, and to ask just what might be accomplished by this particular intervention and what harms might result.

COMMUNITY: An Examination of Two Forms of Cultural Violence

We live in a violent culture. As the U.S. Catholic bishops have noted, "No nation on earth, except those in the midst of war, has as much violent behavior as we do—in our homes, on our televisions and in our streets."[62] In this section we will examine two manifestations of this cultural violence; the plague of domestic violence, and our nation's burgeoning prison industrial complex. We will also look into the myths and institutional practices underlying domestic violence and the explosion of our prisons, and suggest some possible Christian responses to these forms of cultural violence.

Domestic Violence

"Domestic violence is the most common form of violence in our society and the least-reported crime."[63] Every year fifteen hundred women in the United States are killed by their current or former boyfriends or spouses, while another three to four million are battered by such men. More than 50 percent of women in this country are battered at some point in their lives. More than a third are assaulted repeatedly each year. Assaults by intimate partners result in more injuries that require medical treatment than rape, auto accidents and muggings combined. "In the U.S. nine out of ten women murdered are killed by men known to them; four out of five are murdered at home."[64] Still, fewer than 7 percent of marital assaults are reported to the police.

Ideologies. The widespread practice of domestic violence is supported by a number of mistaken beliefs or myths. The first is the sexist assumption that men are superior to women and entitled to control them. A recent Vatican statement, on "The Roots of Violence Against Women," notes that "there is moreover no doubt that violence against women has as its root cause a diffuse, mostly unexpressed conviction that women are not equal to men and that therefore it is normal for a man to subject women to his own will or to have them serve his pleasure."[65] Unfortunately, as we read in Elizabeth Schüssler Fiorenza and Mary Shawn Copeland's *Violence Against Women,* these sexist and patriarchal beliefs have, down through the ages, found ample support and expression in some of the teachings and practices of most Christian churches. Thus, both Catholic and Protestant communities need to accept responsibility for promulgating attitudes that have contributed to the violence being perpetrated against women and children.[66]

A second troubling myth is that violence is an appropriate way of solving interpersonal problems. Violence is a learned behavior, and children exposed to domestic violence are a thousand times more likely to abuse their own spouses or children, while those who see a lot of violent entertainment are noticeably more aggressive and violent in dealing with others. Whether the influence stems from home or TV, too many of our children are being taught that violence works. So too, domestic violence sometimes continues because victims mistakenly believe that they are obliged to accept this abuse for the sake of their marriage and/or children, that they are somehow responsible or at fault for what is going on or that leaving the relationship or marriage would be sinful. Finally, many in our culture continue to believe that domestic violence is a family matter and that the criminal justice system ought not to intervene.

Some Embedded Practices. A number of differing social practices have helped to perpetuate domestic violence. Traditional family structures have generally not favored an equal sharing of authority, labor or finances between wives and husbands, but encouraged women to be disproportionately compliant and dependent. When advertising and pornography treat women as sexual commodities and pervasive discrimination keeps them from achieving equality with men in politics, economics, education, culture and religion, this can only lead to an even sharper imbalance of power between spouses. In particular, the economic dependence of so many women (whose labor goes largely unnoticed and unrewarded) means that in separating from their abusers they risk impoverishing themselves and their children. In a society where divorce results in a woman's standard of living dropping by 73 percent and a man's increasing by 42 percent and where domestic violence is the largest single cause for women going on welfare and the main reason for homelessness among women and children, it is easy to see why so many feel trapped in abusive relationships.

Other practices that add to the problem of domestic violence involve the failure of our society to offer sufficient protection and assistance to victims. First, in spite of the fact that women are at the most risk of assault and/or murder during or after separating from their abusers, there is a drastic shortage of safe places for those seeking to escape from domestic violence. Nationwide, shelters have space for only about 60 percent of those seeking help. During 1994 shelters for battered women in Los Angeles County had to turn down nearly nine thousand requests for assistance. Second, despite improvements in police procedures, domestic violence continues to be a grossly underreported and underprosecuted crime, and protection orders are often ineffective and inconsistently enforced. Third, certain insurance companies have gone so far as to deny health, life or disability coverage to abused women, arguing that they have a "preexisting medical condition" and that they are too risky to insure.

Christian Beliefs. Although certain Christian teachings and practices have been distorted by the sin of sexism, the notion that men are superior to women or have a right to dominate them is antithetical to true Christian beliefs. The Vatican document on "The Roots of Violence Against Women" argues "that the traditional constant teaching of the Catholic Church affirms the equal dignity of men and women, male and female, and [teaches] therefore that they have the same rights. Both are creatures of God, made in the image and likeness of the Lord."[67] And in an ecumenical statement addressing domestic violence, a group of Canadian church leaders argued that "the violent actions taken by men against women, because they are women, reflect a lack of understanding in our society about how men and women ought to relate to each other. They violate the basic Christian values of justice, equality, respect, dignity and peace; they go against the call to practice kindness, gentleness, faithfulness, mutual support and to love one another as ourselves."[68]

Furthermore, as the U.S. Catholic bishops have argued, "violence against women, in the home or outside the home, is *never* justified. Violence in any form—physical, sexual, psychological or verbal—is sinful; many times it is a crime as well....[Indeed,] violence, whether committed against family members or strangers, is antithetical to the Judeo–Christian messages of love and respect for the human person."[69]

And while Christianity places a high value on the sanctity of marriage, a group of Canadian Catholic bishops have recently noted that "the Catholic Church teaches that a woman has the right and sometimes the duty to protect herself and her children by leaving a violent situation when it occurs." Indeed, they go on to say to the victims of domestic violence, "Women, many of you have suffered greatly from abuse. We assure you that our church does not insist that you stay in these situations."[70]

Finally, Christianity does not teach that victims are responsible for the violence directed against them or that the call to forgive and love our enemies means that women should passively accept unjust attacks directed against them or their children. Rather, Christian teaching affirms the inviolable dignity of the human person and argues that injustice in all of its forms is to be uncovered, confronted and resisted.[71]

Structural Reforms. To address the problem of domestic violence we need to make changes in how we behave as a community. Our churches, schools and government must support effective educational programs in which we publicly and repeatedly address the scope, seriousness and harms of this abuse and offer its victims and perpetrators help in breaking the cycle of violence. We need to confront and reform patriarchal and sexist structures that discriminate against and objectify women. In particular we need to support reforms ensuring economic justice for women, such as affordable and accessible child care, fair taxation, pay equity, etc. Also, we must provide effective protection and support for those threatened by domestic violence. There must be sufficient and safe shelters and housing for battered women and their children, adequate assistance in finding employment and securing health and child care, and comprehensive protection from those who would assault and/or kill them. Welfare laws and practices, housing policies and health-care provisions must not penalize women seeking refuge from their abusers, but should instead be geared to offer support and assistance to these victims of violence. Finally, we must make every effort to lower the levels of violence in our communities, to teach and practice more effective and nonviolent means of communication and conflict resolution, to instruct our children on the harms and costs of violence and to create a society built on justice for all.

Prison Industrial Complex

In the past quarter-century the United States has built the largest prison system in the world.[72] With more than two million people crammed into its prisons and jails, America has five times the prisoners it had in 1970 and incarcerates more of its citizens than any other nation, about half a million more than China. Indeed, our national incarceration rate is six to ten times that of Western European democracies, with sentences two to three times longer than those served in such nations. Each year this burgeoning prison system costs taxpayers about $40 billion and must make room for anywhere between fifty and eighty thousand new inmates.

Most of this recent escalation is the fruit of America's war on drugs, which has disproportionately (but not unexpectedly) targeted America's poor and minorities and resulted in our prisons being flooded with a growing number of people convicted of nonviolent crimes. Today about 70 percent of the prison inmates in the United States are functionally illiterate, about 70 percent were victims of child abuse, about half are African Americans and between 60 and 80 percent have a history of substance abuse. Moreover, less than a third of those currently being sent to prison have been convicted of a violent crime.

Ideologies. The explosive growth of America's prisons has been fueled by four questionable beliefs. There is the myth of leniency, the notion that America's high crime rates are the result of our unwillingness to punish offenders severely enough. Although the United States has much tougher sentencing policies than other Western democracies, a huge number of Americans continue to believe politicians who complain that our treatment of criminals is too lenient, and that we need to "get tough" on crime by passing even stiffer penalties.[73]

There is also the myth of deterrence, the idea that prisons are an effective—perhaps even the most effective—crime-fighting tool and that incarcerating more people for longer periods will lower crime rates. Unfortunately the statistics do not bear this out, but suggest instead that prisons and stiffer penalties produce mixed and often minimal results in dealing with crime. As criminologist Michael Tonry notes in *Malign Neglect: Race, Crime and Punishment in America,* "For at least twenty-five years researchers have shown and honest politicians have known that manipulations of penalties have relatively little or no effect on crime rates."[74] And indeed, in 1973 the National Advisory Commission on Criminal Justice Standards and Goals argued that "The prison, the reformatory, and the jail have achieved only a shocking record of failure. There is overwhelming evidence that these institutions create crime rather than prevent it. Their very nature ensures failure. Mass living and bureaucratic management of large numbers of human beings are counterproductive to goals of positive behavior change and reintegration."[75]

And there is the myth that America's explosive prison growth is needed to address our spiraling rates of violent crime. The truth is, however, that although the United States has approximately 100,000 convicted murderers in prison, the vast majority of those currently being incarcerated in this country have been convicted of nonviolent crimes.

Furthermore, there is the questionable belief that prisons are effective and morally appropriate tools for dealing with a wide variety of social ills. This is not a new myth in America. When Alexis de Tocqueville visited this country in 1831 he reported that the United States had been swept up in "the monomania of the penitentiary system," convinced that prisons were "a remedy for all the ills of society." Nearly 170 years later Elliott Currie reports that our society still relies on prisons "to contain a growing social crisis concentrated in the bottom of our population....A growing prison system is what we have *instead* of an antipoverty policy, instead of an employment policy, instead of a comprehensive drug-treatment or mental health policy."[76]

Some Embedded Practices. Two interlocking practices have been at the heart of America's expanding and overcrowded prison system. There has been the government's long-running war on drugs, a battle relying primarily on punishment over prevention or rehabilitation and prosecuted mainly against the poor and minorities. Since the early 1970s America's war on drugs has been the single most important factor in the explosive growth of a prison system increasingly populated by persons convicted of nonviolent crimes. And, as Michael Tonry notes, "anyone with knowledge of drug-trafficking patterns and of police arrest policies and incentives could have foreseen that the enemy troops in [this] war on drugs would consist largely of young, inner-city minority males. Blacks in particular are arrested and imprisoned for drug crimes in numbers far out of line with their proportion in the general population, of drug users, and of drug traffickers."[77]

Then there is the trend toward stiffer and stiffer penalties. As Norval Morris points out, "a substantial reason for the doubling and redoubling of the incarceration rates in the U.S. in the period from 1970 to 1994 was the profound change in sentencing practices, federal and state....over the period we are considering more convicted offenders were selected for prison, and they were sentenced to longer terms of imprisonment."[78] Indeed, throughout the past three decades flexible sentencing policies that gave parole boards a great deal of discretion have been increasingly replaced by minimum mandatory sentences and so-called three-strike laws, which greatly increased the length of jail terms and contributed to massive overcrowding.

Christian Beliefs. Christian thought has consistently affirmed the right and even the responsibility of the state to punish wrongdoers. This may be done to restore public order by exacting retribution for crimes committed against persons and the community, or to protect the common good by preventing further criminal acts. Still, in general Christian teaching also asserts that the rehabilitation of offenders must be an important part of a society's response to crime. Since "those who commit crimes do not give up their dignity as persons...we must not develop a criminal justice system which is founded on revenge and without the elements of mercy and forgiveness."[79]

So too, Christian thought affirms that our use of punishment must be proportionate. This means that prisons are not a cure for all the social ills confronting our society and that even if we could "solve" the problems of poverty, homelessness, unemployment, and mental illness by locking more and more people up, it would be wrong to do so. A proportionate use of punishment also means that even in fighting crime there are a number of strategies which are more effective and humane than incarceration and that we are obliged to seek out a variety of preventive measures and alternative punishments before turning to imprisonment. Also, proportionality means that our prison sentences ought not to be excessive or reflect a desire for vengeance, but should be a fit response to the crime committed and ordered to the rehabilitation of offenders.

In particular, as noted in the Evangelical Lutheran Church of America's statement on community violence, Christians have good reasons to be critical of the "tough on crime" attitude that seeks to solve social ills by locking up more and more people.

> "Tough on crime" policy stances are often proposed in response to the fear of violent crimes. Such stances have their place, but also their limits. Although police and prisons help to protect society, they have no real effect on the causes of violence.…Instead of addressing the root causes of violence, "tough on crime" measures can blind us to the injustices that breed violence in the first place. [Indeed,] prisons can often become "schools" that harden criminals, making them even more disillusioned and enraged.[80]

Structural Reforms. With a homicide rate that dwarfs that of other modern societies, there is little doubt that the United States has a massive and distinctive problem with violent crime.[81] Unfortunately, there is also little evidence that America's campaign to build the largest prison system in the world has proven to be a particularly humane, just or effective response to this problem. Without denying the need to punish wrongdoers or hold them accountable for their actions, Christian thought calls for a reformed criminal justice system "balancing the protection of society with opportunities for healing, retribution and rehabilitation," a system committed to justice for the community, victims, and offenders alike.[82]

In order to effect the reforms needed, three changes must be made. We need to move away from our disproportionate reliance on punishment as a tool for addressing a wide variety of social ills. Confronting poverty, unemployment, homelessness and mental illness—and the violence and suffering they generate in our society—requires developing and maintaining a network of adequate social programs, not a slew of new prisons. At the same time, in our continuing wars on drugs and crime renewed emphasis needs to be placed on prevention, alternative penalties, rehabilitation and the needs and concerns of victims. More of our energies and resources must be invested in programs addressing the underlying causes of crime. We need to provide less costly and more humane alternatives to incarceration and offer help to those needing drug rehabilitation, job training and a smoother, supervised reintegration into society. In particular, we need a greater commitment to assisting the victims of crime in their search for justice and healing. And finally, we must revamp our present sentencing policies, especially for nonviolent offenders, bringing them more in line with those of other modern democracies.

Cases and Resources

Along with the introductory case on violence in the media, the following cases should provide you with a chance to apply this book's method of moral decision making to a number of issues concerning violence in our society, and the list of resources should prove helpful in resolving the cases and/or learning more about these issues.

Case #2: What to Preach?

It's 9:30 on Tuesday morning at the Sunnyside Cafe, and Father Mike Angelini is having his weekly coffee and conversation with Reverend Carol Gunnersman. The pastors of neighboring Catholic and Lutheran congregations (St. Vincent's and St. Paul's) in downtown Orangeville, Mike and Carol have been getting together once a week for the past three years, sharing an hour or two of conversation in a booth at the Sunnyside. Some Tuesdays the talk is about theology, sometimes about parish politics, but mostly it's a chance to brainstorm on ideas for next Sunday's sermon. If asked, both Mike and Carol would agree that these dialogues have enriched their preaching, but neither would say they always come to the same conclusions about what ought to be said from the pulpit. This week is a case in point.

The previous February a young Orangeville school teacher by the name of Catherine Mangione had been brutally slain right in front of her three-year-old son Robert during an attempted carjacking. Because her assailant Jeffrey Harston was a recent parolee with two previous felony convictions, the case got a lot of media attention. Soon it was a cause célèbre for political candidates promising to "get tough on crime" and vowing that if elected they would put Harston and his type on death row.

After many delays and a lengthy process Harston was recently found guilty of first-degree murder, and the trial is currently in the penalty phase, where judge and jury hear testimony as to whether the defendant should receive a life sentence or the death penalty. One of the people testifying this week is Catherine's husband, David, who is also a cousin of Mike Angelini and a member of St. Vincent's parish. Although he knows the Catholic Church has been increasingly critical of capital punishment, David has let it be known that he will be asking the jury to hand down a judgment for the death penalty. And indeed polls in Orangeville and elsewhere indicate that about 73 percent of folks favor Harston's execution.

Mike, who has been struggling with his own responsibilities in this matter, discovered to his chagrin last night that the gospel reading for this Sunday is the parable of the prodigal son (Luke 15:11–32), which tells of God's boundless mercy for all sinners. This morning he finds himself wondering aloud to Carol just what he ought to say in Sunday's sermon. On the one hand he feels a duty to be supportive of Dave and Robert, and indeed all of Catherine's family. He has even agreed to accompany Dave to the trial. What does he owe to the victims of this awful violence? Can he really speak to them about forgiveness? On the other hand, it seems clear to him that capital punishment is inconsistent with the Christian call to forgiveness and that as a preacher of God's word he is obliged to address his congregation and community's continued support of this practice. How can he preach on God's mercy in Orangeville this week without talking about Catherine Mangione and Jeffrey Harston?

Carol's problem is a little different. Like Mike, she is convinced that capital punishment is wrong and fully supports the Evangelical Lutheran Church in America's social statement opposing the death penalty. Still, she is a bit concerned about using the pulpit to address what seems like a secular or political issue. If I do this, she wonders, should I preach on land mines next week or Kosovo the week after that? Should the Sunday sermon be what the church is saying about the hot-button political topic of the week, or should it be about preaching the good news of Jesus Christ? Wouldn't it be better to speak about the radical demands and costs of forgiveness and let people draw their own implications about particular policies?

Mike isn't sure. After all, their congressional representative, a politician who regularly speaks about the importance of biblical and Christian values and who defends the death penalty as taking "an eye for an eye," is a member of Carol's congregation, as is the city's prosecutor and seven of its judges. Shouldn't somebody say something to these folks about Christianity and capital punishment?

The coffee has cooled off and Mike and Carol are still uncertain as to what they should do. Paying the tab, Carol agrees that whatever they say on Sunday, they need to find a way to speak God's grace to a community scarred by violence.

Case #3: To Ban or to Buy?

Carrie Wilson has a problem, and she's not at all sure what she ought to do about it. A thirty-seven-year-old assistant bank manager, she and her two teenaged daughters, Maggie and Jennifer, live in a modest brick rancher located in an older working-class neighborhood about twenty minutes from the downtown

Denver branch office where she's worked for the last eight years. During most of that time she has been quite happy to be living in this neighborhood. The schools are fairly good. The commute to work is easy. Her neighbors have been quiet, hard-working folks who mind their own business, and she has felt safe.

In the past year, however, two things have happened that have made her feel less safe and led to her present dilemma. Beginning in the previous fall, there have been several break-ins and burglaries in Carrie's neighborhood. And though most of these property crimes have involved no bodily harm to the victims, three people have been assaulted in their homes, one of them quite seriously. One of these assaults took place in a house a block and a half from Carrie's home at 3:15 in the morning. On top of this, one bright Wednesday morning this past April a student at Maggie's high school walked into the cafeteria with two handguns and a semiautomatic rifle. An hour and forty-seven minutes later seven teens and two teachers were dead, and thirty-three other students and four cafeteria workers were wounded. The boy in question shot himself twice before police could disarm or capture him, and died in the ambulance taking him to the local county hospital.

During the weeks and months since the shooting the students at Maggie's school have received plenty of counseling. A police officer has been assigned to patrol the grounds and hallways during school time. Metal detectors have been installed at all school entrances. Youngsters making violent threats or attempting to bring weapons onto school property have been suspended or expelled, and their names given to the local police.

Still, many in the community remain deeply concerned that a disturbed sixteen-year-old boy was able to get his hands on a small arsenal of weapons and bring them into a school. The local papers and radio call-in shows have been filled with concerned and often angry voices debating the need for more gun-control measures, especially for laws that would help keep weapons out of the hands of children.

At Carrie's church she has been approached by two social-concern groups petitioning local congressional representatives to support new gun-control legislation, and at a recent adult ed class there she learned some disturbing things about Americans and firearms. With more than 192 million privately owned guns in this country, there are firearms in one out of every two American households, and these weapons are used in more than ten thousand murders a year.

Indeed, some studies suggest that the presence of a gun in the house triples the risk of homicide and increases the chance of a suicide by as much as fivefold.

But when Carrie talks about this problem with her father, he dismisses these concerns as a lot of liberal hogwash, reminding her that she too had grown up in a house with guns. He also notes that he and her three brothers have used rifles and pistols for hunting and target shooting for years, without ever having an accident or shooting a neighbor, relative or themselves. "You've eaten game I shot with a rifle," he reminds her, "and eggs from hens that would have been fox food if we hadn't shot the nasty little predators.

"On top of that," he argues, "there are some studies that indicate that guns are used more than a million times a year to fend off criminals. You ought to see about getting a handgun to protect you and the girls from the criminals operating in your neighborhood. I could help you shop for one and get you signed up for a safety course so you won't hurt yourself or the girls. It would make your mother and me feel a lot safer about the three of you."

Driving home that evening with the girls asleep in the back seat Carrie wonders—buy a gun, ban a gun? What to do? Will purchasing a gun make her and the girls safer? Or will it add to the violence of their community or society? What sort of a witness would that be for her neighbors, for her daughters? Are there other measures she and her neighbors could take that would be better solutions to the problem of crime? What to do?

Case #4: Jails for Jobs?

On a warm autumn evening State Senator Ellen Costanza is sitting in her office listening to Bob Hughes, her campaign manager, and she is not happy. Just a month away from the close of a very tight race for reelection, Ellen's marginal lead is evaporating. Bob warns her that unless she does something significant in the next few weeks she can forget a second term, and all the good she might have accomplished as a newly appointed member of three important senate committees.

The something significant Bob has in mind is SR375, a new piece of anti-crime legislation pending before the senate. Calling for tougher sanctions and mandatory minimum sentences for a broad range of felonies, SR375 also includes $780 million for the construction of several new correctional facilities *and an additional $120 million to help put three to five thousand more police officers on the streets.*

Bob is convinced that coming out in support of this legislation is, at present, just about the only way to save the election.

"Ellen, this bill is just what the doctor ordered. First, by supporting it you show the voters and the media that even with your opposition to the death penalty, you are still tough on crime. In an instant our challenger's number-one issue evaporates, and that 'law and order' prosecutor from downstate has to start talking about jobs and education, topics you can beat him on any day of the week. Second, this bill means jobs, and I mean good jobs, for our district. We may not be in the 'rust belt,' but in the last two decades we've lost thousands of high-paying factory jobs to overseas plants and seen two military installations close up shop. Todd Meyers, the bill's main sponsor and the chair of the allocations committee, has made it clear he wants you on board and that if you give him lots of support before the election, then one of those new prisons will be built in our district. That's going to mean a lot of work for a lot of folks— steady, long-term work with pensions and health care.

"Now Ellen, I know you have some concerns about building more prisons. But you want the government to do more about domestic violence and to put pressure on deadbeat dads. Well, sometimes people have to be put in jail to make them see the light or to protect other folks from their violence. And finally, making a compromise here means you get to do a lot of good work toward education, housing and aid to farmers. Do you think our challenger is going to do any of that if we just roll over and let him win?"

Perhaps. Perhaps this legislation would save her campaign and allow her to do real good. Certainly bringing thousands of high-paying jobs to her district would help a lot of folks. But is SR375 really a good idea? True, Ellen's state does have a high rate of violent crime, though not as high as it was in the early '90s, and a lot of people do need to be punished for their offenses, particularly when they are violent. But does that mean that minimum mandatory sentences are a good idea or that we ought to address overcrowding in our burgeoning prison system by building more and bigger prisons? Will putting more police on the streets really help? How much? Are there other alternatives that might be more effective, or humane?

And just what will happen in her district in five or ten years when hundreds and then thousands of these criminals, most of them from downstate, are released from jail? How many will settle in the local community, and what sorts of problems will they bring to the area? Will there be a "crime leak" from the local prison, contaminating neighborhoods and towns in the area?

And if the state spends $900 million on this piece of anti-crime legislation, what sorts of programs will be cut to pay for new prisons and police? Will the money come out of education, housing, health care? Should Ellen put her signature on this bill? Should she be one of the swing votes to push it over the top?

Sitting there in her office with Bob, Ellen is pretty sure she's going to have to think long and hard about this. Bob, on the other hand, is certain she only has a few weeks to decide.

Case #5: Blockade or Invade?

Harold Grodecki is staring at his computer screen and the stack of notes in front of him, trying to decide just what to put in the conclusion of his report for Senator Desmet, a moderate junior senator from Illinois and a ranking member of the Senate Foreign Relations Committee. In three or four days the senator will be voting on a nonbinding resolution supporting the president's decision to send U.S. troops into a mid-sized Caribbean island-nation plagued by long-term tyranny and civil war. And as Desmet's senior political analyst and longtime friend, Grodecki has been asked to draw up a policy paper with specific recommendations.

For the last two and a half decades former General and now President Eduardo Sabas Escobar has headed a right-wing military government, which, with the aid and support of the island's fourteen leading families, has systematically oppressed, impoverished and terrorized the vast majority of the nation's 4.7 million citizens. He and his associates have removed all democratic institutions and silenced all criticism and opposition through imprisonment, torture and state-sanctioned execution squads. A dozen years ago, after the killing of a popular cleric, a small resistance movement took hold in the southern regions of the island, spreading from hard-to-reach mountain villages where the military had little control to coastal towns and rural communities in the country's central plain. At its high point four years ago the rebels had gained partial control of nearly a third of the island. But government forces, relying in part on weapons and training previously obtained from the United States in exchange for cooperating in regional antidrug measures, have waged a brutal bombing campaign, destroying dozens and dozens of towns and small cities and turning 1.2 million of the island's population into internal refugees.

Escobar and his colleagues have been condemned by Amnesty International and Human Rights Watch. Meanwhile, UN diplomatic efforts by the OAS (Organization of American States) have met with no success, and U.S. attempts to pressure the government have failed miserably. In desperation, but without the support of the OAS (which is suspicious of U.S. intervention in the region), the United States and several European nations have instituted economic sanctions against the government.

Unfortunately, this seems to have produced little in the way of positive effects. Cut off from trade with the larger world, unemployment and poverty have gotten worse for the vast majority of the population, and food and medical supplies are reported to be in short supply. Meanwhile, the military's war against its own people grows increasingly violent, and there are reports of mass graves on the outskirts of several mountain communities recently retaken by the government.

Harold has several concerns about the issue before him. Like the leaders of the OAS, he is conscious of the United States's dubious track record in Central and South America, often intervening in ways that shored up or installed right-wing governments opposed to genuine democratic reform. He also wonders what the costs of an invasion would be—not just in resources and personnel, but in human suffering and death, both to American troops and to the people of this island nation. How long would it take to defeat Escobar's forces? Would it be a swift, nearly bloodless process or a long, bitter conflict? Could it be done without getting bogged down in a long civil war, without worsening the situation for those who have already suffered so much? And what sort of support could the United States hope to get from the UN, from the OAS, from other nations in the region? Was there any sort of consensus outside of Washington that this was the right thing to do? Finally, what approach would minimize the harm to civilians: continuing the blockade, sending in an invasion force, initiating a limited bombing campaign or relying exclusively on diplomatic efforts?

On top of these questions, Harold suspects that after over two decades of military dictatorship, a dozen years of civil war and fourteen months of economic sanctions, the nation's political and economic infrastructure is probably in tatters. That means it's unlikely the crisis can be resolved simply by sending in some troops and removing the dictator. Regional experts have suggested that a good deal of nation building needs to be done. The military will have to be disarmed. There will have to be time for the development of new political parties and preparations for free elections. And, of course, the country will need significant aid, and all sorts of political and economic institutions will require help being rebuilt. Harold is not at all sure American voters would support such an extended process. But if things are done in a shoddy, haphazard way, won't that lead to another military takeover and crisis a few years down the road?

Harold wonders just what the right thing to do might be. What should he recommend to the senator—blockade, invade, or what?

Resources

Center for Defense Information (http://www.cdi.org), 1500 Massachusetts Ave., NW, Washington, DC, 20005; (202) 332-0600. For information about military expenditures and disarmament.

The Children's Defense Fund (http://www.childrensdefense.org), 25 E Street, NW, Washington, DC 20001; (202) 628-8787. For information about threats to our children and a variety of education and advocacy programs on their behalf.

Death Penalty Information Center (http://www.essential.org/dpic), 1320 Eighteenth St., NW, Washington, DC 20036; (202) 293-6970. Information and statistics on capital punishment.

Handgun Control and the Center to Prevent Handgun Violence (http://www.handguncontrol.org), 1225 Eye Street, NW, Suite 1100, Washington, DC 20005; (202) 289-7319. For information on firearms and current legislative initiatives.

National Coalition Against Domestic Violence (http://www.ncadv.org), P.O. Box 18749, Denver, CO 80218-0749; (303)

839-1852. For information and resources regarding domestic violence and child abuse.

National Conference of Catholic Bishops/United States Catholic Conference's Office of Social Development and World Peace (http://www.nccbuscc.org/sdwp), 3211 Fourth Street, NE, Washington, DC 20017-1194; (202) 541-3180. For information on Catholic positions and initiatives regarding peace and violence.

National Council to Prevent Child Abuse and Family Violence (http://www.nccafv.org), 1155 Connecticut Ave., NW, Suite 400, Washington, DC 20036; (202) 429-6695, (800) 222-2000. For information and initiatives on domestic violence and child abuse.

Pax Christi (http://www.nonviolence.org/pcusa), 532 W. Eighth St., Erie, PA 16502; (814) 453-4955. A Catholic education and advocacy group working for peace and disarmament.

Southern Center for Human Rights (http://www.schr.org), 83 Poplar Street, NW, Atlanta, GA 30303-2122; (404) 688-1202. A public interest law firm working for impoverished prisoners, and committed to combating cruel and unusual punishments.

CHAPTER FOUR:
Human Sexuality

Case #1: "To Live Together"

Father Bill Warner, the pastor of St. Luke's, looks at the three couples seated in the living room with him and wonders yet again just what he should say. It's Wednesday evening, and he and Mary and Carl Jeffries are having their fourth meeting with two engaged couples preparing for weddings next spring or summer. Mary and Carl are in their mid-forties, with three children, and, along with Bill, have run the parish's marriage prep program for the last three years. Married nineteen years and active members of St. Luke's for more than a decade, they have enjoyed mentoring young (and sometimes not-so-young) couples in their preparations for married life, and Bill has found their experience and insights deeply enriching for his own understanding of marriage.

Tonight the conversation is about marriage and sexuality, and for the past twenty minutes the discussion has been about the church's teaching regarding premarital sex. There is, to say the least, not a great deal of support for this teaching among the four participants, and though they are sympathetic to the church's concerns, Mary and Carl don't seem convinced that a total ban on premarital sex always makes sense.

Orlando and Carrie initiated the conversation by admitting that they had gotten an apartment together in September. Graduate students in biology and engineering, the two have been dating since their sophomore year in college and got engaged this past July.

"We've been together for better than four years now," Carrie notes, "and our commitment to one another is very real. We took a long time with each other before sleeping together, and we are planning to marry in May and have children as soon as we have enough income to support and care for them."

"And it's not just about sex," Orlando notes. "Carrie and I are paying our own way through school. We've got jobs and loans and are carrying a full load of courses. Living together saves us five to six hundred dollars a month and allows us to spend a lot more time with each other. What's more, living together allows us to support each other in ways we could not do apart."

Mike Archer has been nodding throughout a good deal of this conversation. Fifty-eight and a widower for the past six years, Mike has been a lifelong Catholic and raised four daughters and a son. For the past three and a half years he and Helen Percy have been seeing each other, and though they are not going to move in together before their July wedding, Mike has spent more than a couple of nights over at Helen's. It is clear from his tone and posture that he is not comfortable talking about these matters, but also that he feels quite strongly about them.

"Helen and I are not a couple of kids just out of school," Mike says, nodding briefly to Carrie and Orlando. "I was married to Jeannie for twenty-six years, and nursed her for the last three. I've dated other women and was sexual with one of them, though I wish now we hadn't taken that step. It didn't make sense with who we were or where we were going. But I do love Helen, and I've known I was in love with her for more than a year. We've decided to wait till my boy Zach was out of school and we could start our life together in a new place, and we're waiting to have Helen's marriage annulled. But in the meantime we are two healthy and loving adults who want to be together. Jeannie and I waited till we were married to have sex, but we were nineteen and twenty-one, and we were only engaged for three months. And, trust me, Jeannie was pregnant before our honeymoon was half over."

Looking up from her hands Helen joins in. "Bill, I was in one of the world's all-time worst marriages. Steve hit me and was unfaithful to me. He drank and went through jobs and promises like tap water. I was a single parent for fifteen years, and have been alone—or wished I was alone—for almost thirty. Loving Mike and being loved and touched by him has been the holiest part of my life, and has given me the strength to go through this annulment process, and the courage to believe that marriage can be a sacrament. How can that possibly be sinful?"

Father Bill looks to Mary and Carl, but it is clear that they are waiting for him to take the lead here. He knows from other conversations that they too believe that most people should wait till marriage before sleeping together. That is certainly what Carl has told the parish youth group on more than one occasion. He also knows that they too, like Mike and Jeannie, did wait until after the wedding. But he can tell that they, like him, are a bit stymied by the cases in front of them. What should he, Bill wonders to himself, tell Carrie and Orlando, and/or Mike and Helen?

Introduction. Sexuality is an extraordinarily important and often profoundly joyful dimension of our lives. Indeed, our sexuality is a fundamental element of our personhood and affects every aspect of our humanity. As the Catholic ethicist Christine Gudorf has noted, "Sexuality is foundational in human beings.…[it] affects the structure of our brains, the way we relate to persons, the way we understand our world and attempt to structure our lives, our occupations, our choices around sexual activity, our personality traits, and our social status."[1]

And our sexuality is also extraordinarily good, even blessed. In fact, our sexuality is a sacrament of God's intimate, ecstatic, faithful and creative love, and our identity as sexual beings is a basic part of our being made in the image and likeness of God. For we have not been created as androgynous creatures, but as women and men with a deep and embodied appetite for wholeness, life and joy. Our sexual drive and affections are not sinful distractions, but part of a deep, God-given hunger to be at home in our own bodies and to be connected with our embodied sisters, brothers, parents, children, lovers and friends. Indeed, even for the vowed celibate our sexual passions and attractions are a primary means of building the intimate and caring bonds and communities enabling us to flourish as persons.

Still, our sexuality can also be extremely puzzling and sometimes profoundly troubling. Often it seems like we live in a world both obsessed with and deeply confused about sex. If movies, TV shows, CDs, music videos and commercials are any indication of popular tastes, then most of us enjoy stories and songs laced with liberal doses of sex. Along with violence, sex is the spice in our entertainment, the sweetener that has us coming back for more. And yet, no other pleasure seems to make us feel as guilty, nor does anything seem to stir our righteous indignation like other people's sexual sins or indiscretions. As Nathaniel Hawthorne pointed out long ago in *The Scarlet Letter,* there is no blood sport as satisfying as casting stones at a sexual sinner. Sex. We love it. We hate it.

Recently our confusion and ambiguity about sex has been heightened by radical challenges to traditional beliefs about gender and sexual orientation, technological developments allowing people to (among other things) have sex without babies and babies without sex, increasing concern about population growth and the spread of AIDS. Along with a growing number of social scientists, feminist and homosexual voices have challenged traditional ideas about sexual roles and rules, as well as accepted notions of parenthood, family and marriage. Contraceptive and reproductive technologies have uncoupled the link between intercourse and childbirth and created a range of new options and problems. Fears of an overcrowded and hungry planet have generated pressure for a wide range of population-control measures. And the spread of AIDS has touched and frightened many of us, challenging us to rethink our attitudes toward sexual freedom and rules, as well as our treatment of society's sexual outcasts.

Nor has our church or Christianity at large been untouched by this confusion about sex. For more than a generation Catholics and other Christians have been immersed in a sustained and spreading argument about the meaning and place of sexuality in our lives and about a variety of sexual topics and issues. Questions regarding divorce and remarriage, contraception, mandatory celibacy, sterilization, premarital sex, reproductive technologies, gender roles and/or sexual orientation have fueled dialogue, debate, dissent and division within Catholicism and other Christian churches.

What, then, are we as Christians to make of sex? How are we to understand our sexuality, or the sexuality of others? Is our sexual drive a gift from God or a sign of our sinfulness? And what does it mean to be a woman or a man, gay or straight? How are we to live out our sexual identity and orientation? How are we to behave or relate to one another? What norms or rules should we follow about sexual behavior in and out of marriage? What is—or should be—the connection between sexual intercourse and marriage or parenthood?

In this chapter on sexual ethics we try to address some of these questions from a Christian perspective. Our goal here is to think about the ways in which our Christian faith challenges us to live out a call to discipleship and holiness in the context of our sexuality. We will attempt here to discover what experience, Scripture, tradition and reason have to tell us about the differing moral challenges facing us in this critical area of our lives.

As with other chapters, we begin this one with a brief historical sketch, looking at the story of Christian sexual ethics in three phases. Next, we turn to character, attempting to name some virtues that would help us to live out our Christian vocation in the context of our sexuality and our roles as friends, spouses, parents and citizens. Then we will look at three rather controversial choices in sexual ethics—extramarital sex, birth control and homosexuality—and ask about some possible Christian responses to these issues. Following that, we will address two social or structural sins relating to sexuality—sexism and sexual ignorance—and we will suggest some Christian responses to these evils. Finally, the chapter will close with four more cases addressing different sexual questions or issues, and a set of resources for further study.

The Story of Christian Sexual Ethics in Three Phases[2]

Phase One: The New Testament Era. Born into an age shaped by Greek, Roman and Jewish thought and practice, Christianity's emerging sexual ethic both reflected and challenged these differing worldviews. The ancient Greeks and (especially) Romans held marriage up as a civic duty and ideal, but granted men a great deal of sexual freedom, allowing homosexuality, prostitution, concubines, sex with slaves and divorce. Women in these patriarchal societies were held to more rigid sexual standards and treated as subservient beings or property. At the same time Greek and Roman thinkers tended to denigrate the body and were generally suspicious of sexual pleasure. Stoic philosophy in particular considered the sexual drive an unruly, even dangerous passion requiring the regulation of reason and justified only when directed at procreation. Judaism, on the other hand, had a more positive view of human bodies, sexuality and marriage. According to Genesis, women and men had been fashioned "in the image of God" and were "very good," and their coming together in one flesh continued the creative work of God. Still, Jewish society was also deeply patriarchal, and women were not treated as equals.

At the heart of New Testament ethics is Jesus' proclamation of the reign of God, and at the center of this proclamation is a radical call to holiness and an equally radical command to love. At the same time early Christians believed that they were fashioned in God's image *as* embodied spirits and that in the mystery of the incarnation and Christ's death and resurrection God had taken on and redeemed their very flesh and was calling them to a bodily resurrection in Christ. [3] Thus, these early disciples did not think of themselves as *having* bodies, but as *being* bodies made sacred and redeemed by the grace of God. And so how they treated their own bodies and the bodies of their neighbors was very important.

One result of this twofold call to conversion and profound respect for human embodiment is that "the disciple of Jesus is to live out his or her sexuality in a way that is different from the way that others live out their sexuality."[4] In particular, New Testament authors urge Christians to reject all forms of "sexual immorality" *(porneia)* and behave in ways that honor the sacredness of their bodies, the bodies of their neighbors and the corporate Body of Christ to which they belong. At the same time, Jesus' announcement of God's reign, as well as his own treatment of the marginalized and disenfranchised, also challenges the earliest Christian communities to reform or dismantle unjust structures of sexual violence and oppression and to stand with the outcasts and downtrodden. Thus, as biblical scholar Raymond Collins and Catholic ethicist Lisa Cahill note, the sexual ethics of the New Testament church often (though not always) challenges patriarchal and hierarchical structures that alienated and marginalized women and other sexual outcasts.[5] Unfortunately, these challenges grew significantly weaker as later Christians came to accept a more patriarchal sexual ethic.

In general, then, the earliest Christian communities affirmed an ethic that saw sexuality as part of a call to holiness, rejected what were seen as the excessive and disordered sexual appetites of the world around them (or of their own past lives). They also challenged members to embrace a countercultural witness of sexual restraint and offered some challenges to patriarchal structures and practices. The New Testament authors and communities also held up celibacy and the single state as a viable, holy way of life. In a world where marriage and parenthood were the expected, even mandatory, states of life, this somewhat revolutionary praise of celibacy and the single state was no doubt seen as a liberating option for many and probably drew numerous converts to the early Christian church. Still, part of this praise of celibacy was very likely grounded in part in the expectation that Christ would return shortly, and so there would be little time for marriage or raising children.

Phase Two: Augustine and the Focus on Procreation.[6] In the fourth century Augustine, who was to influence the next sixteen hundred years of Christian sexual ethics more than any other author, defended marriage and procreation against attacks by Manichaean writers condemning both practices. Augustine valued marriage for the procreation of children, the fidelity of its spouses and its indissoluble union, but like his opponents, he was suspicious of the sexual drive. For him, Adam and Eve's fall from grace had rendered sexual passion and pleasure unruly and disordered, and sexual intercourse was now tainted by concupiscence, or the lingering effects of that original sin. Indeed, he believed it was only when a married couple engaged in sex for the purpose of procreation that they could avoid sin.

Unfortunately, subsequent Christian authors and tradition tended to affirm Augustine's pessimistic view, agreeing that procreation was the only morally justifiable reason for intercourse. Married persons who made love to avoid sexual sins like adultery or masturbation were seen as guilty of slight or venial sins, while those motivated primarily by sexual pleasure might well be committing a serious or mortal sin. Furthermore, all sexual acts not open to the procreation and raising of children were seen as sinful by their very nature. In time these rigorous teachings were encoded in the penitential books and canon law of the medieval church, and later became the source for the catalogue of sexual sins found in the manuals of moral theology used until the mid–twentieth century to train candidates for the priesthood.[7]

Along with this pessimism, two other troubling tendencies have influenced Christian reflections on sexuality since Augustine: a disproportionate attention to celibacy (at the cost of marriage) and a denigration of women.

In spite of his defense of marriage and procreation, and the church's elevation of marriage to a sacrament (consummated by the act of conjugal love), Augustine and his successors often saw marriage as a second-class vocation, comparing it less favorably to celibacy and the priesthood or vowed religious life. For much of the past sixteen centuries there has been a kind of two-tiered Christianity within Catholicism, with clerical celibates seen as the moral and spiritual superiors of their married sisters and brothers. Gratefully, much of this tendency was undone by the bishops of Vatican II, who declared that all Christians, married or celibate, have a full vocation to holiness.

Furthermore, although there have clearly been exceptions, in general, Christian teachings and practice have not treated women as equals or full partners in the history of salvation. On the one hand, throughout much of the history of Christianity the church and religious life offered women their only real opportunities to attain a serious education or exercise real leadership. Still, major male Christian writers of the past two thousand years have generally seen women as intellectually, spiritually and morally inferior to men, and often portrayed them as the sources of (usually carnal) temptation. Official teachings have often called women to subservience and obedience, excluded them from leadership in their homes or church and tended to limit their identity as persons or disciples to their (usually misunderstood) reproductive role.[8]

And yet the Christian tradition has also affirmed the goodness and holiness of human sexuality and increasingly appreciated the friendship between women and men that characterizes the sacrament of marriage. Thomas Aquinas offers an example of the tradition's developing optimism about human sexuality. For though, as Catholic theologian Lisa Sowle Cahill notes, Aquinas "saw the female sex in pejorative terms, and as destined for a procreative role," he also gave considerable attention to the loving friendship that marriage is meant to be and did not see the enjoyment of sexual pleasure as wrong "as long as it is properly contained within the marital and procreative union."[9] Aquinas also saw sexual love and pleasure as part of the sacramentality of marriage.[10] And so, Aquinas and theologians like Alphonsus Liguori offered an increasingly optimistic and more positive vision of human sexuality than Augustine's theology alone.

Phase Three: The Twentieth Century. Three major trends have shaped the development of Christian sexual ethics over the past century. The link between sex and procreation as well as the preeminence of procreation as the primary purpose for sexual intercourse have been called into question. Modern feminism has challenged patriarchal notions of family, marriage, gender and sexuality and called for a sexual ethic grounded in mutuality and equality. And those in the social sciences (especially psychology) have joined with homosexual men and lesbian women to call for a reexamination of church and biblical teachings about sexual orientation, the morality of homosexual acts and the possibility of state or church-sponsored unions.

At the Lambeth Conference in 1930 the Anglican Church broke with longstanding Christian moral teaching and approved the use of contraceptives. In the decades that followed nearly all Protestant churches affirmed this decision, foregoing a sexual ethic that saw procreation as the only or primary purpose of sexual intercourse. And though official Catholic teaching continues to see contraception negatively, the bishops of Vatican II and recent popes have accepted the use of natural family planning (i.e., rhythm and its revisions), affirming that human sexuality has two equally important purposes. It is to be both unitive and procreative, an expression of love and a participation in God's creativity.

In large part, new technologies have been behind the deemphasis on procreation. Convenient, readily available and generally effective means of birth control have given couples and individuals (especially women) significantly more freedom regarding sex's procreative dimension. The recent appearance of a variety of reproductive technologies has also raised dramatic questions about the links between marriage, parenthood, sexual intercourse and reproduction. Other factors too have contributed to a decreasing stress on procreation. The global population has grown more than fivefold in just over a century. The roles of women in society and family have undergone a critical transformation. And modern psychology and philosophy increasingly stress the affective and interpersonal nature of human relations and sexuality.

A second trend influencing contemporary Christian sexual ethics has been the growth of modern feminism. In "Peace on Earth," Pope John XXIII pointed out that "women are gaining an increasing awareness of their natural dignity. Far from being content with a purely passive role or allowing themselves to be regarded as a kind of instrument, they are demanding in both domestic and public life the rights and duties that belong to them as human persons."[11] This discontent has led many Christian feminists to propose a sexual ethic that gives full weight to the dignity, equality and experience of women, rethinks notions of marriage, family, sexuality and gender in light of these feminist values, and tries to reform or dismantle sexist and patriarchal structures wherever they appear.

Finally, in recent decades there has been a growing debate about homosexuality, and in particular about biblical and church teachings regarding the morality of homosexual acts and unions. Contemporary psychology no longer views homosexuality as a mental disorder and, in general, seems suspicious of attempts to "convert" or reorient homosexual persons. Biblical scholars and theologians have raised questions about the contextual meaning of scriptural passages condemning homosexuality. And large numbers of homosexual men and women have come out of the closet and into the society, challenging anti-gay myths and stereotypes, demanding fairer treatment as persons, citizens and believers.

Most Christian churches, including the Catholic Church, see one's homosexual orientation as a discovery, not a choice, and therefore not sinful. Again, most Christian denominations oppose discrimination or bias against gays and lesbians, and recommend compassion and understanding in the pastoral care of homosexual persons. Still, debates about the morality of homosexual acts and unions continue. A significant number of Christian believers and communities embrace a qualified or full acceptance of homosexual acts and unions, arguing that for gays and lesbians homosexual love in a committed and monogamous relationship is the natural or God-given way for them to express their sexuality. At the same time, official teaching in the Catholic Church and a number of other Christian churches continues to insist that homosexual relations are not morally acceptable. Catholic theologian Richard Sparks has put it this way, "…if sexual intercourse is about two-in-one-flesh intimacy and about an openness to the possibility of procreation…homosexual genital acts are missing at least one of these two requisite dimensions."[12]

CHARACTER: A Call to Embodied Holiness

Sexuality is not just about sexual or genital acts. Nor is it solely a matter of our biological drive to procreate or our attraction to romance. Indeed, as we have already noted, sexuality is a fundamental and pervasive dimension of our identity as persons and our vocation as Christians. It is an essential element of who we are and who we are called to be.

As Pope John Paul II has noted, we human beings are "embodied spirits" created in the image and likeness of God and called to a radical holiness and community-building love.[13] And "our sexuality plays a crucial role in our ability to answer this call to love" and holiness.[14] As Christian ethicist James B. Nelson notes, sexuality is "God's ingenious way of calling us to communion through our need to reach out and touch and embrace....It is both the physiological and psychological grounding of our capacity to love,...[and] a sacramental means for the love of God."[15] Elsewhere Nelson notes that "the mystery of our sexuality is the mystery of our need to reach out to embrace others both physically and spiritually. Sexuality thus expresses God's intention that we find our authentic humanness in relationship...[and] is intrinsic to our relationship with God."[16] The Jesuit theologian Vincent Genovesi likewise notes that "sexuality is an integral or essential element in the task we face of becoming fully human. It is also a crucial factor in the mission we enjoy as Christians, namely, to continue or extend the reality of God's love for all people. For it is our nature as sexual beings that enables us to be lovers."[17]

As we have noted elsewhere, in general we live out our Christian vocation to love within the roles and relationships making up the fabric of our daily lives and creating a web of moral bonds tying us to companions and neighbors near and far. Thus, we are called to be holy and to love not just as persons, but as friends, spouses, parents and citizens. And the ways we live out our vocation in these various roles will shape and express our character as Christians, while making the world around us more or less loving.

Before determining the specific "sexual" virtues required of friends, spouses, parents or citizens, we will try to name some of the basic convictions or commitments that ought to characterize the approach of any Christian to sexuality. Genovesi suggests that "it is love which must be the context for our expression of sexuality," and the first conviction of Christians must certainly be that we are to express our sexuality in a genuinely loving fashion.[18] As Nelson notes, sexual love is "other-enriching; it has a genuine concern for the well-being of the partner" or neighbor.[19] Paul's poetic description of love in 1 Corinthians 13:4–7 offers us an excellent set of criteria for genuine love, including its sexual dimensions. In addition, Christians must also be committed to expressions of sexuality that are character-ized by justice, respect, fidelity, mutuality and equality, and must resist every sort of sexual abuse, manipulation, violence, domination, oppression or marginalization. Good or moral sexuality can never fail to take the mystery, dignity and sanctity of other "embodied spirits" with the utmost seriousness. Moreover, any adequate Christian sexual ethic will call for a profound honesty and integrity in sexual relations, demanding a coherence between our actions and the actual depth or intimacy of our relations. It will also require trust, commitment and a wealth of generosity. So too, a genuinely Christian sexual ethic will be life affirming and socially responsible, open to a call to generativity (usually in the form of parenthood) and service to the larger commu-nity. Finally, Christians should understand sexuality and sexual love as a gift from God, a joyful dimension of our selves and our lives inviting us to deeper communion with our neighbor and creator.

Specific Roles

Friends. Hopefully we all have some experience of friendship. Taking a cue from Christian ethicists Paul Wadell and Gilbert Mei-lander, the special relationship we call friendship is close to the core of human flourishing.[20] Two character traits related to human sexual-ity that seem especially important for friends are the ability to be *affectionate* and (as part of this) the ability to be *honest*.

To be a sexually good person and, more specifically, to be a good friend, is to be good at being *affectionate*. Now surely there are a vari-ety of ways to show affection, just as there are a host of different forms of friendship. The blessing that a good friendship can be seems to cut across lines of age and gender: both children and the elderly know about friendship; and hopefully we adults can name both men and women we call friends. There is no neat or simple recipe to fol-low for being appropriately affectionate in these diverse relationships. Even so, what genuine affection always entails is the ability to express

...d care in concrete, enfleshed ways. And yes, very often this means the ability to touch, to manifest one's love for a friend physically in some way.

How can we discern what kind of touch, what kind of expression of affection is appropriate, and when and where might it be best offered? A number of authors have suggested that sexuality is not unlike language. Sexuality is about relationship and what we are called to do is express ourselves sexually in ways that are not only loving, but indeed appropriately loving. Perhaps the word for this is *honesty*. We need to relate to one another sexually, to speak a sexual language that is *consistent with the level of intimacy and commitment* in the various relationships that are part of our lives. Put differently, we must learn how to "speak" in ways that are appropriate for our diverse friendships. We must speak honestly with our bodies. Yes, as friends we must "speak" affectionately, but we must do so truthfully.

Spouses. Many of us have entered into the sacrament of Christian marriage, understood to be a holy covenant of love and life between a man and a woman. Marriage is meant ideally to be a living sign of God's passionate, faithful and enduring love. This covenant presumes the giving of oneself totally to another in a bond that is faithful, fruitful, exclusive and permanent.[21]

What kinds of virtues are most appropriate for spouses, especially for partners in Christian marriage? How should Christian spouses strive to be in their relationship with one another? They should seek to be Christlike, making manifest the love of God through their own love of one another. Furthermore, along with embracing a Christlike love for each other, Christian spouses also need to practice a sexual love that is *passionate, mutual, generous and faithful.*

Christian faith takes very seriously the belief that all of God's creation is good and that the love of human beings for one another—in all of its dimensions, spiritual and sensual—is very good. Christian married love, at its best, is invited to be a living and joyful celebration and sacrament of the goodness and holiness of human love. This should be evident in the way in which Christian spouses live their lives, in their gentleness, tenderness and playfulness with each other, in the ways they attend to, care for and show kindness to each other, and in the generosity and zeal with which they love. Without arguing here that Christian spouses must abound in "public displays of affection," it does appear that in some manner the *passionate* nature of this love should be evident, even transparent in their life together. For it is the passionate love of God that Christian married couples are called to make manifest.

A second quality that needs to mark the love of Christian married couples is *mutuality*. Indeed this must be a critical element of that special friendship we call marriage, and both husband and wife must come to this communion as partners and friends. The love and service they offer each other and their children or families is to be given freely and fully by both husband and wife. There must be a mutual give and take when dividing up tasks or making decisions. Each person needs to be willing to be corrected and taught by the other, and to give and receive mutual gifts of love.

This mutuality between spouses is particularly important because we continue to live in a world where women and men do not share power equally and where women are still too often marginalized, victimized or simply ignored. In both the public and private realms we still experience that relationships between women and men are often distorted by practices and structures of manipulation, oppression, suspicion and competition. Thus, it is critical that Christian marriages be a countercultural sign and a school of virtue for our children. In this way Christian marriages can remind us and our world that women and men are indeed capable of relating to one another in ways that are marked by genuine collaboration and respect, and with a sense of fundamental equality and *mutuality*.[22] These marriages should reflect the command of Galatians 3:28 that in the Christian community there is to be no preference for Jews over Greeks, free over slaves, or men over women.

At the same time spouses need to be generous. Marriage is more than a minimal contract where each party gives exactly 50 percent. If marriage, like any great work of art or creation, is to be more than the sum of its parts, then it must be fed by a generous, risk-taking love. Nor should the sexual love of spouses be aimed only at their own narrow good. For the two-in-one fleshness of marriage is to be creative. It is to reach out to others, to children, family, neighbors and the community. The generosity and creativity of spousal love will normally bring children into the world and take care that they are loved and nurtured. But this same generosity might also reach out in love and compassion to the larger community in a variety of other ways: in caring for the sick, in bringing beauty into the world, in struggling for justice or in tending the earth. Different couples will be called to express their creativity in different ways.

Finally, a quality that needs to mark the love of Christian spouses, and indeed mark the character of spouses themselves is *fidelity*. Like God's covenant with humankind, the covenant of Christian marriage is a covenant that is meant to be faithful, exclusive and permanent. Undoubtedly it has never been easy to keep commitments, certainly not permanent ones. That certainly seems to be the case today. This is not to say that one should stay in genuinely abusive or oppressive relationships. But in a culture that often seems suspicious of our ability to make and keep commitments, the *faithful,* exclusive and permanent sexual love of husbands and wives mirrors God's faithful love for us in a way that is particularly important for the men and women of this age.[23]

Parents. Many are parents; many more aspire to be. By way of extension many of us find ourselves in parental roles, fulfilling critically important child-caring responsibilities not only for our own children, but for others' as well. Dozens of character traits or virtues are important for those who fulfill such roles: strength, gentleness, creativity, patience and a sense of humor, to name a few. Two other virtues seem especially important. We might name them by invoking the words of Ecclesiastes (3:1–5): "For everything there is a season…[including]…a time to embrace, and a time to refrain from embracing."

Parents must be good at embracing, literally and symbolically. To put it differently, those who parent must be good at "being with," at demonstrating *care* in very concrete, embodied ways. For parents are to create a safe place, a nurturing environment for their children. They are to hold and to cherish their young, to stand by and with them.

Who does not know this? What could be more obvious? And yet, tragically, how many of us know the stories of children whose fundamental experience of one or the other of their parents was one of absence? The role and responsibility of parents is not to make life easy or pain-free for their children. But it is to make manifest to their children that they are not alone, to be with them in whatever it is that life brings, to hold and embrace them in tender ways, with embraces that have no other agenda but to communicate loving presence and care.[24]

But the other insight from Ecclesiastes is that there are times to refrain from embracing, literally and symbolically. For parents these ought not be occasions of abandonment, but instead times of letting go, times when it is important to demonstrate to our children and to ourselves that our children are not "ours," that in some manner they can and must "stand on their own." In a word, as a kind of virtue, parents must become good at *letting go.* In some paradoxical way, the ability to create enough space for their children to grow, and someday to go out on their own is part and parcel of genuine care. This means that every parental embrace must be free from any form of abusiveness or manipulation. And it also means that however caring and tender they may be, parental embraces must contain within them a certain freedom, an awareness that a child is a gift, not a possession.[25] As the years pass, the loving parent must make ever more room for the maturing freedom and wisdom of their child. They must wish and plan for the child to become an adult.

Citizens. We don't experience friendship, much less the intimacy of a committed sexual relationship, with everyone. In fact, such relationships are relatively small in number. Still, as citizens we are connected to all the other people and groups in our local and global communities, and the choices we make about sexuality in this role affect their lives. Social structures and practices, as well as laws and policies have an effect on how women and men, gay and straight, the single and married, as well as widows and the divorced are treated and/or flourish in our society. The decisions we make as citizens make it easier or harder for women to gain full equality, for single and/or working parents to take care of their children or for homosexual persons to secure their basic rights. The laws we pass and the cultural norms we enforce make it more or less certain that women, children, homosexuals and all people will be free of sexual harassment, violence and abuse. These choices we make as citizens will also improve or reduce the chances that our adolescents will make good choices about sexuality. What we do as citizens shapes the sexual life of our society.

And just what virtues would we need as citizens if we want to make certain that all persons and groups are treated fairly, if we want to assure that we are truly a just and moral sexual society? We propose three character traits or virtues. As citizens we must practice *respect* and *compassion* in our dealing with all persons and their sexuality, and we must stand in *solidarity* with all victims of sexual injustice, harassment and violence, defending their inherent and abiding dignity and rights.

From a Christian perspective respect for others in regard to sexuality begins with the conviction that all people are fashioned in the image and likeness of God and as such have a fundamental and equal dignity as persons, a sanctity that merits our recognition and respect. At a minimum this means that we are to conduct ourselves toward all people in a respectful manner. Whether we are speaking of persons of a different gender or orientation, or those struggling with a sexual dysfunction or anomaly, there can be no justification for any form of prejudice, discrimination, harassment, abuse, ridicule, marginalization or violence.[26] Given the sanctity and fragility of human sexuality, abuse of another person in this dimension of his or her life is a particularly heinous and often devastating form of violence. So *respect* is the "bottom line" in our relations with other persons and groups, the minimal requirement for how we relate to everyone in regard to sexuality as in all things.

Another critical virtue we require as citizens is *compassion* for the frailties and failures of others. In John 7:53–8:11 the evangelist tells the story of a woman caught (alone?) in the very act of adultery. Jesus warns an angry mob that their self-righteous rush to judgment may be more of a sin than this woman's weakness. And as we learned not long ago in the public feeding frenzy over the sexual sins of a president (and of some of his harshest critics), casting stones at sexual sinners remains a popular "sport" among politicians, the press and some prominent clergy. Sexuality is a powerful, often frightening dimension of our lives. It is a place where we often feel vulnerable, frail and out of control. And it is a place where few of us can claim we have made no mistakes, hurt no one else. All too often this insecurity and fear is projected as rage onto those whose failings have become known to the public.

Down through the ages this rage against the sexual frailties of others has been expressed in a variety of ways. We have cast stones at sexual sinners, burned them at the stake, put them in the stock or forced them to wear a scarlet letter. More recently this anger has found expression in the finger-pointing that is sometimes directed at single mothers trying to raise children alone. It has also been seen in the indifference to the plight of AIDS patients or in the cruel suggestion that this epidemic is an expression of God's wrath against homosexual persons, prostitutes or drug addicts. Whatever its form, Christian citizens do well to remember that Christ was much better known for showing compassion to sinners than for siding with the self-righteous.

Though we need to show respect for all persons and compassion for all sinners, we also have a duty as citizens to challenge evil and immorality, to be vigilant in our protection of victims of sexual injustice, abuse, harassment and violence. Children must be kept safe from sexual predators. Women and homosexual persons must be protected from discrimination, harassment and violence. We must stand in solidarity with the victims of all sexual sins and crimes.

CHOICES: Three Issues of Sexuality

When it comes to Christian sexual ethics there is no shortage of controversial questions. In this section we will examine three issues: extramarital sexual relations, birth control and homosexuality. As Christians, how should we think about and respond to these controversies? Which choices represent both good sexuality and good discipleship?

Extramarital Sexual Relations

The Voices of Experience

The Voice of History. The majority of preliterate and ancient societies allowed or tolerated premarital sex under certain conditions, and most societies tend to ignore or say little about postmarital intercourse (sex between separated, divorced or widowed persons) and masturbation (which produces no heirs or new family ties). At the same time the prohibition of adultery has been a fairly constant part of marital law or custom in nearly every human community, though generally framed and enforced more severely against women than men. In ancient Greece and Rome monogamous marriage was the expectation for men and women. Therefore incest, bigamy and adultery were all forbidden. Still, only brides (and not grooms) were truly expected to be virgins. Married men were allowed concubines as well as sex with prostitutes and slaves.[27]

As we have already seen, the Christian tradition has taught that sexual intercourse outside of marriage is immoral. Since the primary (or exclusive) purpose of sexuality was the procreation and raising of children and since marriage was seen as the only safe and stable place for this process, Christian authors and authorities consistently argued that any genital sexual acts outside of marriage were wrong. "Only within marriage" was echoed by medieval scholars like Aquinas, repeated by reformers like Luther and Calvin, and taken up by eighteenth-century philosophers like David Hume, Jean-Jacques Rousseau and Immanuel Kant. It has been the fairly constant and consistent stance of official Christianity and much of Western civilization.

Still, Christianity's prohibition of nonmarital sex was not the only factor discouraging persons from having sex outside of marriage. As Christine Gudorf notes, high rates of venereal diseases (which were untreatable and incurable), the unavailability of effective contraceptives, high rates of infant and maternal mortality and the relatively late age at which persons achieved sexual maturity all supported and made more defensible Western society's restriction of sex to the marriage bed.[28]

Contemporary Voices. Christianity's ban on nonmarital sex has been debated and questioned for a good part of the twentieth century, with most critics downplaying the procreative purpose of sexual intercourse. The introduction and widespread accessibility of relatively safe, reasonably effective and inexpensive contraceptives have raised questions about procreation as the presumed primary or exclusive goal of sexual activity. So too, the risks posed to the human community and planet by population growth, as well as rapidly declining infant mortality rates in developing nations and the increased costs of raising and educating children in developed countries have led many to reevaluate the importance or primacy of procreation.

Meanwhile, a growing number of voices from psychology, theology and elsewhere have increasingly stressed the importance of intimacy, companionship, pleasure and nurturing love as important goals and purposes of human sexuality. At the same time, improvements in our diet and health mean that women and men now reach sexual maturity in their early teens, while economic and educational trends result in postponing marriage to the early- to mid-twenties. When combined with high divorce rates and increased longevity, the result is that more and more people are spending large parts of their adult lives outside of marriage, a place where the traditional Christian ethic has demanded celibacy.

Not too surprisingly, then, studies indicate that in the United States and Europe there has been a steady increase in premarital sex over the past century, with about 75 percent of American men and more than half of the nation's women having had sexual intercourse before marriage. There has also been, it seems fair to say, a growing tolerance of this practice, and of cohabitation of couples before and outside of marriage. While percentages do not necessarily dictate good morality, we do well to listen to and respond to the voices of cultural experience.

Not everyone is in favor of abandoning the traditional ban on extramarital sex. Concerned with the trivialization of sexuality in our culture and popular entertainment, with the large numbers of unwed mothers living in or on the verge of poverty, and with the dangers of AIDS and other sexually transmitted diseases, many in our society and churches, including the Catholic Church, continue to call for abstinence before and outside of marriage. So too, others, who agree that intimacy and mutual pleasure are goals of human sexuality, argue that sexual intercourse represents the fullest self-disclosure one person can offer to another, and thus calls for a level of commitment and fidelity only found within that covenanted friendship we call marriage. In the Catholic tradition, Pope John Paul II, drawing especially on the work of Pope Paul VI, has made this point consistently and eloquently in his teachings on marriage.[29] Such voices often remind us of the importance of the virtue of chastity, which does *not* require that we deny our sexual nature, but helps us to express our sexuality in ways that are appropriate for who we are and where we are in our relationships and commitments.[30]

Voices from the Margins. Large numbers of people now find themselves single for significant periods of their adult lives. For a variety of reasons, many of them unchosen, they are temporarily or permanently unable to marry. There are students facing years of further study, young (or not so young) people who are currently unemployed or underemployed, and divorced, widowed or abandoned spouses caring for children or elderly parents. There are people who are disabled, chronically ill or suffering from emotional or psychological difficulties or scars. And there are gay and lesbian people. Any or all of these persons may find they have few or no real prospects for marriage. Yet they have no less need for the companionship, intimacy, pleasure or nurturing support they might find in a relationship that may involve sexual expressions of care and love. Some Christian theologians and pastoral ministers ask if such persons should always be required to embrace celibacy.

At the same time it seems fair to suggest that many young people in our culture currently feel pressure to be sexually active before they are ready for the emotional and personal challenges of genuine sexual maturity and commitment. All too often the entertainment media trivializes sex and presents sexual encounters as light, frothy moments without any real importance or consequences. In many popular sitcoms and films everyone goes to bed with everyone else and it ends up meaning little if anything. This hardly prepares folks for the mystery or wonder of genuine human love and its appropriate sexual expression.

Scripture. In both the Hebrew and Christian Scriptures monogamous marriage is believed to be the appropriate and ideal moral context for genital sexual expression. We see the fundamental importance and goodness of marriage in the second creation account of Genesis 2:18–24. Here we learn that God has fashioned women and men to be intimate and loving partners joined in a communion of "one flesh." The biblical author sees marriage and procreation as sacred duties. "It is not good," we are told, "that the man should be alone.…Therefore a man leaves his father and mother and clings to his wife, and the two of them become one flesh."

There are a number of indications in the Hebrew Scriptures that sex was to be restricted to the marriage bed. Adultery, which was defined as sexual intercourse between a married or betrothed woman and any man other than her husband, was seen as a grave sin and a capital crime (Lev 20:10), for which both parties were to be executed. Prior to marriage young women lived in their father's household and were expected to be chaste. Any man who seduced an unbetrothed woman was obliged to marry her and pay her father a "brideprice," while anyone who raped a young woman who was already engaged was to be stoned. And any groom who could prove his bride had not been a virgin could have her executed by stoning (Deut 22:13–29). At the same time, concern about the "improper emission of seed" resulted in biblical prohibition against masturbation and homosexual acts, and there were numerous condemnations of incest.

Although the Hebrew Scriptures portray monogamous marriage as the presumed moral setting for sex, several exceptions to the rule against nonmarital sex were made, holding men and women to very different standards. First, in spite of laws aimed at outlawing this practice, both married and unmarried men were generally permitted to have sex with prostitutes. (It was not adultery for a married man to sleep with a prostitute or an unmarried woman, and infidelity by a married man was criticized but not punished.[31]) Second, because of concerns about procreation, paternity and property, married men were allowed to have additional wives, take a concubine or divorce and remarry when faced with a childless marriage. And third, the practice of "levirate marriage" meant that the brother of a dead man might be expected to sleep with his widowed sister-in-law in order to raise up heirs for his deceased sibling.

As Lisa Cahill notes, in the New Testament "heterosexual marriage is certainly assumed to be the proper context of sexual behavior." Indeed, "the positive biblical vision of sex focuses on faithful, heterosexual marriage, and sex outside of that context is clearly not part of the normative picture for the early Christians."[32]

Biblical authors consistently remind Christians that they are to avoid adultery and all sorts of sexual immorality *(porneia),* including incest, fornication and debauchery (terms not always clearly defined), and prostitution. In Matthew 5:27–32 Jesus not only instructs his audience not to commit adultery, but also warns against any lustful coveting they might commit in their hearts. And the author of Hebrews 13:4 tells his readers to "Let marriage be held in honor by all, and let the marriage bed be kept undefiled; for God will judge fornicators and adulterers."

In his extensive treatment of sexual questions in 1 Corinthians 5–7 Paul recommends that married and unmarried Christians should remain in their present situation, presumably because Jesus' second coming seemed imminent, but goes on to advise both women and men that they should indeed marry if they cannot practice self-control or if their sexual passions are too strong. Such marriages, Paul assures his readers, are not sinful. Again, the clear implication is that sexuality belongs in marriage.

Before closing our reflections on Scripture, however, two final points need to be made about New Testament sexual ethics. First, in proclaiming the reign of God Jesus challenges his disciples to reject (among other things) patriarchy and sexism, and build communities in which women and men are equal and mutual partners. Second, in both his words and deeds Jesus rejects any sexual ethic that would allow the "pure" or self-righteous to "cast stones" from on high. Let us examine these points a little further.

Throughout the New Testament there is evidence that Jesus challenged patriarchal and sexist practices, that he broke bread with, befriended and included women among his disciples; indeed, women were the first witnesses of the resurrection. We also know that in the earliest Christian communities women exercised roles and duties traditionally reserved to men. In Galatians 3:28 we read an early baptismal formula informing us "there is no longer male and female; for all of you are one in Christ Jesus," negating notions of male superiority.[33] And in 1 Corinthians 7 Paul stresses that both spouses have mutual duties to each other and that each is to be concerned about pleasing the other. Therefore, any authentic Christian sexual ethic must aim at the full equality and dignity of women and men.

Finally, in John 7:53–8:11 we have the famous account of Jesus and the woman caught in the act of adultery. Here the biblical author makes it abundantly clear that the mob that has come to accuse and punish this woman ought not sit in self-righteous judgment. None of us is so innocent that we can afford to "cast the first stone." This does not mean that Christians are not called to repent of their sexual immorality or that sexual sins are not important. Pastoral and prophetic challenge may be called for. It is however, a reminder that our sexual sins are often a sign of our weakness and not our malice, and that compassion and mercy are what Jesus asks of each of us.

Tradition. In the centuries following the birth of Christianity a number of factors shaped the ongoing formation of the church's sexual ethic. Augustine believed that sexual pleasure was disordered and more or less tainted by original sin. Like the Stoics, he argued that sex could only be justified if it was engaged in for the purpose of procreation. According to him marriage—which produced children, called the partners to fidelity and was an indissoluble union—was the only appropriate place for sex. Aquinas also saw procreation as the primary or natural purpose of sexual intercourse in humans and other animals, but added that human parents were responsible for the education and raising of their children and so required the safe and stable environment only marriage could provide.[34] Even more, Aquinas described "the love between husband and wife as the greatest sort of friendship, and as characterized by the highest intensity of all loves, because of their union 'in one flesh.'"[35] In this way he recognized what would later be called the "unitive" dimension or purpose of marital love.

The result of these positions was a longstanding Christian tradition that generally saw "all non-marital sex as immoral, and all sexual activity not procreatively intended as unnatural whether in or outside of marriage."[36] Thus, fornication, premarital sex, prostitution, concubinage, rape and adultery were all deemed immoral primarily because these acts do not provide a stable setting for the education and raising of possible children and, to some extent, because they are not expressions of committed, mutual love. Likewise, nonprocreative sexual acts (like masturbation, extravaginal sex, incomplete sexual acts, homosexuality and bestiality) were seen as unnatural, not open to procreation and thereby wrong. All sexual sins (including forbidden fantasies, glances and touches) were seen as "grave matter" and potentially serious sins. As recently as the early 1960s the eminent Catholic moral theologian Bernard Häring wrote that "every deliberate sexual gratification outside well-ordered conjugal love is a grave sin if it is directly intended."[37] Still, it is also true that many Christian ethicists and pastors often tempered official teachings with a mixture of prudence and compassion, paying attention to the concrete situation, story and intention of persons, and offering pastoral encouragement, advice and forgiveness to their parishioners and those they counseled.

In general Protestant reformers like Martin Luther and Calvin had a more positive view of marriage and did not base their approval of this institution on the command to procreate. Still, both Luther and Calvin opposed premarital and extramarital sex, as well as homosexual relations, arguing that marriage was indeed the appropriate place for sex. In differing ways each saw marriage as the cure or corrective for unruly sexual desires.[38]

Over the past half century a number of Christian ethicists have questioned traditional Christian sexual ethics and the ban on all non-marital sex. In general the criticisms fall into four categories. First, there is a concern that Christian sexual ethics has been overly suspicious of pleasure in general and sexual pleasure in particular. This negative view of all or most bodily pleasure has often resulted in unnecessary ignorance, shame and scrupulosity. Second, some ask whether Christian sexual morality has paid too much attention to the structure and purpose of physical acts (like coitus or masturbation) and not enough attention to the persons who perform them. Some contemporary ethicists suggest that morality ought to be more about persons and relationships and not so much about do's and don'ts.[39] Third, traditional sexual ethics has paid little, if any, attention to the voices and experience of women. Often the tradition was based on a faulty biology of the day and an anthropology that understood all females as passive and inferior, a distracting temptation to men. Fourth, the focus on procreation undervalued the fact that for humans sexuality is also (some say primarily) about companionship, intimacy, committed union and its accompanying pleasure.

Some Catholic ethicists, like Philip Keane and Vincent Genovesi, offer fairly modest revisions of the ban on nonmarital sex, suggesting it may be overstating the case to say that *all* instances of premarital sex are objectively wrong. Instead, they propose that in some exceptional circumstances, even though premarital sex may not embody the fullness of the ideal of sex within marriage, sex between a nonmarried but committed couple may not only involve a lesser degree of culpability or sinfulness, it may even be morally justified.[40] While not accepted by official Catholic authorities and other more evangelical denominations, this discussion of possible exceptions to longstanding absolute prohibitions seems to be the locus and focus of sincere, sometimes heated intra-Christian study and debate. Such nuanced discussion seems likely to continue for the foreseeable future.

Other Christian moralists, like Karen Lebacqz and Christine Gudorf, call for a more sweeping revision of traditional sexual norms and the ban on premarital sex. Lebacqz argues that "a new ethic for single sexuality is needed, for the tradition that requires celibacy in singleness is not adequate."[41] And Gudorf argues that "given both effective contraception and acceptance of other ends for sex than procreation, traditional reasons for limiting sex to marriage are no longer compelling."[42]

At present the Catholic and some Protestant churches continue to affirm traditional sexual norms and the ban on nonmarital sex, though the reasons for such a ban have evolved somewhat. More and more arguments against premarital sex are based on the notion that sexual love demands the sort of commitment and institutional supports found only in marriage. As Christian ethicist Richard Sparks presents this tradition, "sexual intercourse is…an expression of deep interpersonal intimacy and commitment," which only makes sense in the context of marriage, where two persons "pledge to be there for one another, in good times and bad, in sickness and health, for richer or poorer, until death."[43]

Still, the criticisms and recommendations mentioned above, as well as a rejection of these norms by many Christians, make it clear that the Christian tradition concerning sexual activity is currently not "fixed" or unchanging. So as we attempt to take a stand on sexual moral issues today we do well to pay attention to the voices of the tradition, and the voices heard in sometimes heated and, at its best, respectful debate.

Formulating a Christian Response. In light of all that has been said, then, what sort of stance ought Christians to take regarding extramarital sexual relations? Should the ban on all nonmarital sex be maintained, modified or abandoned?

Some Basic Convictions. There are strong reasons to argue that marriage is the ideal and appropriate context for genital sexual relations. Sexual intercourse involves a radical gift of the self to another and symbolizes a profound "two-in-one-flesh" communion. This gift and communion call for the sort of public and purposeful commitment and promise of fidelity found in marriage, and the sacrament of marriage offers Christian couples abundant grace and support in loving and caring for each other. Furthermore, the potential and enduring link between sex and the procreation of new life and the need children have for a safe and supportive environment make marriage a particularly apt setting for sexual intercourse.

Also, whatever norms we discern or maintain about premarital or extramarital sex must be consistent with what we now know and are continuing to learn about the mystery of human sexuality and must be relevant to the lived experience all sexual persons, married and single alike. Our reflections on the "nature" and purposes of human sexuality must attend to the best scientific information and philosophical insights currently available to us. And we can hardly afford to ignore the fact that the sexual reality and experience of many people has been changed by the widespread use of contraceptives, the need to address population growth and the long periods of adulthood more and more people are spending outside of marriage. Christian sexual norms must take these realities into consideration. This does not mean bending to them, but neither can it mean ignoring this cultural and experiential data.

Furthermore, all people need to be wary of the temptation to "cast stones" at sexual sinners. At the heart of the gospel ethic is a command to love one another as God has loved us, and as we love ourselves. In his own day Jesus challenged purity codes that drew sharp lines between the clean and unclean that rendered women and men whose sexual lives were not immaculate outcasts and pariahs. Particularly in the area of sexual morality and norms it is good to remember Matthew 9:13, where Jesus tells his listeners, "I desire mercy, not sacrifice," and "I have come to call not the righteous but sinners."

Some Difficult Questions. If marriage is the ideal and appropriate context for sexual intercourse, are there other situations in which genital sex might also be appropriate or at least permissible? Even if these other contexts are less than ideal or lack some perfection, could there be enough value or good achieved in these encounters to justify them morally? Is it true, as Keane and others suggest, that under certain conditions "preceremonial" or premarital sex between two engaged persons could be morally acceptable? Or is Lebacqz correct when she argues that while sexual relations between single persons are fraught with more dangers and risks than those protected by marriage, intercourse between unmarried adults can in certain settings be both good and moral?

And, given what we now know about the sexual and psychological development of adolescents, should we reevaluate the traditional absolute prohibition of masturbation? Are Gudorf and others right when they suggest that an act that seems to be a normal part of the sexual maturation of nearly all men and most women could hardly be a grave sin? In an age when we are less inclined to be persuaded by arguments against "wasting seed," what should Christian teaching about the ethics of solitary sex be?

Still, if Christian ethics were to allow for sexual acts or intercourse outside of a monogamous marriage, how exactly would we distinguish between premarital or extramarital sex that was moral (or permissible) and that which was not. Clearly, there are differences between premarital sex between two engaged persons and casual sex with near-strangers, or adultery, or prostitution, or rape, or incest. But by what criteria exactly would we measure "good" sex for single persons? Would it be enough to say that it should be mutually loving, consensual and pleasurable, and that it should express a deep level of respect, intimacy and vulnerability? Should the parties know each other very well, be willing to share parts or all of their lives with each other, be open to having children together? What specifically would we demand of sexual acts outside of marriage? In short, how much commitment and what level of personal intimacy should be required for a couple to be genitally active?

It seems clear that these questions cannot be answered easily. Given the difficulties of formulating a sexual ethic for single persons, it is easy to understand the appeal and power of a clear ban on non-marital sex. That appeal, however, has so far not made these questions go away.

Birth Control

The Voices of Experience

The Voice of History. As John Noonan notes in his classic text, *Contraception,* between the end of the nineteenth century and the middle of the twentieth, "...contraception spread throughout the world, [and] the planning of births became a generally accepted ideal in Western and Western-influenced cultures."[44]

One place to begin a history of this transformation is with Thomas Malthus, an Anglican cleric who in 1798 wrote *An Essay on the Principle of Population,* warning of the dangers of overpopulation. Malthus himself did not recommend contraception as a cure for this problem, but British thinkers like Jeremy Bentham and James Mill soon made the connection. In the second half of the nineteenth century "Malthusian Leagues" proposing contraception as a remedy to the ills of overpopulation, poverty and unemployment sprang up in England and several other European nations. In 1913 Margaret Sanger began what would become the American Birth Control League, and by the 1930s much of the medical community in Europe and the United States had been won over to the idea of birth control.

There was significant opposition to this movement. In 1873 the Comstock law forbid the sending of any contraceptive device or advertisement through the U.S. mail, and after World War I several European nations passed laws forbidding the manufacture, possession and distribution of contraceptives, as well as the dissemination of any information about the topic. Still, as Noonan points out, "...by 1930 the birth control movement had in most countries overcome most restraints upon its freedom."[45]

Contemporary Voices. Supporters of birth control and contraception point to several factors leading to the sweeping cultural and moral acceptance of this practice. First, there is the introduction of relatively safe, accessible and reasonably effective means of contraception. In the second half of the nineteenth century inexpensive condoms and diaphragms became widely available, and by the 1960s there was a broad assortment of methods available, including oral contraceptives. Used properly, a number of these methods are seen to be from 95 to 99 percent effective in preventing conception. Second, concerns about population growth and the stresses overpopulation places on global resources, the environment and the economies of many poorer nations and regions have fueled national and international efforts at birth control. Between 1825 and 1998 the world's population grew from one to six billion people and could reach eight billion by 2025. As Christine Gudorf argues, many believe "present levels of population cannot be sustained alongside any process toward just distribution of the resources of the earth."[46] Third, contraceptives have been seen by some as a way of protecting women's personal freedom, equality and health. Not surprisingly, these values are profoundly important in an age increasingly aware of the rights and dignity of women. Again, as Gudorf and a number of feminist authors argue, contraception's role in the unlinking of sexual intercourse from procreation is seen as critical to liberating women from male oppression, giving women control over their own "bodyselves."[47] Fourth, plummeting infant mortality rates and the escalating costs of raising and educating children in industrial and postindustrial societies have eliminated the economic advantages and incentives for large families and demanded more responsible behavior concerning the timing and number of pregnancies. And fifth, as Jean Ponder Soto argues, unlinking intercourse from procreation allows couples to appreciate the interpersonal and spiritual significance of their sexual love and develop a "spirituality of conjugal intimacy," one that takes seriously the conviction that God is present and active in and through sexual intimacy.[48]

Still, not everyone has been happy with the global spread of contraception and birth control. Along with objections from the Catholic Church (to be treated below), there have been other criticisms. Some human-rights activists in developing nations complain about coercive or manipulative policies directed against the poor, while others argue that Western supporters of contraception often ignore or trample on the cultural practices and beliefs of indigenous peoples. There is concern that wealthy nations have sought to export contraception to developing countries primarily because they are concerned with controlling the population (and power) of the poor and are unwilling to limit their own disproportionate consumption of global resources. At the same time, a few critics like Jacqueline Kasun argue that human intelligence will be able to solve any future shortages or stresses placed upon the global environment by population growth, making massive birth control programs unnecessary or wrongheaded.[49] Furthermore, there is concern about the health effects of certain contraceptives, and that the easy availability of contraceptives has significantly undermined society's commitment to abstinence outside of marriage, encouraging irresponsible, immoral and unsafe sex. Nevertheless, few, if any, of these critiques have been directed against the freely chosen use of contraceptives by married persons seeking to limit or space the number of children born to them.

Voices from the Margins. As we have just seen, supporters of contraception want us to pay attention to the experience of women, who have traditionally not had a strong voice in conversations about sexual or marital ethics and whose health and freedom are often at stake in choices and policies about intercourse and pregnancy. Meanwhile, others are concerned that national and international campaigns supporting birth control need to be genuinely focused on the needs of the poor and of indigenous peoples whose cultural practices and beliefs are often overlooked. Finally, both supporters and opponents of contraception are concerned that our young people are protected from sex that is irresponsible, meaningless or dangerous to their health.

Scripture. John Noonan notes three things about the Hebrew Scriptures that are relevant to our discussion of contraception. The biblical authors clearly see the procreation of children as central to marriage and as both a blessing and a command from God. Companionship and love are also important values in marriage, but not as important as procreation. And there is no rule forbidding contraception in any of the Hebrew Scriptures' codes of law.

As Noonan states, "...the most obvious and commanding message of the Old Testament is that marriage and the procreation of children are eminently desirable human goods, which God has blessed."[50] In both the first creation account (Genesis 1:27–28) and God's blessing of Noah after the flood (Genesis 9:1) humans are directed to "be fruitful and multiply." Later, in Genesis 18:9–13, God promises to bless Abraham and Sarah with a child. And when the Lord does favor Sarah and she conceives and bears her son Isaac, the no-longer barren Sarah rejoices that "God has brought laughter for me; everyone who hears will laugh with me!" So too, in Deuteronomy 7:13–14 the Hebrews are promised they will be blessed with many children and that no man among them will be impotent and no woman barren. And the Book of Wisdom reflects at some length on the blessing that children are and the suffering that childlessness can entail (Wisdom 3:13–19).

Catholic ethicists Margaret Farley and Lisa Cahill agree that the Hebrew Scriptures portray procreation as essential to marriage. Farley notes that, "at the heart of Judaism's tradition of sexual morality is a religious injunction to marry. [And] the command to marry holds within it a command to procreate."[51] Pointing to the creation stories in Genesis, Cahill argues "maleness and femaleness have as a purpose the human response to the Lord's 'Be Fruitful.'" This does not mean sexual relations exist "for the sole or even inalienable purpose of pro-creation," but they are definitely linked to procreation. Cahill also argues that there is something countercultural about this biblical con-viction. "Contrary to modern liberalism, the Priestly author places the man-woman relation in the context of the welfare of the cre-ation, rather than the interpersonal communion."[52]

The Hebrew Scriptures also stress the importance of companion-ship and love in marriage. In the creation accounts in Genesis Adam and Eve are fashioned as partners and companions for one another. "This at last is bone of my bones and flesh of my flesh," Adam exclaims in Genesis 2:23. And Genesis 2:24 reminds us that "a man leaves his father and mother and clings to his wife and they become one flesh." So too the Song of Songs celebrates the personal, affec-tionate and spiritual relation of lovers. Still, Noonan notes, for the biblical authors love and companionship were not as important as procreation. When Sarah believes she cannot have a child she invites Abraham to sleep with her slave girl Hagar, hoping to remedy her barrenness. And, as we already noted, biblical norms allowed men to deal with childless marriages by having sex with concubines or slaves, or by divorcing a barren wife and remarrying.

Finally, Noonan reminds us that there is no commandment against contraception anywhere in the Hebrew Scriptures, which contain rules against a variety of other sexual acts, including intercourse during menstruation, adultery, homosexuality, bestiality, temple prostitution and incest. The fact that the ancient biblical codes offer no specific condemnation of contraception, a practice which was clearly known by Israel and her neighbors, leads Noonan to conclude that it is unlikely that contraception was seen as unlawful.

Marriage and procreation are seen in a distinctly different light in the New Testament. Here virginity, which the Hebrew Scriptures held in little or no esteem, is often portrayed as preferable to marriage. In Matthew 19:12 Jesus seems to praise those who have renounced marriage "for the sake of the kingdom of heaven." And in Luke 20:34–36 Jesus says that "those who belong to this age marry and are given in marriage; but those who are considered worthy of a place in that age and in the resurrection from the dead neither marry nor are given in marriage....they are like angels." So too, in 1 Corinthians 7:32–34 Paul writes that "the unmarried man is anxious about the affairs of the Lord, how to please the Lord; but the married man is anxious about the affairs of the world, how to please his wife, and his interests are divided."

Still, the New Testament authors do affirm the goodness of marriage and the sacred character of sexual intercourse. In Mark 10:7–8 and Matthew 19:4–6 Jesus repeats the assertion of Genesis 1 and 2 that the two-in-one-flesh of marriage is ordained by God. And in Ephesians 5:25–33 husbands and wives are directed to love one another, and their mutual embodied love is described as a symbol of Christ's own love for the Christian community. What is different from the Hebrew Scriptures is a decreased emphasis on the importance of procreation. As

Noonan argues, "it is evident that procreation as the primary purpose of marriage is not emphasized in these writings."[53]

Finally, as in the Hebrew Scriptures, we find no specific treatment of contraception in the New Testament. Rather, any ethical position the Christian community is to develop regarding this matter must attend to the larger biblical themes regarding love, sexuality, marriage, procreation and the dignity of women and men.

Tradition. Since he argued that procreation is the only justifiable purpose for sexual intercourse and that "the procreation of children is the first and natural and lawful reason for marriage," it is not surprising that Augustine condemned contraception.[54] In the centuries that followed, his opposition to any sexual acts in which insemination or procreation was frustrated was echoed in the penitential books of medieval monks and church law, and by the thirteenth century Augustine's position was unchallenged as official church teaching. At this point three reasons were offered for the immorality of contraception. Since the medieval church saw the destruction of sperm as a kind of abortion (killing of the person in the seed), contraception was seen as homicide. Because it frustrated the basic purpose of sexual intercourse, it was deemed unnatural (and against God's will). Finally, since it also frustrated the basic procreative purpose of marriage, it was understood as harmful to the marital relation itself.[55] In general, medieval theologians argued that married persons committed a venial or slight sin if they had intercourse for any other purpose than procreation, and forbade sex during menstruation or pregnancy.[56]

The nineteenth century witnessed significant changes in Catholic teaching on intercourse and contraception. At the start of the century the official position was still that married couples must intend procreation when having intercourse. Later, a growing number of moral theologians argued that other purposes, like pleasure, or "promoting conjugal affection," could also be just reasons for making love, as long as the couples did not "positively exclude" procreation and took no steps to prevent sexual acts from being procreative. By the close of the century it was recognized by many theologians that couples could, in certain circumstances, engage in intercourse with the intent of avoiding procreation, using periodic abstinence to make certain that they did not conceive a child.[57]

Still, it was the twentieth century that witnessed the most radical challenges to the church's longstanding opposition to contraception. As previously noted, at the Lambeth Conference in 1930 the Anglican Church approved the use of contraceptives for couples facing "a clearly-felt moral obligation to limit or avoid parenthood, and where there is a morally sound reason for avoiding complete abstinence."[58] In the years that followed most Protestant communities moved away from an absolute ban on contraception. As Noonan notes, by midcentury, "a substantial consensus of Christian thought in the West outside the Catholic Church now approved of some form of contraception."[59]

In December of 1930 Pope Pius XI responded to the Lambeth Conference with the document "On Chaste Marriage," arguing that the procreation of children was the primary purpose of intercourse. The pope allowed that married couples might make love for other reasons, such as "mutual aid" or "the cultivating or mutual love," but they needed to preserve the "intrinsic nature" of the sexual act, meaning they could not "deliberately frustrate" the procreative function of intercourse. To do so would be a grave sin.[60]

But along with the prohibition of contraceptive actions that "deliberately frustrate" procreation, Pius XI's teaching included a statement acknowledging the importance of the mutual "interchange and sharing" of married couples:

> This mutual inward moulding of a husband and wife; this determined effort to perfect each other, can in a very real sense, as the Roman Catechism teaches, be said to be the chief reason and purpose of matrimony, provided matrimony be looked at not in the restricted sense as instituted for the proper conception and education of the child, but more widely as blending of life as a whole and the mutual interchange and sharing thereof.[61]

Foreshadowing later Catholic teaching stressing the "procreative" and "unitive" purposes of sexual intercourse, Pius XI affirms that sex in marriage exists *for* the procreation and education of children, but also that marriage and sexual love in marriage exist *for* and *because of* the "blending of life" and love of the spouses.

Two decades later, in his 1951 address to the Italian Catholic Society of Midwives, Pope Pius XII granted that married persons could have intercourse for the purpose of giving and receiving God-given sexual intimacy and pleasure, and offered the Catholic Church's first public approval of natural family planning. For good reasons, the pope asserted, married couples could limit intercourse to the times of infertility in the woman's menstrual cycle.

Meanwhile, more and more people—both laypersons and theologians—became increasingly vocal about their dissatisfaction with the idea that marriage and conjugal sex are primarily for procreation. Theologians Herbert Doms and Dietrich von Hildebrand insisted that "we should speak rather of the *meaning* of sex than of its *function* [emphasis added]," and that meaning has everything to do with the union and love of the spouses.[62]

In 1965 the bishops of Vatican II addressed the question of marital intercourse in "The Church in the Modern World." According to this document marriage and sexual intercourse have two purposes, procreating children and building up a "community of love," and the first is not more important than the second. Indeed, the bishops refused to speak of marriage in terms of primary and secondary purposes, and stressed instead the significance of conjugal love as the "centerpiece" of the significance of marriage. Emphasizing the importance of sex within marriage, they noted that when sexual intimacy is broken off, the well-being of the couples and of the marriage itself can be threatened.[63]

It was, however, Pope Paul VI's 1968 encyclical "On the Regulation of Birth" *(Humanae Vitae)* that defined what continues to be the official Catholic position on contraception. Although a papal commission consisting of bishops, theologians, experts and laity recommended revisions to the traditional teaching, the pope reaffirmed the church's opposition to the use of artificial contraceptives. The argument was clear. "Each and every marriage act must remain open to the transmission of life," because God has willed "the inseparable connection...between the two meanings of the conjugal act: the unitive meaning and the procreative meaning." And so it is "intrinsically dishonest" for a couple to have intercourse while deliberately inhibiting the procreative purpose.[64]

This encyclical generated quite a controversy within the Catholic Church. In spite of the repeated and consistent defense of this position by Pope John Paul II, many Catholic theologians—clergy and laity—find the teaching unpersuasive. Indeed, more than a few commentators have suggested that because of its stance on this issue a large number of contemporary Catholics no longer think of their church as a source of moral wisdom on sexual questions.

As Vincent Genovesi points out, the criticisms of the teaching on artificial contraceptives fall into two main categories.[65] A number of Catholic ethicists have argued that it is not evident that every act of intercourse must be open to the transmission of life. Catholic teaching allows for intercourse between persons who cannot conceive and for intercourse at times when conception is, for the moment, impossible. In both instances these acts are seen as moral and blessed, even though there is no chance of procreation. At the same time, many Catholic theologians and married persons reject the idea that natural family planning methods of birth regulation are really "natural" (and on that basis permissible), while "artificial" means like condoms and the pill are "unnatural" and forbidden. According to these critics the "nature" of human persons and human sexuality is about much more than the biological structure of organs or actions, and it is a mistake to pay more attention to the physical rhythms of our organs than to the interpersonal, emotional and spiritual goods involved in human sexuality and relational commitments.

Formulating a Christian Response. In light of the above, what is there that we can say about the morality of contraception?

Some Basic Convictions. It is evident that Christian sexual ethics is, at least in part, a work in progress. Neither the Catholic Church nor the larger Christian community any longer holds that procreation is the only or primary purpose of human sexuality or that couples may not take steps to avoid procreation. (The Catholic Church teaches only that they may not use certain means to do so.) Nor is it any longer church teaching that sex during menstruation or pregnancy is forbidden, that contraception involves homicide or that sexual pleasure may not be sought (and given) for its own sake in the context of marital intimacy. As we seek to be faithful to the best elements of our tradition and the fundamental teachings of Scripture we must also attend to new knowledge from the sciences about human sexuality and the human person, and to the changing realities of marriage, parenthood and human population. In the past this sort of attentiveness has at times led to changes in church teaching, and may do so in the future as well. As Noonan concludes at the end of his text, "it is a perennial mistake to confuse repetition of old formulas with the living law of the Church. The Church, on its pilgrim's path, has grown in grace and wisdom."[66]

The challenge before us today is to fashion a Christian sexual ethics that embraces a significantly more positive understanding of the human body, human sexuality, sexual pleasure, and the dignity, rights and equality of women. Since the era of Augustine the Christian theological tradition has suffered in some ways from an overly negative assessment of human embodiment and sexuality. And the Christian tradition, impacting and impacted by its cultural contexts, has been the recipient and bearer of varying levels of patriarchy and sexism. This century's emphasis on the goodness of sexuality and of sexual pleasure within the context of a loving marriage is good news for Christian theological tradition. So too, the contributions of feminist writers regarding the importance of women achieving full equality as persons and partners is good news. The construction of a new, revised or more holistic sexual ethic along these lines is a work-in-progress. Ideally it will be an ethic grounded in a thoroughly positive—but not naïve—account of human sexuality.

For all of our contemporary technical control over fertility and for all of our rightful emphasis on the goodness of sexual expression and sexual pleasure within marriage, it does seem that our culture may be tempted to factor out procreativity too drastically from sexuality. If we take anything with us into the twenty-first century from our biblical heritage and past centuries of Christian tradition, perhaps it is simply that procreativity is an integral element of human sexuality. This is not to say that every act of intercourse within marriage is necessarily about procreation. Nor is it to demean marriages in which procreation is not biologically possible. Rather, it is to suggest that any radical and complete unlinking of procreation from the marital sexual relationship seems to involve redefining both marriage and sexuality in ways that are inconsistent with too much of the truth and wisdom of Christian tradition.

Some Difficult Questions. Official Catholic teaching on birth control is founded on the conviction that every act of sexual intercourse within marriage has two inseparable meanings—unitive and procreative. The wrongness of contraception, objectively, is that it separates one meaning from the other in specific acts of intercourse. Since Paul VI put forth this argument in 1968 a number of voices within the Catholic community have asked whether this is so. Is not this description of what sexual intercourse means within marriage an ideal description of *some* acts of intercourse? Are the meanings of sexual expression in marriage adequately described as unitive and procreative? Does this account of sex within marriage take sufficiently into count conflict situations in which, in the experience of the spouses, a further pregnancy is not at all ideal? Might the unitive and procreative meanings of sexuality apply more generally to the overall marital and sexual relationship rather than every act of intercourse?

Much of what has happened in regard to human sexuality in this past century has been the result of an "unlinking" of procreation and sexuality. Many have welcomed this "unlinking," partly for the advantages it has offered women, partly because it has led to a greater appreciation of the other goods and purposes of human sexuality. Still, it can be asked whether this "unlinking" does not pose its own dangers. Has it contributed to a trivialization of sexuality, particularly among the young and unmarried? In a culture in which the ready availability of birth control unlinks sex from procreation is there a danger that our commitment to chastity or the seriousness with which we treat human sexuality has been undermined? And if this is true, what might be done to reinvigorate our sense of loving commitment and sexual fidelity?

Homosexuality

The Voices of Experience

The Voice of History. In the ancient world there were mixed views on the morality of homosexuality. The practice was accepted in both Greek and Roman society, and the priests of some Middle Eastern cults engaged in homosexual rites. Nor was it forbidden by Islam or Hinduism. A number of primitive cultures have either tolerated homosexuals or, on occasion, treated them as shamans or holy persons.[67] Throughout most of the history of Judaism and of the Christian West, however, homosexuality has been seen as immoral and prohibited. Adrienne Rich notes that in the seventeenth century "the New Haven Colony prescribed the death penalty for lesbians," and until fairly recently sodomy laws prohibiting homosexual acts were widespread in the United States and elsewhere.[68]

During the 1940s and 1950s the Kinsey studies of human sexuality recognized the existence of a homosexual orientation in a minority of the population and contributed to a rethinking of the traditional ban on homosexuality. In the late 1950s and early 1960s legal groups in England and the United States were pressing for the repeal of sodomy laws.

In 1969 a riot outside the Stonewall Inn in Greenwich Village, New York, led to the founding of gay-rights organizations throughout the country. In the decades that followed more and more homosexual person in the United States "came out of the closet," and worked not only for the removal of sodomy laws but also for legislation protecting the civil and political rights of homosexual persons. In 1974 the American Psychiatric Association removed homosexuality from its list of mental disorders and noted that "homosexuality *per se* implies no impairment in judgment, stability, reliability, or general social or vocational capabilities."[69] More recently the World Health Organization has dropped homosexuality from its international index of diseases.

Contemporary Voices. Since the beginning of the 1990s the controversy over homosexuality—both in the churches and larger society—has increased. Most mainstream Christian churches in the United States have been engaged in wide-ranging studies and public debates and disagreements over the morality of homosexual acts, the ordination of homosexual clergy and the possibility of homosexual unions. On several occasions individual clergy, congregations and denominations have been publicly censured or chastised for challenging traditional teaching or practices. Meanwhile, the federal government has wrestled with the issue of gays and lesbians in the military, and both state and local authorities have been involved in debates over human-rights ordinances seeking to protect homosexual persons from harassment and discrimination in the workplace and elsewhere. At the same time there has been increased pressure to allow civil unions or marriage for homosexual couples, or at least to provide homosexual partners with the same insurance, medical and retirement benefits enjoyed by married couples.

Those in support of more liberal or tolerant views regarding homosexual persons and their participation in the public life of the churches and society generally focus on the dignity, equality and rights of homosexual persons, both as citizens and believers. At the same time they also tend to stress the permanent and unchosen nature of a homosexual orientation, and argue that Christ's call to a universal love of our neighbor must take precedence over ancient biblical norms.

Those opposed to a change in the traditional teaching about homosexuality point to biblical passages describing homosexuality as an abomination and to the longstanding teaching of the Christian churches on this question. At the same time they warn of the moral dangers that acceptance of a homosexual lifestyle or agenda might pose to marriage, the family and young people.

Voices from the Margins. Until very recently homosexual persons have made up an invisible, or "closeted" community, with most living anonymously among their heterosexual siblings and neighbors. In his work *The Nature of Prejudice* the psychologist Gordon Allport offered some insight into this self-imposed invisibility when he noted that homosexual persons were the objects of some of our culture's most virulent prejudice and that they would suffer even graver violence if they could be identified and targeted by the larger community.[70] This argument seems to be borne out by the increased reports of "gay bashing," sexual harassment and hate crimes committed against homosexual persons since many began to come out of the closet. One result of the invisibility of homosexual persons has been the widespread presence and acceptance of myths and stereotypes that describe all or most homosexual persons as promiscuous, unbalanced, immature or even as dangerous sexual predators.

By listening to the voices and experiences of homosexual persons the human sciences have discovered the concept of a homosexual orientation and, in the process, have debunked a number of myths about the causes of this orientation. By listening to these voices we have also learned about the cruelties and injustices perpetrated against gays and lesbians by all sorts of prejudice, harassment and discrimination. And by attending to the voices and stories of homosexual persons and couples living up against the plague of AIDS the wider community has come to see that gays and lesbians are also capable of love that is faithful, compassionate and courageous.

Scripture. A great deal has been written in recent years about the Bible and homosexuality, and much of this writing has underscored three points.[71] The Scripture's treatment of same-sex desires and behaviors is quite critical. Ancient biblical authors had little or no understanding of an abiding and unchosen (i.e., discovered) homosexual orientation. And individual passages dealing with homosexual acts need to be examined and interpreted in context if we are to properly understand precisely what is being condemned or called immoral. It is helpful to deal with the first two of these points and the relationship between them before addressing the specific biblical passages dealing with homosexuality.

Reviewing the biblical evidence, Lisa Cahill notes that "same-sex genital activity is certainly repudiated by both Old and New Testament authors," and adds that "throughout the Bible, homosexual activity is associated with idolatry, with transgression against God, and with contemptible habits of alien religious groups."[72] At the same time contemporary biblical scholars and Christian ethicists also agree with Patricia Beattie Jung and Ralph Smith's assertion that "the ancient Hebrew people and St. Paul...had no understanding of the fact that some people might be homosexually (or heterosexually) oriented."[73] This means that when biblical authors condemn same-sex behavior they are assuming that this conduct is between two heterosexual persons who freely (and rebelliously) decide to go against their "nature" and God's divine plan. What is not so clear from the biblical evidence, however, is just what these authors would have said about the morality of a loving, just and faithful homosexual relation between two homosexual persons, who "discover" rather than "choose" their sexual orientation.

The most famous passage in the Hebrew Scriptures cited in defense of a moral prohibition of homosexual acts is the story of Sodom and Gomorrah in Genesis 19. In this tale two angels disguised as men arrive in Sodom at sunset and are offered hospitality and shelter by Lot. Later in the evening, however, all the men of the city gather outside Lot's house and demand that he hand his two guests over to be gang raped. Lot refuses to accede to the mob's savage demands, and the city is soon destroyed by God. Traditionally Christian authors have argued that since the men of Sodom wanted to have sex with two males this is a story simply about the evils of homosexuality. But a growing number of biblical scholars and Christian ethicists argue that it seems much more likely that the crime being addressed here is rape, and the gross violation of Lot's offer of hospitality and sanctuary that this rape represented. As Vincent Genovesi argues, "...the action which the men of Sodom were contemplating would have been an instance of outright lust and homosexual gang rape. As such, the behavior deserves to be condemned, but this text alone can scarcely be used as a justification for prohibiting all homogenital activity."[74]

Two other passages from Hebrew Scriptures are cited as evidence of the immorality of homosexuality. In Leviticus 18:22 we read that "you shall not lie with a male as with a woman; it is an abomination." And in Leviticus 20:13 we are informed that when two men do lie together in such a fashion "both of them have committed an abomination" and must die. Two things can be noted about these citations from Leviticus. First, they form a part of the "Holiness Code" of ancient Israel, a code that was concerned primarily with cultic and ritual purity, with making certain the Hebrews were not defiled or contaminated by contact with unclean things or practices—particularly those of their idolatrous neighbors. As a result, this code forbids a number of practices that contemporary Christians would not see as immoral, including the eating of certain "unclean" foods and intercourse during menstruation. Second, scholars tell us that it is most likely that the condemnations of homosexual acts in Leviticus 18 and 20 are directed specifically against the practice of temple or cultic prostitution. Israel's Canaanite neighbors often used male prostitutes as part of their worship of fertility gods and goddesses, and the biblical authors condemned any association with such idolatrous practices. Thus, it is unclear whether these passages can be seen as offering an absolute ethical condemnation of all homosexual acts.

In the New Testament same-sex behavior is condemned in two lists of vices appearing in 1 Corinthians 6:9–11 and 1 Timothy 1:8–11, though there is some difficulty establishing exactly what practices the Greek terms used in these lists refer to. And in Romans 1:18–32 Paul offers a very clear condemnation of homosexuality, describing it as the fruit of idolatry. Two scholarly points might assist in reviewing these passages. First, as Jung and Smith note, Paul "thought there was something dishonorable about both male and female same-sex desires and something unnatural about same-sex behavior." For Paul these desires and behaviors violated God's plan for human sexuality and were the result of an idolatrous rebellion against God.[75] However, as we have noted, Paul seems to assume that all persons are heterosexual (though that term would have been foreign to him), and so would have seen all same-sex behavior as a *willful* perversion of our God-given nature. Thus it is not so clear what he might have thought about sex between two homosexually oriented persons. And second, it is likely that Paul's criticisms of same-sex behavior were largely in response to the widespread Greek practice of pederasty, which involved adult males having sex with adolescent boys. This practice, involving heterosexual men having intercourse with minors, was inherently abusive and exploitative, and contemporary Christians would find it as objectionable as Paul did. Still, we cannot be certain that Paul's objection to pederasty (or cultic prostitution) justifies a belief that the Bible would condemn all homosexual behavior as we now understand it. Therefore, while there is no doubt that the Hebrew and Christian Scriptures are negative in their assessment of homosexual acts—especially those that are violent, depersonalizing or abusive—it can be argued that the Bible alone leaves open or does not clearly resolve the issue of a loving and committed gay or lesbian relationship.

Tradition. Until the second half of the twentieth century Christian sexual ethics offered two generally undisputed arguments against homosexual acts. Scripture—particularly in the story of Sodom, but also in Paul's letter to the Romans—was understood as having condemned homosexual acts as an unnatural and therefore immoral form of sexual activity. This biblical argument is evident in the writings of Augustine, John Chrysostom and other important teachers and pastors in the early centuries of the church's history.[76] And because traditional Christian sexual ethics accepted Augustine's assertion that procreation was the only justifiable purpose for any sexual intercourse, church teachings condemned homosexual acts as a violation of natural law. Thus Aquinas listed homosexual acts (as well as masturbation and bestiality) as "unnatural vices" that offend against reason and nature.[77] This natural-law argument continues to form the basis of the Catholic Church's opposition to homosexual acts, as seen in the Vatican's 1975 "Declaration on Certain Questions Concerning Sexual Ethics."[78]

Recently some Christian ethicists have offered a third argument in opposition to homosexual acts—that these acts lack the "complementarity" and fullness of heterosexual intercourse and are a form of selfishness. According to this argument women and men are called by God to be sexual partners and companions *because* they are different from one another and because these physical and psychological differences allow them to complement and complete each other. Homosexual intercourse, however, is said to lack this complementarity because persons are making love with a mirror image of themselves and not to one who is radically "other." As one writer has argued, homosexual relations are seen as "an exercise in narcissism."[79]

Currently nearly all Christian denominations recognize the reality in some or most homosexual persons of a permanent and unchosen homosexual orientation. This is a significant break with past teachings, which for centuries had presumed that all persons were heterosexual and that homosexual acts represented a freely chosen rebellion against our heterosexual "nature." As a result of this new insight the Catholic Church and some other Christian churches make a careful distinction between a homosexual orientation (which is seen as not sinful) and homosexual acts (which continue to be forbidden because they violate natural law). According to this view persons with a homosexual orientation are not to be condemned or persecuted, but treated with dignity, respect and compassion.[80] Nonetheless, such persons are forbidden to engage in homosexual acts and are called to embrace lifelong celibacy. The church likewise pledges to defend the basic rights of gay and lesbian persons and to offer them support and care in their efforts to live chaste lives.

At the same time, a growing number of other Christian thinkers and denominations argue that for persons with an abiding homosexual orientation homosexual relations may, under certain circumstances, be "natural" or at least understandable and therefore morally justified. Throughout the past decade there has been a growing debate in both the Catholic and Protestant churches about the morality of homosexual acts, relations and unions.

Criticisms of the traditional prohibition of homosexual acts generally fall into three categories. As noted above, many argue that Scripture cannot be shown to offer a total or absolute condemnation of all homosexual acts. Moreover, the natural-law argument that homosexuality is wrong because it is not open to procreation has been challenged for its possible inconsistency. How, critics ask, can the church oppose homosexual acts for being nonprocreative when it allows a number of nonprocreative heterosexual acts, like marital intercourse between the elderly, the infertile or those practicing natural family planning? Furthermore, if the churches recognize that a significant number of persons have an abiding homosexual orientation, isn't it "natural" (or at least "tolerable") for these persons to seek out homosexual relations that are loving, faithful and just, even if they are not procreative? And finally, some suggest that the argument against homosexuality based on a lack of complementarity implies that all single or celibate persons are radically incomplete and that men and women require a heterosexual relationship to be "whole."

In general, then, we hear three distinctive voices in contemporary Christian sexual ethics regarding the morality of homosexuality. Defending the traditional stance, the Catholic and some other Christian churches teach that while a homosexual orientation is not in itself sinful (though it is disordered) homosexual acts are "objectively" wrong. Pastorally speaking, persons committing them may not always be subjectively guilty of sin.[81] On the other hand, a number of contemporary Christian ethicists, including Lisa Cahill, Charles Curran, Edward Vacek, Philip Keane and Vincent Genovesi have argued that for homosexual persons in a faithful, loving and just relationship homosexual acts might well be moral. This is what Richard Sparks has described as a "qualified acceptance" position, "because it tolerates or accepts homosexual sex by way of exception to the accepted or presumed heterosexual norm," even though not all the theologians listed above consider the homosexual orientation completely "natural."[82] The third voice, that of "full acceptance," sees homosexuality as a God-given and natural way of being sexual persons, in no way inferior to heterosexuality. The English

Quaker church defends this position, as do Patricia Beattie Jung, Ralph F. Smith and James B. Nelson.[83]

Formulating A Christian Response. Where, then, does all this leave us regarding the morality of homosexuality?

Some Basic Convictions. Any conversation about homosexuality needs to begin with the conviction that gay and lesbian persons are, like all of us, children of God, created out of love and in God's image. As such, they must be responded to with reverence and respect. Their full civil and economic rights should be assured and, as the U.S. Catholic Bishops have said, they should find a special welcome in the community of Christ.[84] Furthermore, the experience—especially the moral experience—of gay and lesbian persons must be factored into Christian theological reflection about homosexuality more than has been the case in the past. If Christian ethics is reflection on moral experience in the light of Christian faith, then Christian ethical reflection about homosexuality can be served by paying attention to the experience and narratives of gay and lesbian persons themselves. Finally, Christian ethics regarding homosexuality must be attentive to Scripture and tradition, but it must also be willing to reexamine these sources of Christian ethics in light of what we know today as the phenomenon of the homosexual orientation. As we have already noted, neither the ancient biblical authors nor those responsible for the first nineteen centuries of Christian sexual ethics were aware of a homosexual orientation, but instead believed that all same-sex activity took place between heterosexual persons. This suggests that the activity being condemned in the scriptural passages that relate to same-sex genital acts is perceived far differently from the sexual intimacy of a loving, committed and faithful homosexual couple.

Some Difficult Questions. Does homosexuality represent some sort of imperfection or disorder when compared with heterosexuality? Is the "two-in-one-flesh" union of woman and man in heterosexual love the ideal or norm of human sexuality, and homosexuality a deviation from that norm? Does homosexuality lack the fullness or perfection of heterosexuality? Or, as some suggest, is homosexuality simply another natural and God-given way for human beings to be sexual? Is it a way of being sexual that is equally good, valuable, moral and loving? Or, even if not the ideal, should we be more tolerant and understanding about sexual commitment among those for whom this is their discovered sexual orientation?

If one grants that homosexuality involves some sort of imperfection, brokenness or disorder, does that mean that all homosexual acts are thus immoral? Does the "disordered" or "imperfect" character of homosexual acts distort them in such a way as to make them always and everywhere wrong? Or is it possible that such acts might, in certain circumstances, be both acceptable and moral?

If the Catholic or other Christian churches were to agree that homosexual acts might be moral in the context of a loving, faithful, and committed homosexual couple, should these unions be sanctioned or blessed by the church? Whether such "unions" could be considered marriages or whether they could be considered to be similar to life vows in religious orders are further questions.

Just what does it really mean to say, as the U.S. Catholic bishops have, that gay and lesbian persons "should have an active role in the Christian community"? Can gay and lesbian *couples* find such a place in the Christian churches? In some churches they already do; in others they do not. Can these brothers and sisters of ours find a thorough welcome in our churches if they are welcome as individuals but not as couples, or if they are welcome as couples as long as their committed partnerships are not made public?

Finally, how much of the Christian community's opposition to homosexuality is the fruit of personal bias or even homophobia? To what degree have church teachings and discipline regarding homosexuality, however inadvertently, offered support to prejudice or violence against gays and lesbians, encouraged "gay bashing" or contributed to environments where harassment and injustice were tolerated or overlooked?

Community: An Examination of Two Sexual Sins

Sexism. More and more we are coming to realize that the most pervasive and longstanding social sin in the area of human sexuality is sexism, which is almost universally directed against women and which is also seen in the related sins of patriarchy (male-dominated societies and families) and misogyny (the hatred of women). Sexism, which involves both distorted *beliefs* about the moral, physical and intellectual inferiority of women as well as unjust *practices* that oppress or even do violence to women, is present in the political, economic, cultural and religious structures of every society. In "Partners in the Mystery of Redemption," the U.S. Catholic bishops note that "we are called to recognize that sexist attitudes have also colored church teaching and practice over the centuries and still in our day."[85]

Ideologies. Sexism is grounded in a number of longstanding false assumptions. As the U.S. bishops note, "…it is a profound sin to label woman as the source of evil in the world, as intellectually inferior, psychologically unstable and inclined to sensuality. Yet sexism does just that," and a good deal more.[86] The first error of sexism is to claim that women are not men's equals, that women are by nature or God's creative design, intellectually, physically, spiritually or morally inferior to men. According to this mistaken belief males are the norm or ideal form of humanity, and females are an inferior variant. We see evidence of this mistaken belief in the writings of Plato and Aristotle, in Augustine's contention that women lack reason and only possess the image of God through their connection with men, in Aquinas's assertion that women are misbegotten males and in Pope Pius XI's defense of the inequality of husbands and wives.[87] Given this presumed inferiority, it is only natural that the second error of sexism would be the belief that men have a right to dominate or control women. And so in a patriarchal society it is assumed that both at home and in the public sphere women are to be subject to men's leadership. As the bishops note, "…on the basis of their supposed superiority, some men, clerics included, believe they have the right to dominate women."[88] The third error of sexism identifies women more closely with the body, emotions, sexuality and human sinfulness, and thus sees them as less noble, spiritual and rational than men. As feminist theologian Rosemary Ruether points out, one result of this error is the belief that women are "more responsible for the origins of evil than men, [and] more prone to sin than males."[89] Tainted by their close association with sexuality and sin, women are perceived as sexual temptresses who lead men into sin and who are to blame when men cannot control their own sexual passions. At the same time, the myth that women are more emotional (and thus less rational, supposedly) results in the sexist belief that females cannot be entrusted with leadership, hard thinking or decision making and are to be kept safely tucked in the domestic sphere of the household. A fourth mistaken belief of sexism is that God is male or that only masculine language or images should be used to describe the divine and that only men can "stand in for" or fully represent God in ecclesial settings. And finally, it is a mistaken belief of sexism that women are to be defined primarily by their reproductive or nurturing role as mothers and/or spouses. It is wrong to limit women's identity and development as persons and human beings to their reproductive or "nurturing" role as parents or spouses. We do not do that with men, who are seen first and foremost as human beings and persons and not as fathers or spouses.

Embedded Practices. Sexism and patriarchy are found in a number of practices and structures that marginalize and oppress women. In the workplace women experience discrimination in a wide variety of ways and are often the victims of sexual harassment. In the United States and around the world women continue to be paid significantly less than men with identical or inferior educations. When making career choices, women are usually directed into "pink collar" jobs like teaching, nursing or secretarial positions, and away from higher paying and more prestigious occupations like physicians, attorneys or engineers. When seeking promotions or advancement in the workplace women are likely to run into a "glass ceiling" that excludes them from the upper realms of management. And when women get home at the end of their working day they often discover they have a "second shift" of largely unassisted housework and child care (or eldercare) to be done before they can go to bed. What's more, women who are the heads of single-parent households often find it difficult to locate or pay for adequate child care and receive little support in getting absent fathers to pay necessary child support. Finally, in sweat-shops around the world women are often the preferred employees because they can be paid less and are more easily exploited.[90]

In society at large women experience discrimination and margin-alization in a variety of ways. In most countries women do not have equal access to educational opportunities. In a number of nations women are effectively barred from participating in the political process. In a handful of states women cannot inherit property. In most economies the value of "women's work" at home or in the fields is ignored or discounted. And throughout the world women, who make up half the population, hold less than a fifth of elected national offices. Similarly, most religious communities have effectively excluded women from leadership positions or marginalized their contributions. One result of this widespread disenfranchisement of women has been the "feminization of poverty," which means that around the planet women and the families they head are more likely to be poor, hungry and sick than men. And study after study indicates that women are less likely to receive adequate medical treatment for their illnesses. As Christian ethicist J. Milburn Thompson notes, "no society treats its women as well as its men."[91]

Still, as seen in our treatment of domestic violence, the most disturb-ing sexist practice women in every culture and society must deal with is the experience and constant threat of violence. As Gudorf notes, "there is little doubt that most women live in fear, to greater or lesser degrees, of male anger and aggression."[92] And as Thompson notes, "...this sexual violence is not random; it is aimed at women as women, and meant to frighten and control them. It amounts to 'sexual terror-ism,' a system perpetuated by men for the domination of women."[93]

Christian Beliefs. In spite of the fact that sexism and patriarchy have "colored church teaching and practice over the centuries," the U.S. Catholic bishops condemn sexism as a sin, and contemporary Christian teachings challenge its underlying assumptions. Women and men are fully equal persons before God and each other. As Pope Paul VI noted, "God created the human person—man and woman both—as part of a unified divine plan and in his own image. Men and women are therefore equals before God: equal as persons, equal as children of God, equal in dignity and equal in rights."[94] As just noted, the equality of women and men is grounded in the fact that both are created "in the image of God." Women are made in God's image, not merely in man's. And women are as capable of being images and sacraments of God's presence in the world as men. Women too make up the "body of Christ," and the feminine is as holy as the masculine. All of these are convictions found in Catholic teaching and the writing of Pope John Paul II, who consistently affirms that women and men together reflect the image of our loving God.[95] Given this fundamental equality, women and men are called to be partners and friends, not servants and masters. It is neither natural nor God's intent that women should be subject to men. Instead, as the U.S. bishops note, "...the domination of men over women, the lack of respect for equal dignity in relationships and the failure to respect women as persons are sins of sexism, sins which are rooted in original sin's disruption of the order willed by God."[96] Contemporary Christian teaching rejects any sort of discrimination or prejudice based on gender as unjust and immoral. At Vatican II the bishops argued that "every type of discrimination, whether social or cultural, whether based on sex, race color, social condition, language or religion, is to be overcome and eradicated as contrary to God's intent."[97] And finally, in its "preferential option for the poor," the church is called to stand on the side of those who are marginalized and oppressed by structures of injustice. Given the effects of sexism and patriarchy and the fact that women are invariably the poorest of the poor, Christianity has a special obligation to stand with women and work for their full liberation from every form of oppression and injustice.

Structural Reforms. Addressing sexism is a colossal task that will call for the conversion and transformation of every society and community and of all our political, economic, cultural and religious institutions. Nonetheless, there are a number of identifiable changes that would advance the struggle against patriarchy and sexism. Addressing church leaders, Pope Paul VI noted two goals for which Christians should work. First, the "recognition of the civil rights of women as the full equals of men, whenever these rights have not been acknowledged." Second, the Christian community must seek "laws that will make it really possible for women to fulfill the same professional, social and political roles as men, according to the individual capacities of the person."[98] Pope John Paul II has espoused the same view, noting also that because women tend to shoulder child-care responsibilities more predominately than do men, societies might do well to consider providing "family allowances or grants to mothers devoting themselves exclusively to their families."[99] At the same time there is a need to eliminate discrimination and harassment in the workplace, to remove the "glass ceiling" and to ensure that the overlooked and unpaid labor of child care and eldercare not fall disproportionately upon the shoulders of women. There is a need to ensure that women have fuller access to educational and leadership opportunities, that women are encouraged and empowered to participate more fully in all our political, economic, cultural and religious structures. And, if the Christian and Catholic communities are to be credible witnesses in this area, there is a need for reforms within the churches themselves. The 1971 world synod of Catholic bishops argued that "women should have their own share of responsibility and participation in the community life of society and likewise of the church."[100] And indeed, if sexism and patriarchy are to be overcome, women will need to have a full and equal share of responsibility and participation in the life of the church. They will need to exercise genuine and equal leadership, and to develop and celebrate their full range of gifts and talents as persons and disciples. As Paul tells us in Galatians 3:28, in the Christian community—of all places—there can be no separation of Jew and Greek, slave and free, or male and female, for we are all "one in Christ."

Sexual Ignorance. Citing recent studies, Christine Gudorf argues that "the overwhelming majority of our society is immensely ignorant about sexuality, and this ignorance victimizes many."[101] A 1989 Kinsey

Institute survey indicated that only a fifth of Americans know the correct answer to twelve of eighteen basic questions about sexuality, while researchers at the Alan Guttmacher Institute concluded that only three states and the District of Columbia have adequate sex and AIDS education programs. At the same time many critics complain that the "value-free" or clinical education so many of our young people receive regarding sexuality fails to make a connection with the deeper personal, emotional and moral questions they will need to struggle with in relationship to love, sexuality and procreation. And others argue that the "just say no" approach found in many programs tends to teach negative attitudes about sexuality and fails to prepare persons adequately for rich, happy, and moral sexual lives as adults. Gudorf believes this widespread sexual ignorance is unnecessary, freely chosen by the society at large, and harmful to large numbers of women and men —often resulting in sexual dysfunctions, unwanted pregnancies and sexually transmitted diseases. Not too surprisingly, then, she argues that this sexual ignorance represents a kind of social sin.

Ideologies. A number of differing, and often conflicting, beliefs and attitudes contribute to our society's ignorance about sexuality. Most adults, it seems, find it quite difficult, challenging or embarrassing to speak openly and frankly to young people about sexuality, particularly about their own sexuality and about the deeper emotional and personal questions a conversation about sexuality involves. This may be because many of us see sexuality as an intensely private affair or because we ourselves never had such conversations with our parents or other respected adults, and so lack the language to speak about such things. Or it may be because many of us continue to see sexuality as somewhat shameful or tainted with sin.

In spite of the difficulty and reticence many parents experience when faced with the task of providing their children with an adequate sexual education, many are resistant to school-based programs that teach values different from their own. In a pluralistic society our public schools educate children from a wide spectrum of religious and moral traditions, and while most Americans support the notion of sexuality education in our schools, lots of (often vocal) parents are unhappy with programs that fail to teach their own moral or religious vision. At the same time, a certain number of parents and educators seem to believe that sexuality education in and of itself encourages immoral or unsafe behavior and that our adolescents would be better off left in blissful and innocent ignorance.

And while parents and teachers often wrestle with providing an adequate sexuality education for our young people, our culture's popular entertainments are awash with confusing, titillating and often trivializing messages about sexuality. Often our sitcoms, films, advertisements and CDs seem obsessed with sexual activity, and the message here can be deeply confusing. On the one hand, as Gudorf notes, "sexual activity is celebrated as the human activity necessary to personal development, the only reliable source of intimacy, as the highest, most satisfying pleasure available (outside illegal drugs)."[102] On the other hand, sex is often portrayed as a recreational activity, as an encounter without serious emotional, personal or medical consequences. And often enough other persons, particularly women, are portrayed as sexual objects to be manipulated, possessed and exploited.

Embedded Practices. A number of the practices contributing to and flowing from our society's unnecessary ignorance about sexuality have already been mentioned. Most children in the United States do not seem to receive adequate sexual education from their own parents.[103] This is a particularly serious problem, since young people need much more than clinical or technical information about sexuality. They need trusted adults who will address the deeper human values and issues related to their sexuality. And while three-quarters of our nation's large urban school districts do provide sex education, only a tenth offer information about contraception, pregnancy or fertility before high school, even though increasing numbers of junior-high and grade-school students are sexually active. In many programs adolescents complain about being bored because the clinical information being offered seems disconnected from their experience of love or sexuality. As a result many do not process or retain the information offered in these programs. Furthermore, media messages portray sexual activity as both the source and summit of all human happiness and a casual recreational activity with little meaning and few consequences.

As a consequence of these practices many of our young people receive too little sexuality education, and often get it too late to help them prepare for the onset of puberty or to deal with menstruation, wet dreams or other sexual developments. Because of their sexual ignorance a number of women and men experience unnecessary sexual dysfunctions, including the absence of orgasm, painful intercourse, male impotence and premature ejaculation. And men and (especially) women do not receive enough information about their own and their partner's sexual processes, and thus are inhibited from becoming more attentive, responsive and joyful lovers.

Christian Beliefs. There are a number of Christian beliefs that call us to overcome our society's sexual ignorance. As we noted at the start of this chapter, we hold that our sexuality is extraordinarily good, even blessed, and that it is a fundamental element of our humanity and personhood, affecting every aspect of our humanity. Our sexuality is a sacrament of God's love and a basic part of our being fashioned "in the image of God." There is no room, then, in a Christian worldview, for any fundamental hostility to sexuality or our bodies, and no reason for intentional or unnecessary ignorance about this fundamental dimension of our lives. In and through sexual love we are able to form intimate, committed, mutual and just relations that are themselves embodied sacraments of God's love. And our sexual acts have the capacity of opening ourselves to one another and God's love in a powerful and unique way, and of offering deeply human and sacred love to each other. Therefore, we should be well and richly educated about our sexuality. Our bodies, too, are sacraments of God's presence in the world, the sacred flesh that God formed and Christ took up, and so we have a need and right to know our own embodied selves fully, and not to be ignorant of who we are. Education is a fundamental right of all persons, and education about our own bodies and sexual selves is critical to our flourishing as persons and communities. And finally, as this chapter has made very clear, we face numerous moral challenges and questions in the area of our sexuality. And our ability to make good conscience judgments depends upon our being well informed about the clinical facts of our sexual identity, development and experience, as well as the deeper personal, emotional, psychological and ethical dimensions of our sexuality. Ignorance is never an asset for Christian disciples seeking to discern their moral obligations.

Structural Reforms. We need to address the problem of sexual silence in our homes. Parents, who are our children's first teachers, have an opportunity and a calling to educate their own children about the realities and mystery of human sexuality. At the same time other respected and important adults must be willing to address the questions and concerns of adolescents in congruent and honest ways. In order to assist parents and other adults in this task our churches and other important communities and institutions need to continue developing resources and programs directed at forming healthy, joyful and responsible attitudes toward and understandings of sexuality. We must also find effective ways of addressing unhelpful and distorted images or messages about sexuality that we encounter in the media or on the Web. While protecting other values like free speech, we need to develop tools and practices that will underscore the tremendous importance of human sexuality and take issue with commercial messages that trivialize either sex or reduce other persons to sexual objects. And parents and educators and communities must struggle together to develop flexible but effective educational programs that will give our children the information they need to understand and address their own sexual development and issues, while preparing them to lead rich, moral and loving lives as sexual persons.

Cases and Resources

Along with the case at the start of the chapter, the following four cases are meant to provide you with a chance to apply this book's method of moral decision making to a number of issues concerning violence in our society. In addition, a brief list of resources regarding human sexuality and Christian theology is provided.

Case #2: Sterilization—Once and for All

Julie Koestler is Ann Mangione's best friend. They've known each other since the third grade. Julie was Ann's maid of honor, her daughter's godmother, and for the past year and a half she's been a sympathetic ear at the other end of hundreds of late-night phone calls. As she has told (and proven to) Ann on a number of occasions over the past two decades, Julie would do anything for her. Right now, however, she is trying to figure out if she loves Ann enough to tell her that she thinks she is about to make a very serious mistake.

"I've made up my mind Julie, this marriage can't take the strain of a second child. Mitch is at the end of his rope. His new job is so stressful; he's drinking again—though maybe not as much as six months ago—and I'm afraid it would only make things worse to have another baby. What's more, I don't like what the birth control pills do to me, our life is certainly not organized enough to use natural family planning, and I need to be absolutely sure I don't get pregnant again any time soon. So I'm going to have my tubes tied."

Silence on the phone.

"Hello?... Julie?...Anybody there?"

After another pause, "I'm not sure I think that's such a good idea, Ann."

"What? Why not? You don't really think having another baby is good for our marriage, do you? You told me three years ago you didn't think having a baby was the solution to our troubles, and you were sure right about that! I love Sally, but having her has only made things tougher for the two of us. There's child care and all sorts of other expenses. Mitch complains that we don't spend as much time together, and she was colicky for the first year and a half.

"I feel like I've been living in a tornado for the past two years, and I need to do something that will give me some peace and security, some stability. If I get this operation at least I won't be worrying about another baby. God, it would be so irresponsible to bring another child into this marriage."

"I agree. Having another baby right now seems like a very bad idea. But are you certain sterilization is such a great idea? Ann, you're barely twenty-eight, and your marriage has been in trouble for six of the last eight years. I've got the phone bills and wet hankies to prove it. Do you really want someone

to do surgery on you in order to take pressure off Mitch? You tried having a baby to save the marriage. What makes you think getting sterilized will work any better?"

"What are you saying, that I should get divorced? That Sally and I should walk out? That I should become a single mom? Is that what you're recommending?"

"I don't know. But I don't think going under the knife to save a fragile marriage is such a great notion.

"Look, how are things with you and Mitch? How's the drinking? How long has he had the new job? Are there any signs that things are really different this time?"

"I want to believe that there are, Julie. I need to believe that there are. But of course I've wanted to believe that before too, haven't I?"

Yes, Julie thought, you have. You've stood by Mitch through six jobs and two long drinking spells. You've tried to get him to go to counseling with you. You've asked his own dad to speak to him about his drinking. And you've tried to keep Sally quiet and out of the way when he was annoyed or drunk. You even had a baby to try and save your marriage. You've done everything you could think of doing. But what has Mitch done, and what can you reasonably expect him to do in the future? Good grief, if somebody needs this operation, why not have Mitch get it?

"Ann, I'm not going to tell you to divorce Mitch. If you can save this marriage I'll be happy to come to your twenty-fifth anniversary and lift a glass of champagne to you and Mitch. But, given everything you've been through and tried over the last six years, I think it's a mistake to do something that could be irreversible to your body when Mitch is unwilling to even see a therapist or go to AA. In a couple of years you could be out of this marriage, through no fault of your own. And you very well might want to have another child with someone else. You're awfully young to be saying 'no' to your future in that way. Isn't there some alternative to this?"

The phone is silent on the other end. Ann sits in her kitchen and wonders about Julie's comments and questions. Is this a mistake? What, she wonders, should she do—about getting pregnant again, about the marriage, about Mitch?

Case #3: What to Teach?

Jenny Pistoia has a problem. For the past fifteen years Jenny, a former high school biology teacher, has been the director of religious education at St. Michael's parish, and for the past eight she has run the parish youth group. This month she and the pastor, Ralph McIntyre, are dealing with the teens' questions around love and sexuality, and this week Jenny is supposed to lead a conversation about homosexuality. Ralph has given her some materials from the diocese on the church's teaching on this topic.

This is a hard teaching for Jenny. Her son Tom is a twenty-nine-year-old physician working in the emergency room of Sacred Heart hospital and volunteering one day a week at a local AIDS clinic. He is also gay, and—like her— a practicing Catholic. A dozen years ago Tom had been a seminarian studying for a small missionary community and the pride of his whole family. Even today he tells his mother that he sees his own medical work as part of his "vocation" to serve what his seminary profs used to describe as the anawim, *or "God's little ones."*

Tom is deeply grateful for his years in the seminary, for the friends he made there and for the mentoring he received from some extraordinarily good priests. He is also grateful for a Catholic heritage that has taught him to be conscious of his duties to the poor and marginalized. But what he is not so grateful for, as he sometimes tells Jenny, is what he increasingly sees as a distorted ethical tradition regarding homosexuality and homosexuals.

In his late teens Tom came to acknowledge his own homosexual orientation, and after a long period of reflection and dialogue with his spiritual director he decided that a life of mandatory celibacy was not part of his own vocation or calling. He made no secret of his orientation or decision, though as Jenny would say he didn't wave any flags in people's faces either. Throughout his years in medical school and as an intern Tom was in two significant relationships, but neither developed into the kind of committed and intimate partnership that he was looking for. Then, a year ago, he met and fell in love with Bob, and they are presently planning to move in together, hoping to spend a rich and loving life committed to one another and to sharing their love with family and friends.

Jenny and her husband Stan have met Bob and had him and Tom to dinner. Afterward, Stan, who was unexpectedly gracious to Bob, admitted to Jenny that although he had long struggled with his son's homosexuality he found he was secretly relieved that Tom has found such a decent and loving partner. "I've often worried about Tom growing old alone, never finding someone to be as close to him as you've been to me." Jenny cried when Stan said this, because she too was so happy for their son and because she knew that Tom would not be able to celebrate this commitment in a Catholic ceremony.

For the last several days Jenny has been struggling with what she will say to the youth group about Catholicism and homosexuality. She reviewed the materials Ralph gave her, and though she was pleased with the church's call to show compassion for persons with a homosexual orientation, she found it more and more painful to read what the church had to say about the wrongfulness of all homosexual acts and about the demand that homosexual persons embrace a lifelong commitment to celibacy. At supper on the night of the meeting she talks to Stan and Ralph one last time about her problem.

"I love my church," she tells them, "and I love my son. But I am not sure that my church understands my son or that my son will be able to stay in my church.

"Ralph, I believe in chastity and abstinence before and outside of marriage. Stan and I waited until we were married before we made love to each other, and we've encouraged our children to do the same. But a lifetime of celibacy seems like it would be too hard for most people. You've told me yourself how hard it is for you, and I am not at all certain that it is fair or right to demand that all homosexuals be celibate forever. Can we really be sure that homosexual people who commit themselves to one another in a mutual, loving and lifelong way are wrong or sinful? Isn't there any way for us to support or celebrate the love between two homosexual persons, especially when they want to commit themselves to each other for life? I just don't know what to say to these young people. Or at least I don't know how to be faithful to my church and my son."

Case #4: Hassle at the Office

Cathy Reed is a thirty-two-year-old accountant with a small but estab-
lished firm in the city. Having worked for Grossman, Planchet and
Williamson for five years now, Cathy is very well liked by colleagues and
clients alike, and has been the subject of not a little bragging on the golf links
and in the board room by her immediate boss, Jeffrey Planchet, Jr. Considered
to be one of the brightest and hardest-working accountants at the firm, most of
her colleagues expect Cathy to be made a junior partner within a few years,
and see her as a likely candidate for a senior partnership in her early forties.

Cathy is also a single mother with two children under six. After a stormy
six-year marriage she and her ex-husband Darren Schiller got a divorce. Two
years later Darren had remarried, moved out of state and begun to fall behind
on child care payments. Cathy has had an attorney working on the case, but
since Darren has been out of work for the past nine months she is not hopeful
of getting any significant income for her daughters. Fortunately, her income
from Grossman, Planchet and Williamson allows Cathy to cover the costs of
taking care of herself and the girls, and—most importantly—enables her to
pay for a live-in housekeeper who has been excellent with Sandy and Megan.
With her lap-top Cathy can do a good deal of late-night work at home
instead of at the office, but on several occasions work with colleagues or clients
has kept her out late, and she has been deeply grateful that Carla was there
with the girls.

For nearly a year, however, Cathy has been uncomfortable with the sort of
attention she has been getting from Jeffrey Planchet. Originally solicitous
about the struggles and difficulties Cathy was experiencing over the breakup
of her marriage, Planchet began to say and do things that seemed inappro-
priate. Hugs at parties were held a bit too long, admiring glances and com-
ments about her clothing seemed more frequent, and on two occasions Jeffrey
touched Cathy in ways that were—to her at least—obviously sexual. Then,
two weeks ago, Planchet—a married man in his mid-fifties—requested that
she join him for a business lunch at a nearby restaurant. During the lunch
he admitted that there was no business to discuss, but that he had wanted
some "quality time" with her, to see how she was doing with all the changes
in her life and to tell her how proud he was of her work and how committed

he was to mentoring her professional development at the firm. Brushing her hand as he reached for a breadstick, Planchet assured Cathy that she was well on her way to becoming one of the youngest senior partners at Grossman, Planchet and Williamson.

After a couple of sleepless nights Cathy decided to get some advice and approached Marge Wolski, a junior partner in her mid-forties who had been with the firm since college.

"So, you've been 'Planchet-ed,' eh? I'm sorry. If it's any consolation, it's happened to a couple of other women here over the years, and the consensus seems to be that he's mostly harmless. If you keep your guard up and maintain your distance, the worst you'll have to deal with is a couple of awkward moments and some long doe-eyed looks across a restaurant table.

"You could make a fuss about it with him or Grossman. Billie Hearnes tried speaking to Planchet directly about six years ago, and he cooled his jets. But she also lost some ground here at work—not as many new or big clients—and two years later she ended up taking a job with a smaller firm. Nobody that I know of has ever gone to Grossman, so you could try that. But he and Planchet are pretty tight, and the two other women he did this with are both gone now. If you like, I would go with you to see Grossman, or Gardner in personnel, but all I can tell them are rumors and gossip about things that happened years ago. You let me know what you want, Cathy. It's a hard spot you're in."

That evening, sitting in the girls' room after having read a couple of stories to them, Cathy thought about her "spot." A great job with a great future. Enough income to be able to take care of the girls and not to have to worry about hunting down their deadbeat dad. And the relative certitude that Planchet can be kept at arm's length, and that the hassle will probably never amount to more than a lot of awkwardness and some occasional uncomfortableness. On the other hand, who wants to deal with this kind of unwanted attention and inappropriate behavior from your boss? Who needs a couple of years of this sort of low-level grief? And what would I ever tell the girls if they were to come to me some day with a similar problem?

Nodding off, Cathy wondered what she was going to do.

Case #5: Honor Roll?

Melissa Caliphano is a senior at Ignatius Prep, ten days away from graduation, and the topic of a very heated conversation at this morning's special meeting of the school's administration, faculty and board of trustees. The second brightest student in a class of 438, Melissa's combined SAT scores are well over 1,500, and she has placed first or second on the school's honor roll for the past seven semesters. All of her teachers agree that she is an exceptionally gifted and energetic student, and has—until now—been a shining example of the sort of student "the Prep" wants to model. Melissa has been active with Father Jake's after-school tutoring program for inner-city kids since her sophomore year. She has been the captain of the school's nationally recognized debate team for two years running, as well as a member of the two-time city champion varsity women's soccer team. And she has twice volunteered for a summer "plunge" program that took students to Mexico to help build homes for Habitat for Humanity. Two months ago she was selected as class salutatorian, and six weeks ago she was named to receive one of four diocesan-wide scholarships granted to outstanding honor students.

In the last four weeks, however, it has become increasingly clear to Melissa's classmates and teachers that she is also pregnant. Ten days ago she and her parents were called into the principal's office and asked about her condition. And four days ago she was informed that she would not be class salutatorian, and that Ignatius Prep could no longer support her recommendation for an honors scholarship. The next morning a long and angry piece signed by seventy of her classmates appeared in the op-ed page of the city's newspaper. And over the next few days local radio shows ate up stories about Melissa's "scarlet letter," with hosts attacking and defending the school's decision, and inviting callers to do the same. Meanwhile, the phones at Ignatius Prep have been ringing off the hooks, and 380 members of the senior class have signed a petition calling for Melissa's reinstatement as salutatorian. Michele Grossman, the school's valedictorian, has said she will not attend the ceremony unless Melissa is reinstated.

The meeting this morning opened with the school's principal, Mr. Cruz, offering an explanation for the administration's decision. "Melissa is in many ways an exemplary student, but the public scandal of her sexual activity and pregnancy undermines our school's commitment to certain moral values. To have a very clearly pregnant unmarried young woman represent "the Prep" at graduation as class salutatorian, and to recommend her as an outstanding "honor" student for a diocesan scholarship sends a message that is counter to what we believe in here at Ignatius. And, though this was I assure you not my central reason for acting as I did, it is also a message that would not be well received by this school's alumni. Over the past several days the calls and e-mail traffic from donors and alumni have been running 60-40 against putting Melissa Caliphano on the dais."

After some applause, Mr. Cruz then recognized Rosemary McMartin, who had agreed to speak on behalf of the faculty and students opposed to the school's action. "Thanks Mr. Cruz. I am not here to defend Melissa's sexual activity or to argue that extramarital or premarital sex is right, or consistent with school or Christian values. I don't think they are, and I don't teach my students that they are. But I am here this morning to say that punishing Melissa in this way is wrong-headed and unjust, and that we shouldn't do it.

"Like that unfortunate woman in St. John's Gospel caught in the act of adultery, Melissa Caliphano did not get pregnant alone. She almost certainly had consensual sex with one of her male classmates, a young man who will not get pregnant or lose any scholarships and who is not even being sought out. And, unlike lots of other young women, Melissa has not decided to terminate this pregnancy, even though she would have had to have been a lot dumber than we know her to be to have thought there would be no cost for that choice. Instead, when she found herself in a very tough spot, Melissa Caliphano chose life and love over safety and success. And those are values we do hold dear at Ignatius. Yes, there is a touch of scandal in a pregnant unmarried woman appearing on our dais as an honor student. But there is a much graver scandal in choosing once again to punish women for sexual failings and in failing to recognize the courage it took her to have this child, courage we hope we taught her at this school."

Once again the room was filled with applause, and Ms. McMartin took her seat. At this point Barbara Haughton, the chair of the board of trustees, came to the dais and announced that they and the administration would now gather in the library to vote on the question of reinstating Melissa Caliphano as class salutatorian and recommending her for an honors scholarship. She asked for everyone's prayers that their choice would be the right one.

Resources

The American Academy of Natural Family Planning. Founded in 1981, the center promotes natural family planning methods of birth regulation (NFP) through educational programs and services. Both the rationale and effectiveness of NFP occupy its attention. Available: *www.aanfp.org.*

The Center for Sexuality and Religion. Founded in 1988, this ecumenical center strives—through educational programs and publications—to foster an appreciation for the connections between sexuality and spirituality. Available: *www.ctrsr.org.*

Charles E. Curran and Richard A. McCormick, S.J., editors, *Dialogue About Catholic Sexual Teaching: Readings in Moral Theology No. 8* (New York/Mahwah, NJ: Paulist Press, 1993). This is a very valuable resource for those who wish to delve more deeply into Catholic teaching and tradition on sexuality. The book contains excerpts from official documents of the church as well as articles by theologians—both those who are supportive of Catholic teaching and those who look for change.

Mary G. Durkin, *Feast of Love: John Paul II on Human Intimacy* (Chicago, IL: Loyola University Press, 1983). This Catholic theologian, wife and mother draws on the pope's famous audience addresses on human sexuality (1979–81) to weave together a fine reflection on the connections among sexuality, sacramentality and spirituality.

Kevin T. Kelly, *New Directions in Sexual Ethics: Moral Theology and the Challenge of AIDS* (New York: Geoffrey Chapman, 1998). In addition to Kelly's valuable reflections on the challenge of AIDS, his twenty-two-page bibliography is an extremely useful resource. Those seeking information about various Christian denominations' teachings on sexual issues will find the bibliography's section entitled "Official or semi-official church reports" particularly helpful.

Odile M. Liebard, editor, *Love and Sexuality: Official Catholic Teachings* (Wilmington, NC: A Consortium Book, 1978). Though a bit dated, this is a valuable source of official Catholic teachings on sexuality through 1976.

Origins on Line. The Catholic News Service publishes *Origins,* which makes available to the public the important documents of the pope, various Vatican offices, the U.S. Catholic bishops and individual bishops on important issues of the day, including those related to human sexuality. It is available in print or on line. Available: *www.originsonline.com.*

CHAPTER FIVE:
Environmental Ethics

Case #1: Building in Mexico

Roger Gibson, the vice president for strategic planning at Gibson Boats, is making a presentation this evening to the company's board of directors. Based in Atlanta, the corporation has enjoyed tremendous success over the past decade, becoming one of the most successful manufacturers of pleasure boats in the United States Recently Roger was asked to analyze the market possibilities for boat sales over the next five to ten years and to make recommendations about the company's future directions. This evening he is presenting his committee's report, along with a recommendation that will surprise many.

"Our financial report makes it clear that we should be proud of what Gibson Boats has accomplished. And I would add that much of our success has stemmed from the bold initiatives the board was willing to undertake during the last decade. Gibson Boats has not become the leader it is because we have been timid. And it is in that spirit that the strategic planning committee makes our proposal tonight.

"Currently we are considering three new lines of boats, and to make that possible, we had been thinking about opening a new manufacturing facility just outside of Atlanta. At this time, however, I am asking you to consider a plan to build in Mexico instead. We have been in conversation with developers there and have the opportunity to build a state-of-the art facility near the U.S.-Mexican border at a cost far less than the proposed Atlanta plant.

213

Moreover, once it is up and running we could operate this plant much more economically than would be possible here in Atlanta. All of this, of course, would allow us to make our products even more affordable to the consumer. Let me present the details."

Over the next ninety minutes Roger sketches out the three phases of his "Mexican Development Project." Phase 1 centers on building the facility. The available property is twice the size of what they might have secured in suburban Atlanta, and about a third of the cost, making the possibility of future expansion much more inviting. Building costs will be significantly lower than in the States, due to the availability of cheaper resources and cheaper labor. Phase 2 will focus on initiation of operations in the new facility. This will require the oversight of a management team from the Atlanta facility for a three-year period, after which (this would be Phase 3, he explained later) management of the plant could gradually be turned over to local personnel. After initial start-up costs, the day-to-day operation of the plant will be far more economical than in a U.S. site, not only because of cheaper labor, but also because Mexico's environmental regulations are not as rigid, or as rigidly monitored as those in the States. (Roger immediately explains that the firm would, of course, develop its own environmental impact plan, one that would be both reasonable and effective.) Admittedly, shipping costs will probably be higher with this plan, but they will be more than offset by the savings in other areas.

After his presentation Roger receives comments and questions from the board. Taken by surprise, their initial response seems largely favorable.

Still, Allison Martinez voices two concerns. "As you know," she said, "my husband is from the Dominican Republic, and we have visited there often. Many U.S. corporations have opened plants there, probably for the same reasons we have heard tonight. But I have seen firsthand what living conditions are like in the cities where these plants are located. They are deplorable. I know the people there are happy to have jobs, but the wages they earn do not even come close to supporting a decent standard of living. And I also have concerns about the less-than-clear plan regarding the environment. There probably are exceptions, but all too often, precisely because the Mexican government may be less than vigilant about enforcement of environmental protections laws, the impact on the environment in these regions and on the people who live in them *has been terrible. I am not completely closed to a possible move to Mexico, but I am skeptical. I want to continue to be proud of what this company stands for."*

Everyone listens to Allison, but there are no further comments about the concerns she has raised. Still, Roger knows Allison is well regarded by many members of the board, and that she will keep a vigilant eye on these concerns about the poor and the environment. He also knows these are issues he will need to attend to in making future recommendations.

Introduction. Like Mrs. Martinez, a growing number of us are disturbed about the damage being done to our environment. We are also worried, even frightened, about the ways this damage is now rebounding on us, on our children, and—in particular—on the poor. Not long ago a book on Christian ethics would not have mentioned the environment. But in the three decades since the first Earth Day (1970) millions upon millions of us have been forced to recognize that humans are reshaping the world in which we live—altering creation itself—often in pretty dangerous and possibly irreversible ways. In the last two centuries the human population has grown from less than one to over six billion, and threatens to pass eight billion within three decades. In the same period the industrial revolution and the growth of global capitalism have resulted in a skyrocketing consumption (and pollution) of the earth's resources. Together, these population and consumption explosions have placed a crushing burden on our environment's ability to sustain and repair itself. And in the years to come, unless some significant changes are made, that burden could well overwhelm the world that we (and every other species on the planet) call home.

Our daily papers and evening news programs are filled with stories about the damage we are doing to our environment and about the ways that harm is coming home to roost on humans, particularly the poor. It is now incontestable that the earth's atmosphere is heating up and that the burning of fossil fuels and the release of carbon dioxide and other "greenhouse gases" has fueled this global warming. Studies indicate that the 1990s was the warmest decade on record, that the earth's surface temperature has increased about one degree Fahrenheit in the last century, that this growth has accelerated since 1979 and that we can expect more rapid warming trends and the doubling of carbon dioxide levels in the coming century. Many scientists are concerned that this climate change will produce increasingly extreme weather patterns, including more flash floods, longer and more serious droughts and a growing number of heat waves. Experts are also worried about the ongoing melting of glaciers and the polar ice cap, rising sea levels and coastal flooding, the withering of crops and the outbreak of crop disease, pests and weeds. At the same time there is a deepening fear that global warming is already contributing to the spread of cholera and could bring about increases in other tropical diseases. And while all of us may be threatened by these climate changes, it is particularly the poor who are likely to be hurt by widespread droughts, flooding, crop failures and infectious diseases.

Meanwhile we hear reports about the ongoing destruction of tropical rain forests, home to half of the world's ten million species of life and nearly half of the planet's medicines and pharmaceuticals. This rapid and ongoing deforestation, which is driving more species into extinction than at any time since the disappearance of the dinosaurs, threatens the biodiversity of the planet, the health and stability of our global food supply and the largest pharmacopoeia we will ever have.

Then there are stories about the effects of chlorofluorocarbons (CFCs) on the planet's ozone layer and the threat increased ultraviolet radiation poses to humans and vegetation. And there are plentiful reports about the environmental harm done by all the waste and garbage we produce, by the toxic and dangerous by-products we dump into our rivers or plow into overcrowded landfills. Again and again we read about chemical or oil spills, about nuclear or toxic materials leaking into underground aquifers or about new "superfund" sites that need to be cleaned up. And, of course, we are continuously inundated with tales about the many ill effects of our increasing consumption of and dependence on fossil fuels. As all of us know by now, we are using up nonrenewable resources that pollute our environment and befoul our air instead of developing renewable and clean sources of energy that will leave our grandchildren with a livable planet and a sustainable economy.

Woven into many or all of these stories are four recurring concerns. There is a worry about the damage we are doing to our local and global environment and to all created life on this planet. There is a growing concern about the effect this damage is beginning to have upon the human community, and may have on generations of humans yet unborn. And there is a deepening realization of the connection between poverty and environmental damage—that the poor are often the first human victims of environmental stress and harm and that poverty and environmental degradation can form a vicious cycle, each feeding off the other and creating more of the other. Finally, there is a worry among many that the very economic development needed to pull millions, even billions, out of poverty will only place greater and greater burdens upon our already overstressed global environment.

How, then, are we as Christians to respond to these concerns and to this growing environmental crisis? What are our obligations or duties to "take care" of the earth, to respect nature or to be good stewards of creation? Indeed, what moral claims do other life forms or unborn generations make upon us? How are we to make room for the poor and for other species in the home we call earth? What does Scripture or tradition have to say to us about environmental ethics or responsibility? How should we address the growing environmental stress being placed on our planet by population growth and escalating rates of consumption and pollution? How are we to make choices about economic development and a sustainable, livable environment?

In this chapter on environmental ethics we try to address some of these concerns and questions from a Christian perspective. Our task here is to think about the ways in which a Christian faith calls us to live and act responsibly and peaceably alongside the rest of creation. And so we will, as in other places, explore some of the ways in which Scripture, tradition, reason and experience direct us as Christians to shape our character, choices and communities when dealing with environmental issues.

As elsewhere, we begin this chapter with a brief historical sketch, this time examining three "ages" of environmental consciousness and three Christian metaphors describing the relationship of humans to the rest of creation. Next we look at character, suggesting some environmental virtues we might bring to our roles as consumers, citizens, employers and stockholders. Then we examine three fairly controversial issues about which we need to make informed choices as Christians: the depletion and destruction of global resources, the possibility of environmental racism and the threat of population growth. Following that we look at two factors that are shaping our community's response to the environment—anthropocentrism and consumerism. We examined consumerism in the chapter on economic justice, but here will be looking at its impact on the "economy" of the planet. Finally, we close the chapter with four more cases and a brief list of organizational resources for those interested in learning more about and addressing some of the issues raised here.

A Glance at the History of Environmental Ethics
Humanity and the Earth: Three Ages

How have humans understood our relationship to the environment, and how have we conducted ourselves in this relationship? The work of Larry Rasmussen and certain other Christian theologians suggests that the history of our relationship to the earth could be divided (roughly) into three ages: the land-based age, the industrial age and (in an attempt at being hopeful) the ecological age.[1]

The Land-Based Age. Beginning with the appearance of the first humans and extending until the age of industrialization, this age refers to the period in which humans sustained themselves and derived their livelihood directly from the land. The first phase of this age was the hunter/gatherer stage, during which humans sustained themselves by gathering fruits and vegetables and various types of hunting and fishing. This phase presumed a fairly radical and immediate human dependency on the land for daily survival. Approximately ten thousand years ago a second phase in the land-based age arrived with the development of agriculture, a result of humanity's increasing ability to cultivate the land and make it predictably productive. Even with the increasing complexity of agriculture human communities generally remained deeply conscious of their dependence upon the land and its fruitfulness. Without romanticizing the period, humanity's relationship to the earth during the land-based age was characterized by a certain respect. The earth, which with hard work and proper care sustained human life, was to be respected.

The Industrial Age. With the spread of the industrial revolution, first in western Europe and then throughout the world, humanity's relationship to the land and the earth begins to shift radically. As Rasmussen notes, with "the spread of industrial production, far more persons could be, and were, engaged in nonagricultural endeavors....Commerce and culture could shift from necessarily working *with* natural forces to *overcoming them* for human ends. Production processes and people could both be separated from intrinsic ties to land."[2]

According to Carolyn Merchant this shift brought with it a new worldview, replacing the *organic* worldview of the land-based age, which saw the earth as a life-giving and nurturing mother with whom humans must live in harmony.[3] In contrast, the industrial age presumes a *mechanistic* worldview, in which "the machine has permeated and reconstructed human consciousness so totally that today we scarcely question its validity. Nature, society, and the human body are composed of interchangeable atomized parts that can be repaired or replaced from outside."[4]

Rasmussen and Merchant argue that this mechanistic worldview has reduced nature to a problem to be solved, or an object to be controlled, dominated or manipulated. As an example of this worldview the philosopher Francis Bacon argued that nature should be "forced out of her natural state and squeezed and molded."[5] Rasmussen and Merchant suggest that this kind of objectification of nature and of the earth has fueled a current ecological crisis. They argue that our current problems with pollution, global warming, the depletion of rain forests and other "natural resources," as well as the massive extinction of plant and animal species, all flow from a lack of respect for the earth, and an amazing shortsightedness in regard to human well-being.

The Ecological Age. Ecophilosopher Thomas Berry describes the budding ecological age in the following way.

"Presently, we are entering another historical period, one that might be designated as the ecological age. I use the term *ecological* in its primary meaning as the relation of an organism to its environment, but also as an indication of the interdependence of all the living and nonliving systems of the earth. This vision of a planet integral with itself throughout its spatial extent and evolutionary sequence is of primary importance if we are to have the psychic power to undergo the psychic and social transformations that are being demanded of us.[6]

Berry believes that the current environmental crisis, as well as important works like Rachel Carson's 1962 *Silent Spring* (which dealt with the chemical poisoning of North America) has have alerted many to the need for a new environmental worldview.[7] We require a worldview that sees humans in a deep and integral physical and spiritual relationship with the earth, not separate from it or suspended above it, as a mechanistic worldview would suggest.[8] This is a central insight of "deep ecology," an environmental approach inspired by Arne Naess and later Bill Devall and George Sessions. Deep ecologists insist that humanity must recognize its own fundamental connection with the rest of the universe and acknowledge the intrinsic and not just instrumental value of all creatures and the ecosystem itself.[9] According to Berry, in an ecological age humans are challenged to recognize that they cannot care for themselves and their descendents without also caring for the larger universe of which they are a part.

Christianity and Creation: Three Metaphors

Just as humanity's relationship to the earth has moved through various stages, so too, Christian thought about our relationship to the rest of creation has evolved over the years. Catholic theologian Elizabeth Johnson proposes three models or metaphors the Christian tradition has used to describe humanity's relationship and obligations to the earth: "the absolute kingship model, the stewardship, and the kinship models."[10] As we shall see, fewer and fewer people today endorse a "kingship" model, but the "stewardship" and "kinship" models are espoused currently by many Christian groups and theologians. Johnson makes her case for the "kinship" model.

The Kingship Model. In a 1967 article on "The Historical Roots of Our Ecological Crisis," cultural historian Lynn White argued that the Judeo-Christian tradition—with its biblical instruction that humans are to subdue the earth and have dominion over all things (Gen 1:28)—is largely to blame for the current ecological crisis.[11] As White sees it, Christianity's use of "dominion" language has resulted in environmentally irresponsible and reckless attitudes and behavior by the human community.

Elizabeth Johnson is similarly concerned with the dangers of "dominion" language when she critiques "the absolute kingship model" of humanity's relationship to creation. According to her, this model

> sees humanity separated from the earth and placed in a position of absolute dominion over all other creatures who are made for us. In this view, the creatures of the world are ranked…with greater value being assigned to those up on the great chain of being.…In the progression from the pebble to the peach to the poodle to the person, with women somewhere between the latter two, the higher order of creatures has the right to use and control the lower.…This is the patriarchal pyramid again, resulting in a top-down domination of nature by man.[12]

The Stewardship Model. The Christian tradition has also espoused a stewardship model of humanity's relation to creation, reminding humans that God's creation has been entrusted to our care. In Johnson's view, the stewardship model "keeps the structure of hierarchical dualism but calls for human beings to be responsible caretakers or guardians of the earth and all its creatures.…In this model humanity is still at the top of the pyramid of being but has the duty to protect and preserve what seems weaker and more vulnerable."[13] This model is often found in the writings of many of the mainline Christian churches. In their 1991 statement on the environment the U.S. Catholic bishops argued that we must be "faithful stewards" of the gift of God's creation. Stewardship, they suggested, means that "we must both care for creation according to standards that are not of our own making and at the same time be resourceful in finding ways to make the earth flourish."[14] And in their 1993 social statement, "Caring for Creation," the Evangelical Lutheran Church in America noted that "acting as God's stewards of the earth" means that "we are called to care for the earth as God cares for the earth,…to serve and keep God's garden, the earth,…[and] to live according to God's wisdom in creation."[15] Surely this model is a major improvement over the kingship model, but scholars like Johnson argue that it does not go deep enough in articulating what our relationship to the earth really is.

The Kinship Model. Johnson describes the kinship model this way: "If separation is not the ideal but connection is; if dualism is not the ideal but the relational embrace of diversity is; if hierarchy is not the ideal but mutuality is; then the kinship model more closely approximates reality. It sees human beings and the earth with all its creatures intrinsically related as companions in a community of life.…This kinship attitude does not measure differences on a scale of higher or lower ontological dignity but appreciates them as integral elements in the robust thriving of a whole."[16]

Johnson's notion of kinship does not imply that there are no "distinctions between human beings and other forms of life," only that the relationship of humanity to the rest of creation should be marked not by superiority, but interconnectedness and mutuality. In "Creation and an Environmental Ethic," Catholic theologians Michael and Kenneth Himes demonstrate how the idea of kinship (or *companionship*) is deeply compatible with the fundamental "sacramental vision" of both Catholic and Protestant theology. As the Himes brothers note, it is a basic Christian conviction that "every creature, human and non-human, animate and inanimate, can be a sacrament," a sign of the love and presence of God.[17]

Perhaps no Christian has articulated this human kinship with creation as beautifully as St. Francis of Assisi (1181–1228) did in his famous "Canticle of Brother Sun," which proclaims that humans are sisters and brothers to all creation because we are all fashioned by the creative hand of God. Thomas Berry allies himself with Francis as he calls us to move into "the ecological age," and Johnson envisions herself as a sister with Francis as she invites us to recognize our kinship with all of God's creatures.

CHARACTER:
Who Shall We Be on This Earth?

As the U.S. Catholic bishops note in "Renewing the Earth," we humans are part and parcel of God's creation, and we, who are fashioned in the image and likeness of God, are called in a unique way to love and care for that creation. "Men and women," the bishops report, "bear a unique responsibility to safeguard the created world and by their creative labor even to enhance it.... The human family is charged with preserving the beauty, diversity and integrity of nature as well as fostering its productivity."[18] The Evangelical Lutheran statement on the environment makes a similar point, noting that "Scripture speaks of humanity's kinship with other creatures,...[and] humans, in service to God, have special roles on behalf of the whole of creation."[19] We, who are ourselves creatures, are to take care of creation as God takes care of us.

In the concrete, we tend to live out this calling to care for (and repair) creation within the various roles and relationships that make up the web of our lives as persons and cocreatures. For often it is in our roles as parents, consumers, citizens or perhaps employers or stockholders that we experience and work out our "ecological vocation," that we come to recognize and respond to the moral claims made upon us by our neighbors and all of God's creation. It is also within these roles that we make the sorts of choices that will shape our character and influence the sorts of communities that we create and live within.

Before recommending the particular "ecological virtues" required of Christian parents, consumers, citizens or employers, we will suggest a number of basic convictions and commitments that ought to be characteristic of every Christian.[20] First, aware of our own identity as creatures and of the sacramental nature of all God's creation, Christians need to approach this creation (which manifests the glory and grace of God) with reverence and humility. As St. Francis argued, we are sister and brother to the stars, the seals and the sand, and whatever "dominion" or "stewardship" we exercise toward our fellow creatures is to be a service of love and gratitude offered with a reverent and joyful humility. Second, recognizing our basic interconnectedness with the rest of humanity and creation, every Christian must embrace a spirit of solidarity that is global and environmental. This solidarity demands our commitment to equity and justice for the poor, ensuring that they receive a fair and sufficient share of God's creation. And this solidarity means that we recognize our basic kinship with all of creation and commit ourselves to ensuring that all God's creatures have the space and protection to grow and flourish. Third, to make certain that we have local and global economies that are truly sustainable and that balance the need for jobs and development against the need for biodiversity and a safe environment, we will need to practice prudence, and (particularly those well-off Christians in wealthy nations) a certain simplicity. Creating healthy economies that are just to the poor and respectful of the environment will not be easy and will require a great deal of wisdom and good judgment. And for those of us living in societies where consumption and pollution have already begun to run amok it will also demand that we make some fairly radical lifestyle and structural changes, reflecting a genuine frugality and simplicity of life.

Specific Roles

Parents/Teachers. One of the primary places we experience our ecological vocation is in our roles as parents and teachers. For it is in our homes and schools that our children will first learn about the ties and duties that bind them to the rest of God's creation. It is in these places that they will come to see the world around them as a sacrament of God's grace, a nurturing and welcoming home to be shared with others, or a mass of lifeless matter to be manipulated, consumed and polluted at will. As the U.S. Catholic bishops note, "…it is from parents that children will learn love of the earth and delight in nature. It is at home that they develop the habits of self-control, concern and care which lie at the heart of environmental morality." And it is from their teachers, and from all who mentor and care for them, that they will learn "a love for God's creation, [and] a respect for nature."[21]

Indeed, being a parent or a teacher ties us not only to our own children and students but to all children and students everywhere. It also ties us to our children's children and to our students' students and to generations and generations of children and students yet to come. In parenting and teaching we are paying a debt to those who took care of us, our parents and teachers. And we are keeping a promise to all the children and students yet unborn, to take care of their inheritance. Even more, in passing on life and caring for our young we are connected to all life forms and every creature that gives life to those who come after it. As St. Francis would say, in being parents or teachers we are siblings to every form of life that gives birth and nurtures its young, to every being that produces seed or egg or newborn. Finally, being parents and teachers ties us to the "stuff" of which our children and their flesh are made, to the atoms, molecules, cells, air and water that make us up, and to the vitamins, nutrients, minerals and sunshine that make them healthy, lively and happy. Being a parent or a teacher ties us to all of life and all creation and obliges us to take care and serve that creation with love, awe and respect.

As parents and teachers we can help our children and students to love and care for creation in a number of ways. We can introduce them to the wonders of nature: visit parks, zoos, forests, farms, the seaside or the mountains; teach them to garden, care for pets, keep an aquarium or study the heavens through a telescope. We can teach them about the need to share our planet's bounty with all peoples, to make a place for the poor at the banquet of creation and to make room for and protect all of God's creatures. We can educate them about the dangers of consuming too much and of polluting our water, air and land. We can try

to instill in them a deep sense of reverence and kinship toward all creation. Certainly our most effective teaching tool in all of this will be
our own example. They will watch and imitate how we behave toward
the created world, how we care for the earth and make room for the
poor. They will be taught by how we consume or conserve goods and
energy, how we recycle and reuse or pollute and discard, how we shop
and commute. Thus as parents and teachers we will need to practice
what we preach, embracing a reverence for creation, a concern for the
poor and a simplicity or frugality in our lifestyles. We must live lightly
and respectfully on the earth.

Consumers. A second important way in which we are called to
live out our ecological vocation is in our role as consumers. For the
choices we make as consumers affect others and the environment. Do
we commute by driving alone, carpooling, taking the bus or riding a
bike? Do we buy foods that have been treated with pesticides or
genetically engineered? Do we purchase goods from companies with
poor environmental track records? How often do we shop for the
newest products or recycle or reuse old ones? What do we do with
the waste generated by our consumption?

As we saw in our discussion of consumerism in the chapter on economic justice, America (and much of the industrial West) consumes a
hugely disproportionate amount of the earth's resources. In *Earth in
the Balance* Al Gore noted that "our civilization is holding ever more
tightly to its habit of consuming larger and larger quantities every year
of coal, oil, fresh air and water, trees, topsoil, and the thousand other
substances we rip from the crust of the earth."[22] At present the United
States and other highly industrialized nations (which together account
for far less than 25 percent of the world's population) "consume 75%
of the world resources and account for 75% of all solid and toxic
waste."[23] Needless to say, these patterns of consumption and waste—
which increased steadily throughout the 1990s—threaten both the
poor and the planet. Indeed, as Pope John Paul II has argued, these
avaricious and addictive patterns of consumption are an injustice
against "masses of people living in conditions of misery at the very

lowest level of subsistence," and pose a real threat of "ecological break-down."[24]

If we are going to be responsible consumers, then, we need first to embrace a spirit of repentance, turning away from greedy and addictive consumption and seeking to reverse the harms we have done to our neighbor and planet. As the U.S. Catholic bishops argue, "...we in the developed world are obligated to address our own wasteful and destructive use of resources as a matter of top priority."[25] Examining our individual and collective consciences as consumers, we will need to acknowledge our ecological sins and begin to work toward a certain amount of environmental sobriety.

In line with this repentance or sobriety, we will need as consumers to practice justice toward the poor, to future generations and even to all of creation. As consumers that means we will need to pay a fair price for products and services, a price that will allow the poor to support themselves without needing to further harm or degrade their environments. Indeed, we must be willing to pay for the full environmental costs of producing, delivering and disposing of the goods and resources we use. Otherwise, these costs will be borne by the poor or passed on to future generations. And it also means making choices as consumers that do not endanger the poor or the environment through continued deforestation, pollution, soil erosion, extinction or global warming.

Practicing this justice and ensuring genuine equity for the poor and sustainability and biodiversity for the environment will require a great deal of prudence and temperance on behalf of consumers. We will need to inform ourselves about the environmental impact of the products and services we buy, and about the environmental practices of the companies we buy from. Most of all, as we noted in our discussion of the duties of consumers in the chapter on economic ethics, we will need to embrace a spirit of simplicity, frugality or temperance. As James Nash has argued, consumers in the United States and other industrialized nations are creating ecological havoc because we are living "beyond our planetary means," writing environmental checks that rob the poor and promise to bankrupt future generations.[26]

Citizens. We also live out our ecological vocation as citizens. In democratic societies we have a voice in the conduct of the communities and nations to which we belong. And we shape those communities and nations—and our environments—by informing ourselves about public policies, becoming involved in community and political organizations, collaborating with others in community projects, and—of course—voting for various candidates and pieces of legislation.

At the same time we are not just citizens of our own particular nation. We are also citizens of the planet, members of a global human community, tied to our fellow citizens in every other land by a web of interlocking rights and responsibilities. And as citizens of the planet we have an obligation to work for a larger, planetary common good.

As citizens of individual nations we are able to make an impact on a number of ecological problems, and should do so. As the U.S. Catholic bishops note, "...as citizens, each of us needs to participate in [the] debate over how our nation best protects our national ecological heritage, limits pollution, allocates environmental costs and plans for the future."[27] As citizens we can and should do things about ensuring clean air and water in our communities, region and perhaps in our country. We can pass laws encouraging more efficient uses of energy by consumers and industry. We can take action to reduce consumption and waste.

Still, many of the environmental concerns and problems that we face—air and water pollution, resource depletion, climate changes, deforestation and the loss of biodiversity—are ultimately beyond the reach of individual persons and local or even national communities. Their causes and cures are too large, too complex for any single person or state to address effectively. These environmental problems and challenges are international, or even global in scope, and they require the combined and coordinated efforts of the whole human community.

Because of this, citizens of every nation must develop a sense of solidarity. As Pope John Paul II notes, "...the ecological crisis reveals the urgent moral need for a new solidarity, especially in relations between developing nations and those that are highly industrialized. States must increasingly share responsibility, in complementary ways, for the promotion of a natural and social environment that is both peaceful and healthy."[28] According to the pope, this virtue of solidarity "is not a feeling of vague compassion or shallow distress at the misfortunes of so many people, both near and far. On the contrary, it is a *firm and persevering determination* to commit oneself to the *common good;* that is to say the good of all and of each individual, because we are *all* really responsible for *all.*"[29] Thus, solidarity enables a person not only to have a feeling of concern or compassion for others, and indeed for all creation, but to make a commitment to stand with the poor and the suffering and to act as advocates on their behalf.

Acting out of this solidarity citizens will need to practice social justice, making sure that they and their country are paying their fair share of the costs of addressing the present ecological crisis and are not consuming more than their fair share of the earth's resources. At the same time many citizens in the United States and other developed nations will need a certain amount of moral courage to speak out on behalf of the poor and the environment, and to call themselves and their fellow citizens to adopt lifestyles that are simpler and more frugal. In a society where more is always better, the idea that we should live more simply so that others may simply live will never be a particularly popular one.

Employers, Board Members and Stockholders. Finally, we also live out our ecological vocations in our roles as employers, board members and stockholders—and indeed a vast number of Americans currently own stocks directly or indirectly through pension plans and mutual funds. Although these various roles are distinct from one another and undoubtedly carry with them differing ethical responsibilities, they do have something in common: employers, board members and stockholders all exercise important roles in the conduct of corporations in regard to the environment.

This is important, for corporations, especially multinational corporations, are critical moral actors in regard to the environment. Without diminishing the real importance of the choices we make as consumers or citizens, it is also true that the conduct of large businesses and corporations has an enormous impact on the health and welfare of the environment. Indeed, given their wealth, power and size, the environmental impact of national and multinational corporations can hardly be exaggerated.

Corporations can harm the environment in two basic ways. First, through their mining, harvesting, manufacturing, delivery, disposal and other processes, corporations are major consumers of energy and other resources, major polluters of our water, land and air, and major producers of toxic waste and garbage. This has long been true in the United States and other developed industrialized nations, but it is particularly troublesome in poorer developing countries where there are insufficient environmental restraints on the conduct of corporations. In these less developed countries—eager for foreign investment and jobs—corporations have significantly more freedom to exploit natural resources and pollute the environment, often without having to pay even a small part of the environmental clean-up or repair bill.[30] Second, when corporations operating in less developed nations exploit local labor by paying workers wages below the subsistence level they contribute to an ongoing cycle of poverty and environmental degradation. As James Nash notes, poverty is a leading cause of ecological disaster, for "poor people are forced to use their natural resources beyond the point of sustainability simply to survive in the present."[31] Thus, corporations that underpay their workers exploit both labor and the environment, adding to deforestation, soil erosion, desertification, habitat degradation and other forms of environmental exhaustion.

Traditionally it has been assumed by many that the primary (even exclusive) purpose of corporations is to make a profit for its stockholders. Indeed, the economist Milton Friedman has argued that "there is one and only one social responsibility of business—to use its resources and engage in activities engaged to increase its profits."[32] Still, corporations and their executives and stockholders also have ties and obligations to a number of other "stakeholders," persons and communities that contribute to or are affected by the work of the corporation. These include, among others, employees, customers, the local and national communities where the corporations are located and the local, regional and global environments affected by the consumption and pollution of these businesses.

Living out our ecological vocation as stockholders, employers and board members demands that we practice social and ecological justice, that we exploit neither workers nor the environment and that we ensure safety and sustainability for both. This will require diligent study and research, and will, yet again, demand prudence and good judgment. It will also mean practicing that solidarity about which we have already spoken, taking a larger and longer view of the common good than one defined by corporate profits.

CHOICES:
What Shall We Do on This Earth?

In this section we will look at three kinds of choices in the arena of environmental ethics. We will ask what is to be done about our depletion and destruction of the earth's resources, take a look at the issue of environmental discrimination or racism, and examine the question of population growth.

Depletion and Destruction of Natural Resources

The Voices of Experience

The Voice of History. Since the invention of agriculture humans have placed a good deal of stress on their local environments. As Clive Ponting argues in *A Green History of the World,* "...the most important task in all human history has been to find a way of extracting from the different ecosystems in which people have lived enough resources for maintaining life—food, clothing, shelter, energy and other material goods."[33] And indeed, humans have generally exploited their environments to the best of their ability (or technology) and have often exhausted these places and been forced

to move on to greener pastures.[34] Ancient farmers eventually transformed Babylon's Fertile Crescent into a desert, and the Roman
Empire's North African breadbasket is now part of the Sahara.

Still, in the past two centuries the environmental impact of
humans has increased exponentially, becoming both global and overwhelming. Improving technologies, the expansion of humans into
every terrestrial ecosystem and the sextupling of the human population have all contributed to the fact that we now find ourselves
affecting our local and global ecosystems in unprecedented and probably irreversible ways. As 3,500 of the planet's scientists argued in a
1992 statement, "...our massive tampering with the world's interdependent web of life...could trigger widespread adverse effects,
including unpredictable collapses of critical biological systems whose
interactions and dynamics we only imperfectly understand."[35]

Contemporary Voices. A growing chorus of experts warn that
humans are living "beyond our environmental means," spending creation's inheritance far faster than it can be renewed or replenished.
We see this dangerous depletion of the earth's resources in a variety of
places. Every year we burn "an amount of fossil fuels that it took a
million years to produce," and currently expect to run out of petroleum in forty years and natural gas in sixty years.[36] A 1998 Worldwatch report notes that "half the forests that once covered the earth
are gone, deforestation has been accelerating in the last thirty
years,...[and] each year at least another 16 million hectares (about 40
million acres) of natural forest are razed—an area the size of Washington state."[37] The Philippines has lost 92 percent of its rain forest.
Brazil has lost 95 percent of its Atlantic coastal forest, and old growth
forests in West Africa, India, Madagascar and elsewhere are a tenth of
their original size. "By the middle of the next century...tropical forest will exist virtually nowhere outside of protected areas—that is,
national parks, wildlife refuges, and other official reserves."[38]

Meanwhile, poor agricultural practices and overgrazing are leading
to the degradation and desertification of more and more of our crop-
lands. Farmers lose about twenty-four billion tons of topsoil from their
cropland every year, and population growth is currently outstripping

the growth of irrigated lands. Furthermore, our expanding use of water for agriculture, manufacturing and other purposes is already straining local and global fresh water supplies. In the United States the Ogallala Aquifer, one of the world's largest groundwater reserves, has already been half depleted from irrigation. Meanwhile, in most of the world's poorest and most populous countries aquifers and groundwater are being drained much faster than they can be refilled by rainwater. About 1.2 billion people have no access to clean water. Nearly three billion have no sanitation (sewage, toilets or latrines). And more than five million die each year of preventable waterborne illnesses like diarrhea, dysentery and cholera.[39]

This depletion of creation's bounty has also led to the destruction and degradation of much of our environment and of a good deal of life on this planet. Our consumption of fossil fuels and production of greenhouse gases has opened a dangerous hole in our planet's stratospheric ozone layer and contributed to a global warming pattern that threatens to unleash all sorts of havoc on humans and other life forms. And as a result of human-induced deforestation and habitat degradation we currently find ourselves in what may be the most massive extinction of species in sixty-five million years. Conservative estimates indicate that we could lose a third of all species on the planet before this process is done. (Others suggest numbers as high as two-thirds.)[40] At present nearly half of the 233 nonhuman species of primates are facing extinction, while about a quarter of the vertebrate species are considered to be in serious trouble. According to a 1998 Worldwatch report, "25% of mammals and amphibian species, 11% of birds, 20% of reptiles, and 34% of fish species surveyed so far are threatened with extinction."[41]

Still, there are a number of "cornucopians," like the late economist Julian Simon, who argue that human inventiveness will be able to solve all the problems created by population growth, consumption and pollution, and that neither our environment nor the human race are seriously endangered by current trends. These critics suggest that the alarms being sounded about global warming, massive extinctions and the depletion and destruction of creation's bounty are fundamentally mistaken and that we need not alter our lifestyles or undergo a radical ecological conversion to save the planet or humanity.[42]

Voices from the Margins. Although we will treat this perspective in more depth in our discussion of environmental racism or discrimination, there are two points to be made here. First, as the World Commission on Environment and Development noted, the economic gap between the world's rich and poor "is the planet's main 'environmental' problem."[43] The global and national economic inequalities we discussed in the chapter on economic justice are major contributors to—and consequences of—environmental degradation. All too often the poor are shoved and squeezed into the most degraded environments, forced to labor under the most environmentally disastrous conditions and pressured to further deplete and degrade these environments simply to stay alive. And so poverty is a major cause and consequence of our exploitation of creation. Second, as we will see later, the poor (particularly women and minorities) tend to receive the least environmental protection and tend to suffer the worst environmental deprivations.

Scripture. As we've seen, a number of critics (like Lynn White) argue that Scripture actually supports humanity's reckless exploitation of creation, calling us in Genesis 1:28 to "fill the earth and subdue it; and have dominion over the fish of the sea and over the birds of the air and over every living thing that moves upon the earth." And indeed, there can be little doubt that many have interpreted "dominion" language as lifting humans above creation, and as giving us permission to take whatever we desired from the earth's bounty or do whatever we liked to our fellow creatures.[44] Still, a closer examination of Scripture gives us a more varied message.

First, as we read in the first creation narrative in Genesis 1:1–31, all of creation has been made by God, and all of it is good, indeed *very* good. "God saw everything that he had made, and indeed, it was very good." Indeed, Scripture teaches not only that creation is good, but that—as the poet Gerard Manley Hopkins notes—"the world is charged with the grandeur of God."[45] In Wisdom 13:3–5 we read that

God's glory and wisdom shine forth in her creation, and in Daniel 3:74–81 (Septuagint) all of creation is urged to sing praises to their creator. In other words, Scripture teaches that *all* of creation is both sacred and a sacrament of God's glory.

Second, Scripture makes it clear that God did not just make the earth, but continues to love and care for all of creation. In Matthew 6:26–30 we are reminded of how God feeds the birds of the sky and clothes the grass in the fields. In Job 38:26 we are told that God makes it rain even in deserts and wildernesses where no human lives. And in Genesis 9:8–17, when God promises never again to destroy the earth, she makes a covenant not only with Noah and his human descendents, but with "every living creature of all flesh that is on the earth." Moreover, in Romans 8:18–25 we learn it is not just humans who are redeemed and saved by Christ's death and resurrection, but all of creation.

Third, Scripture teaches that humans are not *above* or *outside* creation, but part and parcel of the created order. In Genesis 2:7, 9 and 19 we read that humans are made of the same soil and clay that God used to create the plants and trees that cover the earth, the birds that fill the sky and all the animals that roam the planet. And in Job 38–39 and Psalm 104 the biblical authors remind us that humans are not elevated above creation, but live and work alongside all God's other creatures, depending upon God's protection and care like everyone and everything else around them. Added to this, in the New Testament there are a number of passages that display the conviction that it is not only human beings who have been redeemed—re-created—by Christ, but that in some mysterious way *all of creation* shares in Christ's redemptive work (Col 1: 15–20; Rev 21:1–8).

Fourth, in Scripture humans are portrayed as companions to the rest of creation. In Genesis 1:27 we learn that humans are made in the image of God *as* male and female. According to Michael and Kenneth Himes, this means that "God is relational," and that "to be the image of this God, the human being must be relational," not only with other humans, but with all of creation itself.[46] In Genesis 1:31 it is the *whole community of creation* that God blesses as *very* good, a community into which humans come as cocreatures, kin and companions. And in Genesis 2:18 God notes that "it is not good that the man should be alone," and brings forth all sorts of animals as companions from the same soil as humans had been fashioned. Thus, even if the partnership between humans is different from the kinship we have with other creatures, Scripture teaches that humans come to the rest of creation as companions, and not merely as users or consumers.

Fifth, we learn in Scripture that humans have a special role *within* creation, and that this role is one of service and love, to be exercised with wisdom and generosity. In Genesis 2:15 we read that humans are to cultivate and care for the earth. Given the sacredness and sacramentality of all creation, as well as our kinship with the rest of God's creatures, it is clear this biblical call to be "good stewards" means more than a duty to take care of creation as if it were a piece of property, or even a valuable inheritance. Rather, we are, in the language of Christian ethicist Enda McDonagh, to "recognize, respect and respond to" the moral claims made on us by our fellow creatures.[47]

As we saw in the chapter on economic justice, a good deal of our duty to be good stewards has to do with sharing the bounty of creation with other humans, especially with the poor. So in Leviticus 19:9–10 landowners are told to leave the "gleanings" of their harvest for the poor, and in Leviticus 25 those who had accumulated great estates were told to return the lands to their impoverished former owners and to cancel the debts of the poor.

Still, it is also true that Scripture calls us to show a basic regard and respect for creation itself. In Exodus 20:8–11 we read of our duty to let all God's creatures rest on the Sabbath, and in Leviticus 25 the instructions governing the sabbatical and jubilee years instruct the Hebrews to give the land itself a rest every seven years. God has placed moral limits on what we can take from and do to creation, and these limits are not just about taking care of human needs. They are also about reverencing creation itself.

Tradition. It must be admitted that the Christian tradition's record on environmental concerns is somewhat spotty. Given its longstanding support for a notion of human "dominion" that did little to prevent the exploitation of creation's bounty, it's easy to see why Nash believes "Christianity does bear part of the burden of guilt for our ecological crisis."[48] At the same time Catholic social thought has only very recently begun to turn its attention to environmental concerns, and ecology has not yet received the sort of attention it deserves.

Nevertheless, in the past three decades there has been a growing concern about the environment in Christian ethics and Catholic social teachings. In general, most of this concern has been about the dangers our exploitation of creation poses to humanity, particularly to the poor and future generations. In 1971 Pope Paul VI noted that "man is suddenly becoming aware that by an ill-considered exploitation of nature he risks destroying it and becoming in his turn the victim of this degradation," and warned that we were currently "creating an environment for tomorrow which may well be intolerable."[49] That same year the world synod of Catholic bishops criticized rich nations for unfairly depleting and destroying the planet's resources, robbing both the poor and future generations of their rightful share of God's bounty.[50] And in their 1991 statement on the environment, the U.S. Catholic bishops underscored the ways our exploitation of nature threatens humanity present and future, particularly the poor. "The whole human race suffers as a result of environmental blight, and generations yet unborn will bear the cost for our failure to act today. But in most countries today, including our own, it is the poor and the powerless who most directly bear the burden of current environmental carelessness."[51]

This focus on the ways environmental blight harms humanity— and in particular the poor and future generations—reflects three central principles of Catholic social teachings. First, as we are reminded time and time again, "at the center of all Catholic social teaching [is] the dignity of the human person. The human person is the clearest reflection of God's presence in the world; all of the Church's work in pursuit of both justice and peace is designed to protect and promote the dignity of every person."[52] Thus, in many ways Christian reflections on environmental justice have been seen as an extension of Christian social justice, focused on the dignity of the human person.

Harm to the environment is seen as bad *because* it harms humans, and good stewardship is required if we are to be just to other humans. Second, as we saw in our discussion of economic justice, Catholic social thought affirms the "universal purpose of created goods." God's creation is intended for the good of all humans, and the poor and future generations are not to be cheated or robbed by the greed of a few. That would be bad stewardship. And third, the call for "a preferential option for the poor" certainly forbids patterns of consumption and pollution that rob the poor of their fair share of the earth's bounty.

Still, a growing number of Christian voices have begun to argue that exploiting creation is wrong not simply because it harms humans, but because it harms creation itself, which deserves our regard and respect and makes moral claims upon us. In his 1987 encyclical "On Social Concern," Pope John Paul II calls for "respect for the beings which constitute the natural world." And in his 1990 statement on "Peace with All Creation," the pope notes that "respect for life and for the dignity of the human person extends also to the rest of creation, which is called to join man in praising God."[53] And, as we've already noted, both Protestant theologian Larry Rasmussen (among others) and the Evangelical Lutheran Church's social statement "Caring for Creation" remind us of our kinship with other creatures.

Those challenging us to broaden our moral vision and develop a deeper respect for the integrity and blessedness of all creation point to the Christian doctrines of creation and sacramentality. For Christians believe that *all* of creation is fashioned by God, that *all* of creation is very good, and that *all* of creation is shot through with God's grace and grandeur, and mediates that glory and grace to us. Thus, they argue, Christians ought never to see creation as merely an instrument or tool for human satisfaction or happiness.

These Christian voices also challenge us to move beyond a certain anthropocentrism (what Carolyn Merchant has called "homocentrism") and reject a worldview that elevates humans above and outside of the rest of creation. As we saw earlier, Catholic theologians and ethicists like Michael and Kenneth Himes and Elizabeth Johnson and Protestant scholars such as James Nash, James Gustafson and Larry

Rasmussen call for a Christian *ecocentrism* that acknowledges our interconnectedness and our mutual interdependence with the rest of creation. For these authors it is not enough that we repair or rehabilitate our notions of dominion or stewardship so as to reduce or eliminate exploitation. Rather, we need to acknowledge our deeper companionship and kinship with the rest of creation.[54]

Formulating a Christian Response. What, then, ought we to do about the ongoing depletion and destruction of natural resources?

Some Basic Christian Convictions. The mechanistic worldview, which has dominated much of our thinking since the start of the industrial age, needs to be replaced with a more authentically biblical, Christian and ecological perspective. Nature can no longer be viewed as an object to be dominated, manipulated or consumed at will, and humans can no longer consider themselves as above or outside of creation. Instead, Scripture and tradition call us to see the earth as a holy gift of God and a sacrament evoking our gratitude, awe and reverence. These voices also challenge us to recognize our own deep and interdependent connection and kinship with all other creatures, and to reject a hierarchical view that ignores the mutuality of our relation to the rest of creation. And though the sanctity and sacramentality of creation does not mean we cannot cultivate it and feed ourselves from this bounty, it does mean that our use of the goods of the earth should be marked by appreciation, moderation, reverence and justice.

Drawing again from both Scripture and tradition, it is evident that our faith charges us to recognize that the goods of the earth are meant for the use of all. Both the creation narratives of Genesis 1 and 2 and Catholic social teaching's notion of the "universal purpose of created goods" drive home the point that God has given the bounty of creation to be shared with all humanity. And biblical concerns about the *anawim* ("God's little ones"), as well as the contemporary church's call for a "preferential option for the poor" make it clear that we are not to hoard or consume the goods of creation in ways that leave anyone hungry, or thirsty, or naked, or homeless. Though accumulating wealth and amassing larger measures of private property may not in themselves be wrong, they are justified only if reasonable measures have been taken to ensure that the needs of all—especially the poor—have been met first.

Shifting our perspective and priorities in this way will undoubtedly require a radical about-face. Seeing to it that our personal patterns of restraint and conservation as well as our social patterns of production and consumption are more ecologically and socially responsible means we will need to embrace a real conversion in regard to how we live on this earth. The changes called for are not small.

Our use of natural resources will need to be both sustainable and proportionate. We can no longer continue to live beyond our planetary means. We must begin to change our patterns of consumption and pollution in fundamental ways. We can no longer take things out of the earth or nature faster than they can be replenished. Nor can we put things into our environment faster than nature can safely recycle or repair our intrusions. At the same time we must apply a standard of proportionality to our actions. We must be as certain as possible that we are not doing more harm than good to our environment, that we are keeping an accurate audit of our actions, weighing the full and future environmental costs of our construction, consumption and pollution.

Some Difficult Questions. How exactly are we to balance the need for economic growth and development in poor countries with the need to set limits on our growing depletion and destruction of global resources? It is evident that economic development is a necessary part of any solution to global poverty. It is also clear that as the poor gain economic security, population growth begins to level and drop off. But it is just as true that increasing prosperity and industrialization put more and more demands and pressures on our environment. And nearly everyone agrees the planet could not sustain the environmental stress of having poor nations like China and India consume and pollute at the same rate as the United States and other developed countries. What, then, are we to do to create a global economy that is both just and sustainable?

How are we to balance the needs of humans (for jobs, living space, energy) with the needs of other creatures? Admitting that we need to move beyond any notions of dominion or stewardship entitling humans to take and pollute as they see fit, what exactly are to be our priorities when making choices about policies that may have some negative impact on other species or life forms? Are human concerns to be given any priority? How significant should the weight be that we give to other creatures?

Third, how are we to balance our obligations to present and future generations of humans? Do living persons have any priority over future generations of humans? Are present concerns to be treated as equal to future concerns? How are we to make such choices?

Environmental Racism

As we have already seen, there is an intimate connection between poverty and environmental blight. Time and time again the poor are forced to live and work in the most degraded and toxic environments, and their desperate and unjust poverty all too often leads them to further degrade and deplete these environments. Recently there has been increasing evidence that this environmental discrimination is directed not only against the poor, but in particular against the poor who belong to racial and ethnic minorities.

The Voices of Experience. On this particular question it is critical that we attend primarily to the voices of those in the margins, and to those who stand with the human victims of environmental discrimination. Thus, in listening to the voices of experience we will focus first on the victims of environmental racism at home, and then on the voices of the global victims of this discrimination.

The Voices from the Margins: At Home.[55] In its 1987 study, *Toxic Wastes and Race,* the United Church of Christ's Commission for Racial Justice found that in the United States "communities with greater minority percentages of the population were more likely to be the sites of commercial hazardous waste facilities."[56] The study (later confirmed by other investigators) indicated that 60 percent of

African Americans lived in communities with abandoned toxic-waste sites, that three of the five biggest commercial hazardous waste landfills were in predominantly black or Hispanic communities and that minority neighborhoods in major urban areas were much more likely to have garbage dumps, incinerators or landfills sites than their white counterparts.[57] Indeed, the "study researched all 415 of the hazardous waste facilities then in existence in the United States and determined that people of color were about twice as likely as white people to live in the towns that hosted such facilities."[58] What's more, in 1994 the UCC published *Toxic Wastes and Race Revisited,* which found that things had not improved since 1987, but that "people of color today are even more likely than whites to live in communities with commercial hazardous waste than they were a decade ago."[59]

Nor do minority communities receive the same government protection or assistance when it comes to cleaning up toxic sites. A *National Law Journal* article reporting on clean-up efforts at 1,177 toxic-waste sites noted that federal penalties for pollution "in white communities were 46 percent higher than in minority communities, [and that] abandoned hazardous-waste sites in minority areas take 20 percent longer to be placed on the national priority action list than those in white areas."[60]

Not surprisingly, numerous studies indicate that "racial and ethnic communities suffer from the most severe environmental pollution."[61] In Washington, D.C., New York, Chicago, Denver, Los Angeles and San Francisco the air pollution levels are higher in minority neighborhoods, and around the country blacks and Hispanics are more likely than whites to live in areas with poor air quality.

Nor is it only minorities living in cities and towns that suffer from environmental discrimination. In the United States more than 95 percent of migrant farm workers are Latino, African American, Afro-Caribbean or Asian. These workers (and their children) are exposed to a wide range of health risks from pesticides, including a fourfold increase in the risk of skin disease, increased risks of developing several different kinds of cancer and an increased occurrence of sterility, birth defects, brain damage and Parkinson's.[62] Meanwhile, Native American communities bear a disproportionate amount of the environmental burden from the mining and processing of uranium. Members of the Navajo community in particular suffer from a variety of radiation diseases, and many Native American communities have to live with illegally high levels of lead, thorium and radium in their water supply.[63]

The Voices from the Margins: Abroad. Environmental racism, however, is not just a domestic problem. For centuries western European colonial powers drove indigenous peoples off their lands, cut down huge and bountiful forests, polluted the air and water with mining operations and replaced local farmers and subsistence agriculture with massive plantations and ranches, growing cash crops and cattle for export and trade. In the twentieth century rich landowners and multinational corporations (including mining and logging companies, as well as major agribusinesses) have continued these practices, and the results have been devastating for indigenous peoples, trapped in an accelerating cycle of poverty and environmental degradation. When indigenous communities are forced off their lands to make room for plantations and ranches, they must move into more remote and less suitable areas, either cutting down forests and overgrazing and eroding thin topsoil or moving into polluted and overcrowded barrios and slums surrounding major urban centers. Either way, they find themselves in increasingly overtaxed and degraded environments.[64]

At the same time the poor in developing countries find themselves more and more endangered by the export of pesticides, toxic waste, and "dirty industries." International agrochemical companies have been increasingly successful in marketing dangerous pesticides in developing nations, including many that are currently banned in the United States and other developed nations. As a result, one 1990 study indicated that as many as twenty-five million agricultural workers in the developing world are poisoned each year.[65] Meanwhile, as environmental restrictions have been tightened in industrial nations, toxic waste has often been shipped overseas to less developed countries in desperate need of cash but without any resources to protect their citizens from the long-term damage of these hazardous materials. Or, when shipping waste is illegal, "dirty industries" and manufacturing plants are moved in their entirety into countries with lax environmental rules. This is the case with many of the more than 2,000 *maquiladoras* (manufacturing plants) just over the U.S.-Mexican border. Laboring for a fraction of the wages that would be paid to U.S. workers, more than half a million Mexicans find themselves without the environmental protection or safeguards available just a few miles north.[66]

Scripture. Within Scripture we find three themes that are helpful in addressing the problem of environmental racism. First, it seems clear that the bounty of creation is not to be hoarded by a few, but shared among the whole human community, and that those who amass great possessions and drive the poor off the land and into hunger and desperation are sinning gravely. Second, as we saw in our reflection on affirmative action, it is evident that Scripture does not condone discrimination, but calls us to overcome its presence and effects wherever we encounter them. And third, the Bible consistently reminds us to show a particular concern for the *anawim* and to come to the aid of those marginalized, oppressed and disenfranchised by our political, economic and cultural systems. In particular, we are called to make sure that the poor have access to the bounty of the land.

In Genesis 1:28–30 God lays out the bounty of creation and promises not only that there will be food for all humans, but indeed for every living creature. God's creation, then, is meant to provide for everyone. Commenting on this passage, Pope John Paul II has noted, "God gave the earth to the whole human race for the sustenance of all its members, without excluding or favoring anyone."[67]

Not surprisingly, then, the classic Hebrew prophets are scathing in their condemnation of wealthy landowners who drive the poor off their land and deprive them of a share of God's bounty. Isaiah 5:8–10 chastises those "who join house to house, who add field to field, until there is room for no one but you, and you are left to live alone in the midst of the land!...[your] houses shall be desolate...."And in Amos 5:11 the prophet rails against the injustice and greed of the wealthy, saying that "because you trample on the poor and take from them levies of grain, you have built houses of hewn stone, but you shall not live in them...."

And, as we have already noted in other places, Leviticus 19:9–10 and 25 command that provisions be made to ensure that even the landless poor have access to creation's bounty and that no one be permanently disenfranchised from the land. Landowners and farmers are to allow the poor to go through their fields, picking the gleanings of the crop. And in the Jubilee Year the debts of the poor are to be cancelled and they are to be allowed to return to their lands. So too, Deuteronomy 26:12–13 reminds the Hebrews that they are to set aside enough of their harvest so the alien, widow and orphan are likewise taken care of.

Scripture offers a number of reasons to reject any form of racial or ethnic discrimination. In Genesis 1:27 we note that all humans are made in the image and likeness of God, and in Genesis 3:20 the biblical author reports that we are all members of the same human family. In the New Testament we read in Galatians 3:27–28 that "there is no longer Jew or Greek, there is no longer slave or free, there is no longer male and female; for all of you are one in Christ Jesus." And in James 2:1 we find a direct attack on discrimination. "My brothers and sisters, do you with your acts of favoritism really believe in our glorious Lord Jesus Christ?" For Christians, James goes on to note, are not to prefer the rich and well born to the poor person dressed in dirty clothes.

Indeed, if there is any preference to be given, Scripture seems to give it to the *anawim,* who consist of widows, orphans and resident aliens. Time and time again the Bible reveals a God who stands on the side of the marginalized, the dispossessed and the oppressed. In Deuteronomy 24: 17–18 the Hebrews are reminded to take special care of the dispossessed, for they too were once in such a lowly state. "You shall not deprive a resident alien or an orphan of justice; you shall not take a widow's garment in pledge. Remember that you were a slave in Egypt and the Lord your God redeemed you from there; therefore I command you to do this." And in Deuteronomy 10:18 we read that the Lord "executes justice for the orphan and the widow, and...loves the strangers, providing them food and clothing."

So too in the New Testament there is ample evidence that disciples of Christ are to stand with the poor and oppressed. In Luke 4:18–19 Jesus announces that he has come to proclaim good news to the poor and release for prisoners, and in Matthew 25:31–46 we are told that whoever comes to the aid of the least of our sisters and brothers comes to the aid of Christ. Certainly one of the most powerful New Testament parables about our duties to come to the aid of those in the margins is that of the rich man and the beggar Lazarus (Luke 16:19–31). In this tale the nameless rich man commits no real offense against the unnoticed beggar just outside his doorway. Indeed, his only crime is that he does not notice the poor man. And yet for this he is condemned, suggesting that for a Christian overlooking the dispossessed is a serious sin.

Tradition. Throughout the past decade Christian theologians and ethicists like Elizabeth Johnson, Larry Rasmussen, Brian Massingale and Emilie Townes have added their voices to a growing chorus of complaints about environmental racism—as well as other forms of environmental injustice committed against the poor and women.[68] Massingale argues that "there is now mounting, indeed one could say indisputable, evidence that environmental hazards are not randomly or evenly distributed across population groups but rather are borne disproportionately by people of color and the poor."[69] At the same time, there have been statements from the United Church of Christ, the U.S. Catholic Bishops, the Evangelical Lutheran Church and the Vatican's Pontifical Justice and Peace Council noting the ways in which the poor, minorities and indigenous peoples suffer disproportionately from environmental pollution and degradation.[70] As the Lutheran statement "Caring for Creation" notes, "the land and its inhabitants are often disenfranchised by the rich and powerful. The degradation of the environment occurs where people have little or no voice in decisions—because of racial, gender, or economic discrimination."[71]

Christian ethics and Catholic social teachings in particular offer several reasons to oppose environmental racism—or indeed, any form of environmental discrimination against minorities, women or the poor. First, as we noted in our discussions of affirmative action and sexism, the bishops of Vatican II state very clearly that "every type of discrimination…is to be overcome and eradicated as contrary to God's intent."[72] Second, as we have already noted in this chapter and elsewhere, Catholic social teachings repeatedly affirm the "universal purpose of created goods." God's creation is intended for the good of *all* humans, so depriving the poor, minorities and indigenous peoples of access to a sustainable and livable environment is grossly unjust.

Third, as Brian Massingale points out, environmental racism is a serious violation of distributive justice, "which obliges the state to ensure a fair distribution of the benefits and burdens of social life among the members of a society."[73] Indeed, in Pope Leo XIII's encyclical "On the Condition of Labor," we read that the first and chief duty of all rulers is to act with distributive justice toward each and every class. And the pope later notes that "when there is a question of protecting the rights of individuals, the poor and the helpless have a claim to special consideration."[74] Thus, forcing the poor and minorities to bear a disproportionate share of environmental blight and degradation goes against even the most minimal demands of distributive justice.

The fourth and fifth reasons for opposing environmental racism are intimately related: namely, that all humans have a basic and inalienable right to a safe environment and that Christians are to make a preferential option for the poor. As Massingale notes, Pope John Paul II has affirmed the right of every person to a safe environment.[75] In fact, Catholic social teachings have long held that every human person has a right to life and "to the means which are suitable to the proper development of life," including the food, clothing and shelter provided by a safe environment. What's more, the church has also expressed its opposition to "subhuman living conditions…[and] disgraceful working conditions," as they are an "insult to human dignity."[76] Thus, a safe environment is seen as a basic and inalienable human right and one that has been unjustly denied to far too many of the world's poor, minorities, women and indigenous peoples. Furthermore, as we have already noted several times in this text, Catholic social teachings repeatedly call for a "preferential option for the poor." As the U.S. Catholic bishops note, all economic policies and decisions are to be judged "in light of what they do *for* the poor, what they do *to* the poor, and what they enable the poor to do *for themselves.*"[77] And these same bishops note in "Renewing the Earth" that "the option for the poor embedded in the Gospel and in the church's teaching make us aware that the poor suffer most directly from environmental decline and have the least access to relief from their suffering."[78] Clearly, then, environmental racism—displayed in the specific examples of racial discrimination and injustice reported earlier in the "Voices of Experience" section of this choice—is in direct opposition to a commitment to stand with the poor and marginalized.

Finally, environmental racism is in violation of the virtue of solidarity. As the U.S. Catholic bishops have noted, "we are one human family, whatever our national, racial, ethnic, economic and ideological differences. We are our brothers' and sisters' keepers (Gn. 4:9)," and in the face of structural sins like environmental racism this solidarity "requires sacrifices of our own self-interest for the good of others and of the earth we share."[79] It is patently wrong to allow the poor and minorities and indigenous peoples of the earth to pay the greatest cost of our pollution and degradation of the environment.

Formulating a Christian Response

Some Basic Christian Convictions. The biblical and Christian notions of creation, stewardship, the dignity of the human person and "the universal purpose of created goods" teach us the importance of sharing. The bounty of God's creation has been entrusted to us as a gracious gift, to be cared for and shared with the entire human community, and indeed with all our cocreatures. Both Scripture and tradition remind us that we are to treat creation with reverence, that we have a duty to make certain that all of God's creatures are taken care of and that every human person has what is required for their dignity and development.

The biblical concern for the *anawim,* as well as Christian teachings about a "preferential option for the poor," solidarity and the evils of unjust discrimination of every sort remind us of our particular obligations to those in the margins. As disciples of the one who came "to bring good news to the poor…[and] release to the captives," we have a special duty to stand with and work on behalf of all those oppressed and marginalized by any form of injustice. Thus, when it comes to sharing the bounties of God's creation with others, we must make a special effort to see that the poor and those in the margins have a place at the table. They are not to be forced to eat the scraps—particularly not poisoned or spoiled scraps—which have fallen into the dirt.

It seems clear that minority communities and indigenous peoples (as well as women, and the poor in general) are regularly and systematically exposed to a disproportionate degree of environmental hazard and burden. Either they are forced to live and work in the most degraded and inhospitable environments, or they are coerced to accept toxic waste and pollution from other, wealthier communities. This environmental injustice or racism is, from a Christian perspective, an instance of "social" or "structural" sin and a type of "institutionalized violence" waged upon the weakest and most unprotected in our communities. It is a violation of distributive justice and a denial of our solidarity with other peoples. We are obliged to address this wrong and come to the aid of its victims.

Some Difficult Questions. How can impoverished minority communities go about protecting or repairing their environments? In many cases these communities lack the political clout to defend themselves from becoming toxic sinkholes, and they are often so desperate for employment and/or investment that local leaders are willing to accept toxic industries, landfills, hazardous-waste sites or incinerators as part of the price of any economic development. What sorts of structures or policies are needed on the local, regional or national level to make certain that the burdens of environmental degradation do not fall disproportionately on the poor and minorities, or that these communities have other opportunities for economic growth?

How can we make sure that the poor and indigenous peoples in developing nations are not being pushed into more and more inhospitable environments? What sorts of land-reform policies or environmental safeguards are required in these countries to protect the poor and indigenous peoples from being driven off their farms or out of their homelands, or from being forced to engage in environmentally dangerous practices just to stay alive? What sorts of international agreements, investments or aid are needed to ensure that poor nations can develop economically without creating an environmental holocaust for their poor and indigenous peoples? What kinds of trade or business agreements are needed to make sure that less developed nations will not be coerced by multinational corporations to accept practices or industries that are not good for the environment?

Finally, perhaps the most difficult question that needs to be asked has to do with changing our own habits and lifestyles as consumers. Environmental racism and injustice are the results of wealthy communities and nations overpolluting and overconsuming, and then exporting the environmental costs of these practices to poorer and weaker communities. The pyramids of our landfills and toxic-waste sites are being built on the backs of the poor, minorities, women and indigenous peoples. What sorts of changes are we willing to make in our patterns of pollution and consumption in order to reduce the toxic burden of these practices on the *anawim?* How simply are we willing to live so that others may simply live?

Human Population Growth and the Environment

The Voices of Experience

The Voice of History. As Clive Ponting notes in *A Green History of the World,* the threat of overpopulation is not new, but has haunted human societies since the invention of agriculture.[80] Though there were many fewer people on the planet than today, throughout most of the past ten thousand years the vast majority of the population lived under the constant threat of famine, and societies were only very rarely capable of providing their people with an adequate diet. "More often than not, increasing population put ever greater pressure on a limited agricultural system,…[and] the conflict was normally only resolved through mass starvation and death."[81] Still, it is also true that during this period families and communities needed to be very fertile to sustain themselves in the face of disease, high infant-mortality rates and other threats.

About three hundred years ago the rate of population growth, which had remained low and steady throughout most of human history, began to increase. By the end of the eighteenth century the global population was nearing one billion, and there were growing concerns about the dangers of too much population growth. In 1798 Thomas Malthus warned in his *Essay on Population* that population growth was geometric or exponential and so would rapidly outstrip the world's food supply (which only increased arithmetically) and thus precipitate a catastrophe.[82]

Malthus's predictions of an escalating population growth have been borne out by the past two centuries. For although *homo sapiens* has been on the planet for between 200,000 and 400,000 years, Michael Teitelbaum notes that "most of its growth in numbers has occurred in the last 40 years. It took scores of millennia to reach the first billion humans, around 1800; over a century to reach the second billion, somewhere between 1918 and 1927; about 33 years to the third billion, around 1960; only 14 years to the fourth; and 13 to the fifth in 1987."[83] In 2000 the planet's world population was over six billion, and predicted to reach nearly ten billion by midcentury.[84]

Contemporary Voices. In his book *Environmental Ethics: Readings in Theory and Application* Louis Pojman distinguishes three contemporary voices in the debate about population growth: "Doomsdayers," "Cornucopians" and "Cautious Optimists."[85]

According to Pojman, "Doomsdayers" are "those who hold that population growth is a crucial problem and who are pessimistic about our chances for survival if we do not curb [it]."[86] Because these "Doomsdayers" see the situation as desperate, they are open to fairly drastic measures, including, for example, government coercion to reproduce according to strict controls.[87] As Merchant notes, such radical policies have already been implemented in China and India, with China seeking "to reduce population by a government policy of limiting families to one child," and India's government pressuring its employees to be sterilized after three children.[88] Many, of course, object to the ways these radical approaches to the population crisis threaten human freedom.

Pojman's second group are the "Cornucopians," whom we saw earlier. Arguing that population growth is not a problem, "Cornucopians" note that—thanks to human ingenuity and creativity—Malthus's dire predictions about planetary shortages of food or natural resources have so far not come true and "that technology and political changes can accommodate a much larger population than we presently have."[89] If there is a problem of scarcity, these voices contend, this is a problem we can deal with effectively if we have the ingenuity and (more importantly) the political and moral will to do so. What is needed, they suggest, is not governmental intrusion into personal decisions about reproduction, but the will to distribute the goods of the earth justly.[90]

Finally, Pojman suggests, there are the "Cautious Optimists," who "see increasing population growth as a problem, but believe that with economic and political changes (they would say, with economic and social justice), the problem can be solved without population-control policies."[91] The last phrase is important. The "Cautious Optimists" believe that a new approach to reproductive choices is needed but that those choices should not be directed by governmental policies, but determined by the consciences of individual persons and couples. Despite a large diversity of views among these thinkers, they share the cautiously optimistic conviction "that people will voluntarily limit their procreation if they see it is in their economic and social self-interest."

Voices from the Margins. The vast majority of the world's population growth is taking place in poor nations, threatening to overwhelm environments and resources already stretched to the limit and forcing more and more of the world's poor into degraded, depleted and dangerous habitats. "The developing countries add a million people every five days to lands already overworked and depleted of water and cheap sources of energy."[92] Still, many of those working with or concerned about the poor in developing countries express two grave concerns about attempts to identify a population explosion in poor nations as the overriding environmental threat to the planet.

First, as Christine Gudorf notes, for the past half-century the United States and other industrialized nations have sought to limit the growing populations of developing nations. Unfortunately, these programs were often undertaken for reasons that had little to do with the interests of women and men living in these countries and were not infrequently implemented in ways that violated their rights as well as cultural beliefs and practices.[93] And second, the consumption explosion among the world's wealthier nations poses a significantly greater threat to the environment than the multiplication of the poor in developing lands. "The Industrialized countries of the Northern Hemisphere are home to one-fifth of the world's population, yet they consume two-thirds of the world's food, three-quarters of its energy and minerals and 85 percent of its wood."[94] As the poor would remind us, it is the affluence and overconsumption of developed nations that is the real danger confronting our planet's health.

Scripture. From Scripture we learn several things that are relevant to our reflections on the population and consumption explosions. First, the Hebrew Scriptures place a great value on procreation as a command and a blessing, and humans are called to "be fruitful and increase in numbers." Second, however, it is also true that all of God's other creatures are also called to "be fruitful and increase" and to fill the earth, the sky and the seas. Thus, third, the biblical command for humans to procreate must be viewed in light of their twin duties to make room for and to care for other humans and the rest of creation.

As we saw earlier, John Noonan notes that "the most obvious and commanding message of the Old Testament is that marriage and the procreation of children are eminently desirable human goods, which God has blessed."[95] In both Genesis 1:28 and 9:1 God commands humans to "be fruitful and multiply, and fill the earth." And throughout the Hebrew Scriptures fertility is seen as a blessing, and the Israelites' ancestors are repeatedly promised that God will give them descendents as "numerous as the stars of heaven" (Gen 26:4) "and as the sand that is on the seashore" (Gen 22:17). Naturally, given the various threats to their survival, it is hardly surprising that the ancient biblical authors saw the multiplication of their descendents both as a divine mandate and as evidence of God's blessing. And yet, as we have already seen, in neither the Hebrew Scriptures nor the New Testament does Noonan find any commandment against contraception, nor any evidence that the ancient Hebrews thought the practice was unlawful.

It is also important to note that it is not only humans who are called in Scripture to "be fruitful and multiply." In the first chapter of Genesis God creates a great bounty of living beings; plants, birds, fishes and animals of every color, stripe, size and shape. And God provides them with land and sky and sea for their habitats, water for their drink, sunlight and darkness for their warmth and rest, and all sorts of food for their nurturing. And they too are to fill the earth, the skies and the seas with their young.

The point here is that since *all* God's creatures are to "fill" the earth, none are to overfill it or to crowd out God's other creatures or to deplete, degrade or destroy their habitats. Instead, we are to make room for the growth of all God's creation and to share the common space of our land, sky and seas.

Above and beyond this duty to share the planet with all God's other creatures, however, Scripture assigns humans a special obligation to be good stewards of creation, and Lisa Cahill suggests that the biblical command to "be fruitful and multiply" must be read alongside the command to be good stewards. For the ones who are to "fill the earth" in Genesis 1:28 are also the ones who in Genesis 2:15 are to till the garden and look after it. And the ones who are fashioned in the image of God as male and female are also the ones who have a special role and responsibility toward the rest of creation.

Thus, according to Cahill, the biblical evidence indicates that human procreation is "designed" not simply for the good of a particular couple and not simply for the good of the human species (although these are both important), but also for the good of the whole of creation. As Cahill sees it, the biblical author of Genesis 1:28

> places the man-woman relation in the context of the welfare of the creation, rather than of interpersonal communion. Even their sexual coming together is in fulfillment of their responsibility to propagate the inclusive community of their species, and so to support the maintenance of the created orders. Male and female relations, it can be said, find definition and meaning in "the common good."[96]

This means our decisions and actions in regard to procreation should be made not only with the welfare of the couple in mind, but also with the welfare of "the common good" in mind, that is, the welfare of the human community and even the rest of creation.

Tradition. To see what the Christian tradition has to contribute to the conversation about population growth we turn now to two points. First, we examine just what the tradition has had to say about the biblical mandate to "be fruitful and multiply." Then we focus on that same tradition's recent warnings about the dangers and injustices of the "consumption explosion" going on in wealthier nations.

Turning again to Noonan's text *Contraception,* we discover a curious point about Christian teachings on procreation. Both the ancient Hebrews and Romans placed a great deal of emphasis on the duty to procreate and multiply descendents. And, as we saw earlier, throughout most of its history Christianity has opposed contraception and taught that procreation was the primary or exclusive purpose of sexual intercourse and one of the basic goods of marriage. Still, until fairly recently, Christian authorities have generally not taught that married persons had a specific moral duty to "be fruitful and multiply." Nor have these authorities generally been very interested in urging Christians to "fill the earth" through procreation. So, while early and medieval Christian authors could well have strengthened their arguments against contraception by pointing to the state's need for more members, the church's need for an increase in numbers or heaven's need for more souls, they usually did not do so. As Noonan points out, the major interest of most of these Christian writers "was not in more persons, but in spiritually better persons."[97]

The earliest Christians may have been uninterested in filling the earth with their descendents because they were expecting Christ's speedy return. But it was probably the growing emphasis on celibacy that kept the later Christian tradition from stressing a duty to procreate. Indeed, traditional Catholic theology taught that celibate marriages were valid, and until well into the twentieth century did not recognize a duty of married persons to procreate or "be fruitful and multiply," but only taught that they could not engage in contraceptive acts.

Still, contemporary Catholic teachings on procreation have not been completely uninterested in the problem of overpopulation. In spite of differences over the morality of contraception, both official teachings and a large number of Catholic ethicists and theologians agree that Christian couples are called to "responsible parenthood" and that decisions about procreation should pay attention to the "social conditions" these couples encounter.[98] As Pope Paul VI noted, "the responsible exercise of parenthood implies, therefore, that husband and wife recognize fully their own duties towards God, towards themselves, towards the family and towards society."[99] Thus, in the present day and age responsible parenthood must also mean paying attention to legitimate concerns about overpopulation. Still, Catholic authorities and ethicists have also repeatedly warned against birth-control programs that rely on coercion or manipulation, violating the rights and dignity of parents or trampling on the legitimate cultural practices of communities and societies.[100]

And yet, while acknowledging the environmental dangers posed by a global population explosion, Catholic and other Christian authorities have repeatedly argued that there is a need to address the equally (or, indeed, more) serious threat of the "consumption explosion" going on in the world's developed nations. We sketched out some of the dimensions of this "consumption explosion" earlier in this chapter and have repeatedly noted warnings from the Christian tradition about the injustices of any overconsumption or hoarding of the world's limited resources.

In "Christianity and Social Progress" Pope John XXIII discussed the problem of population growth and implied that the real crisis facing developing countries was a failure to distribute a fair share of the world's wealth and resources to the poor.[101] Pope Paul VI made a similar argument in his letter "On the Regulation of Birth," noting that shortages and hunger in poorer nations were more often to be blamed on "an insufficient sense of social justice," or "selfish monopolization."[102] And in "Justice in the World," the 1971 synod of Catholic bishops noted that our global environment would soon be overwhelmed if the high rates of consumption and pollution found in wealthy nations were extended to the rest of the planet.[103] Finally, as we have already noted, Pope John Paul II not only sees the "consumption explosion" in wealthy nations as an injustice against "masses of people living in conditions of misery at the very lowest level of subsistence," but warns that this overconsumption poses a real threat of "ecological breakdown."[104] Indeed, again and again Christian tradition has argued that the dangers posed to creation by the "consumption explosion" going on in developed nations is just as (or, indeed, more) serious than the threat of the population explosion going on in developing countries.

Formulating a Christian Response

Some Basic Christian Convictions. Population growth is clearly a serious moral issue, one that poses significant threats to the human community, the poor and the global environment, and one that needs to be addressed swiftly, effectively and ethically. In less than two centuries the human population on this planet has more than sextupled, going from less than one billion to over six billion, and it is expected to reach nearly ten billion by midcentury. What's more, the vast majority of this growth is currently going on in poor countries and regions where the environment is already overburdened and degraded. Thus, no matter what we say about the dangers and injustices associated with the consumption explosion going on in wealthy nations, the planet's population explosion is a major problem, and one that Christians and all other people need to take seriously. For whatever else good stewardship means, it cannot mean ignoring or tolerating unrestricted population growth.

In light of the ongoing human population explosion persons and communities everywhere must be committed to "responsible parenthood." This means that in making decisions about family planning and birth regulation individuals, couples and communities need to consider the larger social and global contexts in which they find themselves. It also means that our reflections and teachings on the importance and place of procreation and on the size of families must take into account our duties to the larger human community, to generations unborn and to the whole of God's creation.

In responding to the unfolding crisis of population growth we need to seek out solutions that are truly moral and just. We must reject coercive or manipulative programs that ignore or violate the rights, dignity and conscience of persons and families, or that override or trample the legitimate autonomy and cultural practices of societies.[105] And we must certainly reject solutions that involve abortion, infanticide or euthanasia, or that tolerate the abandonment of large segments of the human community to famine and death. Nor can we accept any response that places an unjust burden on the poor, asking them to make significant sacrifices for the good of the planet while we in the developed world continue to overwhelm the environment with our extravagant levels of consumption and pollution.

Finally, while the issue of population growth is extraordinarily serious and increasingly urgent, the consumption explosion going on in the developed (and spreading to the developing) world is creating even more havoc for our planet and must be addressed immediately. By our profligate consumption and pollution of the world's resources we in the developed world are currently overwhelming God's creation and robbing the poor and future generations of their rightful livelihood and inheritance. Whatever else we say about the dangers of population growth, it is absolutely critical that those of us in wealthy nations make radical changes in the ways we consume and pollute.

Some Difficult Questions. How can we slow population growth in the developing world without using immoral means or encouraging the further spread of the consumption explosion? In the past industrialization and economic development have been the way most nations have gained control of their population growth. As people grew wealthier and healthier there was less pressure to have large families. Still, this path has also created its own environmental time bomb. For while it is frightening to think of ten or twelve billion people on the planet, the idea of six billion humans consuming and polluting at the same rate as Americans or Europeans is probably even more alarming.

Where exactly is the line between programs and policies that educate and encourage couples and communities to embrace "responsible parenthood" and those that manipulate them, or that override legitimate and longstanding cultural practices? Would it be permitted to offer financial incentives or educational and employment opportunities that encourage smaller families, or to penalize or tax those who choose to have more children? How can people be educated to the need for "responsible parenthood" while still respecting the cultural practices and beliefs that give meaning to their lives? What roles should local communities, nation states and international organizations have in addressing the issue of population growth?

How lightly will all of us need to live on the earth to create a safe and sustainable economy and environment for our children and grandchildren? How simply will we need to live so that all others can simply live? How much will we need to reduce our consumption and pollution if we want to prevent an environmental catastrophe? How can we educate and encourage ourselves to be "responsible parents" by not spending our children's inheritance? How can we construct healthy economies that do not depend on deficit spending of our planet's resources?

COMMUNITY: An Examination of Two Environmental Sins

Anthropocentrism. In medieval Christianity pride was the first and deadliest of the capital sins, for it represented an arrogant rebellion against God and a fundamental refusal to accept one's place within the wondrous harmony of creation. In John Milton's epic poem *Paradise Lost* the prideful (and fallen) archangel Lucifer typifies this sinful arrogance when he cries out bitterly, "Better to reign in Hell, than serve in Heaven." At the heart of our current ecological crisis is another sort of prideful arrogance, anthropocentrism, which elevates humans far above the rest of creation and ignores our dependence upon or ties and duties to God's other creatures. This pride has wreaked all sorts of havoc and destruction on our world, polluting our air and water, poisoning and stripping our soil and slaughtering thousands upon thousands of our sibling species. But, like Milton's Lucifer, it often seems as if we would rather reign in an environmental wasteland than serve in an ecological Eden.

Ideology. Anthropocentrism is characterized by several basic beliefs. Humans (because of their free will, self-conscious intellect or immortal soul) are seen as above and separate from the rest of God's creation. Rather than understanding ourselves as part and parcel of the created world and woven into larger and interdependent ecosystems that nurture and sustain a wide variety of creatures, anthropocentrism assumes that humans are elevated above the natural order and free to ignore any larger common good. Indeed, in an anthropocentric worldview human beings are not only at the pinnacle of creation, but all the rest of the natural world exists only to provide for our needs. Both Socrates and Aristotle argued that all the plants and animals had been made for the sole purpose of taking care of humans. And Francis Bacon noted that, "Man, if we look to final causes, may be regarded as the center of the world, insomuch that if man were taken away from the world, the rest would seem to be all astray, without aim or purpose."[106] And since the only value of other creatures is their usefulness to humans, the suffering, death or extinction of other life forms, or even the degradation or destruction of entire ecosystems is not important unless it harms or displeases humans. In this worldview there is no reason for gratitude or compassion toward other creatures, no intrinsic value to preserving species or protecting environments, unless, of course, these virtues or actions somehow help us. Furthermore, anthropocentrism assumes that humans, elevated far above the rest of creation, are entitled to exercise an unrestricted dominion over the world. Not only may we, like all other creatures, take food and drink and shelter from our environment. We are also allowed (even called) to reign over the rest of creation, to do as we like with other creatures (as long as we respect the property rights of other humans), to buy and sell, hunt, kill, torture or drive into extinction. Indeed, several modern thinkers from Francis Bacon to Sigmund Freud have argued that it is humanity's role to tame nature and force it to obey our will.[107]

The ideology of anthropocentrism is nicely captured by Sally Griffin, who notes that "We who are born into this civilization have inherited a habit of mind. We are divided against ourselves. We no longer feel ourselves to be part of this earth. We regard our fellow creatures as enemies."[108]

Imbedded Practices. Throughout history anthropocentrism has been embodied in a number of practices and structures showing little or no regard for the good of other creatures or the integrity of ecosystems and the environment. To begin with, since the development of agriculture numerous human societies from the Mediterranean to Central America to China and the Indus Valley have degraded and exhausted their local environments in an attempt to meet the needs of a growing human population and increasingly complex civilizations. Time after time lands have been deforested, habitats degraded and destroyed, species driven or hunted into extinction and soil eroded and exhausted by the processes of human agriculture and expansion. As the environmentalist Peter Farb noted, "from the very beginning *Homo [sapiens]* has exploited the environment up to his technological limits to do so," the result often being the desertification and collapse of regional ecosystems.[109]

Second, with the onset of European colonialism the extent of human exploitation and degradation of the environment increased significantly. In Asia, Africa and the Americas lush forests and environments rich with a cornucopia of flora and fauna were cut or burned down and replaced with huge plantations producing single and usually foreign crops for export back to Europe. This intensive cultivation of single crops like sugar, coffee, cotton or rubber meant the destruction of native ecosystems, the extinction of a large number of indigenous plants and animals, and often exhausted the soil, requiring the increasing use of fertilizers and pesticides.

Third, European colonialism also widely expanded hunting and fishing for animals, and in the past few centuries species after species has been hunted or fished into extinction by increasingly efficient or reckless methods. In modern times overfishing has led to the collapse of numerous oceanic fisheries around the world, while the fur, ivory and whaling industries have decimated or eliminated all sorts of creatures, great and small. Still, it is mostly through habitat destruction that humans have posed the gravest threat to other species, and at present the ongoing destruction of the world's forests, and particularly its rain forests, is contributing to a massive extinction of plants and animals. As we noted earlier, current estimates suggest that we are in the midst of the greatest extinction of species in sixty-five million years, and one that may take between one- and two-thirds of all life forms before it is over.

Fourth, there is the matter of our treatment of domestic animals. In the drive to produce more and cheaper meat for our dinner tables, humans have increasingly transformed the modern farm into a mechanized factory. Cattle, pigs, chickens and other animals are increasingly raised in extremely small cages, sties or stalls, often chained in place, denied access to light or movement, and fed an artificial diet rich in growth hormones and antibiotics. As Ponting points out, these practices are not new. "For centuries poultry and game birds were reared in the dark, blinded, or in the case of geese, had their feet nailed to the floor, or if they were chickens had their feet cut off, because it was believed that it made their meat more tender."[110] As the ad for one national brand of poultry products used to note, "It takes a tough man to raise a tender chicken."

Christian Beliefs. As we noted earlier in this chapter, many Christians have interpreted the command of Genesis 1:28 to "have dominion over the fish of the sea and over the birds of the air and over every living thing that moves upon the earth" as a justification for anthropocentrism. And the Christian tradition certainly bears some responsibility for the spread of a worldview that attends far too little to our duties and ties to the rest of creation. Still, we have also noted several Christian beliefs that challenge any anthropocentric view of the world.

As we see in the first chapter of Genesis, all of creation has been fashioned by God's hand and all of it is good, indeed very good. This means that the goodness or worth of creation and all of God's creatures does not come from the fact that it or they are useful to humans. Rather, creation is good because God has fashioned it and because God's glory shines forth in its splendor and beauty. Also, God continues to care for and love all of creation, feeding the birds of the sky and clothing the grass in the fields (Matt 6:26–30), and making it rain even in deserts where humans never go (Job 38:26). Indeed, God includes all of creation in the covenant with Noah and in the salvation brought by Christ's death and resurrection. Furthermore, the first two chapters of Genesis make it clear that humans are not elevated above the rest of creation. For in the first chapter the creation of humans is part of the overall creation of the world, and in the second chapter they are fashioned of the same soil as all the plants and animals. And as Michael and Kenneth Himes have argued, Scripture portrays humans as companions with the rest of creation. In Genesis 1:31 God blesses the whole community of creation, a family in which humans are companions

and kin to all other creatures. And in the second chapter of Genesis
God creates all the other animals to be companions for the human
who is alone. Finally, Genesis makes it quite clear that humans do
indeed have a special place and role within creation, but it is the role of
one who serves. In Genesis 2:15 humans are placed in the garden in
order to tend and care for it, and thus to preserve and protect its
integrity, to nurture and sustain its growth and to respect its harmony
as a sacrament of God.

Structural Reforms. The first major step in addressing anthropocentrism is to reeducate our children and ourselves in the fundamental
ways we see the world around us. We need to shift from seeing the
rest of creation merely as a global supermarket or marketplace where
every creature and part of creation is a resource or product to be pur-
chased, packaged or consumed by humans. We need to undergo a
"Copernican revolution" in which we are unseated as the center of
the universe and in which we rediscover our identity as cocreature
and servant within God's harmonious and interdependent web of
creation. Second, we need to take immediate steps to slow down or
stop the ongoing massive extinction of species and degradation of
habitats going on around the planet. It is particularly important that
governments, multinational corporations and international organizations begin moving to halt the destruction of the world's shrinking
rain forests and the elimination of countless species of flora and fauna.
As we have already noted, the loss of these rain forests represents a
fundamental threat to the very biodiversity of our planet and may
constitute a kind of global biocide. Of course rescuing the rain
forests, which are mostly found in developing nations struggling with
widespread poverty and crushing international debts, will require a
commitment to economic aid and justice on the part of wealthy
countries and corporations. At the same time, it is also critical that we
address other practices placing increasing pressure on habitats and
ecosystems around the planet, such as the spread of urban sprawl, the
worldwide growth of dams and the increasing problem of overfishing. Third, we need to make significant changes in the ways we treat
and consume animals. Our national and global cattle industries use a

vastly disproportionate amount of land and grains, poison our environment with the production of methane gas and animal waste, and contribute significantly to the degradation and destruction of rain forests and other environments. And, as we have already noted, few would describe the treatment of livestock on modern factory farms as humane. Nationally and globally we need to reduce our dietary use of meat and introduce a more environmentally balanced menu.

Consumerism. We discussed the social sin of consumerism in the chapter on economic justice and have noted the environmental harms of overconsumption and the consumption explosion going on (mainly) in developed countries several times in this chapter. Here we look at the sin of consumerism as it affects both our relations to other humans and the rest of creation. There are a number of similarities between anthropocentrism, which elevates humans above and beyond the rest of creation, and consumerism, which emphasizes the wants and desires of consumers while ignoring the rights and claims of the poor, of future generations and of the rest of the planet. If anthropocentrism leads humans to forget that they are also cocreatures and stewards of creation, consumerism leads us to forget that we are also sisters and brothers to all the other humans on the planet, and called to show a special regard for those in the margins.

Ideology. In its simplest form consumerism is an addiction to the accumulation of things, and this addiction is supported by several mistaken beliefs. An underlying assumption of consumerism is that possessing or consuming goods will not only meet the basic material needs humans have for food, clothing and shelter, but will also satisfy deeper or higher appetites for human fulfillment, wholeness, meaning and happiness. In a consumerist worldview there are very few hungers (perhaps none) that cannot be satisfied by purchasing something, and "for all the rest, there's MasterCard." Since the consumption of goods is the primary way for humans to achieve happiness or fulfillment, it only makes sense that consuming more and more goods will lead to greater and greater happiness. Thus, there is to be no limit on what we consume. More is always better, and what we have is never enough.

Greed and envy are fundamental virtues in a consumerist world. Also, consumerism reduces humans to mere consumers, or at least presents this as our primary role. We are consumers first, and citizens, cocreatures and fellow human beings second or third, or not at all. And as consumers we are made to buy and possess, to shop till we drop. Indeed, as consumers we have no need to concern ourselves with the fuller social or environmental costs of our consumption. We need not worry if the planet is running out of resources, if ecosystems are being destroyed, or what it will take to clean up habitats that have been degraded or destroyed by our consumption. We only need to ask what this item will cost us at the mall. Furthermore, consumerism places consumers at the center of the universe, envisions the world around us as a huge supermarket and reduces other persons and creatures to mere commodities. In a consumerist mindset all the "goods" of the earth have been placed here for our consumption, and other people are valuable only if they help us acquire what we want. Finally, a consumerist mindset assumes that there is a limitless bounty of supplies and resources to be consumed and that we are doing all our shopping in a supermarket that will never run out of goods.

Imbedded Practices. A number of consumerist practices pose environmental hazards. We will name two. First, there is the long-term practice of humans spending beyond our planetary means, consuming or destroying renewable resources far faster than we or the earth can replenish them, or consuming huge amounts of nonrenewable resources with little or no concern for those who will come after us. Ponting and others have pointed out that at least since the invention of agriculture numerous human societies and civilizations have exploited and taxed their local and regional environments and ecosystems to the point of exhaustion and collapse. As long as the human population remained relatively small the ecological damage tended to be fairly limited and abandoned areas could often replenish themselves in time. But with the expansion of Europeans into every continent and the massive growth in the numbers of humans in the past two centuries our practice of deficit spending has created global environmental problems. The clearest case of this is our present use of fossil fuels, which we are consuming at ever-accelerating rates and with which we are polluting our air and warming our planet in ways that may well be irreparable. But we are also engaged in deficit spending in our present consumption and use of water, soil and timber (especially in rain forests), and, as we have previously noted, we are depleting the oceans' stocks of fish. In a variety of ways our consumerist society is living beyond our planetary means and spending the inheritance of our children and grandchildren.

Second, by encouraging an insatiable appetite for more and more goods, the addiction of consumerism all too often results in the hoarding of creation's bounty by a small elite group of people or nations. This gross inequality is not only unjust, but also exiles vast numbers of the planet's poor and dispossessed to marginal and overtaxed environments. And it forces them to engage in shortsighted and dangerous practices that further exhaust and degrade the wretched, swamped and overburdened patches of earth into which they have been crowded. In an historical essay addressing the environmental impact of economic injustice John Gowdy notes that it has long been true that "justice and equity are important factors in assuring [environmental] sustainability."[111] So too, throughout the colonial period and in contemporary developing nations it has been the crushing and widespread poverty resulting from economic injustice that has placed such grave strains on the environment, and forced millions to scrape and beg for the scraps that fall from the consumer's table.

Christian Beliefs. In the chapter on economic justice we noted a number of Christian beliefs that challenge the addiction of consumerism. Here we will list those that are relevant to consumerism's harmful effects on the environment. According to Scripture and the Christian tradition the primary roles that humans have in relationship to the rest of creation are those of steward and cocreature (or companion), not consumer. As we have repeatedly noted, Genesis describes human beings as part and parcel of God's creation, fashioned of the same soil and clay as the rest of God's creatures; human beings are placed in Eden to care for and tend the garden. We are stewards, not owners of God's creation, and we have been given a

sacred trust—for which we will be held accountable—not a license
to do whatever we like. Also, other creatures are not mere commodities, objects we can consume and dispose of without any moral
restraints. All of creation has been fashioned by God and is a sacrament of God's wonder. And all other creatures are, in a very real sense,
our cocreatures and companions. As Kenneth and Michael Himes
have argued, we are called to an "I-Thou" relationship with all God's
creatures. And as we have seen several times in this book, the hoarding
of God's creation by a small group of people or nations violates the
obligations of stewardship, our duties to the *anawim* (the preferential
option for the poor) and the principles of Catholic social teaching.
From the Hebrew prophet Isaiah to Pope John Paul II our religious
ancestors and teachers have cried out against the greed and injustice
at the heart of the consumerist mindset. God's bounty is to be shared.
Finally, as stewards of God's creation we have duties to all those who
will inherit the earth, to our children and theirs. The virtues of temperance and prudence call us to live and consume within moral
boundaries and to preserve and protect the rich inheritance that has
been entrusted to us to hand on to those who will come later.

Structural Reforms. Addressing the environmental harms of consumerism means making several significant, even radical economic,
social and political changes. We need to start living within our environmental means and to take steps to reduce and eventually eliminate
national and global patterns of "deficit spending" of creation's bounty.
Shifting to a sustainable economy would require that we only
"spend" the world's renewable resources at a rate at which they can
be replaced or repaired. For those of us in developed nations that
would certainly mean that we need to make radical changes in our
consumption of energy and other resources, and to spend a significantly smaller proportion of creation's bounty. It would also mean
that we must all begin to care for and manage the earth's soil, water,
forests and other creatures in ways that do not deplete or burden
habitats and ecosystems beyond their capacity to recover. And it
would no doubt mean that we need to shift away from our present
reliance on fossil fuels and move toward solar and other renewable

forms of energy. We also need to begin to pay the full environmental costs of our consumption of creation. We must acknowledge that creation's bounty is not limitless and that making ceaseless and escalating withdrawals from the earth's oceans, forests and rivers or pouring endless amounts of toxic and other wastes into our environment is, in fact, running up a bill that someone—probably the poor, and certainly our children—will eventually have to pay. Either through taxes or fees consumers and producers need to begin paying the full environmental costs of the goods and services we use, including the cost of depleting limited resources, of disposing of the waste products of our consumption and of repairing and replenishing the habitats and ecosystems stressed or harmed by our use. And we need to redistribute the world's wealth, to address the economic injustices that have contributed to and sustained widespread and crushing poverty in developing nations and to work for a better sharing of creation's bounty among all peoples.

Cases and Resources

As we have done in the other chapters, we conclude with four more case studies on various ethical issues of environmental ethics, along with a brief list of resources available for those interested in pursuing questions of environmental ethics further.

Case #2: Thanksgiving Dinner—No Thank You

Connie couldn't believe what she was hearing. She's not often shocked any more by things her kids say and do, but this shocked her.

"Mom," Angie continued to insist, "I just cannot be there. I was hoping you'd understand more than you obviously do. But whether you understand or not, I just can't go. Believe me, I've given this a lot of thought. It would go against my conscience, it would be wrong for me to take part in Thanksgiving dinner at Grandma's. I know Grandma will be disappointed, but I promise that I will talk to her about it myself beforehand. Grandma loves me—I don't

doubt that. So I'll be as kind to her about it as I can, but I just can't take part in a meal of thanksgiving that has as the main event the eating of an animal. I can't be thankful for that. To me it's wrong."

Connie knew about Angie's vegetarianism. It had developed in her over the past two years at college. It started with cutting red meat out of her diet, mostly, she said, for dietary reasons, but also because the sight or even the thought of blood in her food made Angie cringe. Later it became a more full-fledged vegetarianism—except for fish (Connie thought this was inconsistent). This move toward vegetarianism had been sparked by a couple of things. In a philosophy class Angie had taken in her first year in school the professor (supposedly presenting both views) seemed to steer the students toward becoming vegetarians and away from "speciesism," as she called it. Working on a paper for this class, Angie had come across articles about the ways cattle, pigs and poultry are often treated in modern "factory farms," confined in dark places and fed an artificial diet of growth hormones and antibiotics. She also read some pieces about the negative environmental effects of raising cattle, pigs and poultry, about all the forests that have been cut down to provide grazing and the pollution created by millions of cattle and billions of chickens. Then in a religion class one of her professors told her that in Genesis humans are given the plants for food and the animals for companions. "So you see, Mom, we're not supposed to eat animals."

This change has been annoying to Connie over the last year or so, but Angie hadn't been so militant or righteous about her position until now. Connie had no idea that Angie would ever take things this far. To "boycott" the family's celebration of Thanksgiving (that's the word Connie used) seemed to be going way too far, making her own beliefs more important than the family.

Connie doesn't really know what she can do next, if anything. But she is hoping that perhaps her son Bill can be of help. Bill, who is now twenty-eight, married, and, with his wife Lisa expecting their second child, is a "reliable and steady" young man—that's how Connie describes him. And Angie, seven years younger than Bill, has always looked up to him.

Bill and his family are coming into town next Tuesday—a couple days before Thanksgiving. Connie has asked him to talk to Angie about coming to the dinner in the hope that he might be able to get her to change her mind. Bill, you see, went through a "rebellious phase" (Connie's way of *putting it) that also included becoming a vegetarian for a while. Connie is pretty sure that it was Lisa who changed this for Bill. She has heard Lisa, who grew up on a farm, say that she didn't really see the point of being a vegetarian. "A lot of animals eat meat, why shouldn't we," Connie remembers her saying. Bill seemed to accommodate for Lisa. Connie knows that, more than anything else, Bill thinks that we shouldn't impose our beliefs on others or let our beliefs about things like vegetarianism get in the way of our relationships with family and friends. Connie hopes that Bill can help move Angie in the same direction.*

Case #3: On Becoming a One-Car Family

Dave Sosnowski is very thoughtful, willing to stop and look at an issue from both sides. Often this trait helps him to sort out problems in a balanced and intelligent fashion. Sometimes, like now, it can seem pretty exasperating, both to himself and his wife, Annie Sanchez. For the past several weeks the two of them have been wrestling with the question of whether to replace her twelve-year-old Toyota with another (slightly less-) used car, or to cut back to one car for the family. Annie is ready to get the second car. Dave is undecided.

Both Annie and Dave are teachers. He is a biology instructor at a local community college, and she is a special ed teacher at a center city school in Buffalo. Along with their one-year-old son Jason they live in a three-bedroom colonial in an older suburban development about eight miles from downtown. Annie is pregnant, and they are expecting their second child in late July. Their combined income is modest but sufficient to meet mortgage and car payments, keep their credit cards clear, pay off school loans and put a little aside for the children's education. Ironically enough, Dave makes a little extra money in the summer teaching driver's ed at a local high school.

Dave has a number of reasons for wanting to cut back to one car, or even to do without any car at all. As a biology teacher, he regularly lectures about the interrelationships of all living things in an ecosystem, as well as about the "closed" nature of our air and water systems. And he constantly reminds his students about the environmental harms of cars and light trucks. He tells them that each new car is responsible for about two metric tons of carbon emissions every year, that cars and light trucks account for about a quarter of all greenhouse emissions and more than half of the air pollution created by individual consumers. And he notes that the manufacture and maintenance of our cars (and the roads we drive on) contribute significantly to the pollution of our water. He also reminds them that these carbon emissions make up a huge percentage of the greenhouse gases warming up our planet, and that if the rest of the world were to begin driving cars and trucks at the same rate as us we would need nearly a dozen planets to supply us with enough fossil fuel. Of course we would also need to drive with our headlights on to see through the blinding and poisonous smog. Finally, Dave talks in class about the need to reform our patterns of transportation. And he has spoken up often at various political gatherings in the city, calling for major investment in our mass transportation systems.

Still, the switch to a single car would not be easy for Dave and Annie. At present Dave is able to do most of his teaching in the afternoons and evenings. This means he is home with Jason until 10:30 most mornings, when he takes his son to an in-home child-care setting a few miles away, where Annie picks him up after school. This arrangement allows them to maximize their time with Jason, and it is flexible enough to allow for emergencies. The fact that they each have their own car allows them to manage their flip-flopping schedules with a fair amount of ease. Working all this out with one car would be pretty complicated.

Dave could take the bus to work, but because his home and the school are on different routes he would need to take two buses. Depending on the connection and traffic, the ride would be about fifty minutes to an hour and a half each way, and he would need to walk about twelve blocks from the day-care center to his first bus. He could probably bike the ten miles to work in about forty-five minutes, but Buffalo's winters are cold and snowy, and cycling on slush or black ice would be pretty tough and dangerous. And for several months of the year he'd be biking home in the dark. Annie is not amused by this option. There isn't anybody at Annie's school she can car-pool with, and the neighborhood where she teaches is not one where she feels safe taking a bus. Dave could car-pool with a colleague in the department, but their schedules are pretty different, and it would mean putting Jason in day care for several more hours a day.

*So they are trying to figure out what to do. It seems scandalous and hypo-
critical for him to drive to work when he knows and teaches others about the
environmental harms of a two-car family. But the sacrifices he and Annie—
and the children—would need to make to cut back to one car seem daunting.
What to do?*

Case #4: The American College in the Ecological Age

*Brother Andrew Pistoia, O.F.M., is the president of St. Francis College, a
small, Catholic liberal arts school in western Montana. Founded in 1889 by
a group of Italian and German Franciscans, the college has long enjoyed a fine
reputation as a liberal arts school and teacher's college, and includes two former
senators, a governor, an attorney general and three bishops among its alumni.
In the early 1990s Brother Andrew took over as the college's sixteenth president and committed himself and the school to an aggressive building program
and funding campaign. Within the first two years in office "Brother Trump"—
as some of his fellow Franciscans occasionally (and not always playfully) refer
to him—had hired a vice president for development, added thirteen corporate
leaders and a former senator to the school's board of trustees and brought in the
first eight million dollars of a thirty-million-dollar campaign. Five years later
he has brought in over forty-three million dollars, increased enrollment by 23
percent, broken ground on a new science building and library, as well as two
new dorms and an expanded (and state-of-the-art) athletic facility. He has
also secured funding for six new chairs in business, biology, nursing and chem-
istry, and is currently negotiating an arrangement with three corporate sponsors
for a new M.B.A. program.*

*This afternoon, Brother Andrew has come to the board with what he
thinks is an exciting opportunity for St. Francis. Working with Senator Slip
Watson, a conservative and pro-business Republican, and the CEOs of the
state's largest timber and mining corporations, Brother Andrew has been able
to secure 7.6 million dollars toward the construction of a new science building and the establishment of a chair in environmental sciences. The building
and chair will be named after Senator Watson's grandfather, a former lumber
tycoon, and will be committed to "a balanced and moderate protection of the*

environment." Construction on the new building could begin within seven months.

Many on the board are impressed and pleased with the proposal, and four of the trustees note that such a program would be very good for St. Francis and could offer an evenhanded response to some of the more radical environmental positions currently being taught to young people. Still, not everyone is happy.

One of the other Franciscans, Father Frank Barrella, admits that he is pleased at the idea that the school might finally be developing a chair in environmental studies but expresses grave reservations about the direction Watson and the other contributors would want the college and program to move in.

"We are Franciscans, Andy. And I don't want to get romantic about 'brother sun' and 'sister moon,' but it seems clear to me that a genuinely Franciscan view of our duties to God's creation are at odds with what Watson and his colleagues think of as a 'balanced and moderate protection of the environment.' Time and again the senator and these CEOs have chosen profit over habitat protection, and both of these corporate donors have had major hassles with the EPA, even under Republican administrations. Heck, one of them is being sued by the state's attorney general for the clean-up costs of two massive open-pit mines. I think we need to do something about educating our students about the environment, but I don't think where we need to go as a school is where Watson and these other donors are headed."

Kathryn Collingwood, the faculty representative to the board, nodded and added her own concerns.

"Brother Andrew, nobody can say you haven't made an impact at St. Francis. And though I have often had reservations about your corporate model of higher education, I'm grateful for the wage hikes you've been able to achieve through your fundraising. And I'm grateful for the other ways an increased endowment and friendlier ties with the business community have improved things here at St. Francis.

"Still, like Father Frank, I'm concerned about this offer. I think the environment is going to be the moral, economic, scientific and political issue facing our children and grandchildren. And I think that Christianity and Catholicism and this school have been dragging their heels on the question. We're in a region where mining and lumber and cattle are major industries,

*and some of our students will run these companies one day, and most will
live in the environments affected by them. We need to help prepare them for
that future, and we need to do it in ways that are consistent with what we
believe in, as Christians. I have twenty copies of a chapter from a book by
the environmentalist Thomas Berry here. It's called 'The American College
in the Ecological Age,'*[112] *and I'd like to ask that we all read it before making
any decision about this proposal."*

Brother Andrew paused, picked up a copy of Berry's article and looked
around the room.

*"OK folks, let's take a break. I'd like to read Kathryn's chapter for next
month, and to talk over this issue with all of you at our next meeting. Frank,
I don't want to take St. Francis in the wrong direction on this, but I also don't
want to say goodbye to 7.6 million dollars without a good reason. Let's see if
we can't figure a way to help our students and honor our tradition without
having to stand on the street and beg for coins. That's one Franciscan tradition
I'd just as soon skip."*

Case #5: Environmental Racism: Someone's Backyard

*"You just don't get it, do you Melissa?" Tina asked with exasperation.
"You live in your lily-white neighborhood, where people would never even
try to get away with something like this. And if they did, you and your
neighbors would make certain your council leaders put a stop to the idea of
putting a city incinerator or landfill anywhere near your precious homes,
schools or malls. But you come down to my neighborhood sometime, and I'll
show you around. I'll show you an incinerator a half mile from where I live
just like the new one they want to put in. And I'll show you factories polluting the air and the soil right before your very eyes, and abandoned
"brownfields" everywhere you look, plots of land so filthy with pollution
that they're good for nothing. And there isn't anybody doing anything about
it, or at least anybody with any real clout. And I'll show you little children
playing in buildings with old leaded paint chips on walls and floors, buildings that were supposed to be torn down years ago, but the owners of those
buildings are long gone, and so the city just lets them sit there. Now you tell
me, girl, would that go on where you live?"*

Melissa responded with hesitation. "I'm sorry if what I said angered you, Tina. I didn't mean to say that it's a completely level playing field, that people who are poor aren't exposed to a lot more harms and hazards than other people are. I know they are. What I was trying to say is that I don't see how that means there's something racial going on. I think this is about economics, not race. It's just that there happen to be more blacks and other people of color who are poor than there are whites."

"And I'm sorry that this is awkward and painful for you, Melissa, but I just don't think you really know what you're talking about."

Tina was speaking more deliberately now, trying not to fall into the stereotype lots of her classmates had of angry black women. It was just that the question of environmental racism was so academic and abstract to Melissa and most of these other students. But she and her neighbors on the West Side lived with society's sludge and toxins every day.

"When you say there just happens to be more blacks than whites who are poor, or there just happens to be more blacks and Hispanics and other minorities crammed into the city's most polluted and impoverished and abandoned neighborhoods, you make it sound like an accident. You make it sound like racism wasn't behind this unfortunate little turn of events. Like the middle and upper class were just unfair to poor people, and it was some curious oddity that so many of these poor people just happened to be people of color.

"And Melissa," Tina says, leaning over and pointing a finger at her classmate, " when you say that the poor and blacks 'are exposed' to more environmental hazards than the middle class, you make it sound like God or nature pollutes these neighborhoods. You expose them Melissa, you and your middle-class and white parents and neighbors. Every time you tell the city officials 'not in my backyard' you are telling them 'put it in their backyard,' and they, Melissa, just happen to be poor and black. And I don't think either of those facts is an accident."

"All right, class," the instructor interrupted, "it looks like we're out of time, but certainly not out of energy. Tina and Melissa, I think I have an idea for your term paper project. I'd like you two to collaborate on an essay laying out what you both think would be a just method for the city to use in selecting the site for the new incinerator. You can describe what role you think class and race

play in our current decisions about the environment, and what we ought to do about it. One of the city council members is on the college's board of directors, and I'll invite him to class next month to hear your report and to respond to it. Are you interested?"

"Yes!"Tina answered. "I definitely am."

"Yes, I think I would be too." Melissa nodded.

"Good, see everyone Thursday."

Resources

Environmental Protection Agency *(www.epa/gov)*, Ariel Rios Building, 1200 Pennsylvania Ave. NW, Washington, DC 20460; (202) 260-2090. The federal agency committed "to protect human health and safeguard the natural environment."

Friends of the Earth *(www.foe@foe.org)*, 1025 Vermont Ave., Washington, DC 20005; (202) 783-7400. A national environmental organization dedicated to preserving the health and diversity of the planet for future generations.

Greenpeace USA *(www.greenpeaceusa.org)*, 702 H St. NW, Washington, DC 20001; (800) 326-0959. Greenpeace is the leading organization that uses peaceful and creative activism to protect the global environment.

National Audubon Society *(www.audubon.org)*, 700 Broadway, New York, NY 10003; (212) 979-3000. The National Audubon Society seeks to conserve and restore natural ecosystems, focusing on birds and other wildlife for the benefit of humanity and the earth's biological diversity.

National Wildlife Federation *(www.nwf.org)*, 1400 16th St. NW, # 501, Washington, DC 20036-2263; (202)797-6800. The National Wildlife Federation is the nation's largest member-supported conservation group, uniting individuals, organizations, businesses and government to protect wildlife, wild places and the environment.

Sierra Club *(www.sierraclub.org),* 85 Second St., 2nd Floor, San Francisco, CA 94105-3441; (415) 977-5500. The Sierra Club is committed to practice and promote the responsible use of the earth's ecosystems and resources.

Worldwatch Institute *(www.worldwatch.org),* 1776 Massachusetts Ave., Washington, DC 20036-1904; (202) 452-1999. Worldwatch analyzes interdisciplinary environmental data from around the world, providing information on how to build a sustainable society.

CHAPTER SIX:
Biomedical Ethics

Case #1: Taking Care of Dad

Andy Mitchell is, for the moment, resting comfortably in one of the ICU beds on the seventh floor of Ashland Memorial Hospital, the monitor above his head tracking the steady but frail rhythms of his heart and lungs. Outside in the waiting room things are not so calm. Over some stale coffee Mary Jo Hoskins and Phil Mitchell are discussing their father's future.

Andy, a fairly lonely widower for the last fifteen years, has suffered on and off from clinical depression and developed something of a drinking problem. Just under two years ago his first of several strokes left him with slurred speech and an inability to walk or go to the bathroom on his own. Then, over the next four months he suffered three more strokes, which robbed him of the ability to speak or think clearly. As the doctors told Mary Jo and Phil, the "neurological insult" of these recent strokes have left their dad "severely and permanently cognitively impaired."

At this point Andy's children moved him out of the retirement community and into a nursing home, where Mary Jo and Phil attempt to visit him two or three times a week. These visits are hard, as their father is usually unconscious, and when he is awake he is unaware of where he is or who they are, and cannot communicate with them at all.

Neither Phil nor Mary Jo is happy with this turn of events, and both agree that it would probably have been better if one of Andy's strokes had ended his life. Their grandmother had lingered in a vegetative state for two years before dying, and their dad had said repeatedly that he would hate to die that way, indeed, that he would do anything to avoid such an awful death.

"I don't know how much more I can take of this Phil," Mary Jo says over her now empty cup of coffee. "I've been sitting by his bed for a year and a half. I've watched him wither and shrink in that bed, strapped down so he won't pull out his IV. I've listened to his occasional mumblings and helped the nurse's aide clean his sheets. I've read the sports column to him, knowing there's nobody home, and sick that we've got him trapped here, stuck between life and death. And I know—you know—that this is the thing he would have hated the most in the world. This is exactly what he despised about his mother's death, and why he couldn't talk about her for years after she finally died."

"I know, Mary Jo. I've been at his bedside too. And I was probably wrong to oppose putting a 'no-code' on his chart at the nursing home. This dragging him out to the hospital every time he has another stroke or a heart attack is a mistake. I can see that. But I can't support you taking him home to 'help' him die or to have someone else help you help him. That's wrong."

"Why? Why is it better to let him linger, to make him die the worst sort of death, the death you and I know he would never choose to die? Why is it wrong to help him avoid the weeks, months or years of lingering that might be in front of him? If he could end his life now, I think he would."

"And so do I, Mary Jo, so do I. But that doesn't mean I agree or that I would help or go along with you doing it. Dad was depressed and lonely, and his mother's dying frightened him—badly. And he sometimes made bad judgments, particularly when he was depressed. So the fact that he would have done something doesn't mean it's right.

"Look, I am just not certain we have a right to have complete control over our dying or even that we are entitled to a certain kind of death—some perfect ideal where we get to turn out the lights and orchestrate how everything goes. I think Dad would have had a right to turn down and turn off all sorts of treatments, and I'm willing—maybe a little belatedly—to support those wishes. And I think Dad has a right to good care, to be pain-free and to die at home and with his loved ones—if possible. But I don't think he would have had the right to ask me or you to end his life by killing him, and I don't think we have a right or duty to do that for him now that he can't make that request.

"Yeah, it's hard, ugly and painful—mostly for us—but that doesn't mean we're justified in stepping in to take this life."

"OK," Mary Jo says, after a long silence. "Well, let's tell the doctors we want those changes made on Dad's chart. And then I want to look into taking him home with me. I won't do anything for a month or so. Maybe he'll just pass away from another one of these strokes. But if nothing happens before spring, we're going to have this talk again Phil."

Introduction. The art, science and practice of medicine, which has been around at least since the days of Hippocrates, have undergone revolutionary changes in the last hundred years, experiencing tremendous growth and introducing a wide range of wondrous and sometimes worrisome technologies. These changes have in turn led to a host of fresh ethical questions and dilemmas, and have helped bring about the birth of a new field of moral study known as bioethics.

"The twentieth century has seen enormous growth in American medicine—in the amount of money devoted to medical care, the number of persons with access to care, the number of personnel and specialties, the complexity of institutional systems, and the extent of scientific technology."[1] This growth raises significant moral questions for medicine and for the larger society. Who will pay for increasingly more expensive health care? Is medical care a right or a commodity? How are the poor to be ensured adequate access to basic health care? How are we to distribute limited or scarce medical resources? What role should the government have in funding health care, in providing a safety net for the poor, or in overseeing medical research? Indeed, what sorts of limits ought to be set on medical research or spending?

Still, the most striking transformations in medicine have probably come from the development of a vast and growing array of new technologies that have changed—and are continuing to change—the ways we are born, live and die. Developments in reproductive technology and genetics currently allow us to make a wide range of choices about how and when our children are conceived, and offer hope for the diagnosis and treatment of a growing assortment of genetic disorders and diseases, or indeed the creation of a cloned or perhaps a "perfect" offspring. Meanwhile, a battery of life-saving (or at least life-prolonging) technologies keep pushing death back further and further, making it more and more likely that our dying will be the result of someone's choice to finally "let go" and turn off the machines. Furthermore, we increasingly find ourselves needing to make these choices for other people, often people who have left us no instructions.

As a result of these new technologies we are confronted with a growing number of fresh moral problems. First, because new technologies depend on research and experimentation, we need to ask about the rights of human subjects used in this research, and we often need to balance the need to protect their safety against the need for a speedy cure for a disease threatening the lives of millions. Also, because nearly every new technology is initially scarce and expensive we usually need to decide who does and doesn't get access to it. And since new technologies are inevitably in competition with one another for funding, we need to choose which diseases or procedures get our financial backing. In other words, we find ourselves in some sense asking, "Who lives, and who dies?"

And even when these technologies (usually quite expensive and scarce) become standard practice, we will still need to decide just how far we ought to go in resisting or prolonging death. Is the quality of our life more important than the quantity? How much suffering in the face of death is to be tolerated? When can we say enough is enough and let ourselves, or our loved ones, die? And can we ever *do something* to bring death about? Finally, we need to decide just who gets (or has) to make all these choices. Doctors? Patients? Guardians? The courts? And when we make such choices for other people, what sort of norms or guidelines will we follow to make sure we are being fair to those who can't speak for themselves?

In this chapter about bioethics we try to face a number of these questions from a Christian perspective. We ask what Christians believe about medicine, health, death and suffering, and about our obligations to take care of our own health and bodies and to come to the aid of our sick and suffering neighbors. And, listening to the voices of Scripture, tradition, reason and experience, we try to determine how the Christian community calls us to respond to questions about who lives, who dies, who gets health care, how hard should we wrestle against death and who gets to make these choices.

As in other places, we begin with a brief historical sketch, looking at the story of medical ethics in four phases. Next we turn to character, naming some virtues that might be helpful in living out our Christian calling to care for our health and the health of our neighbors, to be good patients, healers and citizens. Then we look at three rather controversial choices in medical ethics—physician-assisted suicide, reproductive interventions and genetic engineering—and ask about some possible Christian responses to these issues. Following that we address two social or structural sins relating to medical care—the commodification of medicine and the denial of death—and we suggest some Christian responses to these evils. Finally, the chapter will close with four more cases and a set of resources for further study.

The Story of Ethics in Medicine

Phase One: The Hippocratic Tradition.[2] The birth of medicine as a profession in the West took place in Greece near the end of the sixth century B.C.E. and was soon followed by the appearance of a number of oaths and other writings on the moral duties and character of the ideal physician. Thus began the field of medical ethics. The most famous of these ancient ethical texts were associated with (but not written by) Hippocrates, a fifth-century-B.C.E. physician and teacher from the island of Cos, who has long been referred to as both "the father of medicine" and "the father of medical ethics."

The Hippocratic tradition and other Greek writings of this period were primarily concerned with developing a professional ethics for physicians, and this focus on doctors' duties to their patients and profession has dominated medical ethics in the West for most of the past 2,500 years. At the heart of this professional ethics is a vision of the virtuous physician, a competent, conscientious and compassionate professional committed to the good of the patient and the skillful practice of the medical arts. Doctors are to be objective and unselfish, to conduct themselves with integrity, grace and decorum, to respect patient confidentiality and to avoid sexual impropriety. They are to refrain from overcharging or harassing the sick about their fees and from offering useless remedies, encouraging false hopes or needlessly prolonging the suffering or death of their patients. And they are to maintain their own health and weight as proof that they have the skills and virtue needed to help or heal others.

The Hippocratic tradition committed physicians to the principles of beneficence and nonmaleficence, meaning that doctors must seek to help patients and should avoid harming them. At the same time, although the Hippocratic oath condemned abortion and assisted suicide, the medical ethics and practice of ancient Greece and Rome clearly allowed for both of these procedures. Indeed, the majority of ancient medical authors did not forbid abortion, the killing of defective newborns, suicide or physicians assisting their patients in this act.

One of the most enduring effects of the Hippocratic tradition's focus on physicians and their duties to patients has been a certain degree of medical paternalism. Traditional medical ethics, written largely from the doctor's perspective, has presumed that medical choices are physicians' choices, that the doctor knows best and that it is the duty of patients (and nurses) to follow the doctor's orders. Until very recently a physician-centered medical ethics has largely ignored or overlooked the autonomy and rights of patients, as well as a number of larger societal questions relating to medicine and health care. As we will see, however, those days are largely over.

Phase Two: Christian and Catholic Medical Ethics.[3] Ancient Greek and Roman physicians were primarily interested in the physical causes of their patients' diseases, but Christians also wrestled with the theological meanings of human illness and suffering, and with the role and place of medicine in their lives. The Christian tradition has generally seen sickness as the result of sin and humanity's fall from grace, as an invitation to share in the redemptive sufferings of Christ or as flowing from natural causes. As a result, Christian writers have encouraged the sick to repent of their sins, to join their sufferings to Christ's and to turn to a doctor. Down through the centuries sick Christians and their loved ones have relied on both prayer and medicine, and have seen the latter as part and parcel of being good stewards of their own health and as a way of reaching out to care for their sick and suffering neighbors.

Indeed, the greatest impact Christianity has had on Western medicine and medical ethics came from its emphasis on compassion for the sick and its demand that physicians and all Christians make a preferential option for those who are ill. Under Christianity compassion for the sick became the central virtue of medical practice. As the medical historian Henry Sigerist once noted, Christianity brought about "the most revolutionary and decisive change in the attitude of society toward the sick....It became the duty of the Christian to attend to the sick and the poor of the community."[4] By the fourth century local bishops and monastic communities were organizing Christian care for the sick and founding the first of what would be a long line of Christian hospitals and health-care institutions.

Christian medical ethics has also been distinguished by its commitment to the sanctity of human life. Arguing that every human life is sacred and that humans are stewards and not owners of their lives, Christians have rejected abortion, infanticide, suicide and euthanasia. Still, the Christian tradition has not seen death as the ultimate enemy, nor supported desperate medical efforts uselessly prolonging a patient's suffering and death.

Beginning in the late middle ages Christian and later Catholic writings in moral theology addressed a number of the ethical choices and cases that physicians confront in their professional lives. By the nineteenth and twentieth centuries Catholic moral theology had developed a body of writings in "pastoral medicine" or medical ethics, which dealt with a large number of moral problems facing Catholic doctors, nurses and hospitals. In general these writings followed natural-law reasoning and emphasized the teachings of the Catholic hierarchy. They also relied on a handful of established moral

principles, including: the sanctity of human life, the procreative purpose of human sexuality, stewardship, totality and certain norms governing acts with good and bad consequences and deeds performed in
cooperation with others.

Phase Three: Nursing Ethics.[5] This story of ethics in medicine
continues with the sad fact that until very recently women were
often treated as second-class persons in medicine, and even now
patriarchy continues to have a significant impact on medical practice.
Western medicine long excluded women from becoming physicians
and sometimes condemned women healers as charlatans or witches.
Ironically, all this is in spite of the fact that women's religious communities have for centuries sponsored and staffed the majority of
Catholic hospitals, and women have nearly always supplied most of
the health "care" provided to the sick and suffering, at home or elsewhere. At the same time male-dominated medical practice and
research have often been conducted as if men were the medical
norm, and women were merely a variant type of person.

In nineteenth-century England nursing was established as a distinct profession when Florence Nightingale founded the first school
of nursing and identified a set of moral norms that would direct
nurses for years to come. Early writings focused on the training and
character of the good nurse, who was to be an educated and skilled
professional, but also (perhaps primarily) a "good woman," and one
who was obedient to the physician. Indeed, until the middle of the
twentieth century nursing journals and professional codes noted that
the nurse's first responsibility was to the doctor and not to the
patient, and argued that "the nurse is under an obligation to carry out
the physician's orders intelligently and loyally."[6]

Since the 1960s feminist thought has contributed to two significant shifts in nursing ethics. First, nurses no longer see themselves as
the physician's handmaid, nor do they envision their primary obligation as serving the doctor's wishes. Instead, their first focus or duty as
medical professionals is to care for their sick patients. Second, challenging what many see as an overly abstract and rule-based approach

to medical ethics, some feminist authors like Nell Noddings have proposed an "ethics of care," focusing on the personal relationships nurses often have with their patients and the critical importance of affections like compassion in good medical practice.

Phase Four: The Birth of Bioethics.[7] Since the 1960s there has been something of an explosion in the field of medical ethics, resulting in the birth of what has come to be known as bioethics and introducing a wide range of new ethical concerns and questions.

One factor contributing to the birth of bioethics has been the introduction of a number of new medical technologies, which have in turn generated a series of fresh and often troubling ethical questions. In the early 1960s life-saving dialysis machines first became available for some but not all patients suffering from kidney failure, and dialysis centers soon needed to deal with the problem of deciding who would receive a life-saving kidney transplant and who would not, as well as who would make those choices. Many felt that such decisions were not merely medical, and required the input of philosophers, clergy and members of the larger community. By the mid-1960s heart transplants and respirators had raised other troubling questions about when people actually died and how far we ought to go to prolong the lives of patients. Questions about when we might withdraw or withhold potentially life-saving or at least life-prolonging measures became particularly troubling when dealing with incompetent or unconscious patients, and families and physicians who were unable to resolve these cases sometimes turned to the courts.

New technologies have also changed the ways people can be conceived and born, and create a host of moral dilemmas for physicians, prospective parents and the wider communities to which we belong. Advances in reproductive technologies and genetics have allowed previously infertile couples to conceive their children through in vitro fertilization, to make use of a donor's sperm, eggs or uterus in the reproductive process, and—perhaps not so far in the future—to clone themselves. Meanwhile, genetic testing allows prospective parents (and others) to discover genetic diseases in themselves or their unborn children, and an unfolding array of gene therapies is becoming available to address these problems, or perhaps to help us fashion more "perfect" children and citizens.

A second factor contributing to the growth of bioethics as a discipline has been the realization that traditional medical ethics did not address all of the concerns related to ethics and medicine. Nor did it pay sufficient attention to all of the players—particularly the patient, but also the larger community.

Since the 1960s physicians have increasingly been forced to surrender their role as medicine's primary stakeholders and decision makers, and the right of patients to make choices for themselves has become for many *the* central moral norm of bioethics. The age of medical paternalism is largely over, and the age of patient autonomy is upon us. In part the focus on patients' rights came in response to reports in the 1960s and 1970s about medical experiments that failed to treat patients as persons or ignored their right to informed consent. And in part the stress on patient autonomy was the result of a growing perception that choices about terminating care and dying were human and moral decisions, and not necessarily medical ones. In this area the doctor, it would seem, did not know best.

What's more, with the growth of modern medicine into a major economic, political and social institution, ethics in medicine is no longer (if it ever was) just about doctors and their patients. There are questions for society about affordable access to health care, about the distribution and delivery of scarce or expensive medical resources and about the share of the national budget that should go to medicine. There are issues that need to be addressed by the churches and religious communities that sponsor hospitals and health-care institutions, and by the private or public insurance and health-management companies that shape so much of contemporary health care in the United States and elsewhere. There are legal, moral, religious and economic concerns relating to the good, just and compassionate practice of medicine, and bioethics seeks to address these issues.

A final factor that has contributed to the development of the discipline and practice of bioethics has been the emergence of various research centers, academic journals and professional organizations devoted to the study of ethical issues in health care. The Hastings Center (1969) and the Kennedy Institute of Ethics of Georgetown University (1971) were two of the first of these research centers. Today many universities support centers for the study of bioethical issues, and the number of journals and professional organizations devoted to bioethics has multiplied.

CHARACTER: Called to Be Disciples "In Sickness and in Health"

As Christians we are called to holiness *and* to wholeness. We humans are enfleshed souls, each of us a mysterious and sacred unity of mind, body and spirit fashioned in the "image of God." Indeed, God has not only formed our embodied spirits, but taken up this sacred flesh and redeemed our whole humanity—body, mind and spirit—through Christ's suffering, death and resurrection.

This means, as Methodist ethicist Paul Ramsey pointed out, that each of us is "a sacredness in the natural, biological order...a sacredness in bodily life...a sacredness in illness and in dying."[8] For Christians the sacredness of our ensouled flesh means three things. As stewards of this gift of life we are to take good and reasonable care of our health and the health of those placed in our care. We are to offer compassionate care and (when possible) healing to our sick, suffering and dying neighbors. And in our own illness and suffering we are somehow connected to the frailty and brokenness of all humanity, and to the suffering and death of Christ.

As in other areas of our life, we live out our call to discipleship "in sickness and in health" within a variety of roles and relationships that tie us to persons and communities near and far. And we seek to live up to the moral obligations generated by these differing roles by putting on and practicing certain virtues. Within the practice of medicine we may find ourselves cast as patients, healers, researchers or citizens. In each of these roles we are tied to others and called to take up those attitudes, affections and habits that will help us to be "good" persons and to do the "right" thing.

Once again, before identifying the specific virtues needed to be "good" or Christian patients, healers, researchers or citizens we offer a short list of basic commitments that ought to shape the approach of every Christian to the practice of medicine. First, the dignity and sanctity of each human person, of each embodied spirit, are at the very heart of Christian ethics. Second, our role as stewards demands that we take care of our health and the health of those left in our care. Third, compassion for the sick and suffering is at the very center of any Christian practice of medicine or health care. Both the Hebrew Scriptures' focus on the *anawim* ("God's little ones") and the New Testament's call for an embodied love for those in need make it clear that disciples of Christ are challenged to care for any neighbor burdened or broken by illness. Fourth, those who are sick and frail need not only our care and treatment, but also our fidelity and trustworthiness. In caring for the ill and suffering, Christians must honor the trust that has been placed in them, and not abandon or take advantage of their superior strength or position.

Specific Roles

Patients. Since the 1960s we have become increasingly aware that patients are persons too, moral agents with a right and duty to participate (as fully as possible) in their own treatment and care, and the primary caretakers of their health when they are not ill. We have long known that doctors and nurses do not heal us without our cooperation, but recently we have come to recognize that persons who are patients are also partners in their medical treatment, and not just the physician's obedient servants. At the same time, our society's growing attention to wellness and preventive medicine underscore the fact that each of us has primary responsibility for taking good care of our own health.

As stewards of our own embodied spirits we have a duty to God and ourselves to take care of our health. We also have a duty to those who depend upon us, to our children and spouses and to all our loved ones. And we have some duty to the larger communities to which we belong and contribute. For their sake too we ought not to abuse our bodies or health and become an unnecessary burden on others.

Being good stewards of our health requires a variety of virtues. Humility and gratitude help us recognize that the life we have is in fact a gift, and encourage us to treasure this gift and take reasonable care of our health. Temperance helps us be wise in regard to the use of food, drink and exercise in the care of our health and life, and prudence helps us to balance the good of our health against other goods in our life.

And what virtues do we require when we are not well? What do we need to be "good patients?" Becoming sick, becoming a patient often involves a series of progressively graver losses. We can lose our sense of well-being or comfort, our strength can fail us, our resistance to infections and diseases may evaporate. Sometimes we can't eat, sleep or concentrate. Often we can't do things for ourselves or even decide what needs to be done. Even our sense of purpose or meaning can come under assault.

In her essay on "The Virtuous Patient," Protestant ethicist Karen Lebacqz argues that when illness has moved out of the wings and onto center stage we need three virtues to be good patients: fortitude, prudence and hope.[9] Fortitude, or courage, enables us to face the losses and suffering of our illness, to come to grips with our temporary or permanent loss of freedom and health. Our courage is one part acceptance, equanimity in the face of suffering. But it is also one part fierce determination to fight and rage against the insults and losses of our sickness. For courage can make us howl against being sidelined and diminished and cry out that we want what we have lost returned to us, and that we are willing and determined to struggle and suffer to make it so. Prudence, on the other hand, helps us to pay attention to what is real, to what is possible (or can be made possible). It helps to guide us when making choices about treatment plans and proposed therapies. It helps us to recognize what each plan will cost us and to know when we have reached the point where we need to start making other plans. And hope enables us to move into our illness and treatment with a vision of what can be, not just here and now, but no matter what happens to us. Like our courage, our hope is made up of parts. It is one part humor, that magical ability to transcend our suffering by discovering or recovering the comic in our lives, the refusal to be drawn into despair's basement. And hope is one part trust, faith in the possibility of the present moment, and in the God who is present in the very midst of our suffering and losses and who does not abandon us even in death.

Health-Care Providers. Since Hippocrates we have known that the physician needs to be virtuous, and in the nineteenth century Florence Nightingale laid out the virtues required of those entering the nursing profession. Still, in hospitals, hospices and nursing homes it is not just doctors and nurses who care for the sick. Aides, technicians, radiologists, social workers, therapists, dieticians, counselors and chaplains share the work of tending the sick and accompanying them along the path of their disease and/or recovery. And in our homes parents care for their sick children and grown children for their failing parents and grandparents.

Whether as trained professionals or family members, the role of caregiver places us in a special relationship with the sick, with those who have come to need and depend on our help. We have a duty to come to their aid, to provide competent, even excellent care. We must work diligently to help them get better and to ease their pain and suffering. We must acknowledge their frailty and dignity and respect their privacy, trust and choices. And we are obliged to keep them company while they struggle and suffer.

What virtues do we need to be good healers, good nurses and doctors, good caregivers? Ramsey argues that the practice of medicine requires at least these five: justice, fairness, righteousness, faithfulness and charity.[10] And in the text *The Virtues in Medical Practice,* Edmund Pellegrino and David Thomasma suggest that the virtuous physician should be trustworthy, compassionate, prudent, just, courageous, temperate and self-effacing.[11] Adding to these lists, Martin Benjamin and Joy Curtis note in an essay on "Virtue and the Practice of Nursing" that the good nurse must be honest, courageous, and just.[12] We offer a combined version of these lists, suggesting that the virtuous caregiver must exhibit five core traits: compassion, fidelity, justice, courage and prudence.

Compassion is the central virtue of Christian medical ethics and should be the first virtue of those who tend to the sick. More than mere sympathy for those in pain, compassion is a sense of solidarity with the sick, a willingness to pay attention to the uniqueness and dignity of each patient and a readiness to share in their suffering, to accompany them on their frightening journey.

Because the health, hopes, bodies and confidences of patients are often entrusted to caregivers, they must be trustworthy and faithful persons. They must keep their word, not making promises they cannot honor. They must keep their patients' secrets and protect their privacy, except when keeping such confidences does some greater harm. And they must be loyal, not abandoning those who have come to depend and count upon them.

Caregivers must also practice justice in the covenants they have entered into with the sick, and with their families. In their relations with their patients they must practice commutative justice, giving a fair exchange for the trust and compensation being offered them. And they must practice a sort of distributive justice in their treatment of all the sick, showing no preference to the rich or powerful, and being sure that every person is treated fairly by them.

So too, caregivers will often need courage or fortitude in their work. It requires a certain amount of "stomach" to face many of the distasteful parts of medicine. And a certain degree of fortitude is needed to keep struggling against daunting illnesses or to encourage one's patients to do the same. Nor is it always an easy thing to face the risk of contagious diseases, particularly when they can be fatal.

Finally, caregivers must be prudent. For they are the ones called upon to make judgments or offer counsel regarding a course of treatment. They will need to say what ought to be done, what would be futile to try and when it makes sense to begin making plans to end treatment altogether.

Researchers. Medicine, however, is not just about providing care. It is also about providing *better* care, about pushing back the frontiers of medical knowledge, about finding cures for diseases and developing more effective and less painful treatments for a variety of conditions. This means that the health-care providers and caregivers discussed above are not the only people who practice medicine. Medical researchers and scientists also provide a critical medical service to both patients and the larger community.

We have a moral obligation to use our God-given intellect to improve our medical knowledge and skills and discover new treatments and cures for those suffering from sickness. We have this duty to those who are currently ill and to those who will be ill in the future. At the same time, we have an obligation to protect the safety, dignity and rights of patients and all persons who become subjects in any medical research. The covenants that tie us to these persons require that we never forget to treat them as partners, overlook their right to informed consent or take inordinate risks with their health or lives. Furthermore, as stewards of our lives and bodies we have a duty to exercise care and caution and to avoid doing what could be irreparable harm to our genes and the genes of our children.

In our role as researchers, then, we need to practice prudence. We need to discern which research projects will provide the most benefit to persons and communities, and what would be the most effective way to go about doing that research. Often enough we have to balance the need to find a quick cure for a deadly illness against the need both to be thorough in our research and to protect the safety of research subjects. And we increasingly need to reflect on the short- and long-term risks and advantages of current and future research in genetics and reproductive technologies, asking just how such research might affect our humanity and our descendents.

At the same time the role of researcher requires the virtue of justice. To begin with, we need to treat research subjects with a basic justice, respecting their rights and dignity as persons. Justice in this setting demands that human subjects not be coerced or manipulated into participating in a research project and that researchers not take undue advantage of particularly vulnerable populations (like prisoners, the mentally handicapped or children). Justice also demands that sick and especially dying patients not be misled about the possible benefits such research could offer them and that no person be exposed to unwarranted or avoidable risks. So too, justice sets some limits on what kinds of things can be done to human subjects, or to their bodies or DNA. There are some things that persons cannot consent to have done to them, even for the sake of medical research. Finally, justice requires that medical researchers should not refrain from working on treatments or medications that could bring relief to millions in poor countries simply because these discoveries would offer little profit to their employers or investors.

Citizens. We also influence the health and health care of others through our role as citizens. As taxpayers and voters we have something to say about how much money the government appropriates for health care, and about how and where those funds are spent. We can decide what provisions are made for the poor, the elderly and minorities, and what kind of access they have to affordable health care. Or we can determine what diseases or research projects get priority and which ones get left on the back burner. We can also put pressure on our legislators to approve or oppose differing types of medical or genetic research, or to support or reject new legislation dealing with abortion, assisted suicide, euthanasia or a growing number of reproductive and genetic technologies. And we can petition our representatives to take action on a broad array of health-related topics, from regulating tobacco advertising to ensuring food safety to limiting environmental pollution.

Catholic social teaching affirms that health care is a basic human good and right. It is demanded by our dignity as persons and required if we are to flourish as either individuals or communities. John XXIII argues in "Peace on Earth" that every person has a "right to life, to bodily integrity, and to the means which are necessary and suitable for the proper development of life."[13] These means include, among other things, "medical care." So too, in their 1981 "Pastoral Letter on Health and Health Care," the U.S. Catholic bishops call upon American society to "move toward the establishment of a national policy which guarantees adequate health care for all" and affirms that "every person has a basic right to adequate health care. This right flows from the sanctity of human life and the dignity that belongs to all human persons, who are made in the image of God."[14]

As citizens called to be disciples, then, we need to practice justice. We do this by protecting the basic right of all persons to life and health care, and by making certain that each group and community gets a "fair share" of our national health-care budget. When evaluating new legislation or funding for various sorts of biomedical research we must be certain that the sanctity and dignity of human life are fully protected. We must also be committed to ensuring that every person and community have access to adequate health care. The current scandal of more than forty million Americans without such access is a violation of social and distributive justice. And our obligation in justice to provide health care for the poor does not end at our own national borders, but calls us to support the same rights for people everywhere.

At the same time we need to practice a certain amount of prudence in our role as citizens. For we have to decide just what portion of our national budget should go to health care and how much we should set aside for other issues and concerns, like education, welfare, transportation, defense, etc. We also need to determine how much of our health-care budget should be put into preventive medicine, hospital care and/or hi-tech research. What are the best uses of our limited medical resources? And we need to decide what mixture of government and private programs would provide the best health care for all our citizens, especially the poor. Furthermore, we have to assess the risks and advantages of a wide assortment of new biomedical and genetic technologies and procedures, and must determine what sorts of legislation would be most effective in protecting the dignity and sanctity of human life. All of these choices call for keen moral judgment and genuine wisdom.

CHOICES: Three Contemporary Issues in Biomedical Ethics

The list of important or controversial issues in biomedical ethics is a long one. The three choices we will examine in this section are physician-assisted suicide, technological interventions in reproduction and genetics.

Physician-Assisted Suicide

The Voices of Experience

The Voice of History. The Hippocratic oath prohibited physicians giving their patients a deadly drug or making any suggestion in this direction, even if asked. Still, as Darrel Amundsen notes, "...assisting in suicide was a relatively common practice for Greek and Roman physicians, and condemnations of the practice were infrequent."[15] Indeed, although Socrates and Plato argue that suicide is normally a violation of religious and civic duties, both they and most Greek and Roman Stoics "justified induced death for severely sick and suffering humans."[16] Aristotle and the Pythagorean school (which may have been responsible for the Hippocratic oath) seem to have been fairly lone voices in their objection to physician-assisted suicide.

With the rise of Christianity, however, suicide and euthanasia came to be seen as grave sins, and Western medicine rejected the practice of assisted suicide as inconsistent with its basic mission. Augustine, who offers the most forceful attack on suicide, argues that ending one's life violates the commandment against murder (Exod 20:13) and precludes the possibility of repentance. In the centuries that followed most mainstream Christian and Western thinkers like Thomas Aquinas, John

Locke, John Wesley, Immanuel Kant and Georg Hegel continued to oppose suicide as immoral, while a minority of dissenters, including John Donne, Michel de Montaigne, David Hume and Arthur Schopenhauer argued that suicide could sometimes be justified.

In the first part of the twentieth century groups supporting voluntary euthanasia for patients suffering from intractable pain surfaced in Great Britain, the United States and elsewhere, and bills allowing for physician-assisted suicide were introduced in several states, though none passed. Much of the support for voluntary euthanasia and mercy killing evaporated, however, when the world learned about Nazi doctors killing the senile, the mentally ill and a wide range of so-called worthless people. Still, by the early 1990s growing fears of a painful, prolonged and undignified death had led to a resurgence of interest in assisted suicide. National surveys indicated that a significant majority of Americans approve of physician-assisted suicide in certain settings, and legislative initiatives in support of this procedure appeared in several states and passed in one.

Contemporary Voices. In 1997 the U.S. Supreme Court determined that states are free to pass legislation regarding physician-assisted suicide. Oregon had already done so in its 1996 "Death with Dignity Act," a law allowing a competent adult suffering from a terminal disease to "make a written request for medication for the purpose of ending his or her life in a humane and dignified manner."[17] As a result, physicians in Oregon are free to act in accord with such requests and have begun to do so. In 1998 sixteen people ended their lives in accord with the guidelines set forth in Oregon's law; the next year twenty-seven people did so.[18]

Those favoring physician-assisted suicide offer several arguments in support of their position. First, they note that allowing patients to choose to end their lives would protect their personal autonomy. Second, they contend that giving patients this choice allows them to avoid a prolonged, painful and undignified death, to meet death on their own terms and to avoid becoming a burden to their loved ones. Third, they argue that there is no significant moral difference between "allowing a patient to die" by terminating all medical treatment and ending this life by a direct act. If the first can be morally justified, they claim, so can the second. Fourth, they believe that serious pain cannot always be sufficiently alleviated and that physicians caring for such suffering patients should be free to help them without fear of criminal prosecution.[19]

Opponents of physician-assisted suicide offer a number of counter arguments. First, they note that the killing of one's patients or participating in their suicide is incompatible with the vocation of physicians and would undermine the trust patients have in their doctors.[20] Second, they contend that there is a real moral difference between allowing persons to die and killing them. The sanctity of human life prohibits directly attacking any life, but it does not require taking every measure to postpone our dying. Third, they argue that compassion for the sick and suffering does not mean taking their lives, but accompanying them through the full process of their dying. Fourth, they express numerous reservations about the consequences of legalizing physician-assisted suicide: that poor or "difficult" patients would be more likely to be "assisted" in their dying; that requests from clinically depressed patients would be accepted; and that assisted suicide could well lead to involuntary euthanasia involving a wide range of incompetent or "unworthy" patients.

Voices from the Margins. Those who support physician-assisted suicide argue that we must not ignore the plaintive cries of conscious, competent patients who beg for release from a painful and protracted death.[21] At the same time, opponents of physician-assisted suicide remind us to be concerned about other voices from the margins: elderly patients who fear becoming a burden to their families, clinically depressed patients who seek suicide as a remedy for a treatable condition, patients receiving inadequate pain management and poor patients lacking access to adequate health care.

One grave concern about physician-assisted suicide is that many patients who are not suffering from a terminal condition or truly intractable pain will be tempted to seek this treatment as a remedy for other problems. Elderly or increasingly frail persons who fear a growing dependence and the "indignity" of becoming a burden upon others could well be drawn (or feel pressured) to seek out suicide as a remedy to their slow decline. Clinically depressed patients, whose condition is highly treatable, could see assisted suicide as a means of escaping their emotional suffering. And patients receiving inadequate treatment for their pain could easily be tempted to turn to suicide as a way out. In each of these cases we need to listen carefully to the cries for help from persons who are frightened, sad and suffering, and we need to respond in ways that are truly compassionate, helpful and appropriate.

Another concern about physician-assisted suicide is that poor patients may find themselves pressured to seek out this treatment much more than those who are fortunate enough to have good health insurance. In a society with spiraling health-care costs, with a growing gap between rich and poor, and with more than forty million people without any health-care coverage, poor and minority patients could have good reasons to be afraid that they might be offered assisted suicide more often than those who could afford to pay for continued and expensive medical care.[22]

Scripture. In turning to Scripture we find four points that are relevant to our reflections on physician-assisted suicide. There is no explicit or direct prohibition of suicide in either the Hebrew Scriptures or the New Testament. There are several accounts in Scripture of persons who take their lives, but no specific condemnation of this behavior. This is true even in regard to Judas's suicide after betraying Jesus (Matthew's Gospel, the only one to discuss the suicide of Judas, actually seems more interested in noting Judas's remorse than in condemning his suicide: Matt 27:3–5). Throughout the Bible human life is seen as a sacred gift from God. As a result, we find both commandments against the taking of life and a general expectation that persons will be good stewards of their lives. And as we have seen elsewhere, biblical authors speak of a duty to show compassion for the weak and suffering, and not to abandon them in their hour of need.

In a recent work on suicide and martyrdom in the ancient world, biblical scholars Arthur Droge and James Tabor note that "the Bible nowhere proscribes suicide," and that later Christian theologians "were hard pressed to find *any* biblical texts that prohibit or speak negatively about voluntary death."[23] Among all the lists of rules and sins found in either the Hebrew Scriptures or the New Testament there is no explicit condemnation or prohibition of persons taking their own lives. And yet we know from elsewhere that the practice of suicide and physician-assisted suicide were both well known and widely accepted in the ancient Greco-Roman world.

What is more striking for Droge and Tabor, though not for a number of other biblical scholars, is that "there are at least seven individuals in the Bible who take their own lives, and none of them is condemned for the act."[24] In the Hebrew Scriptures there are six such persons: Abimelech (Judg 9:50–57), Samson (Judg 16:23–31), Saul and his armor bearer (1 Sam 31), Ahithophel (2 Sam 17:23) and Zimri (1 Kgs 16:18–19). The biblical authors do not criticize any of these individuals for taking their lives, and three of them receive honorable burials. As we have noted, in the New Testament Judas Iscariot (Matt 27:3–5) takes his life in remorse over having betrayed Jesus, and Droge and Tabor argue that Matthew does not see this suicide as an additional sin, but as a sign of Judas's grief.

At the same time, it is clear that throughout Scripture human life is seen as a sacred gift from God, a gift over which only God has full dominion and which we are to care for as good stewards. In the creation accounts of the first chapters of Genesis we read that humans have been fashioned in the image and likeness of God (1:27) and that God has bent down to the earth and blown into our nostrils the breath of life (2:7). Our lives, then, are both sacred and a gift, and we are stewards of this holy gift. As a result, there are biblical commands against the taking of a human life (Gen 9:6 and Exod 20:13) and reminders that only God has full authority over life and death (Job 1:21 and Wis 16:13). Still, while life is sacred, Scripture does not forbid all killing and does not oblige us to make every sacrifice to protect or prolong life. Nonetheless, the Bible's strong defense of the sanctity and giftedness of life must be considered when evaluating the morality of assisted suicide.

Finally, as we have repeatedly noted elsewhere, Scripture consistently affirms our moral obligation to show compassion and justice to those who suffer, making certain never to abandon or mistreat them. Time and time again the Hebrew Scriptures remind us to come to the aid of the *anawim* ("God's little ones") and to help the widows, orphans, foreigners and poor in our midst (Deut 10:18). In the New Testament (Luke 4:18) Jesus announces that he has come to "bring good news to the poor...release to the captives...sight to the blind, [and] to let the oppressed go free." He also commands his disciples to feed the hungry, clothe the naked and visit the sick (Matt 25:35–36), and throughout his life reaches out in compassion to the sick and dying around him. At the very heart of the Bible is a command to imitate the God who hears the cries of the poor and to stand with those who suffer. This call to compassion and justice for those in the margins must also shape our reflections on physician-assisted suicide.

Tradition. Over the centuries Christianity has opposed suicide on five grounds. First, it was a violation of God's sovereignty over human life. As the author of the *Catechism of the Council of Trent* argued, "no man has such dominion over his life as to be at liberty to put himself to death."[25] Second, suicide was a rejection of God's gift of life and contradicted our basic instinct for self-preservation. Thus moral handbooks described suicide as a sin against God and our nature. Third, killing oneself meant breaking the fifth commandment (Exod 20:13) and violating the church's longstanding and exceptionless rule against directly taking innocent human life. Fourth, suicide injured the community, depriving society of one of its members and often enough demoralizing those loved ones left behind. And fifth, Catholic teaching has recently noted that suicide and euthanasia violate our right to life, "a fundamental right," according to the Vatican's 1980 "Declaration on Euthanasia," "which can neither be lost or alienated."[26]

This opposition to suicide, however, has not meant that Catholic teaching requires that dying patients or their doctors do *everything* to sustain or extend their lives. Indeed, the church has long maintained a distinction between "ordinary" (mandatory) and "extraordinary" (optional) medical treatments, arguing that patients were only obliged to use those means that offered them real benefit without incurring undue burden, suffering or cost. As Pope Pius XII wrote, "normally one is obliged to use only ordinary means—means that do not involve any grave burden to oneself or another."[27] Indeed, the pope notes, to ask anything more of terminally ill patients would constitute too grave a burden for them and could well interfere with their preparations for a good death.

As a result, Catholic teaching has supported the use of advance directives and living wills directing medical professionals to withdraw or withhold treatments that no longer offer any reasonable benefit or have become too burdensome for this patient. Catholic thought has also supported effective pain management, even when this involved dosages so powerful that they might hasten the dying process, and many Catholic bishops and ethicists argue that artificial hydration and nutrition may be withdrawn when they serve only to prolong the dying process. Each of these practices has been seen as part of good medicine, medicine directed at the care and accompaniment of the sick and dying.

Nonetheless, the Catholic Church (and Western medicine) has consistently drawn a line between allowing terminal patients to die from their untreatable injuries and diseases and stepping in to hasten this process. It has seen a significant moral difference between discontinuing treatments that no longer offer any real promise of helping the dying and actually killing patients. The first has been seen as ethical, the second as violating some of the most ancient tenets of Christian morality and Western medicine.[28]

Regardless of one's benign intent, official Catholic teaching has seen assisted suicide as a violation of the duty to care for the sick and suffering, to keep company with them as they live up against their dying. As Pope John Paul II notes, "true *compassion* leads to sharing another's pain; it does not kill the person whose suffering we cannot bear...the request which arises [from these patients]...is above all a request for companionship, sympathy and support in the time of trial."[29] The Catholic theologian Richard McCormick makes the same point when he notes that "assisted suicide is a flight from compassion, not an expression of it. It should be suspect not because it is too hard, but because it is too easy."[30]

In recent years some Catholic and wider Christian ethicists have suggested that assisted suicide might be moral in certain limited situations, like that of a dying patient suffering from intractable and unbearable pain. Daniel Maguire argues that in such exceptional cases taking direct steps to end a life would not be an attack on God's dominion over life but an exercise of God-given freedom and responsibility as moral agents.[31] Charles Curran suggests that once persons have begun the final process of dying there is no longer any real moral difference between letting them die and intervening to shorten their life.[32] So too, Lisa Cahill and James Nelson argue that our duty to respect the sanctity of human life and the dignity of persons might not mean we can never directly intervene to end a patient's life.[33]

At the same time, many other Christian and Catholic thinkers continue to warn of the harmful consequences of legalizing physician-assisted suicide.[34] Along with others, John Paris complains that allowing doctors to kill or help kill their patients is not an appropriate way to address legitimate fears of a painful, protracted and undignified death. Adopting physician-assisted suicide as public policy, he argues, will not result in better care for dying or suffering patients. It would, however, "change the traditional role of physician from healer to terminator…[and] add substantially to the range of permissible killing in our society."[35] Furthermore, such a practice, particularly if based on the patient's right to autonomy, would be difficult to control. We might soon be facing requests from and for large numbers of persons who are neither dying nor suffering from intractable pain. And whole categories of marginalized persons (like the poor and the disabled) could be encouraged to seek this remedy.

Formulating a Christian Response. How, then, should we respond to the issue of physician-assisted suicide, either as individuals facing such a decision or request, or as citizens or public officials considering legislation about this matter?

Some Basic Convictions. First, human life is a sacred gift from God, and we are charged to be good stewards of that gift. Indeed, as Paul Ramsey has argued, every human person "is a sacredness in bodily life," and no human person or life is worthless or disposable. Second, the call to show compassion for the suffering is at the very heart of biblical and Christian ethics and has been the cornerstone of Christianity's practice of medicine for two millennia. Whatever else Christians may do in facing the question of physician-assisted suicide, we should not make choices that undermine the sanctity of human life or represent an abandonment of the suffering and dying in their greatest hour of need. Third, while human life is sacred, it is not the overriding value in every set of circumstances. Christians are not obliged to use every means to prolong life, and in certain tragic situations it may be necessary to take a life. Still, the Catholic tradition has long affirmed that the direct taking of innocent life is forbidden. Fourth, while human life is a gift from God, so is human freedom, and personal autonomy is an important moral value, even if it is not the only one. Patients, then, need to be at the center of all decisions made about their care and treatment, particularly those concerned with their death and dying. Fifth, every effort must be made to address growing fears of a protracted, painful and undignified death, committing ourselves as a society to provide adequate and compassionate care for the sick and dying. Killing persons cannot be a substitute for doing the hard work of caring for the suffering. Finally, physician-assisted suicide is not merely a private moral concern. Allowing this practice would have larger institutional and societal implications and consequences affecting the larger practice of medicine and the care of the dying. Any moral judgment about physician-assisted suicide, then, must address these broader concerns.

Some Difficult Questions. Can there ever be an exception to the rule against suicide or the prohibition of directly taking an innocent human life? Does every act aimed at ending the life of a patient represent a violation of God's sovereignty or dominion over life or a rejection of God's gift of life? In the case of a terminal patient suffering from intractable and unbearable pain, does the move from withholding or withdrawing useless care to taking steps to end the patient's life always involve an abandonment of the patient or a violation of the covenant between doctor and patient? Does there ever come a time when care means taking a direct act to end a patient's life?

And if it were determined that physician-assisted suicide might be moral in a very limited number of situations, would it be possible to formulate a public policy regarding this question that did not violate the rights of innocent parties and/or do disproportionate harm to the practice of medicine and the sanctity of human life? What sort of norm would allow for competent dying patients suffering from intractable pain to ask for assistance in ending their lives, while protecting all sorts of other patients from being offered this treatment? How could we ensure that patients suffering from clinical depression would not be assisted in their dying? Or that burdensome or poor patients would not be encouraged to seek this remedy? How could we allow this practice and protect the trust patients have in their doctors, or the integrity of physicians opposed to physician-assisted suicide? How could we protect incompetent patients, or keep physician-assisted suicide from becoming involuntary euthanasia? And how could we make certain that legalizing this practice did not relieve the pressure on the medical community and society at large to provide adequate medical care and pain management to the poor and suffering? All of these questions would need to be addressed in examining the morality of any public policy changes around physician-assisted suicide.

Interventions into Human Reproduction

We move now from a biomedical choice at the *end* of life to consider equally complex and controversial choices related to the *beginning* of human life. And whereas in the chapter on sexual ethics we focused attention on procedures aimed at *limiting* procreation—contraception and other forms of birth control—here the focus is on medical and technological interventions aimed at overcoming infertility or *enhancing* reproduction.

The Voices of Experience

The Voice of History. Prior to the twentieth century not much could be done about a couple's infertility. However, in the 1920s Kyusako Ogino of Japan and Hermann Knaus of Austria did studies on the timing of the fertile and infertile periods in a woman's menstrual cycle. Both researchers determined that "ovulation occurred sixteen to twelve days before the anticipated first day of the next menstrual period."[36] Within a decade this knowledge led to the development of the "rhythm method" of birth regulation. Though most couples used this method to avoid pregnancy, knowledge about the precise time of ovulation offered many infertile couples a low-tech way to enhance the likelihood of conception.

Still, it has primarily been the development of high-tech reproductive technologies that has captured our attention. We will look at three of these: artificial insemination, in vitro fertilization and surrogate motherhood.

Artificial insemination, first used successfully on humans in the late nineteenth century, was introduced more widely in the 1930s and involves "the insemination of a woman by a medical practitioner with semen collected from her husband (*homologous artificial insemination* or AIH) or another donor (*heterologous artificial insemination* or AID)."[37] In this procedure sperm is inserted into the entrance of the uterus by means of a syringe or catheter.

By the early 1950s researchers were able to freeze and thaw viable human sperm, and in 1953 a urologist at the University of Iowa "reported the first human birth resulting from frozen semen."[38] This led to the growth of sperm banks, where husbands could store their frozen sperm for future use in AIH, and where married or single women interested in AID might access donor sperm. Though accurate statistics are hard to acquire, a conservative estimate is that over 300,000 persons in the United States have been conceived through artificial insemination.

In vitro fertilization (IVF) was introduced in England in 1978 and resulted in the birth of Louise Brown—the first "test tube baby."

Since then about 45,000 children have been conceived in the United States using this procedure.[39] Used primarily to treat women with missing or blocked fallopian tubes, IVF normally involves four steps. The woman is given drugs to induce the production of multiple eggs. The eggs are retrieved either through surgery or through a special tube inserted through the vagina and uterus. Then the eggs are fertilized in a glass dish (Latin, *in vitro*) with sperm from her husband or a donor and allowed to develop for a few days. Next, several of these fertilized eggs (sometimes called pre-embryos) are transferred to the woman's uterus. If pregnancy does not result from the first course of IVF, other of her fertilized eggs (which have been frozen and thawed) will be used in up to three or four more cycles. Eggs that are not used are either discarded or stored.

According to Catholic ethicist Thomas Shannon, the typical model of surrogate motherhood is as follows. "The wife is unable to bear a child. The husband then contracts with another woman—the surrogate mother—to artificially inseminate her. She then conceives the child, carries it to term, and relinquishes it to the couple....for which the woman receives a fee, typically $10,000."[40] Of course surrogate arrangements can also take more altruistic forms, such as when a woman agrees to bear a child for her infertile sister.

Contemporary Voices. Supporters of these three (and other) reproductive technologies tend to see artificial insemination, IVF and surrogate motherhood as welcome treatments for infertility, enabling persons and couples who would otherwise be unable to conceive or bear a child to become parents. Many praise these technologies for allowing women and men to overcome biological impediments to parenthood, such as low sperm count or blocked or missing fallopian tubes. Others affirm the freedom these procedures give to single women and homosexual or lesbian couples wanting to have children of their own.

At the same time, those supporting such reproductive technologies do not view these interventions as an attack on the naturalness of sexual intercourse, but as legitimate and moral tools offering prospective parents increased freedom and autonomy when making very human choices about reproduction.

Still, there are a number of concerns raised about these technologies. Some argue that these interventions have crossed the boundary between assisting the natural reproductive process and "playing God." According to this view, fashioning human beings (or embryos) in a laboratory is not a legitimate exercise of human autonomy, but an attack on the sacredness of the human person and a violation of God's dominion over life. Other critics worry about the morality of collecting sperm through masturbation, or freezing, thawing and discarding fertilized eggs. Still others object that the introduction of artificial procedures for insemination, as well as the use of donors and surrogates sever the bonds connecting heterosexual love and parenthood and weaken the very meaning of parenthood.

Voices from the Margins. We need to pay attention to three voices from the margins when analyzing this issue. First, the poor remind us of the high cost of these reproductive technologies. Three cycles of IVF (not at all uncommon) cost more than $20,000 and would not usually be covered by health insurance. In a society with skyrocketing health-care costs and without adequate health care for the poor, spending so much money on reproduction for the wealthy could be a violation of distributive justice and a poor use of scarce medical resources. Second, a number of women have expressed concern that advances in reproductive technology have placed increasing pressure on women to conceive and bear a child, no matter what. As a result, many women have undergone arduous, frustrating and expensive procedures in order to live up to a cultural and sexist stereotype. Third, it needs to be asked whether these interventions encourage us to see children as a gift from God and a sacredness to be treasured and cared for, or as a product to which all persons have a right. Is there a danger that these technologies undermine the awe and reverence we have for our children, leading us to see them as commodities to be produced and purchased according to our tastes?

Scripture. While the biblical authors do not address the question of high-tech interventions in human reproduction, we can find a number of themes and convictions in Scripture relevant to this conversation. In both the Hebrew Scriptures and the New Testament marriage is assumed to be the appropriate and ideal moral setting for sexual intercourse. Particularly in the Hebrew Scriptures, procreation is seen as central to marriage. Indeed, the biblical authors repeatedly affirm that children are a blessing from God. Furthermore, Scripture affirms that God is involved in the creation of human life. And finally, biblical authors acknowledge that the call to "be fruitful and multiply" must be read alongside the duty to be good stewards of creation.

John Noonan argues that in the Hebrew Scriptures marriage is seen as a fundamental good, "and is the ordinary state in which man and woman are sexually related."[41] And indeed, as we noted in our earlier discussion of extramarital sex, there are a number of indications in the Hebrew Scriptures that intercourse was to be restricted to the marriage bed. Lisa Cahill adds that in the New Testament "marriage is certainly assumed to be the proper context of sexual behavior….and sex outside of that context is clearly not part of the normative picture for the early Christians."[42] Thus, we can assume that for the biblical authors there is an intimate connection between intercourse and marriage.

In the Hebrew Scriptures, at least, there is also an intimate bond between marriage and procreation. Indeed, as we have noted elsewhere, the Hebrew Scriptures portray procreation as essential to marriage. For the man and woman who are called to "become one flesh" in marriage (Gen 2:24) are the very ones who receive the procreative command to "be fruitful and multiply" (Gen 1:28). Thus Margaret Farley reports that "at the heart of Judaism's tradition of sexual morality is a religious injunction to marry ... [and at] the core of the imperative to marry is the command to procreate."[43] Furthermore, this command to procreate is addressed equally to both men and women. In Genesis 1:27–28, the man and woman *together* are the image of God and *together* are made cocreators with God in the generation of new human lives.[44]

Indeed, the duty to procreate was seen as so important that biblical norms allowed men to deal with the problem of childless marriages by resorting to polygamy, having intercourse with concubines or slaves, or divorcing a barren wife and remarrying. When Sarah believes she is barren she invites Abraham to have intercourse with her slave girl Hagar (Gen 16: 1–4), and Rachel later does the same thing with her husband Jacob (Gen 30:1–5). And, as we noted earlier, the biblical practice of "levirate marriage" meant that the brother of a dead man might be expected to sleep with his widowed sister-in-law to raise up heirs for his deceased sibling.

Still, in the Hebrew Scriptures procreation is not merely a duty. It is also a blessing. God's promises to bless Abraham and Sarah with a child (Gen 18:10), and when Sarah is favored with a son (Gen 21:6) she rejoices that "God has brought laughter for me; everyone who hears me will laugh with me!" So too, the author of Deuteronomy 7:14 offers the Hebrews God's blessings with the guarantee that there will be "neither sterility nor barrenness among you," and in Wisdom 3:13–19 we are told what a blessing children are, and what sufferings childlessness entails.

While the New Testament continues to affirm the goodness of marriage and sees marriage as the appropriate moral setting for sexual intercourse, it does not stress the importance of procreation in the same way as the Hebrew Scriptures do, and its authors do not portray childlessness as tragic. As Noonan notes, "it is evident that procreation as the primary purpose of marriage is not emphasized in these writings."[45]

In affirming that children are a blessing from God Scripture also reminds us that God is the author and creator of our lives and that the sanctity of each human life comes from the fact that we have been fashioned by God. In both the creation narratives in the first chapters of Genesis God is portrayed as the creator of human life. And the author of Psalm 139:13 praises God, "who formed my inward parts; [who] knit me together in my mother's womb." Still, in Genesis 1:28 humans become cocreators with God, and our role as parents does not place us in competition with the one who has made us, but calls us to exercise our own legitimate authority as ones called to "be fruitful and multiply" and to be good stewards.

Finally, as we noted in the chapter on environmental ethics, the command to "be fruitful and multiply" must be read alongside the command to be good stewards of creation. For the ones who are to fill the earth in Genesis 1:28 are also the ones called to till the garden in Genesis 2:15. Again, as Lisa Cahill notes, the biblical author sees the duty to procreate as concerned not only with the good of a single person or couple, but with the greater common good of the human (and global) community. Thus, decisions about reproductive technologies must also look to larger social concerns about social and economic justice.

Tradition. Catholic teaching on the morality of reproductive technologies has generally focused on three questions: (1) What is the moral status of the embryo? (2) How should we judge the morality of heterologous artificial insemination? (3) How should we judge the morality of homologous artificial insemination?[46] In the following paragraphs we will examine the Catholic Church's official answers to these questions and indicate some concerns and criticisms raised by a number of Catholic and Christian ethicists.

The Human Embryo. Since in vitro fertilization usually involves producing, freezing and destroying a number of "spare" human embryos, we need to know what the moral status of these embryos is and what duties we have toward them. Catholic teaching affirms that "from the time that the ovum is fertilized, a new life is begun which is…the life of a new human being," and that "the human being must be respected—as a person—from the very first instant of his existence."[47] Thus, without necessarily affirming that the embryo is already an individual human person, the church insists that from the moment of conception the fruit of human generation "demands the unconditional respect" due a human being, and "must be treated as a person…and cared for…in the same way as any other human being."[48] Furthermore, Catholic teaching affirms that "any discrimination [against embryos] based on the various stages of life is no more justified than any other discrimination."[49]

This means that the Catholic Church judges the morality of reproductive technologies, at least in part, by how adequately they respect and protect the developing human life of the embryo. Any prenatal diagnosis or therapy that "respects the integrity of the embryo" and "is directed toward its safeguarding or healing" without subjecting it to disproportionate risks is acceptable.[50] But producing or experimenting on embryos "for the sole purpose of research" that will benefit others treats these human lives as mere means and exposes them to "grave and disproportionate" risks. Even more so, the freezing and destruction of "spare" embryos are seen as an affront to the dignity and welfare of developing human life. According to the Vatican's 1987 statement on reproductive technologies, "it is immoral to produce human embryos designed to be exploited as disposable 'biological material,'" and "the freezing of embryos...constitutes an offense against the respect due to human beings."[51]

Still, some Christian ethicists question whether an embryo, particularly in its first weeks of development, does have the same moral status as a human person. Catholic theologian Thomas Shannon, for example, argues that being an individual is a critical part of being a human person, and that in its earliest stages of development the embryo—which is still capable of twinning—is not yet an individual human being. Shannon does not argue that embryos have no moral status or claims, only that the claims they make on us may be different from those of a human person.[52]

Heterologous Artificial Insemination (AID). Catholic teaching opposes heterologous artificial insemination (procedures using donor eggs, sperm or wombs) because it is seen as threatening the sacred ties binding spouses to one another and children to their parents. According to the church, "...respect for the unity of marriage and for conjugal fidelity demands that the child be conceived in marriage," and the introduction of third-party donors "is a violation of the reciprocal commitment of the spouses."[53] Furthermore, "the child has the right to be conceived, carried in the womb, brought into the world and brought up within marriage," and AID violates that right and deprives children of a fundamental connection to their parents.[54]

In general, Catholic and many other Christian theologians agree that the introduction of donors poses a disproportionate threat to the marital relationship and so support the church's opposition to heterologous procedures.[55] Still, other Catholic and Christian ethicists have argued that while the physical and genetic bonds between a married couple and their children are very important, they are not absolutely essential. It is possible, these authors note, to be good parents even when such ties are not fully present. Thus, couples suffering from infertility could be justified in using donor eggs, sperm or wombs to bring a child into their family in this less than ideal but not immoral fashion.[56]

Homologous Artificial Insemination (AIH). Catholic teaching acknowledges that homologous procedures (those taking place within the context of marriage and using only the husband's sperm and the wife's egg and womb) are "not marked by all that ethical negativity found in extraconjugal procreation."[57] Because the child-to-be is the exclusive fruit of the marriage relationship, homologous artificial insemination does not pose the same threats as procedures using third-party donors. Furthermore, the church concedes that the married couple's desire to have a child is indeed praiseworthy, and that the suffering of infertile couples is real and invites a compassionate response.

Still, official Catholic teaching rejects AIH because these procedures separate the process of procreation from the act of sexual intercourse and thus attack what the church sees as the inseparable connection between the procreative and unitive meanings of human sexuality. As the Vatican's 1987 statement notes, "...the procreation of a person must be the fruit and result of married love...[and] fertilization achieved outside the bodies of the couple" is deprived of the unitive meaning of human sexuality and is therefore objectively wrong.[58] Furthermore, the same document expresses concerns that homologous procedures are dangerous because they establish "the domination of technology over the origin and destiny of the human person, and warns about the use of masturbation to obtain sperm."[59]

Nonetheless, a number of Catholic and Christian ethicists are not convinced that homologous interventions are wrong. Richard McCormick, Lisa Cahill and Sidney Callahan, for example, agree that procreation should take place within the context of the marital relationship. They do not concede, however, that procreation should only occur within the bounds of a specific act of sexual intercourse.[60] This position, they argue, is a kind of "physicalism" that equates the moral order with the physical order.

Formulating a Christian Response. In light of all that we have investigated, how should we, as Christians, evaluate these interventions into human procreation?

Some Basic Convictions. We begin with the affirmation, found in both Scripture and the Christian tradition, that the life of every human is sacred and should be treated with reverence and respect. Every human being has been created by God and fashioned in the image and likeness of God, and so the beginning of human life is to be treated as "sacred ground." At the same time, we also believe that God's invitation to "be fruitful and multiply" is both a blessing and a responsibility. Parenthood is a gift and a vocation, and the children we receive from God are likewise a gift entrusted to our care and not a right or a commodity we can lay claim to. Thus, in all of our choices about reproduction we must be certain to take care of our children and to look after their best interests. This does not mean that infertility is not often a source of deep spiritual and personal anguish, that couples should not take steps to address this problem or that medical science's efforts in this area are not welcome. But it does mean that there are moral limits to what should be done to alleviate the suffering that flows from being unable to conceive children and that, as in other areas, we have an obligation to be "responsible" parents.

In recent decades we have learned a great deal more about the details of the development of human life. And though not all agree that a human person is present in the earliest stages of embryonic development, there is a general consensus that human life is present from the time of fertilization. At the very least this means that all prenatal human life makes some real moral claims upon us, and that the loss of this life at any stage of development is to be avoided if possible. It also means that interventions resulting in a loss of prenatal life require more serious reasons to justify them the later they come in the development process.

Finally, the physical and genetic bonds between a married couple
and their children are important, and any reproductive technologies
that break the connections between genetic parenthood, gestational
parenthood and the responsibility for raising children require serious
reasons to justify them.

Some Difficult Questions. A number of thorny moral questions
remain regarding reproductive technologies. First, as Richard
McCormick has asked elsewhere, what exactly is the difference
between acceptable medical therapies aimed at assisting infertile couples conceive and give birth and unjustifiable tampering with the
procreative process? At what point do the interventions of medical
science become an intrusion into the marriage relationship and an
unwarranted exercise of dominion over human life and its creation?
Second, what are the specific moral claims that prenatal life makes
upon the rest of us, and when does it begin to make them? Is every
intervention resulting in the foreseeable loss of embryonic life—even
in the earliest stages of development—a direct and immoral attack on
innocent human life? Could the loss of some human embryos in the
process of in vitro fertilization ever be justified? Or would that always
represent the use of one human being as a mere means? Third, as we
have already noted above, there is a connection among genetic parenthood, gestational parenthood and being the parents who raise our
children. And there is a connection between procreation and marriage and between the procreative and unitive meanings of human
sexuality. In an ideal world all of these connections ought to be protected, ensuring our children and our marriages the best environment possible in which to flourish. Still, if we are to determine the
rightness or wrongness of differing reproductive technologies, we
must ask if each of these various connections must always be protected. Would the lack of any one of these connections always represent an immoral violation of what it means to be a spouse or a parent?
Or is it possible that one or others of these bonds could be broken in
order for an infertile couple to give birth to a child?

Ethical Issues in Genetics

The Voices of Experience

The Voice of History. The modern science of genetics began with an Austrian monk, Gregor Johann Mendel (1822–84), who investigated and charted the processes of variation and heredity in thousands of pea plants. It was Mendel who first identified the "hereditary units" we have come to call genes, and his research in the monastery's garden resulted in our earliest grasp of dominant and recessive traits, showing just how such traits are passed (or not passed) from generation to generation.

Early in the twentieth century researchers discovered that genes are located on threadlike bodies called chromosomes, which are found in the nuclei of cells and composed primarily of DNA (deoxyribonucleic acid) and protein. In 1953 Francis Crick and James Watson discovered the "double-helix" structure of DNA. This "opened the door to significant developments in genetics, which culminated in a capacity to recombine genetic material from one organism to another."[61] Suddenly, it became possible not only to identify and locate many genes associated with specific disorders (like cystic fibrosis, for example), but to remove and replace these unwanted genes with healthy genetic material, offering the hope of eradicating a number of diseases at their very root.

In 1990, the Human Genome Project, a multibillion-dollar federal program, set out to map the human genome and to locate and identify all of what turned out to be the approximately 34,000 human genes and over a billion DNA subunits or bases that make up our twenty-three pairs of chromosomes.[62] By 2001 government researchers and scientists working for a private firm had released a "working draft" of the human genome, taking one giant step toward identifying and treating the genetic source of a wide range of human illnesses. Still, identifying the location of a gene is a long way from knowing what that gene does (particularly in combination with many other genes) and what therapies would safely remedy a specific genetic disease.

Contemporary Voices. Many people today are quite optimistic about the promise of genetics. Some argue that genetic medicine will allow us to cure or eliminate most human diseases, not just treat their symptoms, and could lead to significant improvements in our health, intelligence or even emotional balance. Others believe that genes may hold the key that will unlock the mystery of our humanity, explaining what makes us tick not just physically, but emotionally, psychologically and spiritually as well. Most of these voices of promise seem relatively unconcerned about the risks or dangers of making alterations in our genetic makeup.

Others, however, seem quite troubled by the potential peril of genetics. Some react to what they see as a reductionist view of humanity, and argue that human beings are much more than bags of chemicals. We are not just our DNA, but free and social beings who exist in relationships with God, creation and our neighbors. Others warn that we do not have the authority or wisdom to make changes in our genetic makeup or heritage and that such interference amounts to "playing God" with human nature and could do real and irreparable harm to our humanity and the humanity of our children.

Still, most physicians, scientists and ethicists (particularly Christian ethicists) approach genetics with a certain amount of prudence, aware of both the promise and the peril of this new field. Because of the dangers involved, especially the possible long-term consequences of genetic interventions, we should proceed cautiously, on the lookout for criteria to help us discern between interventions that will promote what is genuinely good for human beings and those which will not.[63] And we will need to think hard about what precisely we mean by such notions as creation, human nature, and the role we human beings, fashioned in God's image, are to play in this universe.[64]

Voices from the Margins. Four groups of persons could be endangered or marginalized by developments in genetics: those predisposed to or suffering from a genetic disease, those identified as carriers of such an illness, those lacking the resources to pay for genetic medicine and future generations of humans who will bear the long-term and unforeseen effects of genetic interventions. As long as genetic screening makes it possible to identify a large number of genetic disorders for which we currently have no treatment or cure, there will be a strong temptation for parents or society to "remedy" the situation of an imperfect fetus through abortion. And in a society (like our own) without universal health care, both insurers and employers will have a strong financial incentive to turn away anyone diagnosed as suffering from or predisposed to a wide range of genetic illnesses. So too, carriers of genetic disorders could be treated as second-class citizens or even nonpersons, denied health care, employment or even the right to life. Furthermore, since in our society gene therapies will be more available to those with wealth or good insurance, it seems likely that the children of the poor could find themselves inheriting not just less income but also poorer genes. Finally, developments in genetic engineering could pose a real threat to the unborn generations of humans whose DNA or even humanity might be adversely affected by interventions done on patients living today. For while one kind of gene therapy (somatic-cell) only affects the patient being treated, another type (germ-cell) makes changes that the patient's descendents will inherit as part of their genetic makeup.

Scripture. Although the Bible does not deal directly with the question of genetic research or engineering, Catholic ethicist James Walter points out that Scripture (particularly in the creation accounts of Genesis 1–2, Psalm 8 and the stories of Jesus' healing of the sick) does have something to say about our moral duties as stewards, cocreators and persons called to share in the healing ministry of Christ. Together, these three biblical themes give us some sense of what we ought and ought not to do when it comes to intervening in human genetics.[65]

Both of the creation accounts found in the first two chapters of Genesis affirm that we humans are not the creators of our world or ourselves, but creatures made by another. Fashioned by the word of God and animated by God's life-giving breath, human beings are not above or outside of creation, but part and parcel of the created order, made of the same stuff as the soil, plants, birds and animals with whom we share this planet. And, like all our cocreatures, we are dependent for our very existence on the powerful and loving hand of God.

At the same time, both of these creation stories also make it clear that humans have a special role within God's creation. Made in the image and likeness of God, we humans have a particular vocation "to till and to keep" the earth-garden in which we have been placed, acting as God's stewards in caring for the rest of creation. As Walter points out, this biblical notion of stewardship "accentuates the fact that humans are entrusted with responsibility for conserving and preserving creation…[and] tends to place limits on human freedom to alter what the divine has created."[66] Thus, stewardship language is often used to warn against the dangers of "playing God" by intervening in areas where creatures have no authority.

Still, as a number of Catholic and Protestant theologians have noted, Scripture also seems to speak of humans as "created cocreators." In Genesis 1:28 God instructs us to "be fruitful and increase, fill the earth and subdue it," implying that human beings participate in the ongoing work of creation. And though the author of Psalm 8:4–6 wonders why God, who has created the majestic wonders of the universe, would even take notice of creatures as small and insignificant as humans, the same writer also notes that "you [O Lord] have made them a little lower than God, and crowned them with glory and honor. You have given them dominion over the works of your hands; you have put all things under their feet." As Walter points out, "…though only God creates *ex nihilo* (out of nothing), we mirror the divine in our capacity to create, even if that ability is restricted to fashioning materials already in the created order. [And] since creation is not complete *(creatio continua),* we have responsibilities to bring it to completion."[67] So too, Pope John Paul II notes that genetic scientists and physicians cooperate "in the work of creation begun on the first day of the world."[68] As created cocreators, then, we work with God, and have more authority and responsibility than mere caretakers or gardeners.

The fact that we are called to be both stewards and cocreators hardly answers all our moral questions regarding genetics. But it does suggest two complementary attitudes that ought to influence us as we try to discern which genetic interventions are appropriate and which are not. In a spirit of humility we are stewards, called to care for the gift of creation we have received; in a spirit of responsibility, ingenuity and perhaps even boldness, we are cocreators, charged to exercise our unique and important role in the universe.

Scripture also reminds us of our vocation to be healers and to join in the healing ministry of Christ. Catholic biblical scholar Donald Senior notes that in the New Testament Jesus is not merely a religious teacher, but also a healer and worker of miracles.[69] The Gospel of Mark stresses the power Jesus has over sickness and Satan, driving out demons (5:1–20) and curing the ill (5:24–34), and points to these wonders as signs of God's "breaking in" to human history in a new way. Luke's Gospel, on the other hand, portrays these miraculous healings as an expression of Jesus' compassion for the suffering and commitment to justice for the poor and oppressed (7:11–17). As Senior puts it, "Jesus was a man so charged with God's own compassion and love that any cry of pain or confusion drew from him an instant response of healing and restoration."[70]

The early Christian community saw itself as charged and empowered to continue this healing ministry of Jesus. Nowhere is this more dramatically displayed than in the Acts of the Apostles, where there are multiple stories of the healing ministry of the first followers of Jesus. Transformed by the power of the Spirit of God, the disciples invoke the name and the power of Jesus as they perform dramatic deeds of healing and transformation. "Peter said, 'I have no silver or gold, but what I have I give to you; in the name of Jesus Christ of Nazareth, stand up and walk'" (Acts 3:6).

Recalling the healing ministry both of Jesus and his disciples does not resolve all our questions about genetics, but it does remind us of our duty to use whatever talents, knowledge and power we have to help the sick and suffering among us.

Tradition. Overall, Christian churches and writers "have a positive attitude toward the developing science of genetics and do not consider genetic engineering as intrinsically problematic theologically."[71] Pope John Paul II has approved of genetic interventions that treat or cure illnesses resulting from chromosome deficiencies.[72] Still, the Christian tradition does have a number of serious ethical questions and concerns regarding both genetic screening and various sorts of genetic engineering, and not every type of genetic testing or manipulation is seen as morally acceptable.

It is now possible to test embryos, fetuses, children and adults for a growing number of genetic disorders or diseases, though such tests are not always accurate, and cures or effective treatments for most of these illnesses are not currently available. Thus, there are some ethical questions about the benefit or usefulness of such tests, particularly when administered to children who may not experience symptoms for decades. In general, Catholic and Christian teachings have argued that all genetic screening should focus on the good of the patient and be conducted in a manner that protects the freedom, privacy and confidentiality of those being tested. People should not be coerced or manipulated into undergoing such tests, nor should the results be used to discriminate against them when it comes to questions of employment or access to health care.[73] Also, counseling, support and adequate medical care should be made available to those who discover that they have or are carriers of a genetic disorder, and recent Catholic teaching notes that children diagnosed with a genetic disease should only be told of their illness when they become adults.[74]

Official Catholic teaching argues that prenatal genetic testing "is permissible, with the consent of the parents after they have been adequately informed, if the methods employed safeguard the life and integrity of the embryo and mother, without subjecting them to disproportionate risks."[75] So, if prenatal testing is offered so parents can better prepare to care for a child with a genetic disorder, or so that a useful therapy might be offered in the womb, it is morally acceptable. But Catholic moral teaching condemns such testing when used to identify and abort embryos or fetuses with significant genetic disorders (or an undesirable gender, height or eye color). And the church opposes genetic screening of embryos "before implantation in the womb...because it represents a selective method that results in the destruction of 'sick' embryos."[76]

As James Walter points out, scientists and ethicists are currently discussing four different types of genetic manipulation: somatic-cell therapy, germ-line therapy, somatic-cell enhancement, and germ-line enhancement. The first two types are therapies, designed to prevent or cure illnesses caused by some genetic defect. Somatic-cell therapies treat genetic defects in the body (somatic) cells of a patient, preventing or curing a disease in that particular person. Germ-line therapies correct genetic defects in the reproductive or germ cells, ensuring that the corrected genes will be passed on to future generations. The second two types of genetic engineering, however, are not therapies, but enhancements, "concerned with improving either various genetic aspects of the patient him/herself [somatic-cell] or with permanently enhancing or engineering the genetic endowment of the patient's children [germ-line]."[77] In somatic-cell enhancement genetic changes could be made in a person's body cells to make them taller, faster or more resistant to infections. Germ-line enhancements would make changes in the reproductive or germ cells and result in passing these improvements on to successive generations. In this way parents might be able to design their children's genetic makeup to fit their own expectations or wishes.

Somatic-cell therapy, which has already been used to treat children with severe combined immune deficiency, has received positive reviews from most Christian and Catholic authors.[78] As we noted above, Pope John Paul II has approved of such therapies as long as they "tend to a real promotion of the personal well-being" of the patient, and the Pontifical Academy for Life has noted that "gene therapy to treat a human disease or predisposition to illness is acceptable as long as the risk is proportionate to the benefit."[79] Christian ethicists have tended to see this form of treatment as similar to other types of medical therapy, though there is concern about the unknown effects of altering our genetic makeup and a general call to exercise caution.

Although it could offer the promise of permanently eliminating a number of genetic diseases, germ-line therapy has not been so well received by the Christian tradition and "remains theologically and morally the most contentious" of the four types of genetic manipulation.[80] The Pontifical Academy has argued that such therapy "is ethically unacceptable because it involves a high-risk technique used on embryos, usually coupled with *in vitro* fertilization and poses a long-term risk to future generations."[81] Other Christian authors and churches have also expressed concerns about the risks germ-line therapies pose to future generations, generations that never consented to have their genetic makeup altered, and generations that some see as being deprived of their right to inherit a genetic endowment that has not been intentionally modified.[82]

The majority of Christian authors and churches have opposed either type of enhancement genetic engineering. Many, like Catholic moral theologian Richard McCormick, S.J., argue that the dubious benefits of building "better" people do not justify the noticeable risks associated with altering the genetic makeup of healthy persons and/or their descendents. They also suggest that in a world where some are genetically enhanced or "perfect," those who are different or "imperfect" could well find themselves discriminated against or marginalized.[83] Others worry about just who would get to decide what represents a "better" or "worse" person, and complain that in a society where tens of millions cannot afford adequate health-care expenditures genetic enhancements would be a violation of social justice.

Formulating a Christian Response

Some Basic Convictions. Five important convictions emerge from our investigation. First, genetics is not an attack on God's authority or a violation of our human nature. Not every form of genetic manipulation or screening is morally acceptable, and genetic engineering, which involves repairing or altering our DNA, poses significant risks and calls for extreme caution. Still, genetics does not in itself amount to a wrongful attempt to "play God." Instead, like other areas of modern science and medicine, this field offers us the opportunity to do great good and challenges us to exercise our moral responsibilities as human beings made in the image and likeness of God. We need to come to the aid of the sick without introducing new harms or injustices. Second, as we try to figure out what genetic interventions we should and should not perform we need to remember that Scripture calls us to be both stewards and cocreators. In a creative, complementary way these balancing categories suggest that both *prudent restraint* and *bold creativity* are part of what it means to be human and should shape our approach to genetic engineering. Third, any genetic screening or intervention must be aimed at the good of the persons being tested or treated, and must protect their safety, health, freedom, privacy and confidentiality without exposing them to disproportionate risks or unjust forms of discrimination. Fourth, social justice demands that we not allow expenditures in genetic research and engineering to undermine or endanger our commitment to provide basic health care to all our citizens. At the very least we must be certain that genetic science does not deepen the chasm between rich and poor. Finally, it would seem that while somatic-cell therapies are morally acceptable, at least for the present both germ-line therapies and somatic and germ-line enhancements are far too risky and dangerous to be considered morally responsible.

Some Difficult Questions. A host of important and difficult questions remains. While the biblical notions of stewardship and cocreatorship remind us that we are called to be both prudent and creative, what do they tell us about the morality of specific genetic interventions? Does the fact that we are stewards mean that we can engage in somatic-cell therapies, but not germ-line therapies or either type of genetic enhancement? Or does our being cocreators mean that we can do any or all of these interventions, as long as we do so carefully and without harming others or violating their rights? Should children undergo any genetic screening, particularly if there is no treatment or cure for the disease they are being tested for, or if the symptoms of this illness will not show up for decades? If so, who would give consent for these minors to be tested, and who would decide if and when they should be informed about their diagnosis? And while genetic information should be kept confidential and not used to discriminate against persons seeking employment or health care, are there any limits to an individual's right to privacy in this area? What rights do spouses, siblings or other family members have to genetic information about their partners or relatives? Moreover, are the differences between somatic-cell therapy and germ-line therapy substantial or merely a matter of increased risk? If the latter, and if the greater risks involved in germ-line therapy could be significantly reduced, should we leave the door open to germ-line therapies somewhere down the road? Also, most Christian ethicists argue against enhancement interventions because of the increased risks and the dangers of abuse, but how firm is the boundary between therapy and enhancement? Would helping a person who was less than three feet tall grow another foot or two be therapy or enhancement? And could we imagine any enhancement interventions that might not result in abuse or discrimination and that would not involve undue risks? Might we imagine some enhancement interventions that could be thought of as appropriate displays of human stewardship and cocreatorship? Finally, what are our obligations to future generations? Do they have a right not to have their genetic endowment intentionally altered, even if there is every reason to believe these modifications will eliminate a great deal of suffering? Do we have a duty to improve their health, and, if so, is there any way to be certain that the changes we make will not do irreparable damage to our descendants, and their humanity?

COMMUNITY:
Two Troublesome Tendencies

The Commodification of Health Care. In a number of articles written over the past decade Catholic moral theologian Richard McCormick complained about the "secularization of medicine," which he described as "the invasion of the [medical] profession by the business ethos."[84] Like many others, McCormick worried that health care was being reduced to a commodity to be bought and sold on the open market, that the medical profession was being transformed into a business obsessed with profits and maintaining the "bottom line" and that the physician-patient covenant at the very heart of medicine was being replaced by a contract between providers and purchasers of medical services.[85] Medical ethicist George Annas offers a similar criticism when he argues that "the new metaphor in medicine is the market metaphor, and it has transformed the way we describe the fundamental relationships in medical care."[86]

According to McCormick and Annas, when health care is reduced to a marketplace commodity the sick and suffering are no longer seen as having any claim on our compassion, or any right to even the most basic health care. In the medical marketplace patients become clients or customers entitled to only those treatments and medicines they (or their insurers) can pay for. As Annas notes, "…there is no place for the poor and uninsured in the metaphor of the market."[87] And when the profession of medicine is transformed into a private financial arrangement between two parties, physicians and other healers have no duty to come to the aid of the sick or to reject immoral requests from patients. Instead, they are merely medical technicians selling their skills to the highest bidder and providing whatever service the customer demands.

Recently the commodification of health care has meant that even our own bodies could be up for sale. There have been a number of proposals for a market in body parts that would include differing forms of remuneration for human blood, sperm, eggs and vital organs.[88] And, in the wake of the Human Genome Project, there have been discussions regarding the patenting rights and ownership of human cells, DNA or cloned human tissue.[89]

Ideologies. The commodification of health care is based on two false beliefs. The first is that health care is merely or primarily a commercial commodity and that the best (or at least the most efficient) way to distribute this good or service is to think of medicine as a business and follow the rules of the marketplace. For when medical providers compete for profits they should become more efficient, resulting in lower prices, wider selection and increased customer satisfaction.

According to this view, then, patients or customers should be able to get whatever medical services they can afford, and the cost of these services should be determined by what people are willing to pay. Unfortunately, this view does not recognize any basic right to health care or any duty to come to the aid of sick persons who are poor or uninsured. In the medical marketplace the sick make no moral claims upon healers or society except to be given the health care they can pay for. Also, this faith in the efficiency or fairness of medical markets overlooks the fact that health care is not just a commodity, but often a necessity, and that the sick are not usually in any position to bargain with health-care providers, but must instead rely on their compassion and generosity, two virtues that customers cannot buy at any price.

The second mistaken belief underlying the commodification of health care is what McCormick has referred to as "the absolutization of autonomy," or the notion that patients or customers are always right and should therefore be able to get whatever medical services or treatments they prefer.[90] As moral agents with a right and a duty to care for their own health, patients are entitled to a great deal of autonomy, and physicians should, within reason, respect their patients' wishes. Still, the absolutization of autonomy refers to the belief that an action or choice is right *because* it is the patient's choice, and that physicians need only ask about a patient's preference and not about whether this represents a moral or immoral choice.[91] According to this view we may buy and sell our organs, tissue, eggs or sperm, opt for any reproductive procedure or technology, or ask for assistance in dying, and the only moral question is whether we are being true to our own desires.

Underlying both of these errors is a certain individualism that assumes that we are not tied to one another in covenants, that healers and society are not obliged to care for or show compassion to the sick and suffering, or that patients have no duties to anyone except themselves.

Imbedded Practices. The commodification of health care is seen in a number of contemporary practices and structures. The first and most striking is the fact that the United States, which pays more for health care than any other industrialized nation and is the world's leader in medical technology, is also the only industrialized nation lacking universal health care for its citizens. Because health care is seen as a commodity and not a fundamental right, more than forty million Americans lack health insurance and find themselves without adequate access to health care.[92] A second troubling practice associated with the commodification of health care is the way for-profit Health Maintenance Organizations (HMOs) are pressuring physicians to pay more attention to shareholders' profits than patients' health. As Annas notes, "…physicians, no longer advocates for patients, are instructed by managers that they are instead advocates for the entire group of covered lives in the health plan. A healthy bottom line replaces a healthy patient as the goal of medicine."[93] Another disturbing phenomenon is the way that Catholic and other not-for-profit hospitals and health-care systems are being endangered by the commodification of health care. In the past religiously sponsored and public hospitals have been able to pay for care for the poor by charging insured patients more, but HMOs and insurance companies no longer allow for such "cost shifting," and more and more not-for-profit institutions find themselves either unable to live up to their mission of service or facing financial ruin and closure.[94] A fourth practice associated with the commodification of health care has been the huge profits of pharmaceutical companies over the past decade, particularly from the sale of essential, life-saving medicines, often in countries where people are too poor to afford these drugs.[95] Most recently there has been a great deal of attention given to the profits being made by international drug companies selling drugs for AIDS in Africa and India, and to the moral obligation to provide these drugs at an affordable price.[96] Finally, as noted above, the commodification of health care has also been seen in recent proposals to develop a market in human blood, organs, tissue, eggs and sperm and to patent human cells, DNA and cloned human tissue.

Christian Beliefs. Christians should be opposed to the commodification of health care for a number of reasons. As we saw earlier in this chapter, Catholic social teaching has consistently held that health care is not simply a commodity, but a basic human right. In "Peace on

Earth" Pope John XXIII argues that every person has a right to life and a right to the medical care needed to sustain that life.[97] And in their 1981 "Pastoral Letter on Health and Health Care," the U.S. Catholic bishops affirm that "every person has a basic right to adequate health care. This right flows from the sanctity of human life and the dignity that belongs to all human persons, who are made in the image of God."[98]

At the same time, Christianity has long argued that medicine is not merely a business, but a ministry, and that we owe the sick and suffering both compassion and care, regardless of their ability to pay. Indeed, the greatest impact Christianity has had on Western medicine and medical ethics came from its emphasis on compassion for the sick and its demand that physicians and all Christians make a preferential option for those who are ill. Under Christianity compassion for the sick became the central virtue of medical practice.[99]

Catholic social teaching also opposes the commodification of health care as inconsistent with the church's commitment to both distributive justice and the notion of the common good. Distributive justice demands that all persons and groups receive a fair share of the community's goods and resources, and Pope Leo XIII argues that the state's first duty is to enforce this justice, particularly on behalf of the poor.[100] Furthermore, Pope John XXIII notes that "the very nature of the common good requires that all members of the state be entitled to share in it."[101] But when health care is treated as a commodity and not a right, tens of millions of America's poor and unemployed find themselves without adequate access to basic health care, while those who are well off or insured can afford the world's best medical treatment. This "health-care gap" is a violation of both distributive justice and the common good.

Structural Reforms. The single most important structural reform needed to address the commodification of health care and the underlying injustices of our present system would be the provision of universal health care. In their 1993 "Resolution on Health-Care Reform" the U.S. Catholic bishops note that "the existing patterns of health care in the United States do not meet the minimal standard of social justice and the common good," and call for a "comprehensive reform that will ensure a decent level of health care for all without regard to their ability to pay."[102] This reform should, according to the bishops, reflect a fundamental respect for the sanctity and dignity of all human life, give special priority to meeting the needs of the poor, overcome the gross inequalities of the present system, and provide universal access to comprehensive health care for everyone in the country.[103]

Until such a comprehensive reform is undertaken, it will be necessary to ensure that Catholic, public and other not-for-profit hospitals and institutions are able to provide indigent care, that the poor have some way of purchasing essential life-saving medicines and that physicians are not pressured by managed-care providers to pay more attention to profits than patients. Recently Michael Place, the president of the Catholic Health Association (CHA), has recommended a number of interim steps, including: (1) an expansion of Medicaid and the State Children's Health Insurance Program (S-CHIP) that would make a larger number of people eligible for health insurance; (2) a program of premium subsidies that would allow more working poor to afford health insurance; (3) an expansion of the Federal Employee Health Benefits Program, making it possible for more people to receive health insurance from this federal program; and (4) government grants to support hospitals and clinics that provide health care to those without insurance.[104]

The Denial of Death. Humans may be the only creatures on the planet who know they are going to die. But because death and its accompanying losses and suffering frighten us so, we are often willing to go to extremes to ignore or deny our mortality. In the late 1960s Elisabeth Kubler-Ross's groundbreaking book *On Death and Dying* showed how desperate many doctors and patients were to avoid talking about or facing death, and how costly that avoidance could be.[105]

More recently a number of ethicists have argued that a "denial of death" may be woven into the very fabric of our contemporary health-care system, and that this tendency has several disturbing effects.[106] Catholic ethicist Philip Keane suggests that modern medicine's many successes in the wars against specific diseases have encouraged a naïve optimism about our ability not just to postpone, but to eliminate death. Beneath this optimism, however, Keane senses "a fear of death and a desire to avoid dealing with death at all costs."[107] Medical ethicist Daniel Callahan makes a similar point when he argues that the most serious problem facing us in health care today is that we have failed to accept the fact that "we are bounded and finite beings, ineluctably subject to aging, decline and death. We have tried to put that truth out of mind in designing a modern healthcare system, one that wants to conquer all diseases and stay the hand of death."[108]

As we will see below, a health-care system committed to conquering death directs physicians and patients to do everything possible to postpone and prolong our dying and very little to help us prepare for it or do it well. It also spends a disproportionate amount of our society's resources trying to purchase a few more weeks or hours of life in an ICU while failing to provide basic medical care to millions.[109]

Ideologies. There are four mistaken beliefs associated with modern medicine's denial of death. To begin with, there is the notion that death is the ultimate enemy of medicine and represents the physician's final and absolute failure. Here death is not seen as a necessary part of life, but an unjust attacker that must always be repelled or forestalled. In this view death is an absolute evil, and we must do whatever we can to purchase even a few more hours of a patient's life. As Richard McCormick notes, this position represents "a kind of medical idolatry" in which physical life is transformed from a basic to an absolute good.[110] Next, there is the idea that modern medicine can and should conquer death and that this goal ought to be a central part of its mission. Because of its many successes medicine has been able to postpone death for many, raising the expectation that death itself could be vanquished. As Keane reports, "there are many persons who probably expect that next month's *Reader's Digest* will carry the headline story that death has been conquered forever."[111] As a result, death is no longer seen as inevitable, but as a biological accident or medical failure. And our health-care system, which has taken on the task of curing our mortality, finds itself much better at raging against death than at helping patients and their families prepare for it.

Given the belief that death is the ultimate enemy or a tragic medical failure, it is not too surprising that so many of us also think that our dying is too painful, frightening or morbid to speak about. For centuries physicians in the West argued that it would do no real good to tell their patients of a terminal diagnosis and followed the advice of Hippocrates to keep silent about such things. Even today, with all our advanced directives and living wills, many physicians, patients and their families still find it too hard to speak openly and honestly about death. Perhaps we are afraid of upsetting others. Perhaps we are afraid of acknowledging our own mortality.

Finally, at least some of our fear and denial of death has to do with our fear of becoming dependent on others. In our individualistic culture many have come to believe that our dignity and worth as persons comes from our independence and our ability to control our lives. And so we become deeply frightened at the thought of dying in ways that have us depending on others or unable to control our bodies. Indeed, many are so frightened that they would be willing to take their own lives or ask their physicians to help them do so.

Imbedded Practices. Several practices are connected with modern medicine's denial of death. First, there is the tendency to resist death with every possible means, waging an escalating and seemingly endless battle against our mortality. Unfortunately, this trend, instead of eliminating death, has often resulted in an increasingly protracted, painful, costly and isolated kind of dying. As Daniel Callahan suggests, the extra months or years we purchase "come at the price of more illness, greater suffering and higher health costs" and tend to produce a "wild" sort of dying that is more and more frightening and burdensome to patients and their families.[112] Second, in our efforts to postpone and avoid death we fail to prepare ourselves to die well. When asked, most people indicate that they would prefer to die at home, in the company of friends and family. They would also like to have a minimum of pain and sufficient time to put their affairs in order and say farewell. But in a health-care system that expends so much of its energy combating death, not nearly enough gets done to make certain patients experience a "good death." Studies indicate that physicians often have little or no sense of their patients' wishes about end-of-life care, and that patients and their doctors rarely communicate about such topics.[113] Other studies suggest that not enough has been done to treat the pain and suffering of dying patients and that far too few terminal patients are offered the option of hospice care.[114]

According to Callahan, a third practice associated with modern medicine's denial of death is our personal and cultural obsession with good health. Committed to opposing death on every front, we sound an alarm at each new perceived danger and throw millions, if not billions, at every new research protocol that might add a week or a month to our lives, even though more modest expenditures on preventive and basic health care would be a more effective and equitable use of resources. And on the individual level we obsess over diet and exercise regimens and become enraged when a friend or relative who neither smoked nor drank succumbs to cancer or heart disease, as if this were an insult to our sense of justice.[115]

Ironically enough, the move to legalize euthanasia and physician-assisted suicide may well be the fourth practice tied to modern medicine's denial of death. For as McCormick and the Catholic bishops of Ohio point out, much of the support for euthanasia and assisted suicide comes from the growing fears many people have of a prolonged and painful death in an intensive care unit, and from the mistaken belief that the only way to ensure that one dies well in such a setting is to take control and end one's life.[116]

Christian Beliefs. The Christian tradition has a number of reasons to be critical of any denial of death embedded in our contemporary health-care system. For Christians life is a basic good, but it is not the only or highest good. As Pope John Paul II notes, "the life of the body in its earthly state is not an absolute good for the believer."[117] Not surprisingly, then, Catholic medical ethics has long taught that physicians and patients need not do everything possible to prolong life or postpone death. This is particularly true if the measures in question are too burdensome or costly for a patient or interfere with a dying person's efforts to achieve other personal or spiritual goals—like a good death.[118] Nor has Christianity taught that death is an absolute evil or that it represents the physician or patient's ultimate failure. For the Christian's faith in the resurrection means that life does not end with death, but is merely changed, and that not even death will destroy us or separate us from God's love. Death, St. Paul tells us, has lost its ultimate sting and power. True, faith in the resurrection does not take death away, nor keep us from sorrow or loss. But such faith does make it possible to face death with genuine hope and not terror or despair.[119]

The Christian tradition also rejects the notion that we need to fear death and dying because it involves the loss of independence or control, or that it would be better to take our own lives than to suffer the supposed indignity of needing others to care for us. No one wants to be a burden, and it is painful to lose control of one's body. But Christian thought and Catholic social teaching both affirm that our worth and dignity as persons come from the fact that we are fashioned in the image and likeness of God, and not from the fact that we are powerful or independent. In the course of our lives all of us experience both independence and dependence. We give to and receive from others, and we are not less human or dignified in either of these moments.

Structural Reforms. In order to come to grips with the problems associated with and flowing from a denial of death, modern medicine must first, as Philip Keane puts it, come to an "acceptance of death as a part of life."[120] Callahan makes a similar point when he argues that "a medicine that embodied an acceptance of death within it would represent a great change in the common conception of medicine, and might then set the stage for seeing the care of the dying not as an afterthought when all else has failed but as itself one of the ends of medicine."[121] And so physicians and patients must be educated to the fact that death comes to us all, and that eliminating death is not part of the mission of medicine.

At the same time our contemporary health-care system must do a better job of preparing persons for a good death. As Callahan argues, "the goal of a peaceful death should be as much a part of the purpose of medicine as that of the promotion of good health."[122] This means that attempts to treat or cure disease cannot go on indefinitely, but need to stop in time to make preparations for a good death. It also means that physicians and patients and their families and clergy need to have open and honest conversations about death and dying, conversations that are about more than when to discontinue treatment, that include discussions of what a good death would be like and how one might prepare for it. And it means that there needs to be a commitment to provide adequate pain management for the dying and a greater support of hospice and other programs that help patients and their families prepare for death and live as fully as possible until death. Finally, a commitment to a good death means recognizing that dying is not merely a medical event, but primarily a human one. For while physicians and nurses can do many things to make our dying less painful, protracted and isolated, the work of dying well (like that of living well) is ultimately up to patients and their loved ones and clergy. And so the task of medicine is not to orchestrate a good death, but to create a space for people to die as well as they can.

Cases and Resources

In addition to the "Taking Care of Dad" case that opened this chapter, the following four cases are offered for your reflection and analysis, and there is a brief list of resources that may be helpful for those interested in learning more about biomedical ethics.

Case #2: To Merge or Not to Merge?

Sitting in back of the sisters' chapel on the top floor of St. Catherine's Hospital, Sister Angela Hastings drums her fingers lightly on the file she has come to pray over this morning. The file contains a proposal for a merger from Merrick Health Systems, a fairly large for-profit health-care chain based in St. Louis and operating four hospitals and seven nursing homes here in the Cleveland area. If accepted, the merger could well rescue the financially strapped St. Catherine's, a 127-year-old Cleveland institution that has served generations of poor and working-class immigrants and African Americans. But it could also mean a radical change in the character and mission of St. Catherine's, a change that might make it unrecognizable to the Sisters of Charity who founded and have sponsored it for over a century. And next week Sister Angela, who may well be the last member of her religious community to serve as president of this hospital, will need to make her recommendation to St. Catherine's board of governors about the merger.

At sixty-two, Sister Angela has plenty of fond memories of St. Catherine's, and has seen a great deal of change in the hospital over the past four decades. Arriving here as a young ER nurse in the mid-1960s, Angela joined a nursing staff that included twenty-seven other sisters from her community, as well as fourteen sisters serving in administrative positions. At that time St. Catherine's was one of seven Catholic hospitals in the Cleveland area, a number that would grow to twelve in the late '70s and then decline to its present four. Especially during her first twenty years at St. Catherine's, Sister Angela was often struck and gratified by the hospital's commitment to serving the city's poor. This commitment was evident on the floors, in the emergency room and in the visiting-nurse program. But it was particularly clear in St. Catherine's maternity ward, which was known citywide for its excellent care of indigent mothers and their struggling newborns. As one of Cleveland's previous bishops had once proudly bragged, "No poor pregnant girl will ever be turned away from St. Catherine's."

Today, however, things are quite different. There are only two sisters on the nursing staff, both in their early sixties, and Sister Angela is one of just three sisters working in administration. The other two, Sister Beatrice and Sister Margaret, are both older than Sister Angela and due to retire within the next two years. Meanwhile, eight Catholic hospitals in the area have either closed or been swallowed up in mergers over the past two decades. And for the past decade St. Catherine's mission to serve the poor has been under attack on several fronts.

With the growth of managed care and for-profit hospitals and health-care systems, more and more attention is being given to cost cutting and the bottom line. Health care, Sister Angela thinks, is being taken over by a corporate or business mentality, and the competition for paying patients has become fierce. Insurance companies and HMOs encourage more and more out-patient surgery and shorter and shorter stays in the hospital and will no longer allow hospitals to charge their insured or covered patients enough to pay for care for the poor. Meanwhile, the costs of new technology are always climbing, and there are huge cuts expected in Medicare and Medicaid, which provide more than 30 percent of St. Catherine's revenues.

This financial crisis has had devastating effects on a number of hospitals in the area. Along with the eight Catholic hospitals that are gone or taken over, two of the city's public hospitals have been forced to close their doors. This has meant even more poor people coming to St. Catherine's ER and maternity ward, and an escalating deficit that could put Sister Angela's hospital out of business in another year or two.

The offer from Merrick is attractive for a couple of reasons. First, St. Catherine's would continue to exist under its present name, and most of its current 874 employees would keep their jobs. The new (and financially solvent) St. Catherine's would not do abortions or sterilizations, thus at least partially protecting its Catholic identity. On the other hand, there would be a change of philosophy, with a greater focus on the institution's fiscal health and profit margin. There would be no preferential option for the poor, and—except in extraordinary circumstances—indigent or nonpaying patients would be directed to one of the remaining public hospitals. Finally, St. Catherine's maternity ward would be closed.

The bishop has told Sister Angela that he opposes this merger because a for-profit St. Catherine's could not maintain any real commitment to serve the poor. Still, he will not order her or her community to reject Merrick's offer, or declare publicly that the hospital is no longer Catholic. Instead, he will pray that she and the board are guided by God's wisdom.

Sitting there in chapel, Sister Angela wonders again what choice would be the most faithful to St. Catherine's mission, and to the people she serves in Cleveland and on the floors of her hospital.

Case #3: Test Tube Child

In their early thirties, Sam and Sarah Rossi have been married, indeed, happily married, for just over nine years and have most of the things they want in life. Both of them have jobs they like and are good at. Sarah is a very popular math teacher at St. Anne's High School and Sam is a hardworking CPA at a small family-owned firm in town. They also have a nice home, savings in the bank, a small circle of good friends and lots of loving relatives.

What they would like, however, is at least one more loving relative—a child of their own. After putting off efforts to have a baby for the first six years of their marriage, Sam and Sarah decided they had enough financial security to start a family and to let Sarah stay home with their newborn for a few years. So they began trying to conceive a child. Because both of them came from large families and because each of Sarah's sisters had had two children within the first three years of marriage, it never occurred to Sam or Sarah that there would be any problems. Nor, unfortunately, did it occur to them to keep their plan a secret.

As the months and years rolled by without any sign of a pregnancy Sam and Sarah were at first surprised and puzzled, then confused and dismayed. Sarah's sisters offered support, advice and shoulders to cry on. Their parents put on a brave face, but were clearly saddened and disappointed. Sam's mother promised to pray to some saint who was supposed to be the patron of infertile couples. Discussions about turning the den into a baby room sputtered and died out, and their lovemaking became more and more focused on conceiving a child, losing much of its spontaneity and playfulness. Each month their hopes would climb and then plummet, and going to family events or baby showers became more awkward and painful. A gap seemed to be opening up between them and all their friends and relatives having babies. The world was being divided into the fertile and the infertile, and they couldn't seem to cross the bridge.

In time they decided to get medical help, which resulted in a long series of examinations and tests. Several months ago their physician at the fertility clinic informed them that the problem they were having conceiving a child was due to Sarah's obstructed fallopian tubes and recommended that they consider in vitro fertilization. This procedure, which involved fertilizing some of Sarah's eggs with Sam's sperm in a laboratory and then introducing these fertilized eggs into her uterus, was supposed to offer the best hopes for conceiving a child.

But there are problems with this solution, at least for Sam and Sarah, both of whom are practicing Catholics. Sarah has had some conversations with a priest who teaches at St. Anne's, and knows that her church is opposed to in vitro fertilization because it separates lovemaking and conception, and because it usually involves freezing or destroying a number of fertilized eggs. Neither she nor Sam are persuaded by the first argument, but she is troubled by the thought that some of her fertilized eggs, which the church teaches are human life, could be discarded like pieces of property.

"I know a two- or four-celled embryo is not a baby," Sarah has said. "But it is something, maybe someone, and the thought of just freezing or throwing away what might be a life seems wrong.

"And I can't help wondering if it wouldn't be better to adopt, or to become foster parents. Maybe we're just being selfish. I know the baby wouldn't have our eyes or nose, but there are so many children out there who need parents, and here we are, healthy, well-off and oh so hungry for a child."

Sam has no answers to these comments. He too is confused. Like Sarah, he wants a son or daughter that will really be his and Sarah's, a child born of their flesh. He wants to be able to give their parents a grandchild. And, most of all, he wants to remove what feels like the "stain" of their infertility, to be able to make love to his wife without obsessing over whether this particular act will lead to a conception.

But what should they do? Even with "in vitro" there are no guarantees of success. Sarah's cousin Maura tried this method unsuccessfully for several years, and the cost and stress made a shambles of her marriage. On the other hand, one of Sam's clients had twins the first time out, gorgeous, healthy girls, and then had another baby two years later from the same batch of eggs. And if they adopted, or took in foster children, lots of things could go wrong there too. Oh, what are they going to do?

Case #4: Genetic Screening: "What Do You Want to Know?"

David and Nancy Holtschneider have been married for six years, are in their late twenties, have a five-year-old boy (Alex) and are expecting their second child in four months. They are also having one of the worst months of their lives, certainly the most frightening and disturbing one either of them can remember. And David blames his sister Michelle.

Put up for adoption as small children, David and Michelle were raised by Jim and Sandy Holtschneider and shown all the love and care any children could receive from a set of parents. Still, Michelle, who recently became a mother herself, has long been curious about their biological parents, and a little over a year ago began to look for them in earnest.

Two months ago Michelle located Cindy Mason, her biological mother, and flew to Houston, where Cindy was living with her current husband. With

Cindy's help Michelle was then able to track down her and David's biological father, Jeffrey Bateman, a Vietnam veteran who had passed away three years earlier in a V.A. hospital in San Antonio. What she learned about Jeffrey, however, frightened Michelle deeply. He had died at forty-seven of Huntington's disease, a progressive, incurable and fatal hereditary disease of the nervous system.

In the weeks that followed Michelle discovered that the symptoms of Huntington's disease (or Huntington's chorea) appear between the time a person is thirty-five to fifty years old and progress from occasional jerking to wild, violent and totally incapacitating spasms that only stop when a person is sleeping. These motor problems are accompanied by a series of increasingly severe mental and emotional difficulties, and death usually occurs ten to twenty years after the onset of the first symptoms.

She also discovered that Huntington's disease was what the doctors called an autosomal dominant genetic disorder, meaning that each child of a person with this disease has a 50 percent chance of inheriting it. And she learned that it was possible for her and her daughter, as well as David, Alex and his unborn child to be tested for the disease, but that there was at present no treatment or cure available.

Without consulting a genetic counselor or anyone else, Michelle decided to tell David and Nancy what she had learned, and informed them that she was going to be tested for Huntington's, and—if she had the disease—was going to have her daughter tested as well.

David was furious and terrified. Nancy was just terrified.

"Why did she have to tell me this?" he yelled. "Why did she have to go looking for those people? And then when she found them, why did she have to bring this garbage into our lives? There is nothing that getting tested can do for me or for Alex. And so now I either live with the agony of wondering if this sickness is going to cripple and kill me, or spin the wheel and maybe find out for sure that it is! And, if I'm unlucky, I get to wonder if my son has it and if our unborn child has it. And, of course, we get to torture ourselves with the thought of an abortion. Or we get to haunt ourselves for years with regret that we didn't terminate the pregnancy."

Yes, Nancy thought, we get to live under this cloud, waiting to see if a ticking bomb will go off in my husband, and then—if it does—waiting to see if it will go off in one or both of my children.

So let's not test David. Let's just shut this out of our minds and go on with our lives as if Michelle hadn't dropped this uninvited news on us. After all, if David does get tested and has the disease, won't that be worse? Won't we be looking for symptoms in every twitch? And won't he be afraid of switching jobs because his medical records will show he has a "preexisting condition" that the new company's HMO won't want to cover?

But if we don't test David, she wondered, will we hate ourselves later for not checking to see if the baby I'm carrying has this disorder? Will we wish that we had found out and terminated the pregnancy? Can anyone go through this with her husband and then their child, or children? Can any child go through this with a parent and see it coming down the road for them? And if we do test Alex, what should we tell him? What should I say to him when and if he sees his father succumbing to this awful disease? Would he have a right to know? Would it help him to know? Oh God, she asked herself, would it be better for any of us to know or not to know, and what good or evil will come from knowing?

"I don't know what we are going to do," David announces, "but I'm making an appointment to see a genetic counselor, preferably one with our religious background, and we are going to talk to somebody. God help us."

Case #5: Health Benefits: "It's Not My Problem"

"Jennie, I appreciate what Father Ralph told you in that class on Catholic social thought, and I believe in workers' rights as much as the next guy. Heck, my dad and Uncle Pete were in the union for forty years, and I paid union dues for six years while I was working in a machinist's shop and going to night school at City University.

"But I'm here to tell you that as the owner of a small business I have no legal obligation to pay for health insurance for my employees. And, given the stiff competition I face and my razor-thin profit margin, there is just no way I can provide coverage for the unskilled women working for my cleaning service, at least not if I am going to pay tuition at a Catholic college where you and your brother can learn about social justice and a preferential option for the poor.

"*I pay worker's compensation and social security, and two dollars over minimum wage. And I give these folks two weeks' paid vacation and a full hour for lunch, which is better than they would get at most of the other services in town. What's more, I give everyone who works for me a bonus at Christmas. If I paid for health coverage for my employees I would probably have to go out of business. We would certainly have to make significant changes in our lifestyle.*"

"*I appreciate that Dad,*" Jennie responds, "*and I get it that it's not your job alone to carry this burden. But the priests at that Catholic college you and Mom were so eager for me and Mike to attend say that folks have a basic right to health care. It's like their right to life, liberty and freedom of religion. And they say—heck the pope says—that our society has a moral duty to provide for that right. Health care's not just a "benefit," it's a right. But at present more than forty million Americans don't have health-care coverage, and a huge percentage of those folks are working-class women and men just like your employees.*

"*Now, we are the only industrialized Western country without universal health care, in large part because lots of folks like you and Uncle Joe—who haven't belonged to a union in years—say we shouldn't have big government or that the free market is the way to take care of things. Well, the free market and competition have got you squeezed so tight you can't provide the basic sort of health-care coverage for your workers that your dad and uncle fought so hard to get for union members fifty years ago. And the government's so small and timid that nobody in Washington has the nerve to suggest major health-care reform.*

"*So that sort of leaves us in a quandary, doesn't it? Either we agree that health care coverage is just a benefit and that the popes and church are wrong to say it's a basic right, or we figure out a way to protect this right for the more than forty million folks who lack access to basic health care. And if you're right that as a small-business owner you simply can't afford to pay for this coverage and keep afloat, then maybe we need to look at the way we provide for health care in this country. Maybe we need some kind of major health-care reform coming out of Washington. I mean, one way or the other, we're going to have to figure out how to solve this problem, aren't we?*"

"*I'll make you a deal, Jennie,*" her father replied. "*You bring home the textbook for that course in Catholic social thought, and I'll read it. After all, I paid for it. And in May when I come to pick you up from school, I'll meet with your Father Ralph and talk to him. But this summer, you'll come to work with me at the office. You'll go over the books and you'll check out all the options for health-insurance plans available to small business owners like myself. And together we'll look at what the politicians in the state capital and Washington are offering in terms of health-care reform. Then, in September, we'll make a plan that you and I and everyone else in this family can actually live with.*

"Of course, we may discover that we can't be just to my workers and pay your tuition at a Catholic college. Or that we need to make significant changes in our lifestyle—which other people in the family might not be so willing to do. Would you be willing to have those conversations and make this deal with me?"

"I suspect that you're bluffing just a bit here, Dad. But it's an intriguing offer, and I'd be silly to turn you down, even if it is also pretty scary. By the way," Jennie wondered, "does this mean the family trip to Costa Rica is off this Christmas?"

Resources

American Society for Bioethics and Humanities. This is one of the largest and most important of the professional organizations that deal with bioethical issues. The ASBH hosts regular conferences and provides publications on various topics. ASBH, 4700 W. Lake Ave., Glenview, IL 60025-1485. *www.asbh.org.*

The Catholic Health Association (CHA). This is a Catholic organization located in St. Louis that sponsors regular conferences on health-care issues (including ethical issues), provides medical-ethical consultation services, makes public policy proposals relating to health care and offers a host of valuable publications. CHA, 4455 Woodson Road, St. Louis, MO 63134-3797.

Encyclopedia of Bioethics. This is a very valuable five-volume encyclopedia of bioethics, recently revised. Articles are by leading scholars. New York: Macmillan, 1995, Warren T. Reich, general editor.

Hastings Center Report. This is perhaps the most popular and well-read professional journal in the United States on bioethical issues. It comes from The Hastings Center, a leading "think tank" on bioethical issues. Garrison, New York 10524-5555.

Health Progress. This is the Official Journal of the Catholic Health Association. It is published every two months, with reader-friendly articles by top scholars—very often dealing with contemporary bioethical issues. See CHA above.

The Human Genome Project, discussed in this chapter, has a very informative Web site that includes information regarding ethical issues in genetics: *http://www.ornl.gov/TechResources/Human Genome/home.html.*

University Centers for Biomedical Ethics. Many major universities in the United States have Centers of Bioethics affiliated with them. These are centers where in-residence scholars do research in issues relating to bioethical issues. The Centers provide various publications and conferences that are often very valuable. A fine example is the "Center for Bioethics" at the University of Minnesota: *www.bioethics.umn.edu.*

Notes

Many of the Catholic Church documents cited in this text are contained in David J. O'Brien and Thomas A. Shannon, eds., *Catholic Social Thought: The Documentary Heritage* (Maryknoll, NY: Orbis, 1997). Page numbers cited in such references will refer to this work, hereafter referred to in the note citations as CST.

CHAPTER ONE

1. Timothy O'Connell, *Principles for a Catholic Morality* (San Francisco: Harper & Row, 1990); Richard Gula, *Reason Informed by Faith: Foundations of Catholic Morality* (New York/Mahwah, NJ: Paulist Press, 1989); Russell B. Connors, Jr. and Patrick T. McCormick, *Character, Choices & Community: The Three Faces of Christian Ethics* (New York/Mahwah, NJ: Paulist Press, 1998).

2. *Catechism of the Catholic Church* (Liguori, MO: Liguori, 1994); Richard C. Sparks, *Contemporary Christian Morality: Real Questions, Candid Responses* (New York: Crossroad Herder, 1996).

3. Vatican II, The Church in the Modern World, *CST,* 192–93.

4. Ibid., 221.

5. Vatican II, Declaration on Religious Freedom, in Joseph Gremillion, ed., *The Gospel of Peace and Justice: Catholic Social Teaching Since Pope John* (Maryknoll, NY: Orbis, 1976), 347.

6. Pope Paul VI, "A Call to Action," *CST,* 266.

7. Daniel Maguire, "Ethics: How to Do It," in Ronald Hamel and Kenneth Himes, eds., *Introduction to Christian Ethics: A Reader* (New York/Mahwah, NJ: Paulist Press, 1989), 533–50; Kenneth Overberg, *Conscience in Conflict: How to Make Moral Choices* (Cincinnati, OH: St. Anthony Messenger, 1991); Richard Gula, *Moral Discernment* (New York/Mahwah, NJ: Paulist Press, 1997); Anne Patrick, *Liberating Conscience* (New York: Continuum, 1996); William Spohn, *Go and Do Likewise* (New York: Continuum, 1999); Timothy O'Connell, *Making Disciples: A Handbook of Christian Moral Formation* (New York: Crossroad Herder, 1998).

8. James F. Keenan, S.J., discusses the four cardinal virtues and proposes a new set of them: "Proposing Cardinal Virtues," *Theological Studies,* 56/4 (December, 1995): 709–29.

9. *Nicomachean Ethics,* II, 6 (1106a, 15).

10. Paul Ramsey, *The Patient as Person: Explorations in Medical Ethics* (New Haven: Yale University Press, 1970), xii.

11. Mark O'Keefe, *What Are They Saying About Social Sin?* (New York/Mahwah, NJ: Paulist Press, 1990), 29.

CHAPTER TWO

1. For an introduction to the biblical roots of Catholic social teachings see chapters one and two of Fred Kammer, S.J., *Doing Faithjustice: An Introduction to Catholic Social Thought* (New York/Mahwah, NJ: Paulist Press, 1991), 13–59.

2. John Atherton, ed., *Christian Social Ethics: A Reader* (Cleveland, OH: Pilgrim Press, 1994), 12–22.

3. Marvin Krier Mich, *Catholic Social Teaching and Movements* (Mystic, CT: Twenty–Third Publications, 1998), 6–17.

4. Atherton, *Christian Social Ethics,* 22–34.

5. For further reading on the development of Catholic social teachings see Peter J. Henriot, Edward P. DeBerri and Michael J.

Schultheis, *Catholic Social Teaching: Our Best Kept Secret* (Maryknoll, NY: Orbis, 1988); Donal Dorr, *Option for the Poor: A Hundred Years of Catholic Social Teaching,* revised ed. (Maryknoll, NY: Orbis, 1992).

6. Pope Paul VI, "The Development of Peoples," *CST,* 243–45.

7. Vatican II, The Church in the Modern World, *CST,* 192.

8. The Evangelical Lutheran Church in America, "Sufficient, Sustainable Livelihood for All: A Social Statement on Economic Life" (Chicago, IL: Division for Church in Society, 1999), 2–4.

9. U.S. Catholic Bishops, "Economic Justice for All," *CST,* 602.

10. For a more extensive discussion of the value of work, see John Paul II, "On Human Work," *CST,* 355–60.

11. Some duties of workers are sketched out in Leo XIII, "On the Condition of Labor," *CST,* 28–29; U.S. Catholic Bishops, "Economic Justice for All," *CST,* 603–05.

12. Pope John Paul II, "Address to Businessmen and Economic Managers," *L'Osservatore Romano,* weekly edition in English (June 20, 1983): 9:1.

13. For a fuller discussion of the duties of managers and the moral obligations of MNCs operating in less developed countries, see Pope Paul VI, "The Development of Peoples," *CST,* 256; U.S. Catholic Bishops, "Economic Justice For All," *CST,* 605–6, 641–42.

14. Pope John Paul II, "On the Hundredth Anniversary of *Rerum Novarum,*" *CST,* 462.

15. Pope Pius XI, "The Reconstruction of the Social Order," *CST,* 51–53.

16. On the duties of stockholders see Ted C. Fishman, "The Joys of Global Investment: Shipping Home the Fruits of Misery," in *Harper's* (February 1997): 35–42; Elizabeth Judd, *Investing with a Social Conscience* (New York: Pharos Books, 1990).

17. Pope Leo XIII, "On the Condition of Labor," *CST,* 26–28; Pope John XXIII, "Peace on Earth," *CST,* 141.

18. U.S. Catholic Bishops, "Economic Justice for All," *CST,* 637.

19. Vatican II, The Church in the Modern World, *CST,* 217–18.

20. For a fuller treatment of the call to simplicity see Duane Elgin, *Voluntary Simplicity,* revised ed. (New York: Quill, 1993); Latin American Episcopal Council, "The Medellin Document on Poverty of the Church," in Joseph Gremillion, ed., *The Gospel of Peace and Justice: Catholic Social Teaching Since Pope John* (Maryknoll, NY: Orbis, 1976), 474–76.

21. For an extensive treatment of the history of welfare in the United States see Thomas Massaro, *Catholic Social Teaching and United States Welfare Reform* (Collegeville, MN: Liturgical Press, 1998).

22. Ibid., 62–67.

23. These arguments are concisely formulated in J. Millburn Thompson, *Justice and Peace: A Christian Primer* (Maryknoll, NY: Orbis, 1997), 55–58.

24. For a spirituality of work based on the Genesis narratives see John Paul II "On Human Work," *CST,* 355–57, 387–88.

25. See Pope Paul VI, "The Development of Peoples," *CST,* 245; J. Philip Wogaman, *Christian Ethics: A Historical Introduction* (Louisville, KY: Westminster, 1993), 47–48; Martin Luther, "The Large Catechism," in Theodore G. Tappert, trans., ed., *The Book of Concord* (Philadelphia: Fortress Press, 1959), 391.

26. Pope Paul VI, "The Development of Peoples," *CST,* 245.

27. Pope John XXIII, "Peace on Earth," *CST,* 132–33.

28. USCC Administrative Board, "Moral Principles and Policy Priorities on Welfare Reform," *Origins* 24/41 (March 30, 1995): 673–77.

29. General Board of Church and Society, "The United Methodist Social Principles: The Economic Community," #67:E; the Presbyterian Church (U.S.A.), "Minutes of the 199th General Assembly," (1987), 582; the Episcopal Church (U.S.A.), "Bringing Christian Response to State Welfare Reform," (November 1996.)

30. For a fuller discussion of the history of racism and affirmative action see the Pontifical Justice and Peace Commission, "The Church and Racism: Toward a More Fraternal Society," *Origins* 18/37 (February 23, 1989): 613–26; Nicholas Lemann, "Taking Affirmative Action Apart," *New York Times Magazine* (June 11, 1995): 36–43; 52–54; 62–66.

31. Arguments critical and supportive of affirmative action are laid out in M. Cathleen Caveny, "Discrimination and Affirmative Action," *Theological Studies* 57/2 (June, 1996): 286–301.

32. Stephen Steinberg, *Turning Back: The Retreat from Racial Justice in American Thought and Policy* (Boston: Beacon Press, 1995), 167–68.

33. Andrew Hacker, *Money: Who Has How Much and Why* (New York: Scribner, 1997), 145–47.

34. Pontifical Commission, "The Church and Racism," 620–21.

35. Pope John XXIII, "Peace on Earth," *CST,* 137–38.

36. Vatican II, The Church in the Modern World, *CST,* 183.

37. U.S. Catholic Bishops, "Economic Justice for All," *CST,* 596, 616–17.

38. Roger Cardinal Mahoney, "Affirmative Action and Catholic Social Teaching," *Origins* 25/6 (June 22, 1995): 89–94; see also Peter J. Chmielewski, "Affirmative Action," in Judith A. Dwyer, ed., *The New Dictionary of Catholic Social Thought* (Collegeville, MN: Liturgical Press, 1994), 12–16.

39. Franklin Gamwell, "Affirmative Action: Is It Democratic?" *Christian Century* (January 24, 1996): 80.

40. The Presbyterian Church (U.S.A.), "Minutes of the 207th General Assembly," (1995): 705–6.

41. Sketches of the history of international debt are offered in Thompson, *Justice and Peace,* 38–40; The Pontifical Justice and Peace Commission, "At the Service of the Human Community: An Ethical Approach to the International Debt Question," *Origins* 16/34 (February 5, 1987): 601–16; "Putting Life Before Debt," a position paper of CIDSE and Caritas Internationalis, 6–10 (http://www.cidse.be/

debt/finaldebteng.html#EXECUTIVE); "How It All Began: Causes of the Debt Crisis," Jubilee 2000 Coalition (http://oneworld.org/jubilee2000/began.html).

42. Veronica Brand, R.S.H.M., "The Poor Pay Twice for the Third World's Debts," *Los Angeles Times* (November 5, 1997): B7; "A Silent War: The Devastating Impact of Debt on the Poor," Jubilee 2000 Coalition (http://oneworld.org/jubilee2000/silent.html); Bread for the World background paper, "Hunger: The Price of Poor Country Debt" (November 1996): no. 137.

43. "Usury," in *New Catholic Encyclopedia* (New York: McGraw Hill, 1967), vol. 14: 498–500.

44. Bernard Häring, *The Law of Christ,* 3 vols. (Westminster MD: Newman Press, 1966), 3: 451–55; John McHugh and Charles Callan, *Moral Theology: A Complete Course,* 2 vols., revised ed. (New York: Joseph P. Wagner, 1958), 64–66, 88–90.

45. Pontifical Commission, "At the Service of the Human Community," 606–16.

46. Pope John Paul II, "The Coming Third Millennium," in *The Pope Speaks* 40/2 (March/April 1995): 109.

47. Pope Paul VI, "The Development of Peoples," *CST,* 253–54; U.S. Catholic Bishops, "Economic Justice For All," *CST,* 640–41.

48. Presbyterian Church (U.S.A.), "Minutes of the 210th General Assembly," (1998): 676.

49. Evangelical Lutheran Church, "Sufficient, Sustainable Livelihood for All," 3.

50. Pope Paul VI, "The Development of Peoples," *CST,* 252.

51. Alexis de Tocqueville, *Democracy in America,* trans. George Lawrence, ed. J. P. Mayer (New York: Doubleday, 1969), 506.

52. For a fuller treatment of American individualism see Hacker, *Money: Who Has How Much and Why,* 31–38; Robert N. Bellah et al., *Habits of the Heart: Individualism and Commitment in American Life*

(New York: Harper & Row, 1986), 142–63; Massaro, *Catholic Social Teaching and United States Welfare Reform,* 61–67.

53. U.S. Catholic Bishops, "Economic Justice For All," *CST,* 579–80.

54. Thompson, *Justice and Peace* 45–47.

55. Hacker, *Money,* 46–56, 223–40; Robert H. Frank and Philip J. Cook, *The Winner-Take-All Society: Why the Few at the Top Get So Much More Than the Rest of Us* (New York: Penguin Books, 1996), 89–99.

56. Hacker, *Money,* 38–43; Juliet B. Schor *The Overspent American: Upscaling, Downshifting, and the New Consumer* (New York: Basic Books, 1998), 3–24, 67–109; *Affluenza,* a PBS video narrated by Scott Simon (KCTS/Oregon Public Broadcasting, 1997); see also the *Affluenza* Web site at http://www.pbs.org/affluenza.

57. Allen R. Myerson, "U.S. Splurging on Energy After Falling Off Its Diet," *New York Times* (October 22, 1998): A1; Thompson, *Justice and Peace,* 63–81; *Affluenza,* a PBS program narrated by Scott Simon.

58. Neil Postman, *Amusing Ourselves to Death* (New York: Viking, 1986), 104–05, 126–37; Benjamin Barber *Jihad vs. McWorld* (New York: Ballantine, 1996), 59–62.

59. Vince Passaro, "Who'll Stop the Drain: Reflections on the Art of Going Broke," *Harper's* (August 1998): 35–42; Schor, *The Overspent American,* 3–24, 67–109.

60. Pope John Paul II, "On Social Concern," *CST,* 412.

61. Evangelical Lutheran Church in America, "Sufficient, Sustainable Livelihood for All," 7.

62. U.S. Catholic Bishops, "Economic Justice For All," *CST,* 600–601.

63. The advantages of a progressive consumption tax are outlined in Frank and Cook, *Winner-Take-All Society,* 212–17.

CHAPTER THREE

1. Roland Bainton, *Christian Attitudes Toward War and Peace* (Nashville: Abingdon, 1960), 66–84; Lisa Sowle Cahill, *Love Your Enemies: Discipleship, Pacifism, and Just War Theory* (Minneapolis: Fortress Press, 1994), 39–54.

2. Bainton, *Christian Attitudes,* 53, 66.

3. Cahill, *Love Your Enemies,* 58–61.

4. The Calhoun Commission, "The Relation of the Church to the War in the Light of the Christian Faith," in Richard B. Miller, ed., *War in the Twentieth Century: Sources in Theological Ethics* (Louisville, KY: Westminster, 1993), 111–12.

5. U.S. Catholic Bishops, "The Challenge of Peace: God's Promise and Our Response," *CST,* 523–31; the Evangelical Lutheran Church in America, "For Peace in God's World" (Chicago, IL: Division for Church in Society, 1995), 5; the United Methodist Council of Bishops, "In Defense of Creation" (Nashville, TN: Graded Press, 1986), 33.

6. Pope John XXIII, "Peace on Earth," *CST,* 151.

7. Vatican II, The Church in the Modern World, *CST,* 222.

8. The Presbyterian Church (U.S.A.), "The Minutes of 192nd General Assembly" (1980), 70; The Evangelical Lutheran Church in America, "For Peace in God's World," 2, 6.

9. U.S. Catholic Bishops, "The Challenge of Peace," *CST,* 523–31; the Lutheran Church in America, "Peace and Politics" (LCA:1984), 5; The Evangelical Lutheran Church in America, "For Peace in God's World," 6; The Presbyterian Church (U.S.A.), "The Minutes of the 200th General Assembly," (1988), 446.

10. U.S. Catholic Bishops, "The Challenge of Peace," *CST,* 504.

11. For a discussion of peaceable virtues, see the U.S. Catholic Bishops "The Harvest of Justice Is Sown in Peace," in *Origins* 23/26 (December 9, 1993): 452.

12. Vatican II, The Church in the Modern World, *CST,* 196–98.

13. Ola W. Barnett, *Family Violence Across the Lifespan: An Introduction* (Thousand Oaks, CA: Sage Publications, 1997), 4–5; 187–8.

14. U.S. Catholic Bishops, "The Challenge of Peace," *CST,* 557.

15. Timothy O'Connell, *Making Disciples: A Handbook of Christian Moral Formation* (New York: Crossroad Herder, 1998), 87–101.

16. Barnett, *Family Violence,* 4.

17. For an extensive discussion of this issue, see Sissela Bok, *Mayhem: Violence as Public Entertainment* (Reading, MA: Addison–Wesley, 1998); Scott Stossel, "The Man Who Counts the Killings," *Atlantic Monthly* (May 1997): 86–104.

18. For more information on this topic, contact the Children's Defense Fund, on the Web at http://www.childrensdefense.org, or Handgun Control Inc., at http://www.handguncontrol.org.

19. Pope John XXIII, "Peace on Earth," *CST,* 132.

20. For more information about this topic, see William Greider, *Fortress America: The American Military and the Consequences of Peace* (New York: Public Affairs, 1998), and contact the Center for Defense Information at http://www.cdi.org.

21. For a comprehensive treatment of this question, see James J. Megivern, *The Death Penalty: An Historical and Theological Survey* (New York/Mahwah, NJ: Paulist Press, 1997).

22. Michel Foucault, *Discipline and Punish: The Birth of the Prison,* trans. by Alan Sheridan (New York: Random House, 1995), 3–69.

23. For more information on discrimination and the death penalty visit the ACLU Death Penalty Issue Page at http:/www.aclu.org.

24. Megivern, *The Death Penalty,* 9–19.

25. Megivern, *The Death Penalty,* 10–12; Jeremiah McCarthy, "Capital Punishment," in Judith A. Dwyer, ed., *The New Dictionary of Catholic Social Thought* (Collegeville, MN: Liturgical Press, 1994), 109.

26. *Catechism of the Catholic Church* (Liguori, MO: Liguori, 1994), #2266.

27. Thomas Aquinas, *Summae Theologiae,* II–II, 64 & 108.

28. Aquinas, *Summae Theologiae,* II–II, 64.

29. Pope John Paul II, "The Gospel of Life," *Origins* 24/42 (April 6, 1995): 693.

30. Pope Pius V, *The Catechism of the Council of Trent for Parish Priests* (New York: Joseph P. Wagner Inc., 1952), 421.

31. U.S. Catholic Bishops, "Statement on Capital Punishment," *Origins* 10/24 (November 27, 1980): 373–77.

32. For a fuller list of churches calling for the abolition of capital punishment, visit Envisioning: Religious Organizing Against the Death Penalty Project, at http://www.envisioning.org/abolition.

33. Pope John Paul II, "The Gospel of Life," 709.

34. U.S. Catholic Bishops, "Statement on Capital Punishment," 373–77.

35. United Methodist Church, "Resolution on Capital Punishment," adopted by the 1980 General Conference, Indianapolis, IN.

36. "On File," *Origins* 24/28 (December 22, 1994): 466.

37. For a history of nuclear deterrence, see Helen Caldicott, *Missile Envy: The Arms Race and Nuclear War* (New York: Bantam Books, 1986).

38. President Jimmy Carter, "Farewell Address to the American People," January 14, 1981.

39. For a defense of the morality of nuclear deterrence, see William V. O'Brien, "The Continuing Problem of Deterrence," in John A Coleman, ed., *One Hundred Years of Catholic Social Thought: Celebration and Challenge* (Maryknoll, NY: Orbis, 1991), 317–28.

40. General Lee Butler, Speech at the State of the World Forum, San Francisco, October 3, 1996.

41. U.S. Catholic Bishops, "The Challenge of Peace," *CST,* 504.

42. Sandra Schneiders, "New Testament Reflections on Peace and Nuclear Arms," in Philip J. Murnion, ed., *Catholics and Nuclear War* (New York: Crossroad, 1983), 91–105.

43. Walter Wink, *Violence and Nonviolence in South Africa: Jesus' Third Way* (Philadelphia: New Society Publishers, 1987), ch. 2; Marcus J. Borg, *Meeting Jesus Again for the First Time* (San Francisco: Harper, 1994), 46–61.

44. For a concise discussion of the church's tradition on nuclear weapons and deterrence see Thomas A. Shannon, *What Are They Saying About Peace and War?* (New York/Mahwah, NJ: Paulist Press, 1983), 30–46.

45. Pope John XXIII, "Peace on Earth," *CST,* 148–49.

46. Vatican II, The Church in the Modern Word, *CST,* 222.

47. U.S. Catholic Bishops, "The Challenge of Peace," *CST,* 562.

48. The United Methodist Council of Bishops (U.S.A.), "In Defense of Creation: The Nuclear Crisis and a Just Peace," in Richard B. Miller, ed., *War in the Twentieth Century: Sources in Theological Ethics* (Louisville, KY: Westminster/John Knox, 1992), 427–30.

49. For statements by religious groups or leaders calling for nuclear disarmament visit the Web site of Abolition 2000 at http://www.napf.org/abolition2000/religious.html.

50. U.S. Catholic Bishops, "The Challenge of Peace," *CST,* 523–35.

51. U.S. Catholic Bishops, "The Harvest of Justice," 456–60.

52. Richard A. McCormick, S.J., "Nuclear Deterrence and the Problem of Intention: A Review of the Positions," in Murnion, ed., *Catholics and Nuclear War,* 178–80.

53. Kenneth R. Himes, "The Morality of Humanitarian Intervention," *Theological Studies* 55/1 (March 1994): 82–105.

54. For a sketch of contemporary Catholic teaching on this topic, see Kenneth R. Himes, "Just War, Pacifism and Humanitarian Intervention," *America* (August 14, 1993): 10–15, 28–31.

55. Pope John XXIII, "Peace on Earth," *CST,* 132–35.

56. H. George Anderson, "Statement by the Presiding Bishop on the Crisis in the Balkans," April 9, 1999. To be found at

http://www.elca.org/ob/kosovo.html. Also, see the Lutheran World Federation Council, "Statement on Humanitarian Intervention," LWF Documentation no. 31 (December 1992), 71.

57. Pope John Paul II, "Principles Underlying a Stance Toward Unjust Aggressors," *Origins* 22/34 (January 28, 1993): 587.

58. Pope John Paul II, "The World's Hunger and Humanity's Conscience," *Origins* 22/28 (December 24, 1992): 475.

59. Himes, "Just War," 14–15, 28–29; LWF Council, "Statement on Humanitarian Intervention," 71.

60. U.S. Catholic Bishops, "The Harvest of Justice," 460–61.

61. Himes, "The Morality of Humanitarian Intervention," 98–104.

62. U.S. Catholic Bishops, "Confronting a Culture of Violence," *Origins* 24/25 (December 1, 1994): 423.

63. U.S. Catholic Bishops, "When I Call for Help: Domestic Violence Against Women," *Origins* 22/21 (November 5, 1992): 355.

64. Elizabeth Schüssler Fiorenza and Mary Shawn Copeland, eds., "Violence Against Women," *Concilium* 94/1 (Maryknoll: Orbis, 1994), viii.

65. Vatican Delegation "The Roots of Violence Against Women," *Origins* 23/21 (November 4, 1993): 369.

66. Fiorenza and Copeland, eds., *Violence Against Women,* x–xvii. See also, Social Affairs Committee of the Assembly of Quebec Bishops, "A Heritage of Violence: A Pastoral Reflection on Conjugal Violence," *Grail* 8 (June 1990): 77–88.

67. Vatican Delegation, "The Roots of Violence Against Women," 371.

68. Canadian Church Leaders, "Violence Against Women," *Origins* 21/47 (June 17, 1992): 789. See also the Evangelical Lutheran Church of America's "Resolution on Domestic Violence" (1995 Churchwide Assembly Action CA95.7.62).

69. U.S. Catholic Bishops, "When I Call for Help," 356.

70. Northern Canada Bishops, "Responding to Family Violence," *Origins* 26/39 (March 20, 1997): margin notes, 635–36.

71. Marie Fortune, *Violence in the Family: A Workshop Curriculum for Clergy and Other Helpers* (Cleveland: Pilgrim Press, 1991), 137–51; Fiorenza and Copeland, eds., *Violence Against Women,* viii–xvii.

72. Statistics in this section were taken from Eric Schlosser, "The Prison Industrial Complex," *Atlantic Monthly* (December 1998): 51–77; Elliott Currie, *Crime and Punishment in America* (New York: Metropolitan Books, 1998): 12–36; Norval Morris, "The Contemporary Prison: 1965–Present," in Norval Morris and David J. Rothman, eds., *The Oxford History of the Prison: The Practice of Punishment in Western Society* (New York: Oxford University Press, 1995): 227–59.

73. Currie, *Crime and Punishment,* 38–53.

74. Michael Tonry, *Malign Neglect: Race, Crime and Punishment in America* (New York: Oxford University Press, 1995), 17. See also Currie, *Crime and Punishment,* 53–66; Morris, "The Contemporary Prison," 257.

75. Cited in New York Catholic Bishops, "Reforming the Criminal Justice System," *Origins* 12/36 (February 17, 1983): 572.

76. Currie, *Crime and Punishment,* 33–34.

77. Tonry, *Malign Neglect,* 4.

78. Morris, "The Contemporary Prison," 242.

79. New York Catholic Bishops, "Reforming the Criminal Justice System," 571.

80. Evangelical Lutheran Church of America, "Message on Community Violence," (April 18, 1994).

81. Eric Schlosser, "A Grief Like No Other," *Atlantic Monthly* (September 1997): 37–38, 75–76; Currie, *Crime and Punishment,* 16–26.

82. New York Catholic Bishops, "Reforming the Criminal Justice System," 571. See also the 1972 statement of the Presbyterian Church in the United States, "Prison Reform" (UPCUSA, 1972): 174,

426–31, as well as the 1978 PCUS General Assembly statement, "The Church and Criminal Justice" (PCUS, 1978): 194–204.

CHAPTER FOUR

1. Christine Gudorf, *Body, Sex, and Pleasure: Reconstructing Christian Sexual Ethics* (Cleveland, OH: Pilgrim Press, 1994), 54.

2. For a history of Christian sexual ethics see: Margaret Farley, "Sexual Ethics," *Encyclopedia of Bioethics,* rev. ed., vol. 5, Warren T. Reich, ed. (New York: Simon & Schuster Macmillan, 1995), 2363–75; Dennis Doherty, "The Tradition in History," in Dennis Doherty, ed., *Dimensions of Human Sexuality* (Garden City, NY: Doubleday, 1979), 39–78; Lisa Cahill, *Sex, Gender and Christian Ethics* (New York: Cambridge University Press, 1996), 121–216; Anthony Kosnik et al., *Human Sexuality: New Directions in American Catholic Thought* (New York/Mahwah, NJ: Paulist Press, 1977), 33–52.

3. Pope John Paul II, "The Apostolic Exhortation on the Family," *Origins* 11/28 (December 24, 1981): 441.

4. Raymond F. Collins, *Sexual Ethics and the New Testament: Behavior and Belief* (New York: Herder & Herder, 2000), 183–85.

5. Collins, *Sexual Ethics,* 186–87, 192; Cahill, *Sex, Gender and Christian Ethics,* 150–60.

6. Farley, "Sexual Ethics," 2367–68.

7. Doherty, "The Tradition in History," 42–54.

8. Christine Gudorf, "Sexism," in Judith A. Dwyer, ed., *The New Dictionary of Catholic Social Thought* (Collegeville, MN: Liturgical Press, 1994), 877–81.

9. Cahill, *Sex, Gender and Christian Ethics,* 192–93.

10. Ibid.

11. Pope John XXIII, "Peace on Earth," *CST,* 137.

12. Richard C. Sparks, *Contemporary Christian Morality: Real Questions, Candid Responses* (New York: Crossroad Herder, 1996), 75.

13. Pope John Paul II, "The Apostolic Exhortation on the Family," 441.

14. Vincent Genovesi, S.J., *In Pursuit of Love: Catholic Morality and Human Sexuality* (Collegeville, MN: Liturgical Press, 1991), 141. See also the U.S. Catholic Bishops' *Human Sexuality: A Catholic Perspective for Education and Lifelong Learning* (Washington, DC: U.S. Catholic Conference, 1990), 15–27.

15. James B. Nelson, *Embodiment: An Approach to Sexuality and Christian Theology* (Minneapolis, MN: Augsburg Publishing House, 1978), 105.

16. Ibid., 18.

17. Genovesi, *In Pursuit of Love,* 157.

18. Ibid.

19. Nelson, *Embodiment,* 118.

20. Paul J. Wadell, *Friendship and the Moral Life* (Notre Dame, IN: University of Notre Dame Press, 1989); Gilbert C. Meilander, *Friendship: A Study in Theological Ethics* (Notre Dame, IN: University of Notre Dame Press, 1981).

21. Pope Paul VI, "On the Regulation of Birth," in Joseph Gremillion, ed., *The Gospel of Peace and Justice: Catholic Social Teaching Since Pope John* (Maryknoll, NY: Orbis, 1976), 430–31.

22. See Margaret A. Farley, "Feminist Ethics," and Susan A. Ross, "Feminist Theology: A Review of Literature," both in Charles E. Curran, Margaret A. Farley and Richard A. McCormick, S.J., eds., *Feminist Ethics and the Catholic Moral Tradition* (New York/Mahwah, NJ: Paulist Press, 1996), 5–10, 11–20.

23. Vatican II, The Church in the Modern World, *CST,* 196–201.

24. Milton Mayeroff, *On Caring* (New York: HarperCollins, 1971); Nel Noddings, *Caring: A Feminine Approach to Ethics and Moral Education* (Berkeley, CA: University of California Press, 1984).

25. Sacred Congregation for the Doctrine of the Faith (CDF), "Instruction on Respect for Human Life in Its Origin and on the

Dignity of Procreation: Replies to Certain Questions of the Day," *Origins* 16/40 (March 19, 1987), 708.

26. A plea for respectful and nondiscriminatory attitudes toward homosexual persons is made by the U.S. Catholic Bishops in *Human Sexuality: A Catholic Perspective for Education and Lifelong Learning,* 54–56; Protestant ethicist James B. Nelson makes a similar point in a discussion of homophobia in his *Body Theology* (Louisville, KY: Westminster/John Knox Press, 1992), 68–71.

27. Farley, "Sexual Ethics," 2363–65; "Sexual Behavior, Human, in *The New Encyclopaedia Britannica,* 15th ed., vol. 27 (Chicago, IL: Encyclopaedia Britannica Inc., 1998), 240–42.

28. Gudorf, *Body, Sex, and Pleasure,* 75.

29. Pope John Paul II, "The Apostolic Exhortation on the Family," 448–49; Pope Paul VI, "On the Regulation of Birth," in Gremillion, ed., *The Gospel of Peace and Justice,* 430–31.

30. *Catechism of the Catholic Church* (Liguori, MO : Liguori, 1994), # 2337–38.

31. On the biblical "double standard" regarding adultery, see Conrad E. L'Heureux's comment on Numbers 5: 5–10 in "Numbers," *The New Jerome Biblical Commentary,* Raymond E. Brown, S.S., Joseph A. Fitzmyer, S.J., and Roland E. Murphy, O.Carm., eds. (Englewood Cliffs, NJ: Prentice Hall, 1990), 83.

32. Cahill, *Sex, Gender and Christian Ethics,* 154–55, 162.

33. Collins, *Sexual Ethics and the New Testament,* 192.

34. John F. Dedek, "Premarital Sex: The Theological Argument from Peter Lombard to Durand," *Theological Studies,* 41/4 (December 1980): 652–60.

35. Cahill, *Sex, Gender and Christian Ethics,* 193.

36. Doherty, "The Tradition in History," 40.

37. Bernard Häring, *The Law of Christ: Moral Theology for Priests and Laity,* vol. 3, Edwin G. Kaiser, trans. (Westminster, MD: Newman Press, 1966), 291.

38. Farley, "Sexual Ethics," 2368–69.

39. The work of Protestant theologian H. Richard Niebuhr has been very influential in stressing persons-in-relationship as the central moral category. See his *The Responsible Self* (NY: Harper & Row, Publishers, 1963); see also R. Melvin Keiser, *Roots of Relational Ethics: Responsibility in Origin and Maturity in H. Richard Niebuhr* (Atlanta, GA: Scholars Press, 1996).

40. Philip S. Keane, S.S., *Sexual Morality: A Catholic Perspective* (New York/Mahwah, NJ: Paulist Press, 1977), 105–10; Genovesi, *In Pursuit of Love* 177–86.

41. Karen Lebacqz, "Appropriate Vulnerability," in James B. Nelson and Sandra Longfellow, eds., *Sexuality and the Sacred: Sources for Theological Reflection* (Louisville, KY: Westminster/John Knox Press, 1994), 256.

42. Gudorf, *Body, Sex and Pleasure,* 32.

43. Sparks, *Contemporary Christian Morality,* 60.

44. John T. Noonan, Jr., *Contraception: A History of Its Treatment by the Catholic Theologians and Canonists,* enlarged edition (Cambridge, MA: Harvard University Press, 1986), 476.

45. Ibid., 414.

46. Gudorf, *Body, Sex and Pleasure,* 38.

47. Ibid., 160.

48. Jean Ponder Soto, "The Church and Marriage: Looking for a New Ethic," in Paul T. Jersild et. al., eds., *Moral Issues and Christian Response,* 6th ed. (Fort Worth, TX: Harcourt Brace College Publishers, 1998), 60–61.

49. Jacqueline Kasun, "The Unjust War Against Population," in Louis P. Pojman, ed., *Environmental Ethics: Readings in Theory and Application,* 3rd ed. (Belmont, CA: Wadsworth Publishing Company, 2001), 331–40.

50. Noonan, *Contraception,* 33.

51. Farley, "Sexual Ethics," 2365.

52. Lisa Cahill, *Between the Sexes: Foundations for a Christian Ethics of Sexuality* (Philadelphia, PA: Fortress Press, 1985), 52–53.

53. Noonan, *Contraception,* 45.

54. Augustine, *Adulterous Marriages,* 2.12.12, CSEL, 41:396, cited in Noonan, *Contraception,* 138.

55. Noonan, *Contraception,* 231–57.

56. In Noonan's view, Aquinas is ambivalent on this, sometimes supporting the view that sexual intercourse in marriage always needed a procreative intent to be justified, and sometimes defending "intercourse which was not procreative." *Contraception,* 351–52.

57. Genovesi, *In Pursuit of Love,* 190.

58. Noonan, *Contraception,* 409.

59. Ibid., 490–91.

60. Pius XII, "On Chaste Marriage," in Odile M. Liebard, ed., *Official Catholic Teachings,* vol. 4, *Love and Sexuality* (Wilmington, NC: McGrath, 1978), 23–70.

61. Ibid., 31.

62. Herbert Doms, *The Meaning of Marriage* (London: Sheed and Ward, 1939). Dietrich Von Hildebrand, *In Defense of Purity* (Baltimore, MD: Helicon Press, 1962), 11.

63. Vatican II, The Church in the Modern World, *CST,* 197–200.

64. Pope Paul VI, "On the Regulation of Birth," in Gremillion, ed., *The Gospel of Peace and Justice,* 432–34.

65. Genovesi, *In Pursuit of Love,* 203–10.

66. Noonan, *Contraception,* 532.

67. Kosnik, *Human Sexuality,* 188.

68. Adrienne Rich, "Compulsory Heterosexuality and Lesbian Existence," in *Blood, Bread and Poetry: Selective Prose 1979–1985* (New York: W. W. Norton, 1986), 29.

69. See Genovesi, *In Pursuit of Love,* 257.

70. Gordon Allport, *The Nature of Prejudice* (Cambridge, MA: Addison Wesley, 1954).

71. Two works seem particularly valuable: Victor P. Furnish, *The Moral Teaching of Paul* (Nashville, TN: Abingdon Press, 1979); and Robin Scroggs, *The New Testament and Homosexuality* (Philadelphia, PA: Fortress Press, 1983).

72. Cahill, *Sex, Gender and Christian Ethics,* 156–57.

73. Patricia Beattie Jung and Ralph F. Smith, *Heterosexism: An Ethical Challenge* (New York: SUNY Press, 1993), 65.

74. Genovesi, *In Pursuit of Love,* 267.

75. Jung and Smith, *Heterosexism,* 80.

76. Kosnik, *Human Sexuality,* 196–200.

77. Ibid., 197–98.

78. CDF, "Declaration on Certain Questions Concerning Sexual Ethics," in Kosnik, *Human Sexuality,* 304–5.

79. Edward Malloy, *Homosexuality and the Christian Way of Life* (Lanham, MD: University Press of America, 1981), 234. For an extensive treatment of traditional moral arguments regarding homosexuality, see James P. Hanigan, *Homosexuality: The Test Case for Christian Sexual Ethics* (New York/Mahwah, NJ: Paulist Press, 1988).

80. U.S. Catholic Bishops, "To Live in Christ Jesus," in John Gallagher, ed., *Homosexuality and the Magisterium: Documents from the Vatican and the U.S. Bishops, 1775–1985* (Mt. Ranier, MD: New Ways Ministry, 1986), 9.

81. CDF, "On the Pastoral Care of Homosexual Persons" *Origins* 16/22 (November 13, 1986): 379; For an explanation of the categories "objectively wrong" but perhaps "subjectively less culpable," see Russell B. Connors, Jr., & Patrick T. McCormick, *Character, Choices and Community: The Three Faces of Christian Ethics* (New York/Mahwah, NJ: Paulist Press, 1998), 38–47.

82. Sparks, *Contemporary Christian Morality,* 77.

83. Jung and Smith, *Heterosexism,* 21–31.

84. U.S. Catholic Bishops, "To Live in Christ Jesus," in Gallagher, ed., *Homosexuality and the Magisterium,* 9.

85. U.S. Catholic Bishops, "Partners in the Mystery of Redemption: A Pastoral Response to Women's Concerns for Church and Society," *Origins* 17/45 (April 21, 1988): 763.

86. Ibid.

87. Augustine, *De Trinitate,* 7:7, 10; Aquinas, *Summa Theologiae,* 1:92:1 ad 1 (New York: McGraw Hill, 1964), vol. 13, 35–39; Pius XI, *Casti Connubii,* AAS 22 (1930), 539–92.

88. U.S. Bishops, "Partners in the Mystery of Redemption," 763.

89. Rosemary Radford Ruether, "Feminist Theology," in Joseph A. Komonchak et al. eds., *The New Dictionary of Theology* (Wilmington, DE: Michael Glazier, 1987), 392.

90. For two moving accounts of some of the ways women have experienced discrimination and oppression, see J. Milburn Thompson, *Justice and Peace: A Christian Primer* (Maryknoll, NY: Orbis, 1997), 98–102; and Lisa Sowle Cahill, *Sex, Gender and Christian Ethics,* 51–55.

91. Thompson, *Justice and Peace,* 98.

92. Gudorf, "Western Religion and the Patriarchal Family," in Curran et al., eds., *Feminist Ethics and the Catholic Tradition,* 262.

93. Thompson, *Justice and Peace,* 100.

94. Pope Paul VI, "Women-Disciples and Co-Workers," *Origins* 4/45 (May 1, 1975), 719.

95. For an insightful analysis of many of the statements of Pope John Paul II regarding the dignity of women, see Leonie Caldecott's "Sincere Gift: The Pope's 'New Feminism,'" in Charles E. Curran and Richard A. McCormick, S.J., eds., *John Paul II and Moral Theology, Readings in Moral Theology No. 10* (New York/Mahwah, NJ: Paulist Press, 1998), 216–34.

96. U.S. Catholic Bishops, "One in Christ Jesus," *Origins* 22/29 (December 31, 1992): 493.

97. Vatican II, The Church in the Modern World, *CST,* 183.

98. Pope Paul VI, "The Role of Women in Contemporary Society," *The Pope Speaks,* XIX (December 8, 1974): 316.

99. Pope John Paul II, "On Human Work," *CST,* 378–80.

100. World Synod of Catholic Bishops, "Justice in the World," *CST,* 295.

101. Gudorf, *Body, Sex and Pleasure,* 18. The discussion of this topic relies heavily on Gudorf's treatment of the causes and harms of sexual ignorance; see 18–24, 51–54, 149–59.

102. Ibid., 19–20.

103. G. Fox, "The Family's Role in Adolescent Sexual Behavior," in Theodora Ooms, ed., *Teenage Pregnancy in a Family Context* (Philadelphia: Temple University Press, 1981).

CHAPTER FIVE

1. Larry Rasmussen, *Earth Community, Earth Ethics* (Maryknoll, NY: Orbis, 1996), 54–74.

2. Ibid., 58.

3. Carolyn Merchant, *Radical Ecology: The Search for a Livable World* (New York: Routledge, 1992), 42–44.

4. Ibid., 48.

5. Ibid., 46.

6. Thomas Berry, *The Dream of the Earth* (San Francisco: Sierra Club, 1988), 41–42.

7. Berry, *The Dream of the Earth,* 54; Rachel Carson, *Silent Spring* (Boston: Houghton and Mifflin, 1962).

8. Berry, *The Dream of the Earth,* 123–37.

9. Arne Naess, "The Shallow and the Deep: Long–Range Ecological Movement"; Bill Devall and George Sessions, "Deep Ecology," both in Louis P. Pojman, ed., *Environmental Ethics: Readings in Theory and Application* (Boston: Jones and Bartlett, 1994), 102–05 and 113–17.

10. Elizabeth A. Johnson, *Women, Earth, and Creator Spirit* (New York/Mahwah, NJ: Paulist Press, 1993), 29.

11. Lynn White, "The Historical Roots of Our Ecological Crisis," *Science,* 155 (March 10, 1967): 1203–7. For a Christian response to this challenge see James Nash, *Loving Nature: Ecological Integrity and Christian Responsibility* (Nashville, TN: Abingdon, 1991), 68–92.

12. Johnson, *Women, Earth, and Creator Spirit,* 29.

13. Ibid., 30.

14. U.S. Catholic Bishops, "Renewing the Earth: An Invitation to Reflection and Action on the Environment in Light of Catholic Social Teaching," *Origins* 21/27 (December 12, 1991): 429. See also Pope John Paul II, "Peace with all Creation," *Origins* 19/28 (December 14, 1989): 465–68.

15. The Evangelical Lutheran Church in America, "Caring for Creation: Vision, Hope and Justice," September 1993. *(http://www.elca.org/dcs/environment.html),* 2.

16. Johnson, *Women, Earth, and Creator Spirit,* 30.

17. Michael J. Himes and Kenneth R. Himes, O.F.M., "Creation and an Environmental Ethic," in *Fullness of Faith: The Public Significance of Theology* (New York/Mahwah, NJ: Paulist Press, 1993), 104–24; 112 cited here.

18. U.S. Catholic Bishops, "Renewing the Earth," 428.

19. Evangelical Lutheran Church in America, "Caring for Creation," 2.

20. For a more extensive list of ecological virtues, see Nash, *Loving Nature,* 63–67; U.S. Catholic Bishops, "Renewing the Earth," 428–31; Rasmussen, *Earth Community, Earth Ethics,* 172–73.

21. U.S. Catholic Bishops, "Renewing the Earth," 432.

22. Al Gore, *Earth in the Balance: Ecology and the Human Spirit* (New York: Penguin, 1993), 221.

23. Rasmussen, *Earth Community, Earth Ethics,* 39.

24. Pope John Paul II, "Peace with All Creation," 466.

25. U.S. Catholic Bishops, "Renewing the Earth," 430.

26. Nash, *Loving Nature,* 41.

27. U.S. Catholic Bishops, "Renewing the Earth, 432.

28. Pope John Paul II, "Peace with All Creation," 467.

29. Pope John Paul II, "On Social Concern," *CST,* 421.

30. Richard T. De George, *Business Ethics,* 3rd ed. (New York: Macmillan, 1990), 399–403.

31. Nash, *Loving Nature,* 52.

32. Milton Friedman, "The Social Responsibility of Business Is to Increase Its Profits," in Tom Beauchamp and Norman Bowie, *Ethical Theory and Business,* 4th ed. (Englewood Cliffs, NJ: Prentice Hall, 1993), 55–60.

33. Clive Ponting, *A Green History of the World: The Environment and the Collapse of Great Civilizations* (New York: Penguin, 1991), 17.

34. Rasmussen, *Earth Community, Earth Ethics,* 38–43.

35. See Dennis Hayes, "Mobilizing to Combat Global Warming," *World Watch* (March/April 2000): 6.

36. Thompson, *Justice and Peace,* 70.

37. Janet Abramowitz, "*Worldwatch* Press Release on Forests," (April 4, 1998): 1.

38. David Quammen, "Planet of Weeds," *Harper's* (October 1998): 62.

39. Jacques Leslie, "Running Dry: What Happens When the World No Longer Has Enough Freshwater?" *Harper's* (July 2000): 37–41.

40. Ibid., 61, 65.

41. John Tuxill, "Worldwatch Press Release on Vertebrate Declines," (May 23, 1998): 1–2.

42. Quammen, "Planet of Weeds," 60.

43. Nash, *Loving Nature,* 50.

44. Ibid., 72–74.

45. Gerard Manley Hopkins, "God's Grandeur," found in *The Norton Anthology of English Literature,* vol. 2, rev. ed. (New York: W.W. Norton, 1968), 1433.

46. Michael J. Himes and Kenneth R. Himes, O.F.M., "The Sacrament of Creation," *Commonweal* (January 26, 1990): 43–44.

47. Enda McDonagh, "The Structure and Basis of Moral Experience," in Ronald Hamel and Kenneth Himes, eds., *Introduction to Christian Ethics: A Reader* (New York/Mahwah, NJ: Paulist Press, 1989), 107.

48. Nash, *Loving Nature,* 72.

49. Pope Paul VI, "A Call to Action," *CST,* 273.

50. World Synod of Bishops, "Justice in the World," *CST,* 290.

51. U.S. Catholic Bishops, "Renewing the Earth," 426.

52. U.S. Catholic Bishops, "The Challenge of Peace: God's Promise and Our Response," *CST,* 495.

53. Pope John Paul II, "On Social Concern," *CST,* 273; Pope John Paul II, "Peace with All Creation," 468.

54. An extremely helpful collection of articles by many of these authors is in Mary Heather MacKinnon and Moni McIntyre, eds., *Readings in Ecology and Feminist Theology* (Kansas City, MO: Sheed & Ward, 1995).

55. For an informed and impassioned description of the practice of "environmental racism" as a new form of "lynching," see Emilie M. Townes, *In a Blaze of Glory: Womanist Spirituality as Social Witness* (Nashville: Abingdon, 1995), 55–60.

56. Vernice D. Miller, "Building on Our Past, Planning for Our Future," in Richard Hofrichter, ed., *Toxic Struggles: The Theory and Practice of Environmental Justice* (Philadelphia: New Society Publishers, 1993), 128.

57. Robert D. Bullard, "Anatomy of Environmental Racism and the Environmental Justice Movement," in Robert D. Bullard, ed.,

Confronting Environmental Racism: Voices from the Grassroots (Boston: South End Press, 1993), 19.

58. Aaron Sachs, *Eco–Justice: Linking Human Rights and the Environment,* Worldwatch Paper 127 (Washington, DC: Worldwatch Institute, 1995), 10.

59. Benjamin Goldman and Laura Fitton, *Toxic Wastes and Race Revisited: An Update of the 1987 Report on the Racial and Socioeconomic Characteristics of Communities with Hazardous Waste Sites* (Washington, DC: Center for Policy Alternatives, 1994), executive summary.

60. Rasmussen, *Earth Community, Earth Ethics,* 75,

61. Charles Lee, "Beyond Toxic Wastes and Race," in Robert Bullard, ed., *Confronting Environmental Racism,* 42; Bullard, "Anatomy of Environmental Racism," 21.

62. Marion Moses, "Farmworkers and Pesticides," in Robert Bullard, ed., *Confronting Environmental Racism,* 162–69.

63. Sachs, *Eco–Justice,* 28–29.

64. Pontifical Council for Justice and Peace, "Toward a Better Distribution of Land: The Challenge of Agrarian Reform," *Origins,* 27/32 (January 29, 1998): 533–34.

65. Sachs, *Eco-Justice,* 39.

66. Bullard, "Anatomy of Environmental Racism," 19.

67. Pope John Paul II, "On the Hundredth Anniversary of *Rerum Novarum,*" *CST,* 462.

68. Elizabeth Johnson, "The Cosmos: An Astonishing Image of God," *Origins* 26/13 (September 12, 1999): 210; Brian Massingale, "The Case for Catholic Support: Catholic Social Ethics and Environmental Justice," in Diana Hayes and Cyprian Davis, eds., *Taking Down Our Harps: Black Catholics in the United States* (Maryknoll, NY: Orbis, 1998), 147–62; Townes, *In a Blaze of Glory,* 55–60; Rasmussen, *Earth Community, Earth Ethics,* 75–89.

69. Massingale, "The Case for Catholic Support," 147.

70. Pontifical Council for Justice and Peace, "Toward a Better Distribution of Land," 533–34; Evangelical Lutheran Church in America, "Caring for Creation," 5; U.S. Catholic Bishops, "Renewing the Earth," 426–27; Bishop William Skylstead, "Letter on Brownfield Areas" (June 9, 1997); United Church of Christ Commission for Racial Justice, *Toxic Wastes and Race in the United States: A National Report on the Racial and Socio–Economic Characteristics of Communities with Hazardous Waste Sites* (New York: United Church of Christ, 1987).

71. Evangelical Lutheran Church in America, "Caring for Creation," 5.

72. Vatican II, The Church in the Modern World, *CST,* 183.

73. Massingale, "The Case for Catholic Support," 153.

74. Pope Leo XIII, "On the Condition of Labor," *CST,* 26–28.

75. Massingale, "The Case for Catholic Support," 152.

76. Pope John XXIII, "Peace on Earth," and Vatican II, The Church in the Modern World, *CST,* 132, 182.

77. U.S. Catholic Bishops, "Economic Justice for All," *CST,* 583.

78. U.S. Catholic Bishops, "Renewing the Earth," 430.

79. U.S. Catholic Bishops, "A Century of Social Teachings" (Washington, DC: National Conference of Catholic Bishops, 2000); U.S. Catholic Bishops, "Renewing the Earth," 429.

80. Ponting, *A Green History of the World,* 88–89.

81. Ibid., 91.

82. Merchant, *Radical Ecology,* 32.

83. Michael Teitelbaum, "The Population Threat," *Foreign Affairs* (Winter 1992): 64.

84. John C. Schwarz, *Global Population from a Catholic Perspective* (Mystic, CT: Twenty–Third Publications, 1998), 22.

85. Pojman, *Environmental Ethics,* 243.

86. Ibid.

87.   Garrett Hardin, "The Tragedy of the Commons," in Pojman, *Environmental Ethics,* pp. 253–54.

88.   Merchant, *Radical Ecology,* 31–32.

89.   Pojman, *Environmental Ethics,* 243.

90.   Jacqueline Kasun, "The Unjust War Against Population," in Pojman, *Environmental Ethics,* 256–66.

91.   Pojman, *Environmental Ethics,* 243.

92.   Barbara Crossette, "U.N. Is Facing Angry Debate on Population," *New York Times* (September 4, 1994): A16.

93.   Christine Gudorf, *Body, Sex, and Pleasure: Reconstructing Christian Sexual Ethics* (Cleveland, OH: Pilgrim Press, 1994), 33–37.

94.   Tas Papathanasis, "Population Debate Misses the Real Issue," *Hartford Courant* (September 30, 1999): op–ed page.

95.   John T. Noonan, Jr., *Contraception: A History of Its Treatment by the Catholic Theologians and Canonists,* enlarged ed. (Cambridge, MA: Harvard University Press, 1986), 33.

96.   Lisa Sowle Cahill, *Between the Sexes: Foundations for a Christian Ethics of Sexuality* (Philadelphia: Fortress Press, 1985), 53.

97.   Noonan, *Contraception,* 81–84, 275–78; 84 cited.

98.   Schwartz, *Global Population from a Catholic Perspective,* 155–85.

99.   Pope Paul VI, "On the Regulation of Birth," in Joseph Gremillion, ed., *The Gospel of Peace and Justice: Catholic Social Teaching Since Pope John* (Maryknoll, NY: Orbis, 1976), 432.

100.   Vatican II, The Church in the Modern World *CST,* 227.

101.   Pope John XXIII, "Christianity and Social Progress," *CST,* 114–16.

102.   Pope Paul VI, "On the Regulation of Birth," in Gremillion, ed., *The Gospel of Peace and Justice,* 439.

103.   World Synod of Catholic Bishops, "Justice in the World," *CST,* 290.

104. Pope John Paul II, "Peace with All Creation," *CST,* 466.

105. Schwartz, *Global Population from a Catholic Perspective,* 195.

106. Cited in Ponting, *A Green History of the World,* 148.

107. Ibid., 148–49.

108. Sally Griffin, "Split Culture," in MacKinnon and McIntyre, eds., *Readings in Ecology and Feminist Theology,* 94.

109. Peter Farb, *Ecology* (New York: Time-Life, 1970), 164.

110. Ponting, *A Green History of the World,* 248.

111. John Gowdy, "Place, Equity, and Environmental Impact: Lessons from the Past," *Ecojustice Quarterly* 14/2 (Spring 1994): 13.

112. Thomas Berry, "The American College in the Ecological Age," in *The Dream of the Earth,* 89–108.

CHAPTER SIX

1. Albert R. Jonsen and Andrew Jameton, "The History of Medical Ethics: The U.S. in the 20th Century," in Warren T. Reich, ed., *Encyclopedia of Bioethics,* rev. ed. (New York: Macmillan, 1995), 1616.

2. Darrel W. Amundsen, "The History of Medical Ethics: Europe: Ancient and Medieval," in Reich, *Encyclopedia of Bioethics,* 1509–15.

3. Ibid., 1516–21; Charles E. Curran, "Roman Catholicism," in Reich, *Encyclopedia of Bioethics,* 2321–30.

4. Henry Sigerist, *Civilization and Disease* (Ithaca, NY: Cornell University Press, 1943), 69 f.

5. Helga Kuhse and Peter Singer, eds., *A Companion to Bioethics* (Oxford: Blackwell Publishers, 1998), 6–7; Martin Benjamin and Joy Curtis, "Virtue and the Practice of Nursing," in Earl E. Shelp, ed., *Virtue and Medicine: Explorations in the Character of Medicine* (Dordrecht: D. Reidel, 1985), 257–74.

6. See Kuhse and Singer, *A Companion to Bioethics,* 7.

7. Jonsen and Jameton, "The History of Medical Ethics," in Reich, *Encyclopedia of Bioethics,* 1616–32.

8. Paul Ramsey, *The Patient as Person* (New Haven:Yale University Press, 1970), xiii.

9. Karen Lebacqz, "The Virtuous Patient," in Shelp, *Virtue and Medicine,* 275–88.

10. Ramsey, *Patient as Person,* xii.

11. Edmund D. Pellegrino and David C.Thomasma, *The Virtues in Medical Practice* (New York: Oxford University Press, 1993).

12. Benjamin and Curtis, "Virtue and the Practice of Nursing," 270–72.

13. Pope John XXIII, "Peace on Earth," *CST,* 132.

14. U.S. Catholic Bishops, "Pastoral Letter on Health and Health Care," *Origins* 11/25 (December 3, 1981): 400–402.

15. Amundsen, "The History of Medical Ethics," in Reich, *Encyclopedia of Bioethics,* 1515.

16. Harold Vanderpool, "Death and Dying: Euthanasia and Sustaining Life: Historical Aspects," in Reich, *Encyclopedia of Bioethics,* 555.

17. "The Oregon Death with Dignity Act," in Margaret P. Battin, Rosamond Rhodes and Anita Silvers, eds., *Physician Assisted Suicide: Expanding the Debate* (New York: Routledge, 1998), 444.

18. These figures are provided in the 1999 Annual Report of the Oregon Health Division: *http://www.ohd.hr.state.or.us/chs/pas/pas.htm.*

19. See Rosamond Rhodes, "Physicians, Assisted Suicide, and the Right to Live or Die," in Battin, Rhodes and Silvers, *Physician Assisted Suicide,* 171–72.

20. Council on Ethical and Legal Affairs, American Medical Association, *Code of Medical Ethics: Current Opinions* (Chicago: AMA, 1997).

21. Timothy E. Quill, M.D., Christine K. Cassel, M.D., Diane E. Meier, M.D., "Care of the Hopelessly Ill: Proposed Clinical Criteria for Physician–Assisted Suicide," *New England Journal of Medicine* 327/19 (Nov. 5, 1992): 1380–83.

22. Patricia A. King and Leslie F. Wolf, "Lessons for Physician-Assisted Suicide from the African-American Experience," in Battin, Rhodes and Silvers, *Physician Assisted Suicide,* 104.

23. Arthur Droge and James Tabor, *A Noble Death: Suicide and Martyrdom Among Christians and Jews in Antiquity* (San Francisco: Harper Collins, 1991), xi, 58.

24. Ibid., xi.

25. Jeremiah Donovan, trans., *Catechism of the Council of Trent* (Dublin: Duffy & Co., 1910), 365.

26. The Sacred Congregation for the Doctrine of the Faith (CDF), "Declaration on Euthanasia," *The Pope Speaks* 25/4 (Winter, 1980): 291.

27. Pope Pius XII, "The Prolongation of Life," *The Pope Speaks,* 4/4 (Spring, 1958): 395–96.

28. See John J. Paris, S.J., "The Moral Notes: Active Euthanasia," *Theological Studies* 53 (March 1992): 113–20.

29. Pope John Paul II, "The Gospel of Life," *Origins* 24/42 (April 6, 1995): 713.

30. Richard McCormick, S.J., "Technology, the Consistent Ethic, and Assisted Suicide," *Origins* 25/27 (December 21, 1995): 460.

31. Daniel Maguire, *Death by Choice* (Garden City, NY: Doubleday, 1974; revised, 1984), 141–45 (1974 ed.).

32. Charles E. Curran, "The Fifth Commandment: Thou Shalt Not Kill," *Ongoing Revision: Studies in Moral Theology* (Notre Dame: University of Notre Dame Press, 1978), 160.

33. Lisa Sowle Cahill, "A 'Natural Law' Reconsideration of Euthanasia," in Stephen E. Lammers and Allen Verhey, eds., *On Moral Medicine: Theological Perspectives in Medical Ethics* (Grand Rapids, MI:

Eerdmans, 1987), 445–53; James B. Nelson and Jo Anne Smith Rohricht, *Human Medicine: Ethical Perspectives on Today's Medical Issues,* rev. ed. (Minneapolis, MN: Augsburg, 1984), 161–67.

34. See Kenneth Overberg, S.J., ed., *Mercy or Murder? Euthanasia, Morality and Public Policy* (Kansas City, MO: Sheed & Ward, 1993).

35. Paris, "Active Euthanasia," 121.

36. John T. Noonan, Jr., *Contraception: A History of Its Treatment by the Catholic Theologians and Canonists,* enlarged ed. (Cambridge, MA: Harvard University Press, 1986), 443.

37. Nelson and Rohricht, *Human Medicine,* 87; A. S. Duncan, G. R. Dunstan and R. B. Welbourn, eds. *Dictionary of Medical Ethics,* new revised ed. (New York: Crossroad, 1981), 27.

38. Nelson and Rohricht, *Human Medicine,* 88.

39. American Society for Reproductive Medicine, *www.asrm.org/Patients/faqs.html#Q7.*

40. Thomas A. Shannon, *An Introduction to Bioethics,* 3rd ed. (New York/Mahwah, NJ: Paulist Press, 1997), 62.

41. Noonan, *Contraception,* 30.

42. Cahill, *Sex, Gender and Christian Ethics* (Cambridge: Cambridge University Press, 1996), 154, 162.

43. Margaret Farley, "Sexual Ethics," in Reich, ed., *Encyclopedia of Bioethics,* 2365.

44. Thomas H. Shannon and Lisa Sowle Cahill, *Religion and Artificial Reproduction: An Inquiry into the Vatican Instruction on "Respect for Human Life"* (New York/Mahwah, NJ: Paulist Press, 1988), 27.

45. Noonan, *Contraception,* 45.

46. CDF, "Instruction on Respect for Human Life in Its Origin and on the Dignity of Procreation: Replies to Certain Questions of the Day." *Origins* 16/40 (March 19, 1987): 697–711.

47. Ibid., 701.

48. Ibid., 701–2.

49. CDF, "Declaration on Procured Abortion" in Austin Flannery, O.P., ed., *Vatican Council II: More Post Conciliar Documents,* vol. 2 (Northport, NY: Costello Publishing, 1982), 443.

50. CDF, "Instruction on Respect for Human Life," 702.

51. Ibid., 703.

52. Thomas A. Shannon and Allan B. Wolter, O.F.M., "Reflections on the Moral Status of the Pre–Embryo," *Theological Studies* 51/4 (December 1990): 622–25.

53. CDF, "Instruction on Respect for Human Life," 705.

54. Ibid., 704–5.

55. Richard McCormick, "Therapy or Tampering: The Ethics of Reproductive Technology and the Development of Doctrine," *The Critical Calling: Reflections on Moral Dilemmas Since Vatican II* (Washington, DC, Georgetown University Press, 1989), 341; Cahill, *Sex, Gender and Christian Ethics,* 252–54.

56. See Maura A. Ryan's "The Argument for Unlimited Procreative Liberty: A Feminist Critique," *Feminist Ethics and the Catholic Moral Tradition, Readings in Moral Theology No. 9* (New York/Mahwah, NJ: Paulist Press, 1996), 383–401.

57. CDF, "Instruction on Respect for Human Life," 707.

58. Ibid., 706.

59. Ibid., 707.

60. McCormick, "Therapy or Tampering," 333–40; Lisa Cahill, *Women and Sexuality* (New York/Mahwah, NJ: Paulist Press, 1992), 73–75; Sidney Callahan, "The Ethical Challenge of the New Reproductive Technology," in Lammers and Verhey, eds., *On Moral Medicine,* 511.

61. Shannon, *An Introduction to Bioethics,* 128.

62. Human Genome Project Information, "History of the Human Genome Project," *http://www.ornl.gov/hgmis/project/hgp.html.*

63. McCormick, "Genetic Technology and Our Common Future," *The Critical Calling,* 276.

64. M. Therese Lysaught, "From Clinic to Congregations: Religious Communities and Genetic Medicine," in Lammers and Verhey, eds., *On Moral Medicine,* 558.

65. James Walter, "Theological Issues in Genetics," *Theological Studies* 60/1 (March 1999): 124–25.

66. Ibid., 126.

67. Ibid., 126–27.

68. Pope John Paul II, "The Ethics of Genetic Manipulation," *Origins* 13/23 (November 17, 1983): 389.

69. Donald Senior, *Jesus: A Gospel Portrait,* New and Revised Edition (New York/Mahwah, NJ: Paulist Press, 1992), 100.

70. Ibid., 116.

71. Audrey R. Chapman, "Ethics and Human Genetics," *The Annual of the Society of Christian Ethics* 18 (Washington, DC: Georgetown University Press, 1998): 298.

72. Pope John Paul II, "The Ethics of Genetic Manipulation," 388.

73. Chapman, "Ethics and Human Genetics," 295; "On File," *Origins* 29/19 (October 21, 1999): 294.

74. "On File," 294.

75. CDF, "Instruction on Respect for Human Life," 702.

76. "On File," 294.

77. James Walter, "'Playing God' or Properly Exercising Human Responsibility? Some Theological Reflections on Human Germ-Line Therapy," *New Theology Review* 10 (November 1997): 40–41.

78. Ibid., 41.

79. Pope John Paul II, "The Ethics of Genetic Manipulation," 388; "On File," 294.

80. Walter, "Theological Issues in Genetics," 126.

81. "On File," 294.

82. Walter, "'Playing God,'" 42–43.

83. McCormick, "Genetic Technology and Our Common Future," *The Critical Calling,* 266.

84. Richard McCormick, "Value Variables in the Health-Care Reform Debate," *America* 168/19 (May 29, 1993): 12; "The End of Catholic Hospitals?" *America* 179/1 (July 4, 1998): 9; "Bioethics: A Moral Vacuum?" America 180/15 (May 1, 1999): 11.

85. The Ad Hoc Committee to Defend Health Care, "For Our Patients, Not For Profits," *The Journal of the American Medical Association* 278/21 (December 3, 1997): 1733.

86. George Annas, "Beyond the Military and Market Metaphors," *The Healthcare Forum Journal* (May/June 1996): 32.

87. George Annas, "Reframing the Debate on Health Care Reform by Replacing Our Metaphors," *The New England Journal of Medicine,* 332/11 (March 16, 1995): 744.

88. See "Should There Be a Market in Body Parts?" in Carol Levine, ed., *Taking Sides: Clashing Views on Controversial Bioethical Issues,* 6th ed. (New York: Dushkin Publications, 1995), 278–96.

89. See M. Cathleen Kaveny, "Jurisprudence and Genetics," *Theological Studies,* 60/1 (March 1999): 144–47.

90. McCormick, "Bioethics: A Moral Vacuum?" 9, 11.

91. Edmund D. Pellegrino and David C. Thomasma, *For the Patient's Good: The Restoration of Beneficence in Health Care* (New York: Oxford University Press, 1988), 52–53.

92. Michael D. Place, "The Health Care Reform Equation," *America,* 184/10 (March 26, 2001), 8–13.

93. Annas, "Beyond the Military and Market Metaphors," 32.

94. McCormick, "The End of Catholic Hospitals?" 5, 8.

95. Richard Spinello, "Ethics, Pricing and the Pharmaceutical Industry," *Journal of Business Ethics* 11/8 (August 1992): 617–27.

96. Clare Kapp, "Health, Trade, and Industry Officials Set to Debate Access to Essential Drugs," *The Lancet* (April 7, 2001): 1105.

97. Pope John XXIII, "Peace on Earth," *CST,* 132.

98. U.S. Catholic Bishops, "Pastoral Letter on Health and Health Care," *Origins* 11/25 (December 3, 1981): 400–402.

99. Amundsen, "The History of Medical Ethics," 1518–20.

100. Pope Leo XIII, "The Condition of Labor," *CST,* 27.

101. Pope John XXIII, "Peace on Earth," *CST,* 140.

102. U.S. Catholic Bishops, "Resolution on Health Care Reform," *Origins* 23/7 (July 1, 1993): 99–100.

103. For other arguments in support of comprehensive health-care reform, see Gene Outka, "Social Justice and Equal Access to Health Care," in Lammers and Verhey, eds., *On Moral Medicine,* 947–73; Philip S. Keane, S.S., *Health Care Reform: A Catholic View* (New York/Mahwah, NJ: Paulist Press, 1993), 173–82.

104. Place, "The Health Care Reform Equation," 11–12.

105. Elisabeth Kubler-Ross, *On Death and Dying* (New York: Macmillan, 1969).

106. McCormick, "Value Variables in the Health-Care Reform Debate," 7.

107. Keane, *Health Care Reform,* 21–22.

108. Daniel Callahan, *What Kind of Life: The Limits of Medical Progress* (New York: Simon & Schuster, 1990), 23.

109. Ibid., 261–62.

110. McCormick, "If I Had Ten Things to Share with Physicians," *The Critical Calling,* 365–66.

111. Keane, *Health Care Reform,* 21.

112. Daniel Callahan, "Restoring the Proper Goals of the Healing Arts," *The Chronicle of Higher Education* (April 25, 1997) A52; *The Troubled Dream of Life: Living with Mortality* (New York: Simon & Schuster, 1993).

113. Linda L. Emanuel, "Structured Deliberation to Improve Decisionmaking for the Seriously Ill," Special Supplement, *Hastings Center Report,* 25/6 (1995): S14–S18; "A Controlled Trial to Improve

Care for Seriously Ill Hospitalized Patients," *The Journal of the American Medical Association* 274/20 (November 22/29, 1996): 1593–94.

114.   Wayne H. Thaluber, M.D., "Overcoming Physician Barriers to Hospice Care," *Minnesota Medicine* 78 (February 1995): 18.

115.   Daniel Callahan, "Health Care—As a Society, Are We Worried Sick?" *Seattle Times* (February 18, 1990): A21.

116.   McCormick, "Technology, the Consistent Ethic, and Assisted Suicide," 460–62; Ohio Catholic Bishops, "Pastoral Reflections: Euthanasia, Assisted Suicide," *Origins* 23/21 (November 4, 1993): 374.

117.   Pope John Paul II, "The Gospel of Life," 706.

118.   Pope Pius XII, "The Prolongation of Life," 395–96.

119.   James F. Bresnahan, S.J., "Catholic Spirituality and Medical Interventions in Dying," Lammers and Verhey, eds., *On Moral Medicine,* 642–47.

120.   Keane, *Health Care Reform,* 186–87.

121.   Daniel Callahan, "Cramming for Your Finals: Make Death a Part of Life," *Commonweal* (July 16, 1993): 14.

122.   Ibid.